Beyond Impunity:
New Directions for Governance in Malawi

Published by
Mzuni Press
P/Bag 201 Luwinga
Mzuzu 2
Malawi

ISBN 978-99960-76-07-7
eISBN 978-99960-76-08-4

Cover picture: Jacob Nankhonya

Cover: Josephine Kawejere and Daniel Neumann

Editorial assistance: Hope Kaombe

Beyond Impunity: New Directions for Governance in Malawi

Edited by

Kenneth R. Ross

Asiyati Lorraine Chiweza

Wapulumuka O. Mulwafu

University of Cape Town Press

UCT PRESS

with

Mzuni Press

2022

The cover photograph was taken by photojournalist Jacob Nankhonya, Assistant Technical Editor at Nation Publications Ltd, and is used by his kind permission. It shows a demonstration in August 2019 that was part of the "One Million March" that called for the resignation of Jane Ansah, Chair of the Malawi Electoral Commission, in the aftermath of the 2019 Presidential election. The demonstrators are on the road close to Kamuzu Central Hospital in Lilongwe as they had just passed through the suburb of Mchesi. The placard states, "Chisankho cha Tippex takana," meaning "We refuse to accept the outcome of the Tippex election."

"The events of 2019/2020 were momentous not just for democracy in Malawi but for the wider region. This impressive volume brings together critical insights that reveal why the presidential election was nullified, how key democratic institutions emerged stronger than before, and the challenges that still remain. It is essential reading for anyone working on Malawian politics or democratic consolidation more broadly".

Nic Cheeseman, Professor of Democracy, University of Birmingham

"Well researched and written by mostly Malawian scholars using a wide variety of local and international sources and new data collected through field work, this book offers fresh perspectives of an assortment of topical issues from the environment, federalism, and gender to governance, financial management, and trust. It also brings to our attention young scholars writing on Malawi, who offer different perspectives to those we are used to reading and refreshing new ways of looking at the country's historical and contemporary issues."

Diana Cammack, political scientist, South Africa

"Malawi's 'critical juncture' of 2019-20 inspires in this volume a comprehensive look at governance. From public finances to electoral management and violence, from regionalism to natural resource management, and a whole host of other topics along the way, the chapters collected here mark a concentrated effort to rethink Malawi's governance."

Harri Englund, Professor of Anthropology, University of Cambridge

"An extremely engaging and gripping collection that analyses Malawi's democratic project in a historical and contemporary perspective with a depth and breadth that very few existing accounts can rival. This volume is a must read for all academics, researchers, policy makers, journalists, activists, diplomats and development practitioners who want to understand how Malawi works or does not work including its prospects for democratic maturity in a highly dynamic local and global context."

Blessings Chinsinga PhD
Director at Centre for Social Research (CSR) and Professor at the
Department of Political and Administrative Studies, University of Malawi

Acknowledgements

Many hands have played their part in the making of this book. Credit must be given, first and foremost, to the authors whose work it contains. They drafted their chapters at a very challenging time in mid-2020 when Malawi was facing high political tension at the same time as having to cope with the onset of the coronavirus pandemic. Anyone could be forgiven for getting distracted, but the authors stuck to their task and worked through a rigorous process of editing and peer review to produce the result that is now in your hands. We are also much indebted to the anonymous or "blind" peer reviewers who freely gave of their time and expertise to ensure that the essays reached the highest possible standard.

Our sincere thanks are also due to the University of Cape Town Press and Mzuni Press who collaborated to achieve publication in a way that will make the book available to an international audience while also circulating widely in Malawi itself. The rigour of their editorial processes has enhanced the quality of the book and it has been a pleasure to work with them. To their respective editors, Sandy Shepherd and Klaus Fiedler, we owe a great debt of gratitude.

We have also been delighted to cooperate with the Scotland Malawi Partnership and the Malawi Scotland Partnership, playing a part in their Year of Governance Strengthening. A grant from the SMP has enabled the publication of a substantial print-run in Malawi, which will make the book widely available to institutions and individuals who are interested. The Partnership also hosted an 8-part Webinar series based on the book, running from October 2021 to May 2022, which has enabled lively discussion of the book's ideas and done much to make it more widely known.

We are thankful to Josephine Kawejere and Daniel Neumann for the cover design, and to Jacob Nankhonya for allowing us to use his evocative photograph.

Kenneth R. Ross
Asiyati Lorraine Chiweza
Wapulumuka O. Mulwafu

Zomba, November 2021

Contents

Notes on Contributors

Paul Chiudza Banda is Assistant Professor of History at Tarleton State University. He received his PhD in History from West Virginia University. He has authored several book chapters and journal articles, including in *The Journal of the Middle East and Africa* and *The Journal of Eastern African Studies.* His latest book is titled *The State, Counterinsurgency, and Political Policing in Colonial and Postcolonial Malawi, 1891-1994.* His current research interests are in British imperialism; the state in colonial and post-colonial Africa; the history of development in Africa; and the global Cold War.

Mphatso Jones Boti-Phiri is a governance researcher and politician. He is a Member of the Malawi Parliament. Holds a PhD in international security governance and institutional reforms from Coventry University, UK, MA in National Security from Naval Postgraduate School California, USA, and BA in Public Administration from the University of Malawi. A retired military officer, he has taught at Chancellor College, University of Malawi. His research interests include governance, elections and voting behaviour, peace and security.

Henry Chingaipe is Director of the Institute for Policy Research & Social Empowerment (IPRSE). He formerly held academic positions at Chancellor College, University of Malawi, and at the Department of Politics, University of York. He studied Public Administration, Political Science and Development Studies at the Universities of Malawi, Cambridge (UK) and York (UK), where he completed his PhD. His research interests include governance and development, political economy analysis, public policy analysis, public sector reforms and the civic space.

Gowokani Chijere Chirwa is a Lecturer in Economics at Chancellor College, University of Malawi. He obtained his PhD in economics from the University of York, United Kingdom. His research interest is in health economics and micro econometric applications. Of late, he has taken an interest in studying the interplay between politics, economics, health care and health outcomes, in African regions.

Asiyati Lorraine Chiweza is an Associate Professor in the Department of Political and Administrative Studies at Chancellor College, University of Malawi. She holds a PhD in Public Administration from Curtin University, Australia. She has authored several book chapters and journal articles, including in *The Journal of African and Asian Studies, Development in Practice,* and *Public Administration and Development Alternatives.* Her main research interests and expertise are in local governance and development, gender and governance, and public sector ethics and governance.

Joseph J. Chunga is a Research Fellow at the Centre for Social Research at Chancellor College, University of Malawi. He is a PhD candidate in Politics at the University of Cape Town and holds a Master's degree in Political Science and a Bachelor's degree in Public Administration. His research spans a wide range of topics around democracy and governance including elections, public opinion, political economy, and constitutionalism.

Garton Kamchedzera is an Associate Professor in the University of Malawi. He holds a PhD (Cambridge University), an LLM in Law and Development (Warwick University), and an LLB (Hons) (University of Malawi). He specializes in applied law and development research nationally and internationally on child rights, human rights-based approach to programming, governance, and trust-based approaches. His publications include *Article 5: The Child's Right to Appropriate Direction and Guidance* (2012).

Fidelis Edge Kanyongolo is Associate Professor of Law at the University of Malawi and holds a PhD from the University of East Anglia. His research interests include legal philosophy and the politics of law. Among his publications are co-authored articles in the *Journal of International Constitutional Law* and the *Journal of Modern African Studies* and co-edited books including *Democracy in Progress: Malawi's 2009 Parliamentary and Presidential Elections* (Kachere, 2010) and *Democracy Tested: Malawi's 2019 Tripartite Elections* (Pretoria University Law Press, forthcoming).

Gift Wasambo Kayira holds a PhD in history from West Virginia University, USA. He lectures in the History Department of Chancellor College, University of Malawi. Kayira's research interests straddle histories of development and ethnic identities in 20th- and 21st-century Malawi. In addition to book chapters, he has previously published in the *Journal of Eastern African Studies, Journal of Public Administration and Development Alternatives,* and the *African Studies Quarterly,* among others.

Happy M. Kayuni is Professor and Dean of Faculty of Social Science in the University of Malawi's Chancellor College and holds a PhD (Political Science) from the University of Western Cape, South Africa. He also taught undergraduate as well as postgraduate programmes in the University of the Western

Cape and Cape Peninsula University of Technology. He has authored several journal articles and book chapters in the following areas: political governance, gender in politics, public sector reform and management, ethnic identity and international relations.

Dan Kuwali LLD, LLM (Lund), LLB (Hons) Malawi is an extraordinary professor of law at the University of Pretoria, South Africa and a fellow at the Carr Centre for Human Rights Policy, Harvard Kennedy School, USA. He is also the Chief of Legal Services and Judge Advocate General, Malawi Defence Force and Adjunct Professor and Founding Executive Director, Centre for Strategic Studies, Malawi University of Science and Technology.

George Chipembere Lwanda, a strategist, is a 2018 Asia Global Fellow at Hong Kong University's Asia Global Institute, an alumnus of the Mo Ibrahim-SOAS University of London Governance for Development in Africa Initiative and an alumnus of the TRALAC trade law programme. He is currently a senior development coordination officer with the United Nations Development Coordination Office. He holds an MSc in economic management and policy from the University of Strathclyde.

John Chipembere Lwanda, FRCP (Ed & Glas), PhD, is a medical practitioner, writer, broadcaster, social historian and an honorary Senior Research Fellow in Sociology and Politics at Glasgow University. His books include *Promises, Power, Politics & Poverty: Democratic Transition in Malawi (1961 to 1999)* (Dudu Nsomba, 1996), *Politics, Culture and Medicine in Malawi* (Kachere, 2005), *Kamuzu Banda of Malawi* (Kachere, 2009) and *Making Music in Malawi* (Logos Open Culture, 2021). He has written many peer-reviewed journal articles as well as newspaper columns.

Anthony Jeckson Malunga holds a PhD in Development Studies from the University of Dar es Salaam, Master's degree in Women's Law from the University of Zimbabwe and Bachelors in Education, University of Malawi. He is a Consultant at the Institute of Gender and Development and an adjunct lecturer for gender courses at the Faculty of Social Science, University of Malawi. He works with international development organisations. His publications and research interests are in gender, GBV, sexual reproductive health rights and women empowerment.

Bernadette Malunga holds a PhD in Law from the University of Nairobi, a Master's degree in Women's Law from the University of Zimbabwe and an LLB (Hons) Degree from the University of Malawi. She is a Senior Lecturer at the University of Malawi, Chancellor College. She has vast expertise and experience in gender and the law and administrative justice. She is passionate about women's and children's rights and governance.

Laston Petro Manja is a Lecturer in the Department of Economics at the University of Malawi, Chancellor College. With expertise in both macro- and micro-economics, his research interests span from international trade and monetary economics to development economics.

Ngcimezile Mbano-Mweso, is a Senior Lecturer in the Faculty of Law, University of Malawi. She has an LLD from University of Western Cape, an LLM in human rights and democratisation in Africa from University of Pretoria and LLB (Hons) from University of Malawi. She teaches and researches gender, governance, and environmental law. She is also the coordinator of Gender Justice Clinic, a platform for students training, advocacy, research and legal services.

Raphael Mbwana III is an HR advisor for a global corporation based in the United Kingdom. His work involves advising managers on employment related matters and the application of employment law. He actively follows Malawi politics, having lived through the transition from dictatorship to the current multiparty dispensation. Raf graduated from De Montfort University in 2005 with a BA (Hons) in Business & Marketing and works in corporate services where his interest in human capital developed.

Wapulumuka O. Mulwafu is Deputy Vice-Chancellor of Mzuzu University and formerly Professor of Environmental History and Dean of Postgraduate Studies at Chancellor College, University of Malawi. He is author of *Conservation Song: A History of Peasant-State Relations and the Environment in Malawi, 1860-2000* (Cambridge: The White Horse Press, 2011) and co-edited with John McCracken and Kings Phiri, *Malawi in Crisis: The 1959/60 Nyasaland State of Emergency and its Legacy* (Zomba: Kachere, 2012).

Mzee Hermann Yokaniah Mvula is Lecturer in Old Testament Ethics and Applied Theology at Chancellor College, University of Malawi. Mvula is the author of *The Theory, Praxis and Pursuit of Constitutionalism in Democratic Malawi: An Old Testament Ethical Perspective* (Kachere, 2020). He has also published several articles in refereed journals and book chapters. Mvula holds degrees from Africa Nazarene University, Nairobi, Kenya and the University of Malawi. He served as Head of the Department of Theology and Religious Studies, Chancellor College: 2015-2016.

Martin Limbikani Mwale is a final year PhD candidate at the University of Stellenbosch in South Africa, holding a Master of Commerce in Economics obtained from the same institution. He has interests in Development Economics and Spatial Econometrics Welfare Analysis. He is currently evaluating the effects of the Malawi Farm Input Subsidy Programme on women and children.

Tony Kamninga Mwenda is a Research and Policy Associate working with African Institute for Development Policy (AFIDEP). He holds a Master of Arts degree in Economics from the University of Malawi under the collaborative Master of Arts programme (CMAP) supported by the African Economic Research Consortium (AERC). His research interest is in applied micro-econometrics.

Bryson Nkhoma is an Associate Professor of History at Mzuzu University in Malawi, and a postdoctoral research fellow with the International Studies Group at the University of the Free State in South Africa. He holds a PhD in Africa Studies (History) from the University of the Free State. His research interests are: agrarian changes; diplomatic relations; migration. Some of his articles appeared in *Journal of Southern African Studies, South Africa Historical Journal, Southern Journal of Contemporary History,* and *Physics and Chemistry of the Earth.*

Kenneth R. Ross is Professor of Theology at Zomba Theological College, having earlier served as Professor of Theology at Chancellor College, University of Malawi, and as Chair of the Scotland Malawi Partnership. His books on governance in Malawi include *Democratisation in Malawi: A Stocktaking,* co-edited with Kings M. Phiri and published in the Kachere Series in 1998. He is currently Series Editor of the *Edinburgh Companions to Global Christianity* (Edinburgh University Press) and an Advisor to the World Council of Churches.

Ernest Lameck Thindwa is a Lecturer at the Department of Political and Administrative Studies, Chancellor College, University of Malawi. He holds an MA (Political Science) and a BA (Public Administration) both from the University of Malawi. He also holds an MBA from the Maastricht School of Management in Netherlands. He is not only a lecturer in political science and management studies but also an ardent governance activist. His research interest is in electoral and identity politics.

Abbreviations

ACB	Anti-Corruption Bureau
ACHPR	African Charter on Human and People's Rights
ADMARC	Agricultural Development and Marketing Corporation
AFORD	Alliance for Democracy
AIP	Affordable Inputs Programme
APRM	African Peer Review Mechanism
BEAM	Beautify Malawi Trust
BLAFO	Bwalo la Achewa Foundation
CAMA	Consumers Association of Malawi
CCAP	Church of Central African Presbyterian
CDP	Christian Democratic Party
CEDEP	Centre for the Development of People
CEDAW	Convention on the Elimination of All Forms of Discrimination against Women
CHEFO	Chewa Heritage Foundation
CHRR	Centre for Human Rights and Rehabilitation
CILIC	Civil Liberties Committee
CLP	Christian Liberation Party
Concourt	Constitutional Court
CDF	Constituency Development Fund
CPIA	Country Policy and Institutional Assessment
CRC	Convention on the Rights of the Child
CRPD	Convention on the Rights of People with Disabilities
CSO	Civil Society Organisation
CSR	Congress for a Second Republic
DPP	Democratic Progressive Party
EAM	Evangelical Association of Malawi
ESCOM	Electricity Supply Commission of Malawi

FBO	Faith Based Organisation
FISP	Farm Input Subsidy Programme
FPE	Fresh Presidential Elections
FPTP	First Past the Post
GII	Gender Inequality Index
HESLGB	Higher Education Students Loans and Grants Board
HDI	Human Development Index
HRDC	Human Rights Defenders' Coalition
ICCPR	International Covenant on Civil and Political Rights
ICESCR	International Covenant on Economic, Social and Cultural Rights
IDEA	Institute for Democracy and Electoral Assistance
MACRA	Malawi Communications Regulatory Authority
MAFREMO	Malawi Freedom Movement
MAFUNDE	Malawi Forum for Unity and National Development
MCC	Malawi Council of Churches
MCP	Malawi Congress Party
MDF	Malawi Defence Force
MDUM	Medical Doctors Union of Malawi
MEC	Malawi Electoral Commission
MERA	Malawi Energy Regulatory Authority
MGDS	Malawi Growth and Development Strategy
MHRC	Malawi Human Rights Commission
MIF	Mo Ibrahim Foundation
MLS	Malawi Law Society
MOD	Ministry of Defence
MP	Member of Parliament
MPS	Malawi Police Service
MRA	Malawi Revenue Authority
MSCA	Malawi Supreme Court of Appeal

MwA	Mulhako wa Alhomwe
MZIHA	Mzimba Heritage Association
NAC	Nyasaland African Congress
NEAP	National Environmental Action Plan
NEPAD	New Partnership for Africa's Development
NFRA	National Food Reserve Agency
NGO	Non-governmental Organisation
NGO-GCN	NGO Gender Coordination Network
NIS	National Intelligence Services
NOCMA	National Oil Company of Malawi
NONM	National Organisation of Nurses and Midwives
NSC	National Security Council
NSP	National Security Policy
OECD	Organisation for Economic Co-operation and Development
OVOP	One Village, One Product
PAA	Public Audit Act
PAC	Public Affairs Committee
PETRA	People's Transformation Party
PFM	Public Finance Management
PFMA	Public Finance Management Act
PP&DA	Public Procurement and Disposal of Assets Act
PP	People's Party
PS	Prisons Service
SADC	Southern African Development Community
SDGs	Sustainable Development Goals
SBRs	State Business Relationships
TPLF	Tigray People's Liberation Front
UDF	United Democratic Front
UFP	United Federal Party
UN	United Nations

UNDP	United Nations Development Programme
UNESCO	United Nations Educational, Scientific and Cultural Organisation
UTM	United Transformation Movement
VAWE	Violence against Women in Elections
WHO	World Health Organisation
WOLREC	Women's Legal Resource Centre

Foreword

Paul Tiyambe Zeleza

This comprehensive, compelling, accessible and timely volume should be compulsory reading to academics, policy makers, social activists, and the general public in Malawi and elsewhere on the continent. It is the best book I have read recently on the country's complex, contradictory, messy, and disappointing political and socioeconomic dispensation since the dawn of the era of multiparty democracy in 1994. It mirrors the trajectories, and provides critical insights and invaluable lessons on, Africa's enduring struggles to construct democratic developmental states as envisaged by the late great Malawian public intellectual, Thandika Mkandawire.

The quality of the chapters is as impressive as the range of topics covered is exhaustive. Each of the sixteen chapters is extensively researched, cogently argued, and well written. Admirably, the chapters combine copious empirical data and sophisticated theoretical analysis. They often seek to place the developments in Malawi in the wider African, and sometimes global, contexts, thus illuminating the general literature on the political economies of Africa's postcolonies and the global South more broadly. This is one reason this book should appeal to a much wider audience than its Malawian emplacement might otherwise suggest.

The authors represent the cream of Malawian scholars, both seasoned and upcoming, located in the universities, think tanks, and public agencies. Some are renowned public intellectuals who have honed their professional lives and praxis in the often demanding and dangerous whirlpool of social activism. They all write with fervour and a sense of urgency, while maintaining the academic disposition of dispassionate analysis. This is an uneasy balance to maintain, but many are able to pull it off. They seem animated by the lingering spirits of a national intelligentsia from the bygone era of African nationalism that was driven by the historic and humanistic struggles and agendas for self-determination, nation-building, democracy, and development.

The accounts the authors present of the pervasive dysfunctions of Malawi's troubled experiment with multiparty democracy since the mid-1990s, and the endlessly deferred dreams of development, are often dispiriting. Yet, their bleak diagnoses are often accompanied by ameliorative prescriptions that are simultaneously bold and pragmatic. The book exudes a sense of hope that the struggles for a better future will continue. In itself the book represents a testament to the possibilities of the country's democratic dispensation, the need to unflinchingly confront the country's debilitating political and socioeconomic pathologies. Such a text would have been unthinkable during the dictatorship of the founding president, Dr. Hastings Kamuzu Banda.

I found the range of the topics covered exhaustive and deeply engrossing. I am confident other readers will benefit immensely engaging themes of particular interest to them. But I urge everyone to read the whole book as its analytical riches pile almost seamlessly and successively from the opening chapter to the last one.

The book opens with an exquisite examination of Malawi's pervasive and worsening corruption through the creation and sustenance of a regime of what Henry Chingaipe aptly calls "roving banditry." He argues public finance mismanagement escalated after the introduction of the multiparty democratic order driven by a confluence of structural and institutional dynamics and incentives in Malawi's entrenched predatory state and kleptocratic political class. Corruption represents a crippling tax and robbery of development, a massive assault on good governance, and impunity against public morality. His list of public investments that would have been made with funds lost to some of the infamous corruption scandals is truly depressing.

In its trenchant analysis, the opening chapter sets the stage for the subsequent chapters that follow its analytical ethos of unsparing critique of the various dimensions of Malawi's post-1994 crass and inept regimes. In their chapter, Chunga and Kayuni analyze the declining levels of public trust in key governance institutions due to the persistence of neo-patrimonial tendencies, tepid public sector reforms, poor economic management, and the persistence of a political culture of patronage, clientelism, and corruption. This has progressively undermined the legitimacy of the state and consolidation of the country's hard won multiparty democracy.

Declining public trust serves to undermine good governance further in a vicious spiral. Mwale, Chirwa, Kamninga, and Manja elaborate on the growing democratic deficits that has led to declining public trust in the election management body, the Malawi Electoral Commission, increasing propensity of citizens to participate in demonstrations, and growing willingness to evade paying taxes.

The impunity of state actors reached an apogee in the contested May 2019 presidential election. The election drama electrified the nation and catapulted Malawi into the lofty annals of African political history as the second country after Kenya where the courts annulled presidential election results and the first country where the fresh elections were won by the opposition. This is the subject of Garton Kamchedzera's detailed and informative chapter on the 2019-2020 presidential election case in the volume. He sees the case as a battle between impunity with mediocrity and transformational constitutional legality, in which the latter scored a provisional victory.

The disputed presidential election of May 2019 provoked widespread protests. In his chapter, Fidelis Kanyongolo focuses on the legal responses to electoral violence, their limits and implications for democratic governance. Women tend to suffer disproportionately from electoral violence compared to men. In their chapter, Jeckson Malunga, Mbano-Mweso and Wangisa Malunga illuminate the role of different groups of women leaders, namely, those in political leadership, civil society activists, and those in constitutional bodies, in challenging violence against women before, during and after Malawi's 2019 tripartite presidential, parliamentary and local elections.

Ernest Thindwa interrogates Malawi's electoral system. He notes the inherent problems of the simple plurality or first-past-the-post system inherited from Britain, the former colonial power. In the multiparty era it engendered minority governments with declining margins of victory in successive elections and reinforced ethno-regional mobilisation and divisions. Concerted pressures for electoral reform by political parties, civil society organisations, development partners, and public institutions finally succeeded in forcing the adoption of the qualified absolute majority electoral system in the June 2020 fresh presidential election.

A destabilizing characteristic of Malawian and African politics more generally is the perennial instability of political parties, constant fluctuation of electoral alliances, and debilitating weaknesses of opposition parties thanks to the persistence of the patrimonial logic of the one-party state era. Under the winner-take-all system, presidentialism and patronage retain their fierce seductions and sanctions that often cripple opposition parties, politicians, and politics. John Lwanda, George Lwanda and Raphael Mbwana offer a fascinating review of this unsavoury phenomenon and the fate of opposition parties in Malawi between 1994-2020.

The challenges of democratic governance and accountability manifest themselves in multiple arenas and dimensions. In his chapter, Dan Kuwali queries Malawi's challenges in ensuring the professionalism, coordination and interoperability of the country's security organs. He argues that notwithstanding the adoption of the National Security Policy in 2018, democratic oversight of the security sector by the Executive, Judiciary and Legislature, as well as by civil society agencies, remains weak, against which he proposes several reforms and interventions.

Mphatso Phiri scrutinizes a key security agency, namely, the military, in terms of how public finance management is exercised by the Malawi Defence Force in adherence to the principles of good governance and democratic consolidation. The findings are quite troubling. There is little public oversight exerted on the military, certainly not by the Legislature. Instead there is "Executive supremacy" in which the military has been deployed since colonial times as an organ of unaccountable state power. This institutional history and mode of security governance and public finance management became entrenched during the Banda dictatorship and persevered after multiparty democracy.

Another troubling feature of Malawi's multiparty democracy is that it has not made much progress in promoting gender equality in terms of women's political representation in Parliament and other walks of life. This is of course a global challenge as evident in the data from the Inter-Parliamentary Union. Notwithstanding constitutional provisions for gender equality, the country's ratification of regional and international declarations and instruments, and the 50-50 Campaign levels of women's descriptive representation remain low. Asiyati Chiweza attributes this to the structural limitations of neopatrimonialism, patriarchal practices of political parties, cut-throat and personalized winner-take-all majoritarian electoral systems, and the lack of gender quotas.

In addition to the challenges of inclusive gender representation, ethnicity and regionalism continue to cast their divisive shadows on the nation-building and democratic projects of the postcolonial state and society. The divisions have deepened in post-1994 Malawi as the political class mobilizes and retreats into the imagined sanctuaries of ethno-regional identities in their ferocious political struggles for elected power and patronage. Gift Kayira and Paul Banda critically survey the growth of the country's deepening polarisations and the escalating debate on federalism. On compelling theoretical and empirical grounds, they are critical of federalism as the panacea for nation-building and advocate decentralisation and devolution of government as in Kenya notwithstanding the challenges experienced in that country.

Such is the beauty of this collection that the issues of governance are extended to a pressing national, regional, and global challenge, namely, the management of natural resources. Wapulumuka Mulwafu presents a sobering account of environmental degradation and the deepening crisis of environmental management that he traces to the colonial period through the postcolonial era under the Banda dictatorship. The crisis has worsened after 1994 as the state loosened its grip over the control of natural resources without the wider society, confronted by rapid population growth, persistent poverty, and excessive dependence on fuelwood for energy, adequately assuming its environmental protection responsibilities. He proposes a holistic and integrated approach in environmental policy development and implementation encompassing cultural attitudes, state regulation, education, and integrity of the ecosystem.

The state of governance is often thrown into sharp relief during national, regional and global crises. The COVID-19 pandemic, which devastated health care systems, economies, and the lives and livelihoods of tens of millions of people around the world, exposed and exacerbated Malawi's democratic and development tensions and challenges. In their chapter, Nkhoma, Kayira, and Banda offer an extensive and nuanced analysis of the political economy of the pandemic that coincided with the political turmoil of the disputed 2019 presidential election. The pandemic was used by the government and different stakeholders in their contestations over the remit and limits of state power, public health preparedness and interventions, economic support measures and management, human rights and political freedoms.

The volume ends with an intriguing chapter on Malawi's governance crisis in theological perspective by Mzee Mvula and Kenneth Ross. It begins by noting the important role the church played in the struggle for democracy and protection of the Constitution through the influential religious-led Public Affairs Committee, although the church has also exhibited some of the regional divergences and divisions wracking the national polity. The authors focus on three dimensions of governance, corruption and plunder, impunity and accountability, and the question of leadership. They argue that religion can provide theological resources to address the challenges facing the nation. They specifically examine the import of the biblical text, global theological thinking, and local contextual theology as powerful mechanisms to create a more progressive and enlightened political culture so essential for democratic governance reform and renewal.

Clearly, this is an important and powerful collection of essays that readers will engage with great profit. They will better understand the crises of democratic governance that ail Malawi, more than 25 years after the end of the one-party dictatorship. They will also come to better appreciate the struggles and strategies needed to maintain the age-old nationalist and Pan-African dreams of constructing an integrated, inclusive, innovative, and sustainable democratic and developmental state and society dreamt and waged by generations of patriots and public intellectuals.

Nairobi, June 19, 2021.

Introduction: A Pivotal Moment for Governance in Malawi?

Kenneth R. Ross, Asiyati Lorraine Chiweza & Wapulumuka O. Mulwafu

On 3 February 2020, Malawi made history when the 2019 presidential election result was overturned after a panel of five High Court judges identified "widespread, systematic, and grave irregularities" in the polls, declared the result "invalid, null and void", and called for a fresh election. On that historic day the country came to a standstill as people spent the day listening on the radio to the judgment delivered by Justice Healey Potani, Justice Ivy Kamanga, Justice Redson Kapindu, Justice Dingiswayo Madise and Justice Michael Tembo. The judges had allegedly been subject to attempted bribery and threats to their safety. They arrived in court under armed escort and wearing bullet-proof vests. It took the whole day to deliver a summary of their 500-page ruling and by the end of it, fair-minded listeners were convinced that, as had been widely suspected, the previous year's presidential election lacked integrity. After months of high tension, the country could move on to conduct a fresh presidential election. The incumbent Government appealed to the Supreme Court, which upheld the findings of the Constitutional Court in its judgment of 8 May 2020. It was a highly significant moment in terms of the independence of the judiciary, the separation of powers, the accountability of the executive and the supremacy of the Constitution. The more so when the opposition Tonse Alliance went on to comfortably win the election, held on 23 June 2020. It was the first time in the history of sub-Saharan Africa that a flawed presidential election was invalidated, with the opposition going on to win at the polls.

International Significance of Malawi's Constitutional Court Ruling

These remarkable events in Malawi have not gone unnoticed on the international stage. On 26 October 2020, it was announced that Malawi's Constitutional Court judges had won the 2020 Chatham House Prize in recognition of their courage and independence in defence of democracy. "At a time when standards of democratic governance are under threat not only in Africa, but in many democracies," reads the citation, "Malawi's constitutional court judges set an example for their peers across the world by upholding the centrality of the rule of law and separation of powers."[1] Dr Robin Niblett, Director of Chatham House, commented: "This is a historic moment for democratic governance. The ruling by Malawi's constitutional court judges is not only crucial for rebuilding the confidence of Malawi's citizens in their institutions, but also for upholding standards of democracy more widely across the African continent."[2] Soon afterwards further recognition of the significance of the Constitutional Court judgment came when *The Economist* magazine named Malawi as its "country of the year" for 2020. "Malawi is still poor," it commented, "but its people are citizens, not subjects. For reviving democracy in an authoritarian region, it is our country of the year."[3] Likewise, US-based Freedom House found that Malawi was the only country in the world where there was a positive trend in regard to freedom and democracy during the onset of the coronavirus pandemic in 2020.[4]

Enduring Issues of Concern

It is notoriously difficult to assess the historical significance of events while they are still unfolding. Nevertheless, some observers have ventured to suggest that the events of 2019-20 might be remembered as a third major political turning-point in Malawi's modern history, following the attainment of independence in 1964 and the introduction of multiparty democracy in 1993-1994.[5] The reasons for attaching such high importance to the events of 2019-20 are explored in the pages of this book. Its analysis spans a range of issues which, taken together, demonstrate how far Malawi's national integrity and social equilibrium were threatened by negative trends in relation to governance. These came to a head in the political crisis of 2019-20. Some matters have been decisively addressed, such as the electoral system for the election of the president. Others remain on the agenda, such as the need to establish sound

---

1 www.chathamhouse.org/2020/10/chatham-house-prize-malawi-judges-win-election-work accessed 10 January 2021.

2 Ibid.

3 *The Economist*, 19 December 2020.

4 Malika Gharib,"The Pandemic Is Not Good For Freedom and Democracy–But There Are Exceptions", Freedom House Report, 10 November 2020 www.npr.org/sections/goatsandsoda/2020/11/10/930464419/report-the-pandemic-is-not-good-for-freedom-and-democracy-but-there-are-exceptio accessed 13 February 2021.

5 See John McCracken, *A History of Malawi 1859-1966*, Woodbridge: James Currey, 2012, 336-428; Matembo S. Nzunda and Kenneth R. Ross (eds), *Church, Law and Political Transition in Malawi 1992-94*, Gweru: Mambo-Kachere, 1995.

practice in the management of public finances or the effective separation of powers.

The mass demonstrations held in 2019 to protest against the conduct and outcome of the presidential election reflected widespread dissatisfaction amongst the population at large with the way in which Malawi has been governed. The demonstrations were driven not only by the injustice of one flawed election but also by deep concern about long-standing social, political and economic problems that successive governments have failed to address. It is almost thirty years since Malawi changed from a one-party authoritarian regime to a democratic multiparty system of government. As a system of governance, democracy retains high approval ratings in the country. Afrobarometer surveys conducted in 2017 showed that 71% of Malawian respondents support democracy, 84% reject presidential dictatorship, 69% reject one-party rule, and 86% reject military rule. Ironically, while democracy as a system of governance scores well, the same cannot be said about democratic performance. A majority of Malawians say their country is "not a democracy" (14%) or "a democracy with major problems" (42%).[6] A previous assessment of the process of democratisation was equivocal: not progressing much, not backsliding but perhaps stuck in transition.[7] Several post-mortem assessments of the 2014 elections also found a similar result: "that Malawi's democracy is stuck in a period of transition, neither consolidating as a democracy nor regressing to the era of authoritarianism."[8]

Constitutional provisions and subsidiary legislation have established democratic institutions in Malawi. However, the functioning of the democratic institutions is erratic and not always consistent with their legal mandates.[9] The formal rules—no matter how stringently formulated—are often contravened in favour of personalised and irregular agendas.[10] As a result Malawi's political

---

6 Afrobarometer, *Afrobarometer Round 7: Summary of Results for Malawi, 2017*, Zomba: Centre for Social Research, 2018.

7 Lars Svåsand, "Democratization in Malawi: Moving Forward, Stuck in Transition or Backsliding?" *Forum for Development Studies* 38/1 (2011), 1–24.

8 See Nandini Patel, and Michael Wahman (eds), *The Malawi 2014 Tripartite Elections: Is Democracy Maturing?* Lilongwe: National Initiative for Civic Education, 2015; Boniface Dulani, "Progress or Stagnation? Twenty Years of Democracy", in Dan Banik and Blessings Chinsinga (eds), *Political Transition and Inclusive Development in Malawi: The Democratic Dividend*, Abingdon: Routledge, 2016, 15–34.

9 Bertelsmann Stiftung, *BTI 2020 Country Report – Malawi*, Gütersloh: Bertelsmann, 2020.

10 Arne Tostensen, *Malawi: A Political Economy Analysis. A Report commissioned by the Norwegian Ministry of Foreign Affairs,* Oslo: 2017.

governance has since then been characterised as "fundamentally a hybrid neo-patrimonial state where a framework of formal law and administration exists but the state is informally characterised by patronage networks.[11] Over the years this has manifested in various ways which we elaborate below.

Based on the 1994 Constitution, the governance system of Malawi comprises a standard set of institutions, nominally akin to those of a modern, liberal-democratic state: a legislature, an executive and a judiciary as well as a number of institutions of restraint. However, because of executive dominance, the legislature has limited means to perform its oversight task.[12] However, the generally accepted assessment of the judiciary as relatively independent of the executive still holds true.[13]

Political parties in Malawi, although numerous, have, with few exceptions, shallow social roots in the electorate and weak institutional structures. For their part, they are partially committed to democratic principles in their internal affairs. Clientelism remains prevalent and many political parties coalesce around ethnic identities or the personality of a key founding member who may also be a source of funding. Voters tend to rally around political parties due to ethnic identity or clientelism rather than ideological preference. With the exception of the 2009 elections, in which the incumbent DPP garnered support throughout the country, electoral support tends to follow regional-cum-ethnic lines.[14] As a result, Malawian politics are orientated towards personalities rather than ideology or policy issues. Electoral success depends heavily on networks of clientelism and patrimonialism, not on impressive election manifestos.[15] The persistence of patrimonialism and ethnicity means that the structures and culture of democracy remain weak. There is an ever-widening divergence between campaign promises and the lack or slow delivery on such promises.[16]

---

[11] Diana Cammack, Fred Golooba-Mutebi, Fidelis Kanyongolo and Tam O'Neil, *Neopatrimonial Politics, Decentralisation and Local Government: Uganda and Malawi in 2006*, Good Governance, Aid Modalities and Poverty Reduction Working Paper Series, London: ODI, 2007.

[12] Henry Chingaipe, Austin Zvoma and Roosevelt Gondwe, *Political Economy Analysis of the Malawi Parliament: Determinants of Performance and Prospects for Improved Effectiveness*, Lilongwe: Institute for Policy Research & Social Empowerment, 2016.

[13] Rachel Ellett, *Politics of Judicial Independence in Malawi*, Washington D.C.: Freed, 2014.

[14] Arne Tostensen, *Malawi: A Political Economy Analysis. A Report Commissioned by the Norwegian Ministry of Foreign Affairs,* Oslo: Norway, 2017.

[15] Bertelsmann Stiftung, *BTI 2020 Country Report – Malawi.* Gütersloh: Bertelsmann, 2020.

[16] Siame Kameme, "Politics, Democracy and Governance in Independent Malawi: The dichotomy between promises and reality", MPhil, University of Birmingham, 2011.

All political parties have failed to play a meaningful role in spearheading fundamental and sustainable democratic and structural transformation. Once in power they have perpetuated clientelistic behaviour, forged settlements within the political elite to the effect that those well connected to the political establishment have benefited at the expense of national development.[17] According to Prowse and Grassin, vested interests within elite circles swirl around and soak into governance processes, since they always want to ensure that their interests are served.[18]

Neopatrimonial politics and ethnic cliques also affect the ability of the democratically elected representatives to use formal power to govern in Malawi. There are strong indications, however, that between elections, informality often overrides the formal rules and processes and thus undermines the power of elected representatives. For example, a close analysis of some decisions (e.g., appointments to key government positions or removal from key government offices) suggests that informal forces sometimes sway government decisions.

A multitude of civil society organisations (CSOs) play a prominent role in the governance realm, acting primarily to scrutinise the government and as participants in the public debate. Generally, civil society has increasingly asserted itself in recent years. A particularly prominent sub-category of CSOs are faith-based organisations (FBOs). They act independently and collectively —for example through the Public Affairs Committee (PAC), the Malawi Council of Churches (MCC), and the Evangelical Association of Malawi (EAM).[19] FBOs occasionally issue pastoral letters or statements on salient political and social issues—e.g., corruption and elections—that receive coverage in the media. However, they tend to act opportunistically when societal tension is running high, for example around elections, but also when other issues are on the agenda, such as Bakili Muluzi's bid for a third term.[20] They are reputed to make some difference but also experience frustration when up against the powers-that-be.[21] Over the years, some civil society organisations have been infiltrated by pro-government figures, who alongside

---

17 Arne Tostensen, *Malawi: A Political Economy Analysis.*

18 Martin Prowse and Paul Grassin, *Tobacco, Transformation and Development Dilemmas from Central Africa*, London: Palgrave Macmillan, 2020.

19 Arne Tostensen, *Malawi: A Political Economy Analysis.*

20 Joseph Chunga and Arne Tostensen, "Clergy in Politics: The Opportunistic Engagement of Faith-Based Organisations in Malawi's Politics", *Journal of Religion in Africa* 49 (2019), 1–33.

21 Ibid.

some traditional leaders have advanced pro-government interests through spreading misinformation and fomenting scandal among opposition parties and critical civic groups such as the Public Affairs Committee.[22]

Corruption and the abuse of office remain a persistent scourge. Despite the professed commitment to curbing corruption by successive governments since the democratic transition of 1993-94, this scourge remains endemic in Malawi.[23] Chinsinga and Matita note that Malawi's competitive clientelist regime has resulted in patronage-driving policy and is underpinned by rampant fraud, corruption, nepotism, and sheer opportunism with a decentralised rent management system.[24] This perpetuates a political logic in which corruption is tolerated as a means of rewarding loyalists and rents are captured to promote political aims rather than to reinvest in poverty reduction and inclusive growth.[25] Efforts to deal with corruption are piecemeal and half-hearted.[26] It is asserted that due to the dysfunctional-cum-corrupt governance system the economy is stagnant and poverty is pervasive.[27] The latest Afrobarometer survey conducted in 2019 but released in 2020 revealed that a majority (83.5%) of Malawians were of the view that their country was "going in the wrong direction." This view was shared by large majorities in both urban and rural areas as well as across all major political parties.[28]

The Human Development Index (HDI) also highlights Malawi's dire economic situation. In 2020, Malawi's value on the HDI was 0.483—which put the country in the low human development category, at 174 out of 189 countries. Malawi's economy is heavily aid-dependent. Over the years, about 40% of the state budget has been sourced from donors. Access to opportunities may

---

22 Bertelsmann Stiftung, *BTI 2020 Country Report – Malawi.*

23 Blessings Chinsinga, Happy Kayuni and Sidon Konyani, *Governance and Corruption Survey 2010*, Zomba: Centre for Social Research, 2010.

24 Blessings Chinsinga and Mirriam Matita, *The Political Economy of the Groundnut Value Chain in Malawi: its re-emergence amidst policy chaos, strategic neglect, and opportunism*. APRA working paper series no. 56, Brighton, UK: Institute of Development Studies, 2021.

25 Diana Cammack, "The Politics of Chameleons Revisited: The Burden of Malawi's Political Culture", in Martin Ott and Edge Kanyongolo (eds) *Malawi's 2009 Parliamentary and Presidential Elections*, Balaka: Montfort Media, 2010. See further Harri Englund (ed), *A Democracy of Chameleons: Politics and Culture in the New Malawi*, Stockholm: Nordiska Afrikainstitutet and Blantyre: CLAIM-Kachere, 2002.

26 Bertelsmann Stiftung, *BTI 2020 Country Report – Malawi.*

27 Arne Tostensen, *Malawi: A Political Economy Analysis.*

28 Afrobarometer, *Summary of Results.* Afrobarometer Round 8 survey in Malawi. Afrobarometer Briefing, 2020.

depend on one's ethnic identity and connections to ethnic kin. Gender is also a key factor, reflected in the fact that women occupy few influential positions in society. Political equality in terms of gender seems to have retrogressed to the level of 2004. In the 2009 election, 22.3%of the elected MPs were women. This figure dropped to 16.7% in 2014, roughly the same as in 2004. Patriarchy remains a predominant social paradigm in Malawi. The country ranked 163 out of 188 countries on the UN Gender Inequality Index. The Mo Ibrahim African Governance Index 2020 report on gender scores depicts Malawi as a country that is showing deterioration on gender inclusion and equality. The report shows negative trends on political power and representation of women (-12.4 points), equal civil liberties for women (-6.0 points) and violence against women.[29]

Although successive governments have made commendable attempts to set short- to medium-term priorities in their development policies and plans, consistent implementation in accordance with those priorities has been lacking. Malawi seems better at developing and setting priorities than implementing them. Medium-term strategies have been developed in three Malawi Growth and Development Strategies (MGDS I, II and III). Government's inability to follow through on development initiatives is in many ways a function of a widespread unwillingness among successive governments to continue the policy initiatives of previous administrations. Instead, new leaders often start their own projects while abandoning those of their predecessors. Governments remain sensitive to the vagaries of electoral competition and sometimes alter their priorities in order to boost their chances of electoral victory.[30]

Malawi has a long history of public sector reform. There have been 80 reform attempts by successive administrations since independence in 1964, but none have produced the desired results.[31] The Malawi Public Service has persistently experienced poor and declining performance in the delivery of services as well as in the management of public agencies, a deterioration of work ethic, indiscipline and absenteeism and proliferation of fraud and corruption.[32] Two years

---

29 Mo Ibrahim Foundation, 2020 Ibrahim Index of African Governance Index Report, London: Mo Ibrahim Foundation, 2020.

30 For a recent wide-ranging analysis see Matthias Rompel and Reiner Gronemeyer, *Malawi: Economy, Society and Political Affairs*, London: Zed Books, 2020.

31 Arne Tostensen, *Malawi: A Political Economy Analysis.*

32 Government of Malawi, *Malawi Public Service Management Policy 2018 to 2022*, OPC: Lilongwe, 2018.

after the launch of the Public Service Reform Commission report the politicisation of the public service remains deeply entrenched.[33] Despite efforts to instil prudence in the management of public resources, budget discipline is often lax and resources are diverted to purposes other than those intended.

It should be noted that Malawi has acceded to all major international and regional conventions on human rights: (a) the International Covenant on Civil and Political Rights (ICCPR) that includes rights related to elections such as freedom of assembly, freedom of expression, and freedom of association; (b) the International Covenant on Economic, Social and Cultural Rights (ICESCR); (c) the Convention on the Rights of the Child (CRC); (d) the Convention on the Elimination of All Forms of Discrimination against Women (CEDAW); (f) the Convention on the Rights of People with Disabilities (CRPD); and (g) the African Charter on Human and People's Rights (ACHPR). As a signatory to these instruments, Malawi is legally obligated to abide by their precepts. Many of the obligations are enshrined in Malawi's Constitution as the Bill of Rights, while others have been legislated and specified in Acts of Parliament. However, adherence to the legal obligations has been challenging and performance with regard to different rights is uneven.

Genesis of the Book

Concern to address this cluster of issues from an academic perspective prompted a group of scholars, mainly but not exclusively from Chancellor College, University of Malawi, to come together in the aftermath of the 3 February 2020 judgment of the Constitutional Court. Their initial plan was to launch a series of public seminars as a forum for academic analysis of the issues at stake in the life of the nation. However, the onset of the coronavirus and consequent closure of schools and colleges throughout Malawi the following month meant that public events were no longer advisable. There was, however, time available for writing. So, a call for papers was issued with a view to working towards the publication of a book on governance in Malawi. This attracted an enthusiastic response, with more than 30 abstracts being submitted. A rigorous editorial process, including double-blind peer review, shaped the chapters that are now found in this book. The editors acknowledge their debt to all the

33 Lewis Dzimbiri, "Politics and the Public Service", in Banik and Chinsinga, *Political Transition and Inclusive Development in Malawi: The Democratic Dividend*, Abingdon: Routledge, 2016, 75–94.

contributors, who were operating in the challenging circumstances presented by the pandemic.

One creative response to those circumstances has been to develop more online academic engagement. Under the auspices of the Scotland Malawi Partnership, which is generously supporting the publication, there will be an online lecture series in 2021-22, based on the contents of the book. Hence the original idea of a seminar series is being fulfilled in a way that was not expected at the outset. The project has faced significant obstacles that could easily have derailed it but has been motivated by a strong sense that there was a duty laid on the scholarly community to attempt a comprehensive academic analysis of what appeared to be a pivotal political moment in the life of the nation. This is what can be found in the chapters that follow.

Organisation of the Book

The chapters of the book are arranged in a broadly centrifugal pattern, with the early chapters setting out central issues of concern in relation to governance in Malawi while the later chapters examine the issues at stake from a variety of disciplinary and critical perspectives. The multi-disciplinary character of the book means that it is not uniform in terms of methodology. Sources and methods vary considerably among the different chapters, including the use of interviews, statistical data, observations, questionnaires, literature review and documentary analysis. This brings a richness and texture to the analysis that might be difficult to achieve if confined to the methodological approach of just one particular discipline. The complexity presented by the challenges of governance lends itself to an analysis that draws on a variety of methodological approaches.

The first chapter by Henry Chingaipe addresses an issue which, if it is not resolved, threatens to undermine all of Malawi's efforts to attain good governance: the question of mismanagement of public finances. Examining the 2010-2020 decade, the chapter assembles a formidable body of evidence to suggest that misappropriation of government funds was wide and pervasive during this period. The notorious Cashgate scandal of 2013, on this analysis, turns out to be no more than the tip of an iceberg. Chingaipe describes the situation as one of "roving banditry", a metaphor drawn from the history of Warlord China in the 1920s. China's roving bandits worked on a short time horizon, simply concerned to plunder as many resources as possible from the population at their mercy with no regard for the future. Likewise, it is suggested that state elites in Malawi created a felonious state in which they used positions intended to protect and promote the public interest to extract resources for their own benefit. How can we explain the persistence and intractability of public finance mismanagement? Moving beyond technical public accounting and managerial capacity perspectives, Chingaipe takes a political economy approach to explain habitual, non-random public finance mismanagement. He finds that the configuration of political power and the exercise of the state's administrative authority were reconfigured and repurposed by a confluence of informal rules that overlay or displaced formal rules in ways that responded to and reinforced a spoils culture that militated against public finance management.

A pertinent question to ask in light of such evidence of mismanagement of public finances is how far Malawians maintain trust in the organs of the state. This is the question taken up in the next chapter by Joseph Chunga and Happy Kayuni. They observe that the success or failure of government policies and programmes largely depends on the trust enjoyed by such public institutions as the presidency, Parliament, the courts and the police. Using mainly Afrobarometer data sets, the authors examine trajectories of public trust in these key government institutions from 1999 to 2019, explore factors that affect public trust, and assess the implications for state legitimacy and prospects of democracy. Critical perspectives drawn from relevant recent literature demonstrate that public trust has critical implications on the long-term legitimacy and democratic consolidation of any polity. In Malawi, the post-1994 Constitution specifically stipulates that authority of all state institutions is based on sustained trust of the people. This was an attempt to emerge from the shadow of three-decades of strong presidency, a Parliament that was effectively a rubberstamp of presidential decrees and a security service that was politically captured and used to stifle political dissent. However, on the evidence presented here, Malawi's overall trajectory in regard to public trust in state institutions, notwithstanding some variations, is not a healthy one. To reverse the negative trend, the authors suggest there is urgent need for a strengthened anti-corruption drive and a more convincing government performance in regard to management of the economy, particularly concerning food supply.

The question of citizen trust is further pursued by Martin Limbikani Mwale, Gowokani Chijere Chirwa, Tony Mwenda Kamninga and Laston Petro Manja in a chapter that focuses on the correlation between trust in the Malawi Electoral Commission on the one hand and willingness to pay taxes and willingness to participate in demonstrations on the other hand. They examine three cross-sections of Malawi Afrobarometer survey data from the years 2018, 2014 and 2012 and employ probit models to account for chronological variation as regards willingness to pay tax and willingness to demonstrate. The results reveal that increasing levels of trust positively associate with the willingness to pay tax. Further, increasing levels of trust reduce citizens' willingness to demonstrate. These results highlight the importance of fostering credible election management bodies that are trusted by citizens. In terms of economic impact, high levels of trust in these bodies have the potential to simultaneously improve public financing and reduce economy-wide disruptions from protests. Hence there is far-reaching importance to the chapter's finding that trust in electoral bodies is critical in ensuring reduced demonstrations and increased willingness to pay taxes.

Garton Kamchedzera discusses the way in which Malawi's 2019-20 presidential Election Case highlighted the contest between impunity and constitutional legality in Malawi's governance. Impunity with mediocrity is a negation of the key function of the law, to guide behaviour, decision and action. The chapter suggests that by giving consequential directions to Parliament to pass necessary laws and inquire into the competence and capacity of the Electoral Commission, the two courts sitting as a Constitutional Court (Concourt) and the Malawi Supreme Court of Appeal (MSCA) achieved social significance because they showed how the law can resist impunity and mediocrity. The court judgments proved to be a game-changer in Malawi because they insisted on strict performance of duties laid down by the Constitution and required accountability for such performance. Kamchedzera argues that this can be socially and politically transformative since it introduces accountability to the aspirations of the people as expressed in the Constitution. The outcomes of the court cases demonstrated the resilience of the law in calling impunity and mediocrity to account. This has significance not only for the resolution of the political crisis of 2019-20 but for the constitutional accountability of public officials at all times. If it is not possible to require excellence in the discharge of public duty, it can at least be possible to require a reasonable level of fulfilment of constitutional obligation. This can be a significant breakthrough for the people of Malawi who have for too long endured impunity and mediocrity on the part of those entrusted with public office.

Fidelis Edge Kanyongolo takes up the troubling question of election-related violence. For too long a dark shadow of violence has been cast over Malawi's elections and the elections of 2019 and 2020 were no exception. Kanyongolo takes account of reported incidents of violence, considering such factors as geography, age and gender, to build a picture of the nature of the problem. His particular focus is on the legal responses that have been made when violent incidents have occurred. A significant issue inhibiting effective legal response is perceived state capture of such actors as the Malawi Police Service and prosecutorial agencies, resulting in these agents failing to act in an impartial way, and government-affiliated perpetrators believing that they can act with impunity. By contrast, Malawians generally have confidence in the courts to hear cases impartially. However, few trials for cases of election violence have been concluded, or even commenced, and the relatively light sentences imposed on those convicted fail to reflect how much is at stake for the nation in the deterrence of election-related violence. Kanyongolo is driven to the conclusion that gaps in the legal definition of election violence, selective law enforcement and prosecutions and operational inefficiencies of legal institutions and processes in the legal responses to violence connected to the 2019 and 2020 elections have jeopardised the rule of law, observance of human rights and the integrity of electoral processes.

The next chapter is also concerned with election-related violence. Anthony Jeckson Malunga, Ngcimezile Mbano-Mweso and Bernadette Wangisa Malunga investigate the role of women leaders in challenging violence against women in elections (VAWE) in Malawi during the May 2019 tripartite elections. Their evidence suggests that VAWE played a significant role in threatening and inhibiting full and free participation of women in the electoral process. But when women themselves are in leadership positions can they challenge such violence? The chapter considers three categories of women leaders: women in political leadership, civil society women's rights activists, and women leaders in constitutional bodies with the legal mandate to act against VAWE. It shows that having women occupying significant positions of leadership does not, by itself, guarantee that they will be effective in countering VAWE. Their own personal motivation is a significant factor but there are also forces at play that can limit their effectiveness even if they are personally committed. The aim of the chapter is to assess how far women leaders in the three categories were able to challenge or curb VAWE and whether they can be regarded as game-changers or not. Its findings present a mixed picture, with both successes and failures. Some women leaders can be identified as game-changers while others cannot. By identifying factors that make for success or failure on this score, the chapter offers an original contribution.

When the Constitutional Court gave its momentous judgment on 3 February 2020, it was the decision to nullify the 2019 presidential election that initially caught the eye. Arguably, however, even more influential was its interpretation of the constitutional provision that the president be elected by a "majority" of the electorate. In the conduct of Malawi's elections since 1994 this had always been interpreted as a matter of "first-past-the-post", i.e. the candidate with the highest number of votes was declared to be the winner. This practice was found by the court to be unconstitutional and it interpreted the term "majority" in the Constitution as meaning that the president must secure more than half of the votes cast (50%+1). In practice, this would involve a "run-off" in the event that no candidate secured more than 50% of the votes in the first round of voting. Ernest Thindwa explores the debate over this issue that took place in the years prior to the judgment. He also exposes the anomalous situation in which Malawi approached the 2020 presidential election, with the winner required to secure 50%+1 of the votes but no provision being made for a run-off. Finally, he assesses how far the new interpretation of the Constitution resolves Malawi's electoral reform agenda and how much remains to be done, for example to create an electoral system that promotes national cohesion rather than fragmentation.

In a democratic political system, while attention might focus primarily on the party in government, there is a crucial role for the opposition in holding government to account. The fate of the opposition in Malawi is the question addressed in the next chapter by John Chipembere Lwanda, George Chikondi Chipembere Lwanda and Raphael Mbwana. They consider the political parties that have formed the opposition during Malawi's democratic era but also, given the weakness of opposition parties for most of the period, they take a broader view and consider agents of civil society who at times have channelled opposition to the government more effectively than the political parties. They note the *aona nyekhwe* slogan which became a catchphrase of the DPP regime during the 2018-20 period, a successor to the *wina alira* and *muona mbwadza* of earlier eras—all slogans designed to intimidate any opposition and to suggest that things will not end well for anyone who opposes the government. Besides being implicitly threatened the opposition has also been bought—"fed scones"—by being given just enough government patronage to ensure that they will not bite the hand that feeds them. It took an unusual constellation of forces for the opposition to prevail in the political crisis of 2019-20: a broad coalition between the opposition parties and civil society pressure groups and an activated rural and urban civil society, supported by the "guardian angels" of the Malawi Defence Force and the Judicial System. Still, it remains to be seen whether old dynamics of government hegemony reassert themselves or there can be a place for an opposition that is neither threatened nor bought but an effective force in ensuring government accountability.

Dan Kuwali takes up the question of democratic oversight and accountability of the security sector in Malawi, taking account of the different agencies involved and reviewing the functioning of the National Security Policy, introduced in 2018. A fundamental problem in Malawi has been the manipulation of security sector agencies for political purposes, at the expense of their independence and professionalism. For example, during the political crisis of 2019-20 the Malawi Police Service was widely perceived to be serving the narrow political interests of the governing party rather than ensuring the safety and security of all citizens on an impartial basis. While the 2018 National Security Policy aims to achieve integration and democratic accountability of all security agencies operating in the country, Kuwali finds that they are still prone to operate in silos and are vulnerable to political manipulation. He advocates the strengthening of an institutional framework that enables the security sector to operate professionally, in a way that is independent of political control while being fully accountable for fulfilling its constitutional role. There is need, he argues, for greater awareness of their respective responsibilities among both political leaders and senior officers of the security agencies. Much remains to be done before Malawi will fulfil the aspiration of the 2018 National Security Policy and have an integrated and collaborative national security framework with a robust democratic accountability.

Mphatso Jones Boti Phiri offers a case study of the issues at stake by focussing on the operations of the Malawi Defence Force, with particular attention to issues of accountability in financial management. He utilises the concept of historical institutionalism to appreciate the broader policy trajectory and historical environment in which the military in Malawi has operated with regard to governance and financial accountability. From colonial times, through the period of one-party rule and throughout the democratic period, a consistent feature of Malawi's governance has been executive supremacy in regard to the funding and operation of the Armed Forces. Even after the democratic Constitution of 1994 vested significant powers of oversight in Parliament and the Ministry of Defence, these powers have not been exercised at all effectively. A tacit understanding has maintained that the accountability of the military is directly and only to the office of the president. In practical effect, this means that there is no public scrutiny of financial management in the Malawi Defence Force. Through his close attention to the military context, Boti Phiri raises an issue that calls for attention in many other sectors also: excessive concentration of power in the office of the president inhibits the development of healthy democratic accountability.

In the next chapter, Asiyati Lorraine Chiweza draws our attention to the quest for inclusive governance through increased women's representation in elected bodies. This has been a feature of Malawi's governance landscape since democratisation in 1994 and it gained new impetus in 2009 when the government in collaboration with non-state actors introduced a gender parity funding scheme, popularly known as the 50-50 Campaign. While the campaign was initially deemed successful in 2009, the declining women representation figures in both 2014 and 2019 elections have triggered debate about the effectiveness of such schemes in improving gender parity in national elected decision-making bodies. Using a review of existing literature this chapter seeks to explain the reasons for the campaign's mediocre performance. It focuses on the nature of the actors who have been driving these campaigns and examines how far there is congruency between the locus of the underrepresentation problem and the campaign interventions. It concludes that although Malawi has relevant legislation, policies, and strategies to increase women's participation in politics, the campaigns since 2009 have been largely driven by a multitude of non-state actors who design and fund a variety of positive action interventions that have been disjointed, short-term, and scarcely address the underlying reasons for the underrepresentation of women.

Gift Wasambo Kayira and Paul Chiudza Banda take up a theme that has long caused concern to observers of Malawi's political scene: the tendency towards fragmentation on ethnic and regional lines. They bring a fresh line of analysis by considering the proposal for a federal system of government, which has been widely canvassed in recent years. They problematise the idea that Malawi could easily be divided into three homogeneous self-governing regions. For Kayira and Banda this might lead simply to a replication at regional level of divisions currently experienced at national level. Far from being homogeneous, each region is made up of a variety of ethnic, linguistic and religious groups. Therefore, in a federal system many of them might find themselves being marginalised by the dominant group in their region. This does not mean, however, that the authors wish to advocate the continued centralisation of power at the national level. They propose that Malawi consider the Kenyan model where power has been devolved to 47 districts, each with its own elected governor. This, they argue, has resulted in a more equitable distribution of national resources and has given each district the opportunity to drive its own development. Rather than adopting a federal system that would perennially set large regional power-blocs against one another, might Malawi benefit from devolution of power and resources to district level?

Wapulumuka Mulwafu brings an original slant to analysis of Malawi's environmental crisis by examining it in relation to issues of governance. Since the transition to multiparty democracy in the early 1990s, Malawi has experienced serious challenges in the provision of energy and water services as a result of an escalating environmental crisis. While it may be inaccurate to correlate the environmental crisis with multipartyism per se, Mulwafu argues that degradation of the country's natural resource base, on which both energy and water supplies so fundamentally depend, has accelerated rapidly in the post-dictatorship period. While orthodoxy explains this exacerbating problem in terms of population growth and poverty, this chapter argues that the cause can be attributed to a governance crisis. The crisis is characterised by weak management systems occasioned by withdrawal of the state, attitude of populist leadership, and redefinition of the rights of citizens. The chapter goes beyond banal description of environmental challenges in Malawi and seeks to understand the origins and development of the governance crisis. An historical analysis is employed in order to explain changes over time and how the state has either facilitated or mitigated against the occurrence of the crisis.

The next chapter addresses the very contemporary issue of the Covid-19 pandemic. Bryson Nkhoma, Gift Kayira and Paul Chiudza Banda observe that the Malawi Government has struggled to implement measures to contain the pandemic. Before any Covid-19 case was confirmed, President Peter Mutharika declared a national disaster towards the end of March 2020. However, in mid-April when the government declared a country-wide lockdown to stave off the spread of the virus, Civil Society Organisations (CSOs) challenged this decision as insensitive to the interests of the poor, most of whom engage in the informal economic sector and have limited access to health care facilities. The question posed is what do such contestations reveal about the nature of the state and Malawian politics? The chapter shows how the CSOs and other opposition groups have used the Covid-19 pandemic as a platform to confront the state on certain social ills relating to the country's development and people's welfare. By successfully blocking public health measures raised to mitigate the pandemic, the CSO's actions point to how state power is contested in ways that reveal the very limits of the Weberian model of governance in democratic societies—one that accords unlimited power to the state. Experience with Covid-19 has demonstrated the limits of state power and highlighted the need for inclusive models of governance.

In the final chapter, Hermann Mvula and Kenneth Ross turn our attention to another dimension of Malawi's self-understanding, i.e. that it claims to be a "God-fearing country". Theological perspectives are therefore of significance for political life, as was famously illustrated by the Catholic Bishops' Lenten Letter of 1992 and more recently by their Pastoral Letter of 23 May 2020. This chapter revisits a 1995 essay by Kenneth Ross that attempted a theological analysis of the exercise of power in Malawi. It assesses how far the issues raised have been successfully addressed in the subsequent years and how far they remain unfinished business. It then draws on three theological resources to bring fresh perspectives to bear on Malawi's contemporary political challenges: (1) the biblical text, (2) global theological thinking and (3) local contextual theology. From this base it interrogates such features of Malawian political life as impunity of the powerful, regionalism, elitism, balance of powers, patrimonialism, corruption, patronage and clientelism, inequality, and popular participation. It concludes that Malawi's failures in governance are derived more from a faulty political culture than from any shortcomings in the constitutional and political structures of the country. The resource it highlights is Malawi's religious culture, suggesting that there is a constructive role for it to play at the deep level of the cultural forces that shape governance.

Significance of the Book

The various chapters of the book, taken together, shine searchlights from many different angles on the governance challenges facing Malawi in the third decade of the 21st century. The events of 2019-2020 provide a litmus test of how far the nation of Malawi has come in consolidating its democratic institutions as well as aligning itself with good governance practices. Coming on the heels of an unprecedented tussle among the three arms of government, this book provides a rich context in which to understand the broader spectrum of governance issues in Malawi. Triggered by the outcome of the controversial May 2019 presidential election, which was nullified by the Constitutional Court ruling of February 2020, many questions emerged regarding the principles and practice of governance in Malawian society. What constitutes a credible election? How can the process and outcome of an election promote good governance? How can the electorate's trust in the election process be enhanced? How can right-holders hold duty-bearers accountable?

Building on the considerable body of literature that offers analysis of the conduct of successive elections in Malawi, this book addresses questions that came into particularly sharp focus in 2019-20.[34] The book was drafted in the heat of that crisis. Hence for the most part it has an effective cut-off date of 23 June 2020 when the Fresh Presidential Election was held. It does not make any attempt to consider developments subsequent to that date. However, many of the issues that came into focus in 2019-20 remain decisive for governance in Malawi in the present and future. Key lessons have been learnt on how elections should be managed and who should endorse the results. For a long time, cooperating partners who funded a substantial chunk of the budget, together with foreign observer missions, had a symbolic role in certifying credibility of elections. Their role is likely to change in future elections in the country.

The book's scope, however, is not confined to technical questions on the conduct of democratic elections, important as these undoubtedly remain. It places such questions in the context of a broader analytical framework that allows for exploration of many different dimensions that bear on Malawi's governance. A long-running concern has centred on the question of whether the structures of democracy are functioning in Malawi simply as camouflage for the undemocratic forces that are actually in control.[35] The crisis of 2019-20 has brought into fresh focus the issue that Malawi's democratic transition did not effectively replace the old order. Instead, the transition brought in largely cosmetic reforms to the governance system. While much emphasis had been placed on holding regular elections and establishing institutions of governance,

---

[34] See Matembo S. Nzunda and Kenneth R. Ross (eds), *Church, Law and Political Transition in Malawi 1992-94*, Gweru: Mambo-Kachere, 1995; Martin Ott, Kings M. Phiri and Nandini Patel (eds), *Malawi's Second Democratic Elections: Process, Problems and Prospects*, Blantyre: CLAIM-Kachere, 2000; Martin Ott, Bodo Immink, Bhatupe Mhango, Christian Peters-Berries (eds), *The Power of the Vote: Malawi's 2004 Parliamentary & Presidential Elections*, Zomba: Kachere, 2004; Martin Ott and Edge Kanyongolo (eds) *Malawi's 2009 Parliamentary and Presidential Elections*, Balaka: Montfort Media, 2010; Nandini Patel and Michael Wahman (eds), *The Malawi 2014 Tripartite Elections: Is Democracy Maturing?* Lilongwe: National Initiative for Civic Education (NICE), 2015; Nandini Patel and Fidelis Edge Kanyongolo (eds), *Democracy Tested: The Case of Malawi's 2019 Tripartite Elections*, Pretoria: Pretoria University Law Press, 2021.

[35] See Kings M. Phiri and Kenneth R. Ross (eds), *Democratization in Malawi: A Stocktaking*, Blantyre: CLAIM-Kachere, 1998; Nandini Patel and Lars Svåsand (eds), *Government and Politics in Malawi*, Zomba: Centre for Social Research, 2013.

structural forces of power abuse and impunity remain deep-rooted. The litany of cases of political leaders trying to subvert the constitutional order and tilt towards bad governance is a reflection of the unfinished business of the transition process. For example, the abortive attempt to introduce the third term bill, rampant corruption, and executive arrogance by blatantly violating human rights are all indicators of impunity and an affront to good governance.

The element of impunity by duty-bearers who are supposed to be upholding principles and practices of good governance has resulted in tensions and conflicts with citizens, as seen in many of the chapters in this volume. There is a general appreciation that ideas of good governance have now become entrenched in the minds of citizens and that everyone including duty-bearers have a crucial role to play in safeguarding the citizens' constitutional rights and democratic choices. In a society where political leaders had for too long taken the electorate for granted and freely manipulated systems for their own interests, the 2019-2020 events have become a watershed with far-reaching consequences for the future.[36]

First, the events have shown that Malawi's democracy is gradually maturing, notwithstanding recurrent setbacks. Second, they demonstrate the resilience of the people of Malawi, as their achievements in upholding democracy and constitutionalism during the crisis of 2019-20 are unparalleled in post-colonial African history. It may well be the case that a culture of resistance to oppressive laws and policies as well as repugnance to bad aspects of governance has been well established. Starting from the 1990s when Malawians challenged Dr Kamuzu Banda‘s dictatorship to Bakili Muluzi‘s third term bid, to Bingu wa Mutharika‘s dictatorial and nepotistic policies as well as Peter Mutharika‘s culture of impunity, Malawian citizens have shown that they are expecting more than rhetoric from their duty bearers. Third, the military has shown that it is not only an apolitical institution but an active facilitator in promoting democracy and good governance in the country.

A crucial issue that surfaces time and again throughout this volume is the tendency in Malawi for the executive arm of government, particularly the office of the Presidency, to accumulate power, resources and authority—at the expense of the legislature and the judiciary. In this regard, the court judgments

---

36 Some of these aspects have been discussed in Wapulumuka Mulwafu, "Afterword for Malawi Special Issue on Enduring Concerns and New Directions", *Journal of Southern African Studies* 46/2 (2020), 375-379.

of February and May 2020 can be understood as restoring a proper balance between the three arms of government. When he was displeased with the court judgments, former president Peter Mutharika attempted to argue that Parliament was superior to the judiciary in a vain attempt to avoid having to face a fresh presidential election. This may have been part of a strategy to serve his narrow political interests at the time but it exposed trends that have been emerging in the country over time. As a law scholar, the former President was not unaware of the salience of the doctrine of separation of powers but perhaps he was mired in a situation where he felt he had to advance the agenda of his political clientele. It may not be unreasonable to conclude that the DPP regime wanted to create a myth of executive supremacy over the other branches of government. In the absence of clear evidence, we can only speculate that this may have been part of the political manoeuvring to create a hegemonic system of governance dominated by the DPP. Not surprisingly in the tense political atmosphere, some political sycophants went overboard to utter rhetorical statements to the effect that the DPP party would rule Malawi forever.

Another issue that arises frequently in the following pages concerns the power of money in relation to governance in Malawi. In an earlier article, John Lwanda has bemoaned the unbridled influence of money in politics particularly in silencing critics or inciting violence against citizens.[37] That trend, which started in colonial times and reached its climax during the Muluzi administration, appears not to be abating. If anything, it has continued to exist in different forms: buying individuals so that they abandon their ethical principles and integrity in order to side with the government—not biting the hand that feeds them. In other cases, government has been infiltrating opposition parties and groups to co-opt or silence them through offers of money and other perks.

While political parties the world over will always fight to retain their influence in or control over government, one particular political idea appears to have taken hold in Malawi. This is the attempt to create an insular system of governance premised on the assumption that Malawians will not easily react or challenge those in power. It is advanced by an elitist group of people who criss-cross political parties while looking for opportunities for personal gain. Instead of establishing institutions and systems of electing leaders who qualify in their own right, post-Banda Malawian politics has been dominated by family

37 John Lwanda, "Kwacha: The Violence of Money in Malawi's Politics, 1954-2004", *Journal of Southern African Studies* 32/3 (2006), 525-44.

dynastical cliques. While every citizen has the right to stand for any position in society, it raises serious governance questions when political parties engage in schemes aimed at maintaining dynasties at the expense of party, government and national wellbeing. This issue goes beyond the founder syndrome where the initial leader wants to keep himself or his influence on a particular party. But the trend in Malawi is that despite the differences in party affiliation, some leaders appear to be convinced that they are privileged and destined to rule the country on an indefinite basis. This has led to the entrenchment of a system of assembling and sometimes recycling leaders who share the ideology of plunder as the key driving force for joining politics. Once in power, their main interest appears not to be that of serving Malawians but self-serving interest to plunder resources and consolidate their positions. They are happy to keep in power a dynastic leader who is equally grateful to those who surround him. To secure their own interests they will go all the way to ensure that structures of good governance are diluted or compromised, including the elections management system.

While this book is multi-disciplinary in character and offers a many-sided analysis of Malawi's governance challenges, a consistent thread running through the text is the issue of impunity in the exercise of government. If there is a thesis that unifies the book, it is that the significant strengths of Malawi's democracy have too often been undermined by a culture of impunity at the heart of government. This sets an agenda not only to ensure that adequate structures of democratic accountability are in place but also to undertake fundamental attitudinal change, particularly among those entrusted with political office. The people of Malawi, through their handling of the political crisis of 2019-20, have made it clear that they expect to see such change. We hope that the analysis offered in this book might be one small contribution towards the fulfilment of their expectations.

Conclusion

This book can be expected to be of immense value to scholars, researchers and everyone else interested in understanding governance issues in Malawi, both past and present. Apart from providing a synthesised and multi-dimensional perspective on governance, the book goes beyond analysis of official narratives and offers fresh perspectives which are crucial for democratic consolidation in the country. It will likely secure a place in Malawi's historiography as a useful source book for a broad range of disciplines including law, politics, history, and development studies.

Chapter 1

A Decade of Governance as "Roving Banditry" The Political Economy of Public Finance Mismanagement in Malawi, 2010 -2020

Henry Chingaipe

"The whole entire Government of Malawi is a criminal enterprise...That is what I discovered."

Paul Mphwiyo, Former Government Budget Director[1]

Introduction: Setting the Context

The sixth day of July 2020 was perhaps the zenith of Malawi's third critical juncture i.e. a moment of heightened expectations for political and socio-economic change.[2] While the previous critical junctures had led to political independence from the British and from the stranglehold of a one-party post-independence state, respectively, the critical juncture of June 2020 heralded widespread expectations of change in the totality of the configuration and exercise of political power that had defined and set the country on a low equilibrium trajectory of governance and development since the transition to multiparty democracy in 1993. It promised a simultaneity of democratic governance and socio-economic development. The euphoria was reinforced by the inaugural speech of President Lazarus Chakwera, who had been elected in a fresh presidential election following the nullification of the presidential election held in May 2019.[3] President Chakwera spoke candidly about "clearing the rubble"—a theme that spoke directly to public finance mismanagement and corruption in the public sector that had become an identity tag for Malawi:

---

1 Shaun Raviv, "Cashgate: How a Scandal started by a Poor Housemaid ended up taking down the most Powerful Woman in Africa", *Latterly Magazine*, 14 May 2018, 8.

2 Giovanni Capocia, "When Do Institutions 'Bite'? Historical Institutionalism and the Politics of Change", *Comparative Political Studies* 49/8, 2016, 1095-1127; Henry Chingaipe, "Business and the State in Malawi: The Politics of Institutional Formation, Maintenance and Change", PhD, University of York, 2010.

3 Constitutional Reference No. 1 of 2019: *Dr. Saulos Chilima and Dr. Lazarus Chakwera v. Prof. Peter Mutharika and the Electoral Commission*, Lilongwe: High Court of Malawi.

> Before we can begin to rebuild, we must clear the rubble of corruption, for it has left our taxes in ruins; we must clear the rubble of laziness, for it has left our infrastructure in ruins; we must clear the rubble of passivism, for it has left our rights in ruins; we must clear the rubble of donor dependency, for it has left our dignity in ruins; we must clear the rubble of regionalism, for it has left our nationhood in ruins; we must clear the rubble of negativity, for it has left our resolve in ruins; we must clear the rubble of impunity, for it has left our governance institutions in ruins; and we must clear the rubble of unprofessionalism and incompetence, for it has left our services in ruins. The ruining of national treasures of both nature and state is a sin of my generation that I am bound by God to confess and bound by you to correct.[4]

President Chakwera's speech of hope was delivered against a background of worsening public perceptions of corruption, regarded by many as a side effect of democratisation and neoliberalism in a context of a weak state and weak markets. Throughout the decade, corruption was regarded by many as the number one enemy of public finance management. As shown in the figure below, the corruption perception index (CPI) ranged between 34 and 37 indicating strong perception of the prevalence of corruption even though this

Figure 1.1: *Corruption Perception Index for Malawi*
(https://www.theglobaleconomy.com/Malawi/transparency_corruption)

this represented a significant improvement on the scores of the previous decade. (Note: a score of 100 means no corruption).

---

4 Lazarus Chakwera, "Inaugural Address by the State President of the Republic of Malawi", 6 July 2020 at Kamuzu Barracks of the Malawi Defence Force.

Control of corruption—a World Bank Governance Indicator—has also remained weak despite political rhetoric by the various political regimes. In fact,

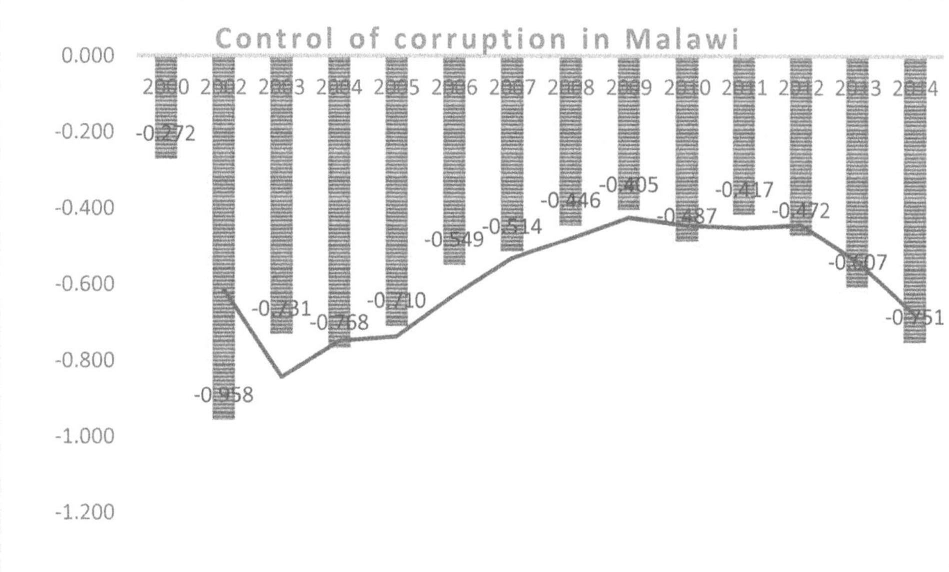

***Figure 1.2:** Control of corruption estimate. World Bank Governance Indicators.*

each political regime in the decade out-competed its predecessors in introducing new ruses or schemes for stealing public finances. The anti-corruption approach has been so ineffective that the estimate of control of corruption for Malawi has been very low since 1996 when the World Bank began collecting data on this variable of governance. The figure above shows the trend of control of corruption between 2001 and 2014—the estimate lies between -2.5 (weak) and 2.5 (strong).

Thus, Chakwera's inaugural speech signalled a shift to state-society relations that would uphold the social contract between state elites and the citizens, on which basis the Malawi government bears responsibilities to provide public goods and services to citizens.[5] Like any government, its capacity to deliver on this obligation is dependent on the quality of its public finance management i.e. its ability to *mobilise, manage, prudently spend and enforce accountability for public resources.* Political Science literature shows unequivocally that the way in which and the purposes for which a government mobilises revenue, allocates and spends and accounts for public money bestows on the state its character. In this regard, governments find their place on a continuum that has on the

---

5 Jean-Jacques Rousseau, *The Social Contract*, ed. Maurice William Cranston, Harmondsworth: Penguin, 1968.

negative end those that are sub-optimal in the delivery of public goods and services. Depending on the nature and degree of abuse of political power, bureaucratic authority and public finances, these states are variously described as predatory, patrimonial, captured, kleptocratic, fragile or weak.[6] On the positive end of the continuum are governments that deliver public goods and services to optimal levels, described variously as developmental, effective and people-centred.[7] For governments that deviate from their purposes and obligations under the social contract, public finance mismanagement is invariably one of the core factors that explain sub-optimal performance in the delivery of public goods and services and forms the pith of criminal enterprises within the government institutional framework.[8]

Public finance mismanagement is part of the explanation of Malawi's low human capital and social development. Wastage (inefficient use) and appropriation of public finances for private ends (corruption) by those privyleged to access the resources through political and bureaucratic positions and ties have denied many ordinary citizens the basics of life that constitute the necessary conditions to unleash the potential of human development. Malawi's Country Policy and Institutional Assessment (CPIA) Report of 2020[9] shows that the country's institutional and policy framework had stagnated with a rating of 3.2 (6 being highest), in a fourth successive year since 2014, implying that Malawi's policy orientation was neither reducing poverty nor enhancing economic growth.[10] While the country has institutions with largely the right forms and mandates for prudent management and accountability for public finances, public finance mismanagement is a common, almost institutionalised occurrence. This is despite multiple and concurrent efforts by government supported by donors to improve public finance management systems,

---

6 See David Held (ed), *States and Societies*, New York: New York University Press, 1983; Jabusile M. Shumba, *Zimbabwe's Predatory State: Party, Military and Business*, Scotsville: University of KwaZulu-Natal Press, 2018.

7 A. Ndahiro and J. Rwagatare (eds), *Rwanda: Rebuilding of a Nation*, Kampala: Fountain Publishers, 2015; Adrian Leftwitch, *States of Development: On the Primacy of Politics in Development*, Oxford: Wiley, 2001.

8 Jean-Francois Bayart, Stephen Ellis and Beatrice Hibou, *The Criminalization of the State in Africa*, Oxford: James Currey, 1999.

9 World Bank, *Country Policy and Institutional Assessment – Malawi*, Washington: World Bank, 2020.

10 "Growth, Poverty Reduction Stalls", *Weekend Nation*, 24 August 2019. The CPIA score assesses four thematic categories: economic management, structural policies, social inclusion, equity policies, and public sector management and institutions

prudence in public procurement and public expenditure. For example, between 1995 and 2018, more than 25 projects were implemented in Malawi by the World Bank with direct focus on improved public finance management systems and enhanced prudence in public procurement and public expenditure.[11] Besides World Bank interventions, there have been several other efforts by various stakeholders. Previous CPIA assessments have consistently shown that governance improvements have resulted in organisational and institutional reforms that are primarily in better *"form"* (i.e. new laws, systems, procedures) without the expected change in *functional* performance (i.e. reduced corruption, greater efficiency and compliance to the new reforms).[12] This is typically the case of PFM in Malawi. Thus, the fundamental question that concerns this chapter is why public finance mismanagement persists in spite of having the right institutions of accountability with largely the right mandates.

Analytical and Methodological Framework

Roving Banditry

The metaphor of roving banditry has its origins in Mancur Olson's interpretive reading of the history of Warlord China during the 1920s on which basis he developed a theory of state capacity for development that is intimately bound with the character of governments or political regimes i.e. dictatorships and democracies.[13] The warlords—men who led some armed band with which they conquered territory, appointed themselves lords of the conquered territory and extracted resources from the population through various ways including taxation. Some warlords, such as Feng Yu-hsiang were "stationary bandits" who established taxation systems for extraction of resources and maintained strong armies to fend off other armed bands and protect their access to the economic surplus of the population while providing minimal public goods and services such as security of the population. Other warlords were "roving bandits", such as Bai Lang (also known as White Wolf) who carried out intense extraction of the economic surplus from the population using a varied set of schemes including forms of taxation, plundered the populations and their

---

11 Katherine Marguerite Bridges and Michael Woolcock, "How (Not) to Fix Problems that Matter: Assessing and Responding to Malawi's History of Institutional Reform", Policy Research Working Paper, No. WPS 8289, Washington: World Bank Group, 2017.

12 Ibid.

13 Mancur Olson, "Dictatorship, Democracy, and Development", *The American Political Science Review* 87/3, 1993, 567-576.

resources for his exclusive benefit and that of his associates and moved on to other territories pretty much like nomads. Thus, for any conquered territory, roving bandits had short time horizons and had no incentive for investing in public goods and services to enable the conquered populations to continue their economic activities and prosper. They conquered, abused the people, plundered the resources and moved on to the next victim as soon as it was no longer viable to remain in the territory. Roving banditry was associated with a nomadic perspective that the new elites had to maximise their economic benefits in the shortest possible time before it was time to move on.

In the literature, roving banditry in PFM is akin to the creation and operationalisation of a felonious state in which the state elites engage in criminal acts using the very same positions of trust that they are expected to use to protect and promote the public interest.[14] There are four key elements of a felonious state that are born out in public finance mismanagement and characterise roving banditry: Firstly, the use for private purposes of the legitimate organs of state violence by those in authority, and the function of such violence as an instrument in the service of their strategies of accumulation of wealth; secondly, the existence of a hidden, collective structure of power which surrounds and even controls the official occupant of the most senior political office, and which benefits from the privatisation of the legitimate means of coercion, or is able with impunity to have recourse to a private and illegitimate apparatus of violence, notably in the form of organised gangs; thirdly, the participation by the collective and semi-clandestine power structure in economic activities considered to be criminal in domestic and international law; and fourthly, the insertion of such economic activities in international networks of crime or international actors that aid collusive and corrupt schemes for siphoning money.[15]

Applied to public finance mismanagement in Malawi between 2010-2020, roving banditry describes a phenomenon of competitive theft of public resources (money and assets) involving state elites (politicians and bureaucrats) and many of their supporters and beneficiaries who deployed multiple ruses to siphon and privatise public resources in the short periods they had control of

---

14 Jean-Francois Bayart, Stephen Ellis and Beatrice Hibou, "From Kleptocracy to the Felonious State?" in *The Criminalization of the State in Africa.*

15 Ibid, 25-26.

the levers of power of the state, punctuated by pre-determined dates of presidential and parliamentary elections.

Institutional Political Economy Analysis

The analysis was carried out using an integrated framework that drew on institutionalism and traditional problem-driven political economy analysis. This framework was adopted on recognition that public finance mismanagement is driven, firstly, by how political power is configured and exercised and the economic interests of the power-holders. These two elements are primary foci of political economy analysis. Thus, the analytical concern was with the distribution of power among actors, incentive schemes, the competing interests of individuals and groups and the processes that created and sustained these felonious interactions.[16] The economic elements of the analysis focused on economic and financial interests and benefits accruing to the actors.

Secondly, any occurrence of public finance mismanagement entails a breach of specific formal rules. If the mismanagement is habitual and systematic, it signifies a replacement of or an overlay of informal rules on the formal ones to govern the mobilisation, allocation and spending of public finances. Rules that govern behavior are traditional concerns of institutionalism.

Thus, the institutionalist dimension of the analysis focused on identifying formal and informal rules as well as formal and informal power-holders that shaped the ways in which public finances were allocated and expended. In this regard, the analysis adopted the definitions of Helmke and Levitsky who define informal rules as "socially shared rules, usually unwritten, that are created, communicated, and enforced outside officially sanctioned channels."[17] By contrast, "formal rules and procedures are created, communicated and enforced through channels that are widely accepted as official."[18] Thus, legislation such as the Public Finance Management Act (PFMA), Public Audit Act (PAA), Public Procurement and Disposal of Assets Act (PP&DA), Treasury Instruc-

---

16 World Bank, *Problem Driven Political Economy Analysis for Projects*, Washington: World Bank, 2010; World Bank, *Political Economy Assessments at Sector and Project Levels 1*, Washington: World Bank, 2011; Claire Mcloughlin, *Topic Guidance on Political Economy Analysis*, Governance and Social Development Resource Centre, University of Birmingham, 2009; *Political Economy Analysis with a Legitimacy Twist: What is it and why does it matter?* Oslo: NORAD: 2010; Adrian Leftwich, *States of Development*.

17 Gretchen Helmke and Steven Levistky (eds), *Informal Institutions and Democracy: Lessons from Latin America*, Baltimore: Johns Hopkins University Press, 2006, 9.

18 Ibid.

tions and all other regulations and procedures including standards for professional accountancy governing the mobilisation, allocation, spending and accounting for public money are formal rules. All regular patterns of behaviour in public finance management that are not based on or contradict or breach any formally codified rules and regulations are understood to be based on some informal rules that have to be discovered through a diagnostic PEA.

In felonious states, informal rules emanating from particular ways in which political power is configured and exercised, undermine the regulations and procedures for managing public money as they redefine incentives for actors not to comply with the formal rules. When the formal rules, regulations and procedures are ineffective, the informal rules tend to have a substitutive or a competing effect on the formal rules. The effect is *substitutive* when informal rules are used by actors who seek outcomes compatible with formal rules but operate in environments where formal rules are not often enforced. On the other hand, the effect is *competing* when the informal rules structure incentives in ways that are incompatible with the formal rules so much that by following the formal rule, actors violate the informal one and vice versa. Which rule actors follow depends on their calculations of which one protects or enhances their interest. Informal rules with competing effects trump formal rules and generate outcomes that diverge markedly from what is expected from the formal rules.[19]

Data Collection and Analysis Methods

Relevant source materials, including media reports and documents on public finance management in Malawi were gathered and reviewed to extract information that would help address the concerns of the chapter. Furthermore, informative, analytical and scholarly literature on public finance management was reviewed for its insights relevant to the PEA of PFM in Malawi. Key informant interviews were conducted with a limited number of people with direct experiences with public finance management by virtue of their current or previous careers. This being a qualitative study based on observed and experiential narratives, analysis was done using the method of discourse analysis.[20]

---

19 Ibid.

20 Lavinia Suciu, "Discourse and Discourse Analysis: A Retrospective Approach", DOI 10.5772intechopen.82823, 2019; Johnny Saldana, *The Coding Manual for Qualitative Researchers*, London: Sage, 2009.

State of Public Finance Mismanagement and its Developmental Cost

A Glimpse of the State of Public Finance Mismanagement

Evidence of public finance mismanagement in Malawi is not in short supply. Between July 2009 and June 2014, a preliminary audit estimated fraud of public funds at MWK 577 billion, implicating various ministries, departments, parastatal organisations, private suppliers and banks.[21] The estimate was later reduced to MWK 236 billion.[22] The Auditor General handed over 67 case files to the Anti-Corruption Bureau (ACB) for prosecution. Of these 13 were handed over in 2015 but the ACB did not pursue these cases.[23] The Auditor General's reports reveal persistent behavioural patterns of mismanagement and theft of public funds through multiple ruses. The table below gives a summary of expenditure mismanagement in the civil service for three financial years based on the Auditor General's reports.

***Table 1:** Summary view of evidence of public finance mismanagement in the civil service*[24]

Fiscal year	Without supporting documents	Missing vouchers and other documents	Misallocated payments	Arrears from breach of procurement
2014-15	16,367,012,333.28	29,905,112,806.82	4,857,041,661.90	N/A
2015-16	517,115,701.82	158,273,251.61	427,974,099.00	10,3000,137,321.62
2016-17	5,315,251,031.00	2,033,810,685.59	136,178,292.00	23,342,322,940.36

The Auditor General's reports over the years have always been candid and forthright as the findings have been repeated from year to year with minimal

21 PricewaterhouseCoopers' Report, "Final Analysis Report: Reconstruction of the Malawian Government Cashbook for Purposes of Further Investigation."

22 Ibid.

23 Whistleblower Report dated 5 July 2020, submitted to and leaked from Office of the president and Cabinet.

24 Based on Reports of the Auditor General for the financial years ended on 30 June 2015, 2016 and 2017.

uptake and implementation of recommendations to check abuse of resources. The reports are clear on the unwillingness or resistance of the public finance management actors to comply with public finance management operating guidelines, rules and procedures.[25] This system-wide observation by the Auditor General shows that the actors involved in public finance management have incentives not to comply with the formal rules, regulations and procedures for the stewardship of public money. Until those incentives are "discovered" and addressed, no amount of legal and policy reforms will arrest public finance mismanagement.

The findings of the Auditor General are reinforced by media and other reports of public finance mismanagement across the public sector during the decade. Some of the cases that came out during the decade and illustrate the scope and nature of schemes or tactics for abusing public finances in the public sector include the following:

1. Collusion between the Malawi Police Service, The Democratic Progressive Party (DPP), President Peter Mutharika and Pioneer Investments. Malawi Police Service using a forged contract dated 15th June 2015, a forged payment voucher and a forged government cheque paid Pioneer Investments MWK 2,793,087,500 for procurement of food rations for Police Officers. The paid amount included fraud of MWK 466 million singularly approved by a Police Officer as money for retaining contract value against currency depreciation when the contract was only six days old. From the total payment, Pioneer Investment deposited MWK 145 million (about USD 196,000) into the DPP account whose sole signatory was the president.[26] The case came out in public through a leaked investigations report of the Anti-Corruption Bureau.[27]

2. In 2016, the Ministry of Agriculture's Internal Procurement Committee, Office of the president and Cabinet, senior public officials and legislators participated in unlawful sharing of 177 tractors, 144 maize shellers meant for Green Belt Initiative and One Village One Product programmes worth a total of USD 50 million which the Government, with the approval of the National

[25] Report of the Auditor General on the Accounts of the Government of Republic of Malawi, for the year ended 30 June 2018, 7.

[26] *BBC World*, "Malawi's President Mutharika and the Police Food Scandal", 4 July 2018, www.bbc.com/news/world-africa-44714224.

[27] Anti-Corruption Bureau, "Investigations Report: Allegation of Fraudulent Transactions in Ration Packs Contract between Malawi Police Service and Pioneer Investments", REF NO: CR/LL/200/2017.

Assembly had borrowed from the EXIM Bank of India.[28] Meanwhile, the Government is servicing and paying back the loan.

3. First Lady Gertrude Mutharika and her Beautify Malawi Trust (BEAM) forced payments from the National Aids Commission amounting to MWK 67.4 million allegedly for cultural festivities. The Director of National Intelligence at the time also tried to force out a payment from NAC of MWK 43 million but was refused.

4. Between January and June 2018, 4.2 million litres of fuel worth MWK 4 billion was stolen from ESCOM by cadres of the Democratic Progressive Party who were given rights to fuel their vehicles at various gasoline stations on ESCOM account. Information came to light through a leaked internal report of ESCOM. Similarly, party cadres of the DPP, including women dancers and cheering boys whose job was to provide entertainment and political endorsement at political rallies, were put on Government payroll as civil servants (mostly as secondary and primary school teachers). In a similar scheme, the Ministry of Agriculture lost MWK 47 million in 2016 to ghost workers.[29]

5. In 2018, the Lilongwe Water Board was pressured to pay a private company, Gaston Arts, MWK 29.2 million for some nondescript sculpture statues "at Parliament and Capital Hotel Roundabouts".[30] This was reportedly demanded by the First Lady's outfit, BEAM, which had taken upon itself the duty to beautify the city's roundabouts. Lilongwe Water Board obliged as it was a political directive. Lilongwe Water Board sanitised the payment as "part of [corporate social responsibility] CSR." The said company did not even have money for the works and demanded upfront payment of 60% of the contract sum to enable it to carry out the works. While the Parliament roundabout has some statues, the other roundabout has nothing.

The illustrative cases of public finance mismanagement highlighted here indicate a collapsed and defective public finance management system. It is clear that during the decade there were structural, institutional and agency factors that collectively presented perverse incentives for public finance misma-

---

28 The Ombudsman, "The Present Toiling, The Future Overburdened: Report on an Investigation into Allegations of Maladministration and Related Irregularities on the Purchase and Disposal of Farm Machinery under India Line of Credit Worth 50 Million United States Dollars", Lilongwe: Office of Ombudsman, 2016.

29 Archibald Kasakura, "K47M Looted in Malawi Ghost Workers from Payroll of Ministry of Agriculture", *The Nation*, 4 April 2016.

30 Gaston Arts "Request for Upfront payment", addressed to the CEO of Lilongwe Water Board, 21 November 2018.

nagement. With such a confluence of causal and enabling factors, solutions focusing narrowly on fixing the accounting systems were unlikely to arrest malfeasance in PFM and in fact had the potential of deflecting attention away from the real problems that had to be addressed. Technical solutions would amount to much ado about nothing if the incentive scheme that underlie public finance mismanagement remained unaddressed.

Illustrating the Development Cost of Public Finance Mismanagement

A simplified analysis of forgone development investments due to public finance mismanagement (i.e. opportunity cost analysis) shows that if public finances were managed, allocated and spent properly, Malawi's development trajectory would be significantly different and better than the current low equilibrium and grossly sub-optimal situation.

To illustrate the developmental cost of public finance mismanagement in Malawi, we use MWK 90 billion which was misappropriated between 2009 and April 2012 when the government was under the aegis of late President Bingu wa Mutharika and the Democratic Progressive Party (DPP); and MWK 20 billion which was misappropriated in six months when government and the public purse were entrusted to President Joyce Banda and her People's Party (PP).[31] Using the cost figures presented in the national budget of 2014/2015 financial year, here is why public finance mismanagement should make every person genuinely interested in Malawi's national development indignant.

Box 1: Illustrative opportunity costs of public finance mismanagement in the health sector:

- With the MWK 110 billion Malawi's government could have trained over 40,000 medical doctors at College of Medicine (CoM) over a period of 5 years;
- With MWK 110 billion government could have constructed 314 health centres, each with an average of 5 new houses for health care workers;
- In the 2014/2015 national budget, the health sector was allocated a total of MWK 69 billion representing 9.2% of the total budget. Thus, with MWK 110 billion government could have effectively supported the delivery of services in all government health facilities across the country for more than 2 years.

[31] Baker Tilly, "Report on Fraud and Mismanagement of Malawi Government Finances from April to September 2013", Lilongwe: NAO, 2014.

- MWK 20 billion mismanaged during Joyce Banda's first 6 months was enough to provide all health services in Nsanje district for 80 years. This means that MWK 110 billion was worth 440 years of health services in Nsanje at the cost prices of 2014.

Similarly, the opportunity costs in the education sector were significant as illustrated below:

Box 2: Illustrative opportunity costs of public finance mismanagement in education sector

- The MWK 20 billion would educate some 3,311,258 children at primary school, with cost calculated at a UNESCO minimum rate of USD 15 per annum;
- With MWK 20 billion the Ministry of Education could construct over 3,000 classroom blocks, each block with two classrooms;
- With MWK 110 billion government could improve and provide 16,500 classroom blocks and save children from learning in open air under the scorching sun;
- The MWK 20 billion could construct at least 20 new secondary schools or a total of 400 girls' hostels (assuming communities provided bricks, sand and quarry);
- Malawi could have 110 new secondary schools from the MWK 110 billion or 4 Teacher Training Colleges and improve quality of education;
- The MWK 20 billion could enable the construction of 1,176 teachers' houses.

The developmental opportunity cost of public finance mismanagement in a country where every development indicator is at a sub-optimal position should be a concern for all those interested in socio-economic transformation of the country. Significant amounts of resources meant for public goods and services are lost to private consumption of only a few people that are privileged with political and bureaucratic connections to access illicit payments from the public sector. Elements of public finance mismanagement that dominate popular discourses relate to actual expenditures, often identified in audit reports. However, expenditures are a third and last component in the public finance chain. The other two are revenue mobilisation and allocation where also public finance mismanagement happens and precipitate the mismanagement at the expenditure stage. The following section highlights key elements of public finance mismanagement in the other nodes of PFM.

Public Finance Management Chain and Attendant Accountability Mechanisms

Public finance management covers three main nodes: revenue mobilisation, budget allocation and budget expenditure. Statutory law and layers of regulations govern each of these components of PFM. Besides the principles set out in the Republican Constitution, there are three key statutes that constitute the legal framework for public finance management in Malawi. These are the Public Finance Management Act (PFMA), the Public Procurement and Disposal of Assets Act and the Public Audit Act. Other laws that are important to PFM include the statutes governing the work of the Malawi Revenue Authority (MRA), the Reserve Bank of Malawi and other banks in the country. The figure below illustrates the main ways in each stage through which public finance mismanagement occurs.

Revenue Collection

The Government of Malawi mobilises its revenues through taxes, fees and levies administered and managed by various agencies; loans and grants negotiated by the Ministry of Finance in collaboration with other ministries and approved or endorsed by Parliament; proceeds from state-owned enterprises; and, locally generated revenues in local government councils. Revenue mismanagement and misappropriation are part of public finance mismanagement in Malawi even though this is overshadowed by mismanagement related to expenditures. The Public Expenditure and Financial Accountability (PEFA) Assessment for 2018 rated revenue risk management below the level of optimality (B) while revenue audit and investigations as well as revenue arrears monitoring were rated even lower (C). Accounting for revenue was rated at the level of optimality (A) representing improvements over the last few years in availability of information on revenue collections, transfer of revenue collections and reconciliation of revenue accounts. Previous narratives, especially in the aftermath of Cashgate in 2013, held that significant amounts of revenues were misappropriated even before being deposited into the government's account for the consolidated fund.[32] Although the narratives do not constitute evidence, they are not hallucinations or figments of imagination. They are based on observed facts by people working in the systems and sharing information in hushed voices for fear of reprisals.

---

32 Shaun Raviv, "Cashgate".

An interview with an officer of the Malawi Revenue Authority (MRA) suggested that while revenues are audited, the reports are not made public inthe

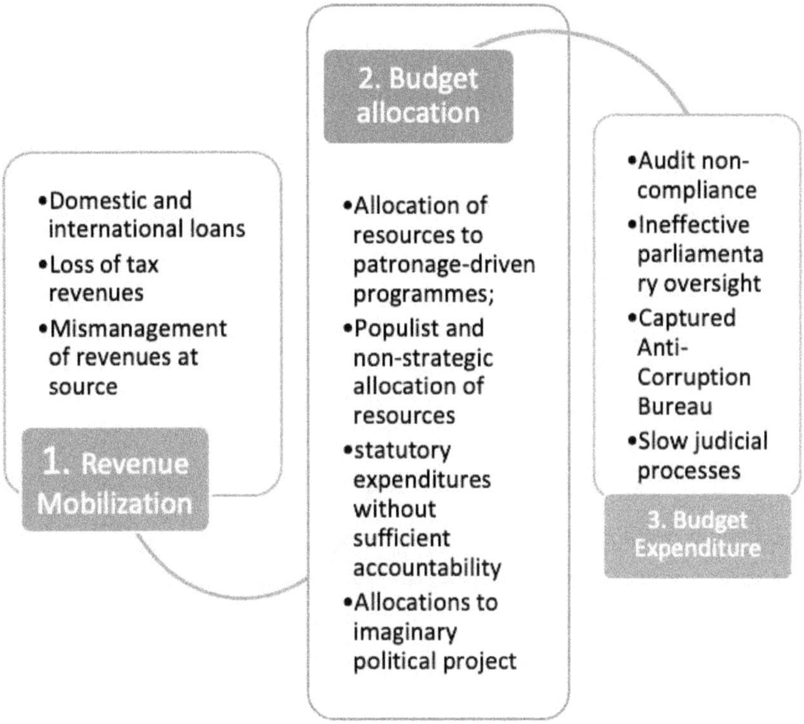

Figure 1.3: *Simplified PFM Chain*

same way expenditure audit reports are: "After the audit is done, Auditor General keeps a report but am not sure if they make it available to the public."[33] This narrative was reinforced by interviews with a former Chairperson of the Parliamentary Committee on Budget and Finance who asserted that throughout his tenure of chairmanship, he did not see any MRA or other Agency's audited revenue account reports. Furthermore, reconciliation of revenue accounts between the Treasury and revenue-collecting agencies was not yet a regular practice, thereby opening up opportunities for abuse of resources. Narratives abound that some or the gravest malfeasance in public revenues mismanagement is orchestrated by inappropriate direct access to revenues by senior political executives for discretionary expenses that are off budget[34] and are not part of the consolidated fund in government's primary account. For instance, an audit established the failure of Malawian missions abroad to

---

33 Interview with MRA officer.

34 Interviews with officers from ESCOM, MRA and former chairperson of Parliamentary Committee on Budget and Finance.

transfer visa and passport fees to government's primary account and the use of these revenues without authorisation.[35] Similarly, in the aftermath of the Fresh Presidential Election in June 2020, there have been more media reports about forgone revenue through ruses involving business persons and supported by political elites and officers of the Tax Authority. The most prominent of these is Cementgate which has gone for trial in the High Court. In this case, a former Chief of Staff and a former Security Aide for President Peter Mutharika, a businessperson and a former Deputy Commissioner of the Malawi Revenue Authority colluded and imported 800,000 bags of cement duty-free under the president's tax account but for the benefit of the businessman, leading to a revenue loss of MWK 1.5 billion.[36] There are numerous reports of aided or abetted tax evasion and avoidance of lawful payments leading to loss of revenue for public coffers.

Loan Contraction as Revenue Collection

In recent years, loan contraction has been revealed to be one avenue through which public finances are mismanaged. The key observation is that the Malawi government borrows significant amounts of money which are not put to the intended use. Some of the loans are basically appropriated by politicians and bureaucrats through various schemes. Nonetheless, loan repayments and servicing become part of statutory expenditure that reduces the amount of resources available in future to finance service delivery and development. The performance of Parliament on loan contraction is sub-optimal thereby committing more future public finances to statutory expenditure in loan repayments, without corresponding tangible development to show. Members of Parliament shy away from asking tough questions when loan authorisation bills are presented for fear of creating the perception that they are anti-developmental as the loans are, officially, procured for development purposes. Furthermore, the law and standing orders of Parliament do not oblige the Minister of Finance to present all documents and speak in sufficient detail about the loan agreements reached with lending institutions. Furthermore, oversight institutions are constrained by considerations of political correctness to track and ensure value for money of the public loans. For example, Parliament approved a MWK 328 billion loan secured from the Indian government for the

---

35 Taonga Sabola, "Audit Exposes Rot in Embassies: Government has K500M debt in Canada", *The Daily Times*, 3 March 2020.

36 Ntchindi Meki, "Cementgate Moves to High Court", *Weekend Nation*, 6 February 2021.

construction of 10,000 modern houses for security agencies (Malawi Police Service; Malawi Defence Force; Immigration Department; and Malawi Prison Service). The Ministry of Lands, Housing and Urban Development was the implementer of the project, while the Ministry of Home Affairs and Internal Security was earmarked as the beneficiary of the project scheduled to run for two years effective 2016.

While the project was well intentioned, this money went down the drain, as there is virtually nothing to show for it.[37] There are many similarly contracted and abused loans including the infamous Tractorgate, as elaborated in the Ombudsman's investigation report.[38] The net effect is that a significant amount of public loans are contracted purportedly for public goods and services but end up lining the pockets of a few privileged individuals while all citizens, through the taxation system contribute to servicing and repaying the loans.

Mineral Resource (mis) Governance Leading to Loss Revenue

Mineral resources can offer greater tax revenues that are critical for eradicating poverty in the country. However, this is likely to happen only if companies are required to pay equitable taxes and royalties; if mining taxes are standardised in conformity with international best practice and not open to ministerial discretion; and if the mining sector is managed transparently. Yet none of these measures are currently in place in Malawi.[39] Government share in royalties is miniscule, tax revenue is far too low as government tends to award long, sometimes very unreasonable tax holidays to mining companies, some tax rates are not standardised thereby opening them up to bargaining by private enterprises and to unregulated discretion of the Minister of Finance,[40] effectively providing enabling conditions for collusive state-business relations in the sector.[41]

Malawi provides tax incentives—reductions or exemptions from paying taxes —to the mining sector exporters and other companies supposedly to encourage investment. One study estimated that tax incentives in the mining sector had cost Malawi a minimum of MWK 86.4 billion (USD 217 million at ruling

---

37 Tom Sangala, "K328 Billion Housing Project for Security Organisations Flops", *The Daily Times*, 31 July 2018.

38 Office of the Ombudsman, "The Present Toiling, The Future Overburdened".

39 Mark Curtis and Rafiq Hajat, "Malawi's Mining Opportunity: Increasing Revenues, Improving Legislation", Lilongwe: Study Report for the Norwegian Church Aid, 2013.

40 Ibid.

41 Henry Chingaipe, "Business and the State in Malawi".

exchange rate) between 2008 and 2012, translating to an average of USD 43.4 million per year. This calculation was based on only two companies. Thus, the overall loss of revenue from mining is much greater. By some estimates, it amounts to an average of MWK 17.28 billion a year which is over 8 times more than the revenues received by the government from mining (according to the 2010 figure of MWK 2 billion).

Two cases illustrate the underoptimisation of collection of revenue from mineral resources for the common good. An Australian company, Paladin, mined Uranium in Malawi under circumstances that were shrouded in secrecy. Paladin negotiated a tax holiday of 15 years, lowering royalty rates from 5% of the sales to 1.5%. The tax holiday and the lowering of royalty rates resulted in revenue loss to the Malawi government amounting to USD 15 million.[42] More recently, Mzimba District Council ordered the shutdown of all mining activities in the district as a reaction to reports that Chinese nationals were flooding into the district to mine gemstones.[43] The district has rock crystals, smoky and rose quartz, that are in high demand and can fetch USD 15,000 per kilogram or more depending on quality and size. However, the Council alleged that the Chinese miners did not have mining licences from the government,[44] and government was not collecting revenue from the mining activities.

The opportunity costs in terms of development outcomes of the lost revenues are significant. It is widely believed that the chaos in the mining sector is not accidental and that it is part of a corrupt scheme between political and bureaucratic elites in government with foreign elements or actors. This belief is reinforced by apparent lack of action by government authorities to act decisively on those elements that come into the public domain or to simply regulate the sector.

Allocation of Public Finances

Parliament's Nominal Role

Although the National Assembly is designated as a resource allocator through the national budget, its role remains insignificant save for rituals that make the

---

42 Staff Reporter, "Questions over 3.6% royalty rate in Kayelekera as Paladin sells Malawi Uranium Mine", www.nyasatimes.com June 25, 2019 accessed on 14 November 2019.

43 Rebeca Chimjeka, "Mzimba Chiefs Stop Illegal Mining", *The Times Group*, October 2019.

44 Ibid.

budget legitimate.[45] The real or effective power to allocate the budget is disproportionately skewed in favour of the Minister of Finance. While recent reforms, such as introduction of the committee cluster system for parliamentary scrutiny of the budget have improved analysis of the minister's budget, they have not given Parliament significant additional influence on the allocations except through hardball, off-the-radar negotiations with the minister.[46]

Populist and Non-strategic Allocation of Resources

Other than expenditures for running conventional and routine government affairs, the allocation of resources is affected by populist and rent-seeking considerations. One scholar and observer of Malawi's political economy has poignantly observed that one of the key problems for Malawi is that political patronage drives policy and programming instead of the other way round.[47] Political elites allocate public resources to programmes and areas where they hope to obtain votes, sustain their political positions or make money for themselves rather than allocating to strategic projects or areas that catalyse long-term sustainable development. For instance, in the national budget passed in October 2019, against popular public opinion and advice from various stakeholders, Parliament approved MWK 1.6 billion for the construction of stadia for two privately owned football teams, Nyasa Bullets and Be Forward Wanderers, to fulfill a wild campaign promise aimed at wooing votes from the Southern Region during the presidential election of 2019. However, judging by popular opinion, government should have allocated these funds to pro-poor services, especially in the health and education sectors, where the scarcity of resources has a huge impact on the delivery of services. Other than electoral advantage, there is no other rationale for such public investment in the private enterprises that are the soccer teams. While the stadia project was taken off the radar by the government elected in June 2020, the budget allocation to another populist programme, the Farm Input Subsidy Programme (FISP), currently rebranded as Affordable Inputs Programme (AIP), increased. The programme

---

45 Lise Rakner et al., "Budget as Theatre: the Formal and Informal Institutional Makings of the Budget Process in Malawi", Working Paper, 2004.

46 Henry Chingaipe et al, "The PEA of the Performance and Effectiveness of the Malawi Parliament", Lilongwe: RNE, 2016.

47 Blessings Chinsinga, "The Green Belt Initiative, Politics and Sugar Production in Malawi", *Journal of Southern African Studies* 43/3 (2017), 501-515, DOI: 10.1080/03057070.2016.1211401; Blessings Chinsinga, "The Political Economy of Agricultural Commercialization in Malawi", Agricultural Policy Research in Africa, Working Paper No. 17, 2018.

which has been implemented since 2005 has too many inefficiencies.[48] Despite recommendations for reforms or abandonment arising from evaluations of the programme, government continues to allocate resources to the programme despite evidence that it benefits more people who are undeserving and worsens public finance management as government tends to spend even more money to procure food to feed the very same people who receive agricultural subsidies for the production of their own food. The agricultural inputs programme has a very low "value for money" score but continues to run because it is a patronage cash cow for politically connected businessmen and bureaucrats and generates votes from farming communities.[49]

Furthermore, some allocations are made to make provision for largesse for patronage and rent-seeking and rent-sharing without serious intentions to deliver the public goods and services in whose name the allocations are made. The same observation goes for the Constituency Development Fund (CDF) which many members of Parliamentregard as their "pocket money"[50] and is generally used for political patronage.[51] Audit reports as well as reports on citizen monitoring of CDF projects highlight wanton abuse and impunity of members of Parliamentin the use of the funds.[52] The Procurement Act and the Public Finance Management Act are often breached for political expediency. Nonetheless, allocations to the CDF have been increasing in spite of public outcry. From MWK 5 million per constituency in 2005 when the funding window started, the allocation stands at MWK 40 million per constituency in 2021.

---

48 Blessings Chinsinga, "The Political Economy of Agricultural Policy Processes in Malawi: A Case Study of the Fertilizer Subsidy Program", Future Agricultures Consortium (FAC), Working Paper 039, nd; Ephraim Chirwa and Andrew Dorward, *Agricultural Input Subsidies: The Recent Malawi Experience*, Oxford: Oxford University Press, 2013.

49 Kim Yi Dionne and Jeremy Horowitz, "The Political Effects of Agricultural Subsidies in Africa: Evidence from Malawi", *World Development* 87 (2016), 215-226; Blessings Chinsinga and Colin Poulton, "Beyond Technocratic Debates: The Significance of Transience of Political Incentives in the Malawi Farm Input Subsidy Program (FISP)", *Development Policy Review* 32/52 (2014), 5123-5150.

50 IPRSE, "Report of Mediation between Members of Parliament and the National Initiative for Civic Education (NICE)", Lilongwe.

51 CONGOMA, "Political Capture of CDF Projects: Malawians Demand Transparency and Accountability", www.congoma.mw/political-capture-of-cdf-projects-malawians-demand-transparency-and-accountability.

52 Rumphi Civil Society Network (RCSN), Constituency Development Fund Tracking Report for Rumphi West, Central and East Constituencies. Action Aid Malawi, 2017 available at https://malawi.actionaid.org/sites/malawi/files/cdf_budget_tracking_report_2017.pdf.

The Auditor General's reports contain repeated findings of misallocations of public funds, unfinished construction works and substandard infrastructure projects where money is siphoned away. The unfinished projects become cause and justification for even more allocations in subsequent years. These acts are not random or accidental and require that Parliament and others undertake even more detailed scrutiny of the budget and carry out analysis of any year's budget in ways that establish backward and forward linkages between allocations.

Undefined Political Projects and Misprocurement Schemes in Statutory Corporations

Mismanagement of public finances in statutory corporations reached nauseating levels during the decade. Utility companies, such as the Electricity Supply Corporation (ESCOM), water boards, regulatory bodies such as Malawi Communications Regulatory Authority (MACRA), Malawi Energy Regulatory Authority (MERA) and Malawi Bureau of Standards and other parastatal organisations that handle significant amounts of money, such as Higher Education Students Loans and Grants Board (HESLGB), National Oil Company of Malawi (NOCMA), Agricultural Development and Marketing Corporation (ADMARC) and the National Food Reserve Agency (NFRA) among others, were mired in financial scams of untold magnitude. Between 2015 and June 2020, during the presidency of Peter Mutharika and his Democratic Progressive Party, money was siphoned from these organisations through demands of payments for unspecified "political projects" of the political party in government and for financing lifestyles of politicians and their associates. The payments were collected by political party agents through various bogus procurement schemes.[53]

The demands for money on the statutory corporations or for entitlements to fringe benefits by the political executive engendered a breakdown in financial discipline, resulting in wanton access to and use of public finances for private ends by staff within the organisations, including entitlements to luxurious fringe benefits such as expensive vehicles, payment of school fees for wards in very expensive private schools, among others.

---

53 Conversations in confidence with two CEOs of affected statutory corporations. For the energy and water sector, see also Henry Chingaipe, "PEA of the Management of Energy (Electricity) and Water Sectors in Malawi", Lilongwe: Democracy Works Foundation, 2016.

Accountability mechanisms for public finances in statutory corporations were very weak throughout the decade. Some of the parastatal organisations were rarely audited and did not submit performance and financial reports to Parliament as required by law, or if they did, Parliament did not discuss them due to crowded business schedules.[54] Thus, there was very little censure and no significant consequences for abuse of public resources in statutory corporations throughout the decade. Once the political executives were taken care of by meeting their demands for money, perpetrators of public finance mismanagement in statutory corporations tended to be secure in comfort while pillaging public finances.

Oversight for Expenditure of Public Funds

The mandate to oversee public expenditures is mostly with Parliament as a primary duty-bearer. Parliament is supported in this role by its oversight agencies, namely the Office of the Auditor General and the Office of the Ombudsman. On the basis of the findings of the Auditor General and recommendations of Parliament, other duty-bearers such as Secretary to Treasury, law enforcement agencies such the Anti-Corruption Bureau and Director of Public Prosecutions are expected to play their roles to ensure accountability for the mismanagement of public finances. However, the oversight function is confounded in many ways. In particular, there is habitual non-compliance by public officers in MDAs with corrective recommendations of the Auditor General, Parliament is institutionally weak to effectively execute its oversight mandate and the Anti-Corruption Bureau lacks operational autonomy to exact accountability for public finance mismanagement in a consistent manner.

Non-compliance with Auditor General's Recommendation

Throughout the decade, the public finance management system showed a very high propensity for breaching principles and rules for managing and safeguarding public resources and persisted in defying recommendations of the Auditor General to improve the situation. As noted in a recent report, "despite providing guidance, most controlling officers [do] not take into action the provided recommendations."[55] As a result, public finance mismanagement

[54] Henry Chingaipe et al., "The Political Economy of the Performance and Effectiveness of the Malawi Parliament", Lilongwe: RNE, 2016.

[55] Report of the Auditor General on the accounts of the Government of the Republic of Malawi for the year ended 30 June 2019.

continued almost unabated despite technical and legal or policy improvements to the system. Although the Office of the Auditor General should be an independent agency of Parliament, it is caught up in the thicket of informal rules that characterise the governance sphere in Malawi in which oversight institutions are beholden to the executive branch of government thereby having their mandates and practices compromised by the idiosyncrasies of political incumbents. This scenario creates a favourable environment for plunder of public financial resources by political elites and their associates, with full knowledge that should the audit office expose the dirt, the configuration of power and their political loyalty would protect them or exonerate them from culpability.

Unfortunately, the Auditor General's mandate stops at making recommenddations. Once the reports are submitted, it is dependent on the goodwill of Parliament to act on the report and on the Secretary to Treasury to take remedial and disciplinary measures against errant officers and for the prosecutorial authorities to weigh in. Except for some cases related to Cashgate, most of the reported cases of public finance mismanagement during the decade were not pursued to their logical conclusion to ensure full accountability. Errant officers were simply redeployed or transferred from one ministry, department or agency to another or in rare cases, they were interdicted to pave way for investigations or to answer criminal charges in court.

Parliament's Weak Oversight

Exercising oversight over public finance management is a core constitutional mandate of Parliament. However, the oversight function of Parliament is undermined by several factors, including inadequate and erratic funding for the work of portfolio committees and the National Assembly; insufficient skilled officers with research capacity to support MPs with competent analysis for enhanced probity; defiance of some controlling public officers when summoned to appear before committees, including the Public Accounts Committee; and asymmetric power relations between Parliament and the executive in favour of the latter.[56] Under the laws, Parliament, just like the Auditor General, lacks sanctioning power. At best, it can only "talk down controlling officers" and make recommendations to the executive, mostly the Secretary to Treasury (ST) (Ministry of Finance) or the Director of Public Prosecutions (DPP) (Ministry of Justice and Constitutional Affairs). However,

---

56 Henry Chingaipe et al, "The Political Economy".

these offices are obliged by the same logic of political loyalty and a requirement never to rock the boat. Thus, the prospect of sanctions on errant public officers in the management of finances is left to chance and is dependent on political considerations. The uncertainty of being caught and the certainty of not being punished for public finance mismanagement or the prospect of a delayed disciplinary or protracted judicial process present incentives for financial malfeasance.

An Anti-Corruption Bureau that Lacks Operational Autonomy

The Anti-Corruption Bureau (ACB) is mandated to take any necessary measures for the prevention, investigation and prosecution of corruption.[57] Within its legal mandate the ACB has powers of oversight on PFM, to ensure that public funds benefit the public; and that the funds are not diverted to private benefit by unscrupulous individuals.

While the ACB has a comprehensive mandate and a required institutional form, its performance is constrained. The key impediments relate to low levels of operational independence in view of high levels of political interference especially in investigating and prosecuting corruption; inadequate funding of operations partly because of genuine resource constraints but also a perceived motivation to stifle its oversight work by the political executive; several institutional and legal requirements that collectively undermine effectiveness; and staff and institutional capacity gaps.[58] Throughout the decade, the ACB appeared and operated as an oversight organisation that had been captured and repurposed by political elites to protect the plunderers of public finances that had some political wherewithal by not investigating them or delaying and protracting the investigations or the prosecutions.

A PEA Explanation of Persistent Public Finance Mismanagement

Why did reforms not yield the kind of PFM that was desirable throughout the decade? Why were public monies mismanaged, pilfered out of the system and remained unaccounted for despite yearly recommendations by the Auditor General and a whole lot of reforms? The pervasiveness of public finance mismanagement and the persistent noncompliance with rules and regulations,

---

57 The ACB is established by an Act of Parliament, the Corrupt Practices Act, Chap. 7, 2004.

58 Henry Chingaipe, "Effectiveness of the Malawi Anti-Corruption Bureau", in Open Society Initiative for Southern Africa (OSISA), *Effectiveness of Anti-Corruption Agencies in Southern Africa*, Johannesburg: OSISA, 2017, 132-66.

show that the formal rules for managing public finances in Malawi have been mostly ineffective. They were supplanted by competing informal rules that were politically engineered to enable ruling politicians and their bureaucratic associates to maximise personal benefits from the positions they held in the configuration of political power and the exercise of administrative authority. Informal rules reinforced a political logic of "feeding off the state" and reinforced the notion of politics of the belly, i.e. a goat eats where it is tethered.[59] The supplanting of formal rules and good practices in PFM was enabled by three core factors, namely the redefining of national interests away from the collective good, the weakening of accountability through appointive bureaucracies and a docile citizenry that hardly engaged in social accountability.

Interests, Capture and Repurposing of the State

Most public finance mismanagement during the decade was not random. It was carried out through deliberate dubious procurement processes characterised by collusion, and involving syndicates of politicians, bureaucrats and genuine and pseudo business enterprises. It represented a conspiracy to feed off the state by pressuring the government or individuals in key government positions to divert resources away from most efficient and socially optimal uses to support private accumulation and unearned luxurious lifestyles. These collusive coalitions overrode, undermined or disabled existing formal public financial management and accountability mechanisms and were abetted by negligent or "captured and repurposed" by controlling officers. The report by PricewaterhouseCoopers, for instance, showed that government had made payments to different suppliers on different dates using the same cheque number. How that is possible defeats even the wildest of imaginations. What is clear, however, is that public finance mismanagement was done in a very coordinated way and in a Mafia-like style.[60]

Appointive Bureaucracies and their Roles in Public Finance Mismanagement

It is apparent that Malawi's bureaucracy is "appointive" in nature. An appointive bureaucracy is a cadre of public servants appointed by the president or his

---

[59] Jean-Francois Bayart et al, *The Criminalization of the State in Africa.*

[60] Frank Jomo, "Corruption bleeds Malawi's wobbling economy", 4 September 2016, https://africanarguments.org/2015/07/10/corruption-bleeds-malawis-wobbling-economy-by-frank-jomo.

proxies into key decision-making positions as agents of the regime and retainers of the president. They use their official positions to pursue and implement schemes of political survival and continuity of the regime.[61] Such cadres create situations in which "the interests of individual incumbents are allowed free rein"[62] and provide the necessary conditions for schemes that plunder or mis-manage public finances. Hence, in appointive bureaucracies, decision-making is appropriated by the sympathisers of the political regime and the internal structures of the bureaucracy are unable to bind the behaviour of individual bureaucrats to the pursuit of common goals.[63] The career bureaucrats wait for signals from the political executive of what is acceptable behaviour and they quickly build their own schemes of survival around those cues, under the pretext of "serving the Government of the day". Thus, politicians with a short-term horizon influence bureaucrats to mismanage public finances. Appointive bureaucracies are responsible for creating what Goran Hyden described as a "social affection economy". In such a state, individuals connected to the political regime pursue favours, gain prestigious status and share private benefits by investing in interpersonal and mutual reciprocities based on reliance on handshakes, rather than impersonal contracts. Hence, sharing private goods is more important than investing in economic growth and collective goods and services.[64]

During the decade under review in this chapter, Malawi mirrored a state hanging on social affinities that thrived on the appointive nature of the public sector. Through this system, as aptly observed by one legal scholar, "a horde of irredeemably unscrupulous people placed each other in strategic positions misappropriate public resources. The horde grew exponentially in numbers to steal and favour each other with opportunities to steal, divert or otherwise misappropriate public resources. The horde grew exponentially in numbers over the years and were widely deployed across the public sector."[65] By 6 July, 2020 when President Chakwera was speaking about clearing the rubble, "there was no public institution that did not have their representative, to do the

---

61 Peter Evans, *Embedded Autonomy: States and Industrial Transformation*, Princeton: Princeton University Press, 1995.

62 Peter Evans, "State Structures, Government-Business Relations, and Economic Transformation", in Ben Ross Schneider and Sylvia Maxfield (eds), *Business and the State in Developing Countries*, 63-87.

63 Ibid.

64 Goran Hyden, *African Politics in Comparative Perspectives*, Cambridge: University Press, 2005.

65 Bright Theu, *Facebook* Timeline post, 9 February 2021, www.facbook.com/bright.theu

needful when need should arise, including aiding their members to evade accountability whenever they [would be] called to account".[66]

Thus, throughout the decade, political interests and incentives for political elites were the major reasons for the mismanagement of public finances. Through their agents planted all over the public sector, politically powerful individuals pulled the strings, motivated public finance mismanagement and benefited from its proceeds. Since the controlling officers and the heads of the watchdog institutions were appointed by the political executive and were made to understand that their primary role was to serve as retainers of their political masters, they ignored the formal mandates and rules of the bureaucratic positions they held for fear of losing their jobs. In some instances, they even created schemes to rationalise abuse of resources. Such was the vicious cycle of public finance mismanagement during the decade. The state was captured and repurposed to serve narrow interests.

Weak Social Accountability Mechanisms for Public Finance Management

During the decade, state-society relations were reconfigured. The classic democratic formulation of a principal-agent relationship in which citizens reign supreme and state elites (politicians and bureaucrats) serve the people, increasingly became subverted and was effectively replaced with a patrimonial and clientelistic relationship. State elites reigned supreme and lived big. Citizens became more subservient, reduced to being subjects, lived on patrimonial crumbs trickling from the high tables of state elites and were useful and relevant mainly in taxation and extraction of economic surplus from them. Critical citizenship, necessary for social accountability, was dampened as the state elites competed against each other in using their positions to maximise privatisation of resources from the public sector. Even a "national psyche was created in which citizens became conditioned to tolerate theft and abuse of public resources, and celebrate the perpetrators."[67]

Thus, social accountability, understood as actions initiated by individual citizens and groups to hold public officials, politicians and service providers to account for their conduct and performance in terms of delivering services, improving people's welfare and protecting people's rights, went down to its

66 Ibid.
67 Ibid.

lowest ebb.[68] Citizens increased their voices demanding accountability through media and other ways but rarely achieved any accountability from public officials on public finance management. Despite numerous revelations in the media on massive looting of public resources, accountability for public finance mismanagement was elusive, except in a few instances where the system had to offer a few sacrificial lambs in order to protect the system from rupture.

Civic actors were disempowered through all sorts of regulatory threats, especially in the last half of the decade,[69] through cooptation of strong voices into the political establishment, violence perpetrated by cadres of the political regime and a propagation of narratives that undermined or discouraged citizen activism in demanding accountable, responsive and inclusive governance.

Conclusion and Recommendations

Public finance mismanagement in Malawi in the last decade was a mirror image of roving banditry perpetrated by state elites (politicians and bureaucrats) and their associates. This was sustained by how political power was configured and exercised to allow a cadre of politicians and their associates to divert resources from public to private purposes. In part, this was reinforced by the logic of a "winner takes all" political system in which there is a real prospect of losing power through elections. The analysis shows that public finance mismanagement underlies all the eight types of "rubble" that President Chakwera outlined in his inaugural address: corruption, laziness, passivism, donor dependency, regionalism, negativity, impunity and unprofessionalism and incompetence. These governance challenges are wholly or in part, direct outcomes of the careless and criminal pillaging of public finances of the last decade, even going back beyond the decade. Thus, a reform of politics, i.e. how political power is configured and exercised, is essential for dividends in PFM reforms. This determines whether formal rules and procedures will be complied with or not; whether people working in the public service will serve as retainers of a political regime or trustees of citizens looking after the greatest good for the greatest numbers of citizens.

---

[68] Claudia Baez Camargo, *Social Accountability: A Practitioner's Handbook*, Basel: Basel Institute on Governance, 2016.

[69] Henry Chingaipe, "Regulatory Threats to the Civic Space in Malawi and their Impact on the Functioning of CSOs/NGOs", Lilongwe: Economic Justice Network, 2020.

Reforms will have to reach institutions of accountability for public finance management. Parliament, the Auditor General and the ACB have segmented, unfinished or inadequate mandates with ultimate authority in offices and incumbents with conflicts of interest. Key institutions of accountability are subjugated to the political executive such that they are stifled and cannot carry out their oversight mandates over PFM with consistency. The situation is exacerbated by the fact that social accountability is still in nascent stages and requires significant social investment in the form civic empowerment of citizens beyond giving them information of their rights.

So what can the new government do to clear the rubble in public finance management? Ethical political leadership with unwavering will to improve public finance management and ensure "value for money" is the key to reverse abuse of public finances. The rhetoric of the new government on this subject, at least during its inception stage, has been correct both in the diagnosis of the status quo and the optimism of the solutions to address the challenges. As observed by the Ombudsman, "to effectively deal with fraud and abuse of public resources and the institutionalised impunity that goes with it, there is need for a good conspiracy of governance and law enforcement institutions."[70] However, as elucidated in examples of abuse, some of these institutions are themselves embroiled in public finance frauds and scams. Malawian institutions are easily repurposed. It depends largely on the interests of those entrusted to run the institutions and their incentives for engaging or avoiding the lures of a felonious system. Any PFM system is only as good as the people who operate it. To clean up the system, the new government will have to identify those officers in the public sector that were agents of the roving banditry that characterised governance in the last decade and remove them from the system while exacting accountability. Furthermore, there is need for public sector reforms that address perverse incentives that fuel public finance mismanagement across the PFM chain, not just expenditures. The direction taken for public sector reforms between 2014 and 2016 was most appropriate but was abandoned as the content of reforms ran contrary to the informal rules upon which the felonious system of roving banditry thrived.[71] Enforcement of existing laws, rules and procedures for PFM requires visible high-level political leadership, able to

[70] Martha Chizuma, Ombudsman of Malawi, quoted in Golden Matonga, "DPP Director of Public Prosecutions Moves in on Covid-19 Funds", *The Nation*, 11 February 2021.

[71] Government of Malawi, "Malawi Public Service Reform Commission. Making Malawi Work", Final Report, Lilongwe: MPSRC, 2015.

mete out punishments for misuse of public money. This is particularly important as a first stage towards attenuating the significance of informal rules that shaped public finance mismanagement during the decade.

Ensuring the operational autonomy of watchdog institutions such as the ACB and the Auditor General from the tentacles of the political elites in the executive is an important milestone to ensure that unscrupulous individuals with political powers or with ties to political elites do not interfere with robust management of public resources. Making the watchdogs more independent requires changes in the policies and laws that govern the appointment of the Auditor General and the Director General of the ACB and in the ways of financing their operations. Shifting the powers of appointment from the president to Parliament for these two important positions will go a long way in promoting ethical, transparent and effective oversight of public finance management. Similarly, parliamentary reforms are necessary for effective oversight on PFM. In particular, mechanisms should be developed to execute resolutions of the Public Accounts Committee on the findings of the Auditor General. Failure to mete out punishment on errant officers lowers the calculation of risk for perpetrators of public finance mismanagement.

Finally, but hardly least in importance, is the need for a deliberate civic empowerment programme to energise citizens on exercising oversight and demanding transparency and accountability for public finance management and to clear the rubble of citizen passivism. This will require the new political leadership to be steadfast and sincere in implementing the Access to Information law to enable citizens and journalists to access information on transactions and deals that can militate against good PFM. Thus, besides the creation of the Ministry of Civic Education and National Unity, Public Trust organisations such as NICE should be supported to enable them to implement a National Civic Competence Programme that goes beyond civic education to catalyse critical and active citizenship on public finance and development outcomes.

Chapter 2

Two Decades of Governance in Malawi: Examining Citizen Trust in Malawi from 1999-2019

Joseph J. Chunga
& Happy Kayuni

Introduction

Increasingly, contemporary political governance studies are acknowledging the role of citizen trust in good governance. In other words, public trust is no longer being taken for granted because it has critical implications for the long-term legitimacy and democratic consolidation of any polity. The success or failure of government policies and programmes largely depends on the trust that respective public institutions enjoy. As Kotze argues, "there is ample consensus in the literature that institutional confidence by the public is needed in democracies … if political stability in established democracies and the consolidation of new democracies are desired."[1] Since the re-introduction of democracy in 1994, Malawi has experienced several political gains and losses which ultimately have affected democratic consolidation or governance. The post-1994 Constitution specifically stipulates that authority of all state institutions is based on sustained trust of Malawians. In the shadow of three-decades legacy of strong presidency, a Parliament that was effectively a rubberstamp of presidential decrees and a security service that was politically captured and used to stifle political dissent, Malawi's democracy project significantly hinges on the extent to which these institutions have been transformed.

Thus, the aim of this chapter is to critically examine trajectories of public trust in key government institutions (Parliament, courts, the Presidency and the police) from 1999 to 2019, explore factors that affect public trust, and discuss implications on state legitimacy and prospects of democracy. These four institutions were particularly identified to represent key elements of the three arms of government (the Presidency and police in this chapter represent the

---

1 Hennie Kotze and Carlos Garcia-Rivero, "Institutions, Crises, and Political Confidence in Seven Contemporary Democracies: An Elite–mass Analysis", *Journal of Public Affairs* 17/1-2 (2017) https://doi.org/10.1002/pa.1642.

executive). Using mainly Afrobarometer data sets,[2] the chapter argues that there is a general decline in public trust of key governance institutions, especially in recent years, hence this is a threat to state legitimacy and prospects of democracy consolidation. The key explanatory factors as regards the declining levels of trust are perceptions of government handling of food challenges and management of the economy (or general performance) and levels of corruption. The identification of these possible explanatory factors was guided by the observations made by public trust studies done by Ramesh and Mattes and Moreno. According to Ramesh, "in the recent past, citizen trust in most public institutions has been alarmingly decreasing owing to politicisation of the public sector, service delivery, political and bureaucratic corruption, lack of transparency, accountability."[3] In relation to public trust, Mattes and Moreno argue that "the strongest determinants are individual perceptions of government performance and government corruption."[4]

This chapter is divided into seven parts. The first part discusses the concepts of governance and trust followed by a section on good governance in Africa. The third section provides a brief background to governance in Malawi then an overview of general trends of trust in presidents, Parliament, police and courts (from 1999 to 2019). The fifth section deliberates the possible explanatory factors and before concluding, the final section discusses the consequences of loss of citizen trust on the state.

The Concept and Governance Consequences of Political Trust

Political trust is defined as "the ratio of people's evaluation of government performance relative to their normative expectations of how government ought to perform".[5] It is an expression of people's confidence in political institutions

---

2 Afrobarometer is a pan-African, non-partisan survey research network that provides data on Africans' experiences and evaluations of quality of life, governance, and democracy. Afrobarometer conducts face-to-face interviews with nationally representative samples. Previous surveys were conducted in Malawi in 1999, 2003, 2005, 2008, 2012, 2014 and 2017. More details on methodology are available on www.afrobarometer.org.

3 Ramasamy Ramesh, "Does Trust Matter? An Inquiry on Citizens' Trust in Public Institutions of Sri Lanka", *Millennial Asia* 8/2 (2017), 123–145. DOI: 10.1177/097639961 7715820,123.

4 Robert Mattes and Alejandro Moreno, "Social and Political Trust in Developing Countries: Sub-Saharan Africa and Latin America", in Eric M. Uslaner (ed), *The Oxford Handbook of Social and Political Trust*, Oxford: Oxford University Press, 2018, 357-82. DOI: 0.1093/oxford hb/9780190274801.013.10.

5 Marc Hetherington and Jason Husser, "How Trust Matters: The Changing Political Relevance of Political Trust", *American Journal of Political Science*, 56/2, 2012, 312-25 [313].

or political leaders. According to Miller and Listhaug, political trust is akin to the "judgment of the citizenry" on the political system and its leadership to ensure that they are responsive to the needs of the people irrespective of whether there are effective checks and balances or not.[6] In other words, political trust acts like the citizenry's underlying sentiment concerning their political system and its leadership.[7] The OECD explains that trust implies that "people must feel they have a real voice; are treated with respect; and receive necessary explanations".[8]

According to Moti, there are two types of political trust: *macro-level or organisational trust* and *micro-level or individual political trust.*[9] Macro-level trust is directed towards a political system and its organisations. He further argues that macro-level trust can also be divided into two: *diffuse or system-based trust*, and *specific or institution-based trust.* In this case he explains that, "diffuse political trust refers to the citizens' evaluation of the performance of the overall political system and the regime. Specific political trust, on the other hand, is directed towards certain political institutions, such as the Congress or the local police force."[10] Unlike macro-level trust, micro-level trust is directed at individual political leaders. Thus, in micro-level trust, "citizens become trustful or distrustful of government—because of their approval or disapproval of certain political leaders".[11] Based on the discussion above, political trust can be said to have taken place when citizens in general have assessed government in terms of its institutions or leadership including the general policy-making process and approved its activities to be unbiased, honest and efficient.

As rightly argued by Turper and Aarts, political trust will always be a critical theme in political science research because, among other reasons, "measuring

---

6 Arthur Miller and Ola Listhaug, "Political Parties and Confidence in Government: A Comparison of Norway, Sweden and the United States", *British Journal of Political Science* 20/3, 1990, 357-86 [358].

7 Kenneth Newton and Pippa Norris, "Confidence in Public Institutions: Faith, Culture, or Performance?" in S.J. Pharr and R.D. Putnam (eds), *Disaffected Democracies: What's Troubling the Trilateral Democracies*? Princeton: Princeton University Press, 2000, 52-73 [53].

8 The Organisation for Economic Co-operation and Development (OECD), *Trust and Public Policy: How Better Governance Can Help Rebuild Public Trust*, OECD Public Governance Reviews, Paris: OECD Publishing, 2017, 13. http://dx.doi.org/10.1787/9789264268920-en.

9 Ukertor Moti, "Building Trust in Government for Good Governance: What can Nigeria and African Governments Learn?" *Nigerian Journal of Administrative Science* 10/1-2 (2013), 3.

10 Moti "Building Trust in Government for Good Governance: What can Nigeria and African Governments Learn?" 3.

11 Ibid.

the level and development of political trust may provide us with important information about the stability of political systems".[12] Most scholarly debates on the consequences of political trust build on the work of David Easton where trust is regarded as a form of diffuse-support input into a political system.[13] From one perspective, low-level political support is regarded as a symbol of critical citizenship which is important for democratic accountability and therefore a positive contribution for democracy.[14] On the other hand, based on empirical research, there is ample evidence that lower levels of trust lead to lower citizen participation but "more often undertake system-challenging political behavior".[15] Low levels of political trust are associated with less law compliance within a society.[16] Hetherington also observes that when there is low level of political trust, it produces a political environment in which political leaders find it difficult to successfully lead or implement policies or even win an election.[17]

The link between trust and good governance is aptly discussed by Ramesh who points out that:

> Citizen trust in public institutions is an indication of successful governance as it has often been viewed as an important element of good governance. Citizen distrust in government and its institutions considerably affects the effectiveness and efficiency of public policies and their implementation … Higher citizen trust in public institutions ensures good governance and successful implementation of policies.[18]

In other words, as governments are busy developing practical ways in which they may be more relevant to the citizenry, there is no way they may bypass the critical element of trust. Thus, the language of good governance is also the language of public trust.

Currently there are several definitions and measures of governance and, according to Fukuyama, these measures do "have a number of limitations …

---

12 Sedef Turper and Kees Aarts, "Political Trust and Sophistication: Taking Measurement Seriously", *Social Indicator Research* 130/1 (2017), 415-34 [415].

13 David Easton, *A Framework for Political Analysis*, Englewood Cliffs, NJ: Prentice Hall, 1965.

14 Pippa Norris (ed), *Critical Citizens: Global Support for Democratic Government*, Oxford: Oxford University Press, 1999.

15 Sedef Turper and Kees Aarts, "Political Trust and Sophistication", 415.

16 Sofie Marien and Marc Hooghe, "Does Political Trust Matter? An Empirical Investigation into the Relation Between Political Trust and Support for Law Compliance", *European Journal of Political Research* 50/2 (2011), 267-91 [267].

17 Marc J. Hetherington, "The Political Relevance of Political Trust", *American Political Science Review* 92/4 (1998), 791-808.

18 Ramesh, "Does Trust Matter?" 123, 126.

since the concept of good governance is not well established".[19] According to Keping, the original meaning of the word governance was "control, guidance and manipulation", but after the 1990s the word came to be associated with political conditions of most developing countries.[20] This chapter is guided by the Mo Ibrahim Foundation's (MIF) definition of governance which states that it is "the provision of the political, social and economic public goods and services that every citizen has the right to expect from their state, and that a state has the responsibility to deliver to its citizens".[21] In academic discourse, the qualifier of "good" was later added to governance mainly to express a "desired value" of governance and also a "precondition for aid recipients" as prescribed mainly by the World Bank.[22] This chapter uses the terms "governance" and "good governance" interchangeably.

The concept of good governance is understood differently by different individuals or stakeholders. Also, there are proponents and opponents of the good governance agenda. According to Gisselquist, proponents argue that application of the concept can influence economic growth and development for countries that are particularly poorly managed. On the other hand, opponents of the good governance agenda "argue that the use of governance criteria in the allocation of foreign aid effectively introduces political conditionalities and imposes Western liberal models of democracy".[23]

In relation to indicators, the World Bank was initially the leading institution in the development of indicators for economic and political governance but, over the years, several institutions have developed their own measures and indicators. Despite the fact that over time several governance institutions developed, the influence of the World Bank and UNDP cannot be discounted. The Afrobarometer governance indicators that this chapter uses are related to the World Bank and UNDP's indicators, such as "political accountability,

---

19 Francis Fukuyama, "What Is Governance?" CGD Working Paper 314, Washington, DC: Center for Global Development 2013, 2. http://www.cgdev.org/content/publications/detail/1426906.

20 Yu Keping, "Governance and Good Governance: A New Framework for Political Analysis", *Fudan Journal of the Humanities and Social Science* 11/1–8 (2018), 1-2. https://doi.org/10.1007/s40647-017-0197-4.

21 Mo Ibrahim Foundation, *2019 African Governance Report,* Mo Ibrahim Foundation, 2019.

22 Mohammed Asaduzzaman and Petri Virtanen, "Governance Theories and Models", in Ali Farazmand (ed), *Global Encyclopedia of Public Administration, Public Policy, and Governance,* Dordrecht: Springer, 2016. DOI 10.1007/978-3-319-31816-5_2612-1.

23 Rachel M. Gisselquist, "Good Governance as a Concept, and Why This Matters for Development Policy", Working Paper No. 2012/30, UNU-Wider, 2012, 1.

freedom of association and participation, rule of law and independence of the judiciary, bureaucratic accountability, freedom of information, a sound administrative system, partnership between the government and the civil society organisations".[24]

Good Governance in Africa

Before discussing governance in Malawi, it is important to provide the wider context by analysing briefly the status of governance in Africa. At a global and regional level, the issue of good governance has taken centre stage. It has also become recognised that social or economic development cannot be achieved if governance is ignored. For instance, through the United Nations, countries of the world in 2015 committed themselves to 17 life-changing goals.[25] These goals, popularly known as the Sustainable Development Goals (SDGs), include among other things ending extreme poverty and ensuring prosperity for everyone by the year 2030. One of the goals listed is good governance (SDG 16). African countries have, through mainly the African Union, since the 1980s demonstrated commitment towards building credible governance institutions. Several studies have shown that the governance situation in most African countries leaves a lot to be desired. Some of the local initiatives to address the problem of bad governance are discussed below.[26]

The African Economic Community for Continental Co-operation (Abuja Treaty of 1991) and the Sirte Declaration (1999)—these two agreements highlighted commitment to good governance and democratic ideals such as the rule of law and human rights.

The New Partnership for Africa's Development (NEPAD) came about as a way to facilitate a constructive association with countries in the west. One of the key elements in NEPAD is the introduction of a self-appraisal on governance known as the African Peer Review Mechanism (APRM). Among other things, it measures performance on political, economic, corporate and socio-economic areas.[27]

---

24 Asaduzzaman and Virtanen, "Governance Theories and Models", 6.

25 United Nations, *Agenda 2030: Sustainable Development Goals*, UN, 2015 www.undp.org/content/undp/en/home/sustainable-development-goals.html.

26 Christine Cubitt "An Introduction to Governance in Africa", *Governance in Africa* 1/1 (2014), 1, DOI: http://dx.doi.org/10.5334/gia.ae

27 Cubitt, "An Introduction to Governance in Africa", 1.

Despite the above-mentioned initiatives, it has become apparent that not much has been achieved. According to Freedom House, governance challenges are some of the key elements "that are holding citizens across Africa back" and negatively affecting the continent's socio-economic progress.[28] In this case, Freedom House identified the five governance challenges as follows: firstly, there is dismal press freedom. This is one type of freedom which had seen the greatest level of decline in the past decade. Several journalists in the region have over the years been harassed or exiled in order to suppress independent reporting. Secondly, there has been a proliferation of restrictive laws. Specifically, draconian laws have been put in place in order to deal with opposition leaders, political activists and civil society organisations who are deemed to be against the government. Thirdly, the region has witnessed entrenched leaders and the abuse of term limits. In this case, several attempts have been made by some political leaders to extend their tenure beyond their country's constitutionally mandated limit. Fourthly, there are weak regional human rights mechanisms meant to protect the citizens of each African country. Although an important regional court was established some years ago, the African Court of Human and Peoples' Rights, it lacks support from its member countries. Finally, there is lack of economic competitiveness in the region. Despite the observation that some of the world's 10 fastest growing economies are found in the region, the majority of the world's least competitive nations are also from the same region.

Agenda 2063 is one of the latest African regional initiatives to address, among other things, the issue of poor governance. In January 2013 the African Union Summit adopted Agenda 2063, which was entitled "The Africa We Want", and it was meant to be Africa's blueprint and master plan for economic growth and sustainable development of the continent. The African Union's Agenda 2063 Aspiration number 3 talks about "An Africa of Good Governance, Democracy, Respect for Human Rights, Justice and the Rule of Law" and one of the goals associated with this aspiration is "Capable institutions and transformative leadership in place".[29] Since Malawi is a member of the African Union and is party to almost all the governance initiatives highlighted above, it is imperative that we understand its governance performance in the context of commitment to these initiatives.

---

[28] Freedom House, "5 Governance Challenges for Africa", *Perspectives*, 12 June 2015. https://freedomhouse.org/article/5-governance-challenges-africa.

[29] African Union Goals & Priority Areas of Agenda 2063, https://au.int/agenda2063/goals.

A Brief Background to Governance in Malawi

From independence in 1964 up to 1994, Malawi's governance system revolved around an individual, Hastings Kamuzu Banda of the Malawi Congress Party (MCP), Malawi's first president who later became the Life President of the country. In other words, the Presidency dominated Parliament and any other policy-making and governance institution in the country. Parliament met to merely rubberstamp what the president had directed. Specifically, parliament-tarians tried to outdo one another in praising the president during their mee-tings. The police and the specially created traditional courts were some of the political instruments used by the president to deal with those who opposed him. During Kamuzu Banda's reign, the bureaucracy was highly regarded, and corruption was reportedly not rampant; however, the chapter does not focus on state institutions during Banda's rule and beyond.

Since 1994, when Malawi re-introduced a multiparty system of governance, the country has had five presidents: Bakili Muluzi of the United Democratic Front (UDF) from 1994 to 2004, Bingu wa Mutharika of UDF and later Democratic Progressive Party (DPP) from 2004 to 2012, Joyce Banda of People's Party (PP) from 2012 to 2014, Peter Mutharika of DPP from 2014 to 27 June 2020 and Lazarus Chakwera of MCP from 28 June 2020 to the present. The re-intro-duction of a multiparty system of government in 1994 provided an opportunity for a renewed democratic political system. Specifically, there was a proper legal and political platform established to ensure meaningful participation of citizens in the development agenda of the country. For the first time in many years, Malawians started exercising some of the most basic rights such as freedom of association and other related rights. Several development plans were developed after 1994 which emphasised governance. This section briefly discusses Malawi's Vision 2020 and the Malawi Growth and Development Strategy (MGDS) III as background to understanding governance programmes.

Launched in 1998, the recently expired Vision 2020 highlights the significance of good governance and in particular chapter 2 of the vision is dedicated to this theme. The vision mentions that:

> The Government will operate in an environment of transparency, accountability and rule of law. There will be effective participation of all citizens in the governing of the country coupled with clear separation of powers between the three branches of

> government: the executive, the legislature and the judiciary. The Government will operate according to the principle of merit in all public appointments.[30]

Building on Vision 2020, Malawi's current medium-term overall development plans are highlighted in the Malawi Growth and Development Strategy (MGDS) III, and chapter 3 of the plan is devoted to governance issues. It recognises that development cannot be achieved if governance of the country is ignored. Specifically, the MGDS III says that:

> Effective governance can improve management, leading to more effective implementation of the chosen interventions, better service delivery, and, ultimately, better outcomes. Good governance is, therefore, the backbone for an efficient and effective public sector and is the anchor for this strategy.[31]

However, despite embracing a multiparty system of governance in 1994 and developing several plans which embraced the concept of governance, Malawi's political governance has since then been characterised as "fundamentally a hybrid neo-patrimonial state where a framework of formal law and administration exists but the state is informally characterised by patronage networks".[32] Specifically, Kayuni and Chinsinga have in their separate works identified the following political economy challenges that Malawi has been facing in recent years.[33]

First is the mismanagement of the transition from a single-party to multiparty system of governance followed by government's failure to effectively formulate, articulate and implement policy alternatives. This was worsened by widespread neopatrimonial tendencies and practices in the running of the civil service. In other words, key positions in the civil service were filled by party loyalists who replaced professional and technically oriented administrators. *Second,* and linked to the above point, is the limited progress in the public sector

---

[30] Government of Malawi (GoM) *Vision 2020: National Long-Term Development Perspective for Malawi*, National Economic Council, 1998, 33

[31] Government of Malawi, The Malawi Growth and Development Strategy (MGDS) III, Ministry of Finance, Economic Planning and Development, 2017, 19.

[32] Blessings Chinsinga, "The Political Economy Context", in Nandini Patel and Michael Wahman (eds), *The Malawi 2014 Tripartite Elections: Is Democracy Maturing?* Lilongwe: National Initiative for Civic Education, 2015, 22.

[33] Happy Kayuni, "Budgeting in African Nations: The Case of Malawi", in Peter Haruna and Shikha Vyas-Doorgapersad (eds), *Public Budgeting in African Nations: Fiscal Analysis in Development Management*, London: Routledge, 2016, 168-185; Happy Kayuni, "Innovation and Thought Leadership in the Public Sector: Reflections in the Context of Malawi's Public Sector Reforms", Norhed conference: Administrative and Political Governance for Inclusive Development, SUM, University of Oslo, 23 November 2016; Chinsinga, "The Political Economy Context".

reform agenda. Malawi has since the Kamuzu era made attempts at reforming the public sector. During the launch of the Public Sector Reform Agenda in February 2015, the former President of Malawi indicated that since 1994 "there have been 79 attempts to reform Malawi's public sector".[34] *Third*, in the quest to gain votes, politicians have promoted a culture of handouts. *Fourth*, the donors have dominated the policy formulation arena and taking into consideration that the donors themselves do not have a unified approach this has resulted in multiple and uncoordinated policy decisions. *Fifth*, although the Malawi Decentralisation Policy launched in 1998 was hailed as a great democratic and developmental initiative which was meant to, among other things, enhance accountability and effectiveness at local level, not much has so far been achieved. *Sixth,* several civil society organisations have emerged to provide significant support to communities in the country in almost all development areas. However, the relationship between civil society and government has not always been harmonious especially those working in the governance sector. *Finally*, taking into consideration that political parties lack an ideological base, Malawi's political culture "is characterised by patronage, clientelism, opportunism and corruption, the centralising, authoritarian tendency of the executive".[35] This situation has negatively affected the quest to build enduring democratic institutions and practices as party leaders seem not interested to champion policy reform but rather pursue personal interests.

General Trends of Trust in Presidents, Parliament, Police and Courts from 1999 to 2019

Respondents to the Afrobarometer surveys were asked: "How much do you trust each of the following, or haven't you heard enough about them to say ... the president, Parliament, the police, and the courts of law?" The response options were: Not at all, Just a little, Somewhat, A lot, Don't know and Refused to answer. As Figure 2.1 shows, with minor exceptions, the trend from 1999 to 2019 indicates that there has been a general reduction in the level of trust (a lot or somewhat) for all institutions.[36] It is interesting to note that all institutions

---

34 *Newstime Africa*, 11 February, 2015.

35 Chinsinga "The Political Economy Context", 25.

36 Note that the analysis in this chapter focuses on levels of trust measured as a sum of people who said they trust the particular institution 'a lot' and 'somewhat'. The remaining percentage represents those who said they do not trust the institutions with small proportions of those who either refused to answer or did not know much to assess. Only in a few cases, we report those who said they 'didn't know'.

received increasing approval or trust between 1999 and 2005. The general reduction started mainly around 2008 to the present. The significant exceptions are with the office of the presidency and courts. The office of the president has witnessed a noticeably significant reduction in trust from 79% in 2008 to 29% in 2014, followed by an increase to 36% and 43% in 2017 and 2019 respectively.

The courts experienced an increase of 9% in the 2017 and 2019 period. Reasons for the precipitous drop (by 22 percentage points) in popular trust in the courts between 2012 and 2017 are not clear, though they may include dissatisfaction with the way the courts were handling politically connected cases, especially

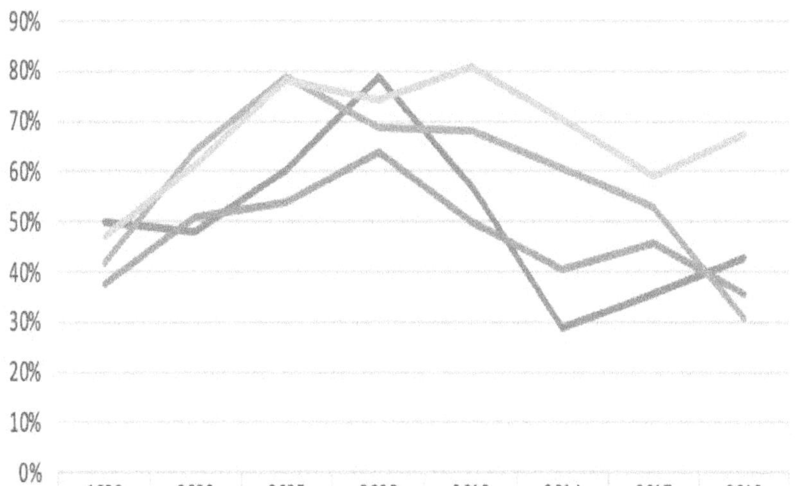

	1999	2003	2005	2008	2012	2014	2017	2019
President	50%	48%	60%	79%	57%	29%	36%	43%
MP	38%	51%	54%	64%	50%	40%	46%	35%
Police	42%	64%	79%	69%	68%	60%	53%	31%
Courts	47%	61%	78%	74%	81%	71%	59%	68%

Figure 2.1: *Trends of trust in presidents, Parliament, police and courts 1999-2019*

related to corruption (this is further discussed below). As Wroe points out, “this kind of reversal provokes only doubts and suspicions among ordinary Malawians about how the country’s justice system works and who it works for”.[37] The data do not suggest that the increase in trust since 2017 is related to the way courts have been handling the recent presidential election case. Compa-

---

37 Daniel Wroe, “Remembering Kamuzu: The Ambiguity of the Past in Malawi’s Central Region”, *Journal of Southern African Studies* 41/1 (2015), 247-61. DOI:10.1080/03057070.2020.1721151

ratively, the courts have enjoyed a higher level of trust over the years and even in cases where the trust had dropped, the drop itself was not as significant as other institutions. The extremely high and low levels of trust in the Office of the Presidency may, as explained below, be due to specific socio-political events that are generally associated with individual presidents during a specified period.

The findings on Parliament in Malawi are not very different from studies in other countries. Globally, the institution of Parliament is experiencing lower levels of trust. According to the 2010-2014 World Value Survey data of 80 countries, which include both new and old democracies, the institution of Parliament "harbour lower levels of trust".[38]

Possible Explanatory Factors

This section discusses some possible explanatory factors concerning the observed general decline in public trust of the governance institutions in Malawi as shown above.

Levels of Corruption

Taking into consideration the argument by several scholars including Mattes and Moreno who believe that level of corruption is one of the major determinants of trust in government,[39] this chapter tried to relate the perception of trust to corruption for each of the sampled institutions.[40] When the data of respondents who perceived the existence of corruption for specific institutions is compared to their perception of trust for the same institutions, it shows that there is a correlation. In other words, the higher the perceived perception of corruption for a specific office/institution, the lower is the trust for the same. In other words, this chapter agrees with other studies which attributed higher levels of corruption to loss of citizenry trust. As Figure 2b shows, over the years the levels of perception of corruption have least been perceived in the courts

---

38 Sören Holmberg, Staffan Lindberg and Richard Svensson, "Trust in Parliament", *Journal of Public Affairs* 17/1-2 (2017), https://doi.org/10.1002/ pa.1647

39 Robert Mattes and Alejandro Moreno "Social and Political Trust in Developing Countries", 2, DOI: 0.1093/oxfordhb/9780190274801.013.10.

40 Respondents to the surveys were asked "How many of the following people do you think are involved in corruption, or haven't you heard enough about them to say … members of Parliament, the president and officials in his office, police, judges and magistrates?" with the following response options: None, Some of them, Most of them, All of them, Refused to answer, or Don't know. The analysis in this chapter reports perceived corruption by percentage of those who responded 'all of them' and 'most of them'.

hence the level of trust has comparatively been higher. More importantly, the levels of trust have almost been consistent over the years just as the perception of corruption has consistently been lower except for the year 2017, as previously explained.

There is a need to explain that corruption has consistently been lower except for the years 2017 and 2014 (Figure 2d). The trust levels fell from 57% in 2012

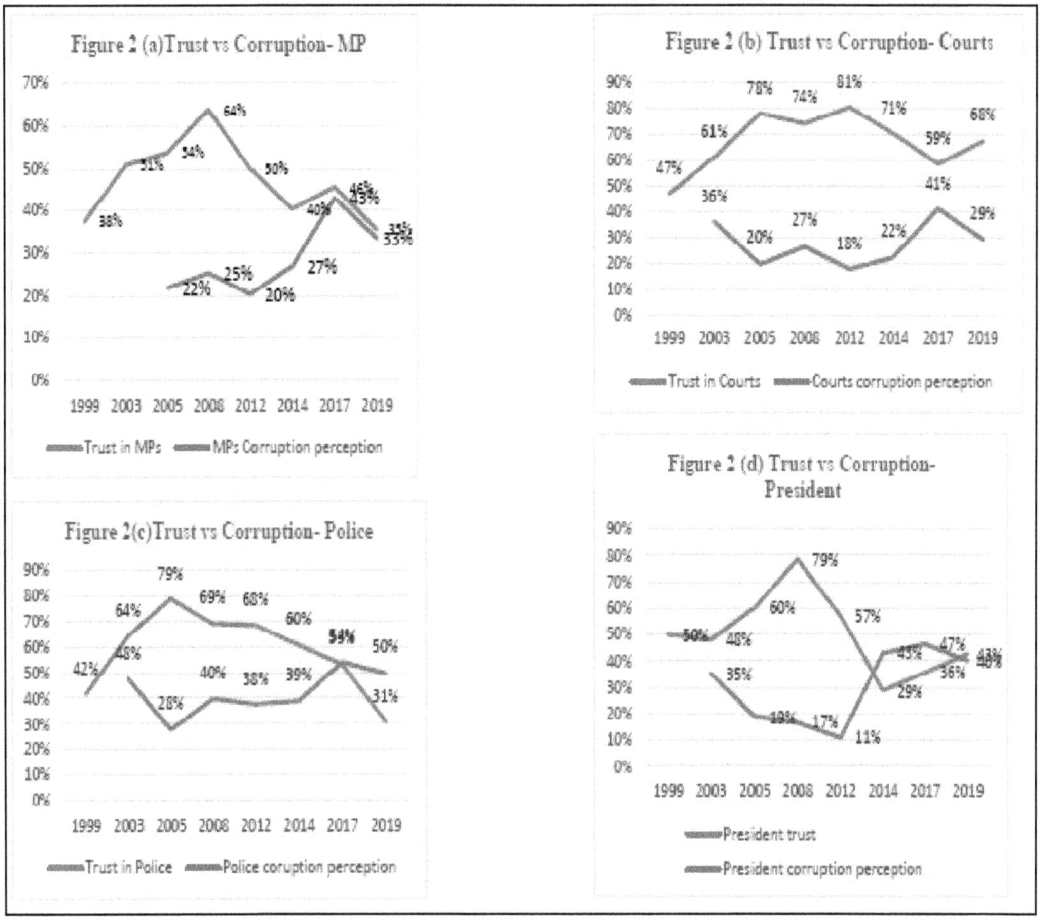

Figure 2.2: *Perception of trust versus perception of corruption (1999-2019)*

to 29% in 2014 and levels of perception of corruption rose from 11% to 43% during the same period. This is the time when Joyce Banda occupied the office of president and, during her tenure, the country experienced the highly publicised infamous Cashgate scandal in 2013—where public officials were accused of siphoning off more than USD 30 million. Although some may argue that Cashgate was not corruption but merely public resource theft, this chapter provides a much broader perspective than just theft. This is the case because Cashgate included direct theft as well as corruptly awarding government contracts to politically connected people. This scandal significantly affected people's trust in the office of presidency. Zimmerman aptly captures this when she argues that:

> In the wake of the Cashgate scandal, public sentiments about the abuse of public resources for personal gain and electioneering were strengthened because of Joyce Banda's refusal to declare her assets as provided for in the Constitution … her apparent reluctance to do so rendered credibility to the speculation that she was directly involved in the Cashgate scandal … Thus some accounts further attribute Joyce Banda's loss to the apparent failure to demonstrate decisive leadership on key national issues, such as: her 'flip-flopping' on how she handled the Cashgate scandal.[41]

It is also worth mentioning that the police experienced the lowest level of trust in 2019 (31%) (Figure 2c). Compared to the year 2005, this was a drop of 48%. It is also not surprising that the levels of perception of corruption for the police had increased from 28% to 50% over the same period.

Government Handling of Food Challenges, Management of Economy and General Performance

When the data (2003 to 2019) of respondents' perception on government handling of some of the most important problems facing the country (food challenges and management of the economy) are analysed in relation to their perception of trust for the office of presidency, it shows that there is a positive relationship.[42] The more people felt that the government had handled well food challenges and management of the economy, the more they trusted the office of the president and vice versa.

For instance, between 2003 and 2008, there was an increase of 37% for respondents who felt that the government's handling of the economy was good and in the same period, trust of the office of the presidency also increased by 31%. Likewise, trust in the office of the presidency significantly declined (by 50%) between 2008 and 2014 while the perception of the government handling of food security and managing the economy also declined by 15% and 38%

---

41 Brigitte Zimmerman, "Voter Response to Scandal: Cashgate", in Nandini Patel and Michael Wahman, *The Malawi 2014 Tripartite Elections,* 215-35 [226, 231].

42 Respondents were asked "How well or badly would you say the current government is handling the following matters, or haven't you heard enough to say: ... Managing the economy ... Ensuring everyone has enough to eat?" The response options were Very Badly, Fairly Badly, Fairly Well, Very Well, Don't Know / Haven't heard enough. The analysis reports those who said well (i.e. Very Well and Fairly Well).

respectively over the same period. Although management of the economy is a major factor in most countries in relation to trust of the office of the president,

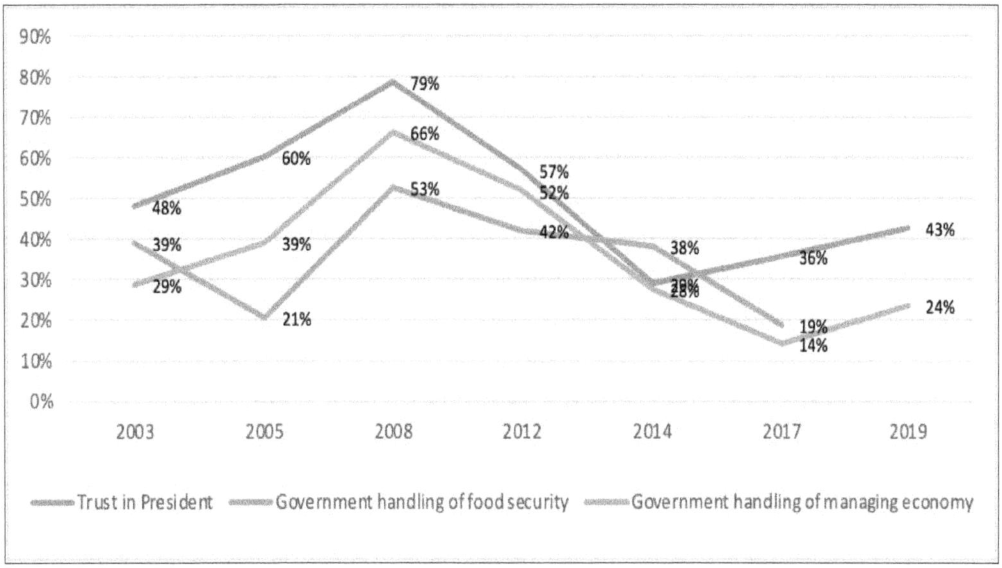

Figure 2.3: *Government handling of most important problems (food challenges and management of economy)*

the case of food security is particularly special in the context of Malawian politics. Mpesi and Muriaas aptly observe how former president Bingu wa Mutharika used food policy to gain popularity ahead of the 2009 elections. Specifically, they argue that:

> Food security is a salient political issue in Malawi. In three subsequent Afrobarometer surveys (2003, 2005 and 2008) the Malawian respondents identified 'food and famine' as the most important political issue in the country … President Mutharika's decision to introduce universal fertiliser subsidies can, in this regard, be interpreted as a political move to get electorate support. … Yet the changing food policies were important for Malawians' trust in the presidency of Mutharika.[43]

It should be mentioned that the key government policy towards food security has been through the implementation of input subsidies on maize which is the country's staple food.

As mentioned above, Ramesh argued that loss of trust is attributed, among other things, to politicisation of the public sector (perception of neutrality) and quality of service delivery. Comparing perception of performance (for

---

[43] Andrew Mabvuto Mpesi and Ragnhild L. Muriaas, "Food Security as a Political Issue: the 2009 Elections in Malawi", *Journal of Contemporary African Studies* 30 (2012), 377-93. DOI:10.1080/02589001.2012.689624.

respondents who perceived performance) in the office of the president to trust, there is a positive relationship. The highest is in 2008 (during the reign of Bingu wa Mutharika) when 83% approved of his performance and 79% indicated trust for the president. The lowest level of trust (29%) was in 2014 during the reign of Joyce Banda when her performance rating was 38%. Factors behind this perception of performance may be attributed to elements mentioned above: Bingu wa Mutharika's handling of food policy and Joyce Banda's perceived connection to corruption scandals.

Consequences of (Loss of) Citizenry Trust: Implications on State Legitimacy and Prospects for Democracy

Declining Support for Elections as a Method of Choosing Political Leaders

Taking into consideration that the president and members of Parliament assume office through the ballot, loss of trust in these offices or institutions has a direct impact on the same method or process which gives them power. In other words, loss of trust has an impact on elections as a way of choosing leaders. Data from 2003 to 2019 shows that there is a general rise in the number of people who think we should choose leaders through other methods than elections because elections produce bad results (see Figure 2.4).[44]

For instance, support for alternatives to elections has increased from 15% in 2003 to 44% in 2019. Support for alternative ways to choose the president and MPs has increased (this is not about abandoning democracy and returning to dictatorship but whether people think elections are delivering the leaders they want). Elections are critical for identifying political leaders and if the citizenry are losing trust in the electoral system then it has serious implications on legitimacy and effective representation. Based on previous observations stated above, this perspective is emerging due to the loss of trust that the citizenry has on these elected leaders.

---

[44] Respondents were asked "Which of the following statements is closest to your view? Statement 1: We should choose our leaders in this country through regular, open, and honest elections. Statement 2: Since elections sometimes produce bad results, we should adopt other methods for choosing this country's leaders". The figure analysis shows those who agreed (strongly or agree) with Statement 1.

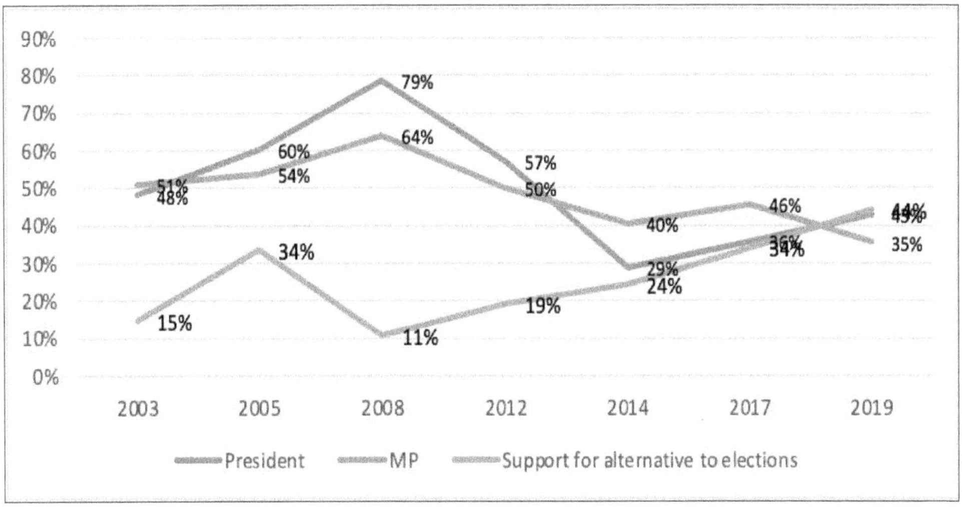

Figure 2.4: *Support for alternative to elections to choose leaders*

Decline in Support and Satisfaction with Democracy Data from 1999 to 2019 shows that support for democracy (democracy is always preferable to other forms of government) and satisfaction with how democracy is working in Malawi are on the decline.[45] This decline is going hand in hand with loss of trust for the office of president and Parliament (See Table 2.1).

Table 2.1: *Support for and Satisfaction with Democracy*

	1999	2003	2005	2008	2012	2014	2017	2019
President	50%	48%	60%	79%	57%	29%	36%	43%
Parliament	38%	51%	54%	64%	50%	40%	46%	35%
Support for democracy	65%	64%	56%	74%	76%	71%	62%	51%
Satisfaction with democracy	57%	47%	26%	57%	53%	49%	37%	35%

In 1999, support for democracy was 65% but it significantly declined to 51% in 2019. Similarly, satisfaction with democracy had declined by 22% during the same period. The decline in support and satisfaction with democracy is

45 Respondents were asked: "Which of these three statements is closest to your own opinion? Statement 1: Democracy is preferable to any other kind of government. Statement 2: In some circumstances, a non-democratic government can be preferable. Statement 3: For someone like me, it doesn't matter what kind of government we have." The analysis reports those who choose Statement 1.
Respondents were asked: "Overall, how satisfied are you with the way democracy works in Malawi?" with response options: The country is not a democracy, Not at all satisfied, Not very satisfied, Fairly satisfied, Very satisfied, Refused, Don't know. The analysis reports those who said that they were satisfied (fairly and very).

emerging from loss of trust in the key governance institutions. This finding is not different from findings in other countries (both developed and developing). However, despite the fact that it is a general trend globally, this doesn't imply that it should not raise concern. For an emerging democracy which is grappling with numerous socio-political challenges, having trust in key governance institutions is not only important but essential.

On Obeying the Law and on Courts Making Binding Decisions

In relation to trust in the police and legitimacy of the police to enforce people's obedience to the law, the proportion of respondents who believe the police have the right to ensure that people always obey laws significantly declined in 2017 and this also matched with the loss of trust in the same year (see Table 2.2).[46] In other words, among the respondents who believe in the legitimacy of the police to enforce laws when matched with their level of trust in the police the results show a decline from 84% in 2014 to 51% in 2017 and trust in the police declined from 60% in 2014 to 53% in 2017.

Table 2.2: *Proportion of people who believe people must obey laws vs trust in the police*

	2003	2005	2008	2012	2014	2017
Trust in police	64%	79%	69%	68%	60%	53%
Proportion of people who believe police have the right to make people obey laws	79%	74%	69%	82%	84%	51%

Concerning the courts, trust for the institution among the respondents who indicated that courts should make binding decisions has comparatively been good over the years except in 2017 when trust plummeted from 71% in 2014 to 59% in 2017. The view that courts have the right to make binding decisions also significantly declined by 16% over the same period[47] (see Table 2.3).

---

46 Respondents were asked: "For each of the following statements, please tell me whether you disagree or agree: The police always have the right to make people obey the law" with response options: Strongly Disagree, Disagree, Neither Agree Nor Disagree, Agree, Strongly Agree, Refused to answer, and Don't Know. The analysis reports the percentage of those who agreed (Agree or Strongly Agree).

47 For each of the following statements, please tell me whether you disagree or agree: The courts have the right to make decisions that people always have to abide by" with response options: Strongly Disagree, Disagree, Neither Agree Nor Disagree, Agree, Strongly Agree,

Table 2.3: *Proportion of people who think courts must make binding decisions vs trust in the courts*

	2003	2005	2008	2012	2014	2017
Trust in courts	61%	78%	74%	81%	71%	59%
Courts must make binding decisions	64%	63%	75%	86%	86%	73%

One of the key indicators of good governance is the rule of law. Hence, when there is a decline of trust in the courts for those who claim that court decisions should be binding then it means some of the key parameters of good governance are under threat.

From 2003, the courts have gradually but increasingly asserted their authority including against the executive. There are many examples. In the Civil Liberties Committee (CILIC) case during the Third Term debate, the court ordered that Muluzi's declaration against demonstrations was unconstitutional. In 2004, the court ruled against Muluzi's Third Term bid. In the 2014 elections, the courts ordered the Malawi Electoral Commission (MEC) to release results even after Joyce Banda had declared that the election was void. In 2020, the courts nullified the presidential election and ordered a Fresh Presidential Election.

Conclusion

Citizen trust is one of the key indicators of successful good governance. The Afrobarometer survey results show that from 1999 to 2019 Malawi has faced a significant decline in trust of key governance institutions. This is especially the case from 2008 following a general positive trend between 1999 and 2008, albeit with some variations in the detailed trends for the institutions analysed in this chapter—Presidency, Parliament, police and the courts. It is known from the literature that citizen distrust in government and its institutions negatively affects the effectiveness and efficiency of public policies as well as their implementation. In other words, the more citizens demonstrate trust in public institutions the more likely it is that government would be able to successfully implement its desired policies. Thus, citizen trust promotes long term stability of the political system. Comparatively, although the courts have

Refused to answer, and Don't Know. The analysis reports the percentage of those who agreed (agree or strongly agree).

also experienced decline in public trust, Parliament and the presidency have experienced a sharper decline. The office of the president carries the public image of the country. Loss of trust in that office implies a serious malaise. Likewise, Parliament, as Holmberg pointed out: "if people do not have faith in the institution making the rules, it is less likely that people live by them … democracy itself is endangered".[48]

It is not surprising that the survey results show that the proportion of respondents who believe people must always obey laws significantly declined in 2017 and this also matched the loss of trust in courts and Parliament in the same year. A growing number of people are losing trust in elections as a method of choosing leaders and there is a general decline in support and satisfaction with democracy. In order to address the problem, the results of this chapter are in tandem with recommendations from studies done elsewhere. Thus, some key explanatory factors or issues that need to be seriously considered if trust has to be restored include: improving the anti-corruption drive and the need for the government to effectively handle food challenges, management of the economy and general public performance.

---

48 Holmberg, Lindberg and Svensson, "Trust in Parliament".

Chapter 3

Trust in Election Management Bodies, Participation in Demonstrations and Willingness to Pay Taxes: Evidence from Malawi

Martin Limbikani Mwale,
Gowokani Chijere Chirwa,
Tony Mwenda Kamninga
& Laston Petro Manja

Introduction

Over the last 30 years, electoral outcomes across the globe have become contentious despite international observers endorsing them as free and fair.[1] Previous literature focused on electoral integrity grounds and establishing institutional consequences of the problem, with inadequate concern devoted to the citizen's behavioural responses.[2] The link between the people's trust of the national electoral bodies and post-elections demonstration protests has not been investigated comprehensively. Furthermore, an extension of the potential after-effects of this lack of trust in the electoral bodies on people's willingness to pay taxes is yet to be known.

Conceptually, a national elections management body that is not trusted could usher in a government that is not legitimate in the view of the citizens. If people do not believe that the outcomes of the elections reflect their choice, they may protest through demonstrations. In cases where the protests do not yield a call

---

1 Peter Burnell, "Zambia's 2001 Elections: The Tyranny of Small Decisions, 'Non-Decisions' and 'Not Decisions'", *Third World Quarterly* 23/6, 2002, 1103–20.

2 Miguel Carreras and Yasemin Irepoğlu, "Trust in Elections, Vote Buying, and Turnout in Latin America", *Electoral Studies* 32/4 (2013), 609–19; F. Barrientos, "Gestión Electoral Comparada y Confiaza En Las Elecciones En América Latina", Mexico, D.F, 2011; J. Hartlyn, J. McCoy and T.M Mustillo, "Electoral Governance Matters: Explaining the Quality of Elections in Contemporary Latin America", *Comparative Political Studies* 41/1 (2008), 73; T.A. Eisenstadt, "Catching the State off Guard: Electoral Courts, Campaign Finance, and Mexico's Separation of State and Ruling Party", *Party Politics* 10/6, 2004, 723–745; J. Foweraker and R. Krznaric, "The Uneven Performance of Third Wave Democracies: Electoral Politics and the Imperfect Rule of Law in Latin America", *Latin American Politics and Society* 44/3 (2002), 29–60.

for re-run or fresh elections, the citizens may become unwilling to support the operations of the new government. One of the ways to show dissatisfaction with a seemingly illegitimate government is unwillingness to pay taxes. This is particularly important in countries that have weak tax collection systems due to high levels of informal business operations as is the case with most sub-Saharan African countries.[3]

One way to improve citizens' trust in electoral management bodies could be through increased transparency and accountability of the electoral processes. These tenets are also relevant for achievement of the UN Sustainable Development Goals (SDGs). For instance, the 16th SDG recognises effective, accountable, and transparent institutions as key to inclusive and peaceful societies for sustainable development. National development strategies implement the SDGs. In Malawi, the country's third growth and development framework—the Malawi Growth and Development Strategy III—operationalises SDG 16 by emphasising the need for transparency, accountability, and institution-strengthening in its governance structures.[4] Fair conduct of elections has also been enshrined in Malawi's 2063 development agenda (MW2063) as one of the country's enablers of effective governance and institutions.[5] MW2063 is aligned with the African Agenda 2063 which also aims at improving institutions.

Malawi experienced state instability immediately after the 2019 presidential and parliamentary elections owing to widespread irregularities in the management of the elections by the Malawi Electoral Commission (MEC). The country is, therefore, a compelling case study on the topic. Using data collected by the Afrobarometer survey, this chapter examines the relationship between citizens' trust in the MEC and demonstration protests, and the association between the trust in MEC and willingness to pay taxes.

The chapter makes two contributions to democratic governance literature. First, it uncovers the potential behavioural response to election results by establishing the link between trust in electoral management bodies and demonstration protests. Second, it shows the link between lack of trust in the electoral management bodies and public finance, an important element in economic development. Results show that increased citizen trust in the Malawi

3 Emmanuel Ekow Asmah, Francis Kwaw Andoh and Edem Titriku, "Trade Misinvoicing Effects on Tax Revenue in Sub-Saharan Africa: The Role of Tax Holidays and Regulatory Quality", *Annals of Public and Cooperative Economics* 91/4 (2020), 649–72.

4 Malawi, "MGDS III: Building a Productive, Competitive and Resilient Nation".

5 National Planning Commission, "An Inclusively Wealthy and Self-Reliant Nation".

Electoral Commission associates with a reduction in willingness to participate in demonstration protests. Furthermore, increased trust in the MEC relates to rising willingness to pay taxes. These findings call for increased efforts to ensure credibility of the electoral processes to win citizens' trust. Increased trust has implications on state stability and public financing. Therefore, research on democratic governance should include examination of people's behavioural responses to trust in electoral management bodies as an important transmission mechanism through which citizens can support operations of government. Conclusions drawn from the chapter can be useful in prioritising both short- and medium-term electoral reforms in many countries.

Related Literature

In the analysis of human post-election behaviour, it is essential to understand whether democratic election outcomes may affect the citizens' behaviour outcomes. Previous evidence from Kenya reveals a positive association between losing elections and protesting the results.[6] The protests particularly erupted between citizens from different ethnic groups, those from different income strata, and where there is power parity between the winner and the loser. Similar traits were found to be fuelling post-elections protests in Nigeria.[7] Therefore, untrustworthy election outcomes affect citizens' behavioural responses especially where there are visibly differentiated social groupings. Arguably, these protests emerge conditional on visible irregularities in the electoral processes that erode citizen trust in the electoral management bodies.

People form expectations about winners of most elections and where the expectations are not met in the presence of perceived anomalies, protests can emerge. For instance, in Russia's 2012 presidential elections, the perceived irregularities and tainted electoral process coupled with the disqualification of potentially strong opponents led to rejection of, and public protests against, the outcome of the elections.[8] A similar case happened in Haiti, where citizens perceived the electoral management process to be corrupt and suspected that elections were rigged. In many African countries, the compromised electoral

---

6 Nkwachukwu Orji, "Responses to Election Outcomes: The Aftermath of 2007 Elections in Nigeria and Kenya", *African and Asian Studies* 9/4 (2010), 436–61.

7 For explanation of the remaining structural conditions Orji "Responses to Election Outcomes: The Aftermath of 2007 Elections in Nigeria and Kenya".

8 Jim Nichol, "Russia's March 2012 Presidential Election: Outcome and Implications", *Current Politics and Economics of Russia, Eastern and Central Europe* 27/3 (2012), 357–73.

processes, and hence protests, are accompanied by election-related bribes that further decrease citizens' trust of the outcomes.

Demonstrations during Malawi's Democratic Dispensation

Malawi obtained its democratic system of governance in 1994.[9] This ended Hastings Kamuzu Banda's one-party rule that had prevailed since the country's independence in 1964. Democracy brought power to the people and one of the salient features of this freedom in Malawi has been the freedom to stage demonstrations whenever citizens are dissatisfied with a regime and its administrative modalities. Over the years, Malawians have taken to the streets to demonstrate over many issues, including economic downturns, proposed constitutional amendments that were not supported by the majority of the citizens and unsatisfactory general election administration and outcomes.

In 1999, Malawians took to the streets following general election results that they deemed unsatisfactory based on the expectations of the majority.[10] In that election, the then incumbent president, Bakili Muluzi, was declared winner in an election in which the opposition leader, Gwanda Chakuamba, was widely perceived as the favourite to win. Chakuamba later challenged the results in court arguing that the election was not free and fair. The court however upheld the results. Protests erupted again in 2002 when Bakili Muluzi attempted to amend the Constitution to allow an extension of presidential term beyond the constitutional two consecutive five-year terms.[11]

In 2007, opposition members of Parliament held the country at ransom when they refused to pass the national budget demanding that the august house first settle a breach of the Constitution by some members of Parliament who had crossed the floor from the opposition to the government side.[12] Malawians

---

9 Lars Svåsand, "Regulation of Political Parties and Party Functions in Malawi: Incentive Structures and the Selective Application of the Rules", *International Political Science Review* 35/3 (2014), 275–90; Jonathan Mayuyuka Kaunda, "The Transition To a Multiparty System and Consolidation of Democracy in Malawi", *Il Politico* 63/3 (1998), 425–48.

10 UCA, "Malawi (1964-Present)".

11 Sean Morrow, "Toxic Mushrooms? The Presidential Third-Term Debate in Malawi", in R. Southall and H. Melber (eds), *Legacies of Power: Leadership Change and Former Presidents in African Politics*, Cape Town: HSRC Press, 2006, 151–74; M. Banda, "UDF Forms 3rd Term Team", *Daily Times*, 18 April 2002; Daniel Nowack, "Cultural Values, Attitudes and Democracy Promotion in Malawi, Bonn: Deutsches Institut für Entwicklungshilfe, 2018. (SSRN Electronic Journal, 2018).

12 Peter Chihana, Marshal Chilenga, Blessings Chinsinga, Rafiq Hajat, Samson Lambani, Nandini Patel, Florence Phiri and Ingo Scholz, "Towards the Consolidation of Malawi's

went to the streets yet again to force MPs to pass the budget before settling the constitutional matter.

The 2011 demonstrations are probably the most tragic in Malawi's recent history. Twenty protesters were shot dead by police during the demonstrations in which Malawians were protesting against a failing economy characterised by scarcity of foreign exchange and fuel.[13] They attempted to force the government to devalue the currency and mend diplomatic relations with donor countries which had withheld donor support due to souring relations with Malawi.[14]

The most recent spate of demonstrations in Malawi followed the contentious 2019 presidential elections. The citizens demonstrated against the outcome of the elections in which the then incumbent, Peter Mutharika (Democratic Progressive Party), was declared winner in an election marred by irregularities. The results were challenged in court by opposition contenders Lazarus Chakwera (Malawi Congress Party) and Saulos Chilima (United Transformation Movement). The court annulled the election results and ordered a fresh presidential poll in which the Chakwera-Chilima electoral alliance triumphed.

The Malawian democratic dispensation reveals that dissatisfaction of citizens in a democracy gives rise to protests, particularly where people's welfare is at stake and where they do not trust the outcomes of elections. Malawi's history of demonstrations is similar to events observed in other countries such as Kenya[15] and Haiti.[16] Nevertheless, not all demonstrations yield what the citizens demand. A case in point is Malawi's 1999 election outcomes which were upheld by the courts despite the protests.[17]

Democracy", 2008.; Louis Chimango, "Section 65 of the Malawian Constitution: The Role of the Speaker, 2005-2009", *Malawi Law Journal* 6/2 (2012), 121–42.

13 Diana Cammack, "Malawi in Crisis, 2011–12", *Review of African Political Economy* 39/132 (2012), 375–88.

14 Samantha Page, "The Development Aid Situation in Malawi", in Samantha Page (ed), *Development, Sexual Cultural Practices and HIV/AIDS in Africa*, Switzerland: Springer International Publishing, 2019, 43–60.

15 Orji, "Responses to Election Outcomes: The Aftermath of 2007 Elections in Nigeria and Kenya".

16 Mamyrah Dougé-Prosper and Mark Schuller, "Haiti's PétroRéalité: Government Corruption Tipped Popular Outrage into the Streets in Haiti, but a Sordid History of U.S. Meddling, Rigged Elections, and Botched Disaster Recovery Also Helped Pave the Way to the Current Protests", *NACLA Report on the Americas* 52/1 (2020), 20–25.

17 Nixon Khembo, Claude Kabemba and Eric Mcheka, "Elections and Democratisation in Malawi: An Uncertain Process", EISA Research Report, 2005.

Arguably, citizens who are not happy with election outcomes could become less willing to finance the operations of the administration that is ushered into power. Such citizens would be less willing to pay taxes in support of the seemingly illegitimate government. Democratic governance literature has not yet explored these potential effects of citizens' electoral management bodies trust on such development outcomes. Nevertheless, governance and development should not be examined in isolation. This is particularly because people elect leaders who envision improving the people's general living standards.[18] This is visible through elections campaigns and manifestos whose content are a promise for development.[19] Therefore, good democratic governance could not be an end itself but a means to an end. This demands linking democratic governance research to development outcomes, beyond the primary focus of citizens' dissatisfaction shown through demonstrations. This chapter, therefore, explores the relationship between democratic governance and development by particularly examining Malawians' willingness to pay tax in response as influenced by their trust or lack of trust in the MEC. Further, we examine whether trust in MEC associates with demonstrations as has been the case with most countries.

Data and Variable Definitions

The Sample

The chapter uses individual-level Afrobarometer data from Malawi. The Afrobarometer is a Pan-African comparative series of public attitude surveys which collects and disseminates information regarding Africans' views on democracy, governance, economic reform, civil society, and quality of life. We particulary use three rounds of the Afrobarometer data collected in 2017, 2014 and 2012. These Afrobarometers have sample sizes of 1,160, 2,349 and 2,360 respectively. These total observations account for the respondents that had

---

18 Nageeb Ali and Charles Lin, "Why People Vote: Ethical Motives and Social Incentives", *American Economic Journal: Microeconomics* 5/2 (2013), 73–98; Christian Gerhardous Joubert, "Followers' Experiences and Expectations of Leadership Behaviours in a Safety-Critical Commercial Environment: The Case of the Air Traffic and Navigation Services Company", PhD, University of South Africa, 2014.

19 Aeron Nahuku, Alinune Musopole, Harrison Bokola and Doreen Nahuku, "Greening up and the Political Manifestos: A Review of Political Party Manifestos on Issues of the Environment in Malawi", *International Journal of Environmental Protection and Policy* 8/5 (2020), 94–99; Joseph Chunga, "Examining the Relevance of Political Parties in Malawi", 2014.

complete information on our topic. The Afrobarometers are repeated cross-sections, sampling different people across the wave.

Outcomes Variables

The response variables in the study are willingness to pay taxes and demonstrate. We measure these outcomes independently. As reported by the Afrobaromenter, willingness to pay taxes responds to a question of whether a respondent would refuse to pay taxes. As shown in Table 3.1, the responses range from never refuses to pay tax, to refuse if given a chance, refused once or twice, refuse several times and refuse all times. Considering that Malawi is largely an informal economy, unwillingness to pay taxes could reveal the persistence of informality. We measure willingness to participate in demonstrations using the same response categories as those presented under willingness to pay taxes. Both outcomes are discretely ordered from 1 (unwillingness) to 5 (very willing).

Main Explanatory Variables

Trust in the MEC is measured in the study as a discrete variable. The question is whether one trusts the MEC or not. The responses include: no trust at all, little trust, somewhat trust and a lot of trust. We split this variable into its four respective categories and construct four dummy variables for the analysis. The reference (omitted) category is no trust at all.

Control Variables

The chapter includes two sets of control variables. The first is from alternative theories of tax compliance and protests including corruption of government officials; access to public services; performance of the president and performance of the member of Parliament. The second are demographic and socio-economic characteristics comprising age, gender, employment status, religion, levels of education and residence (for detailed definition of these covariates and alternative theories of tax compliance and protests see Table 3.2).

Table 3.1: *Variable Definitions*

Variable	Description
Dependent Variables	
Willingness to pay tax	Discrete variable = 1 if a respondent would never refuse to pay tax; 2 if they would refuse given a chance; 3 if they have refused once or twice; 4 if they refused several times; 5 if they refuse often times.
Willingness to demonstrate	Discrete variable = 1 if respondent would never participate in a demonstration; 2 if would participate given a chance; 3 if they have participated once or twice; 4 if they participated several times; 5 if they participate often times.
Independent Variables	
Trust in MEC	Discrete variable = 0 if No trust at all; 1 = Just a little trust; 2 = Somewhat trust; 3 = A lot of trust
Corrupt government	Dummy variable = 1 if the officials are corrupt; 0 otherwise
Access to public services	Dummy variable = 1 if it is difficult to access a primary school enrolment; 0 otherwise
Performing president	Dummy variable = 1 if a respondent agrees; 0 if the respondent does not agree
Performing MP	Dummy variable = 1 if the member of Parliament is performing well; 0 otherwise
Age	Continuous, at least 18 years old
Male	Binary variable = 1 if respondent is male; = 0 if respondent is female
Employed	Binary variable = 1 if respondent is employed; = 0 if respondent is not employed
Christian	Binary variable = 1 if respondent is Christian; = 0 if respondent is not Christian (Muslim or Other)
Education	Categorical variable = 0 if No formal education; 1 = Primary; 2 = Secondary; 3 = Post-secondary
Urban	Binary variable = 1 if respondent is based in urban area; = 0 if respondent is based in rural area
Region of residence	Categorical variable, if respondent is based in: 1 = North; 2 = Centre; 3 = South

Estimation strategy

To estimate the relationship between different levels of trust and willingness to pay taxes and different levels of trust and willingness to demonstrate, we build econometric models specified as follows.

$$y_{ikt} = \alpha_1 Trust_{iht} + \alpha_2 x_{it} + \varepsilon_{it}$$

In equation 1, y is the dependent variable capturing willingness to pay taxes or willingness to demonstrate. The two outcomes have categories with an increasing order: for taxes, 1 (never refuse to pay taxes), 2 (refuse if given a chance), 3 (refuse once or twice), 4 (refuse several times) and 5 (refuse often times); for demonstration, 1 (never demonstrate), 2 (demonstrate given a chance), 3 (demonstrate twice or thrice), 4 (demonstrate several times) and 5 (demonstrate often times). The relationship between trust and these two outcomes is captured by the coefficient α_1. The association between the outcomes and the covariates (vector *x*) is represented by the coefficient α_2; ε_{it} is the error term comprising all other variables that affect the outcomes but are not included in the equation. We estimate separate equations for the three years (2018, 2014, 2012).

In applied economics studies, it is assumed that the true preference of individuals is an unobserved latent factor conventionally proxied by a self-reported response.[20] In this study, the reported response is *willingness* measured on a category scale of 5 where 1 is the least preference and 5 the largest preference. Hence, our estimation procedure needs to account for the ordered nature of the dependent variable and the ordered probit model is the best candidate to derive reliable estimates. Therefore, we estimate equation (1) by ordered probit and take the derivative to the estimates to present marginal effects that can be directly interpreted as probabilities. We present the findings in the next sections.

Empirical Findings

Although our interest lies in presenting the relationship between different levels of trust and different levels of willingness to pay tax and demonstrate, we first provide the descriptive results of the relationship and the distribution of

---

20 Yonas Alem and Gunnar Köhlin, "The Impact of Food Price Inflation on Subjective Well-Being: Evidence from Urban Ethiopia", *Social Indicators Research* 116/3 (2014), 853–68.

covariates for the 3 years of interest (2018, 2014, 2012). Thereafter, we present the regression output of the relationships after controlling all the covariates.

Descriptive Statistics

Table 2.2: *The descriptive relationship between trust and willingness to demonstrate*

Demonstrate	Never	Would	Once or twice	Several times	Oftentimes
No trust at all	58.560	34.240	4.580	1.680	0.940
Little trust	65.380	29.380	3.270	1.060	0.900
Some trust	73.110	22.030	2.430	1.470	0.950
A lot of trust	72.250	23.830	2.530	0.960	0.430

Table 3.3: *The descriptive relationship between trust and willingness to pay tax*

Refuse to pay tax	Never	Would	Once or twice	Several times	Oftentimes
No trust at all	67.910	26.190	2.340	2.060	1.500
Little trust	70.870	24.390	1.470	1.390	1.880
Somewhat trust	79.620	16.390	1.820	1.210	0.950
A lot of trust	77.220	18.820	1.190	1.000	1.770

Table 3.4: *The distribution of control variables by year*

	2018	2014	2012
Corrupt government officials	0.801	0.807	0.680
Difficult to access public services	0.114	0.108	0.809
Performing president	0.314	0.398	0.687
Performing MP	0.285	0.324	0.393
Male	0.506	0.502	0.503
Employed	0.198	0.199	0.364
Catholic	0.218	0.207	0.199
Educated	0.889	0.878	0.885
Urban	0.196	0.187	0.192
Northern Region	0.133	0.432	0.422
Central Region	0.440	0.131	0.130
Southern Region	0.428	0.438	0.448
Observations	1160	2349	2360

SD: Standard Deviation

Table 3.2 shows the crosstabulation (bivariate relationship) between trust and willingness to demonstrate. The columns (from left to right) show increasing levels of willingness to demonstrate. The rows (from top to bottom) depict increasing levels of trust. Just as was the case with willingness to pay tax, more people are not willing to be deviant. In the case of demonstrations, more people are less willing to partake in demonstrations. The percentage of those who would never partake in demonstrations, as shown in column 1, grows as the level of trust increases. Amongst those willing to partake in demonstrations at different levels from column 2 to column 5, increasing trust associates with reducing percentage of demonstrators.

Table 3.3 presents the crosstabulation between trust and willingness to pay tax. The columns (from left to right) show increasing levels of refusing to pay tax while rows (from top to bottom) show increasing levels of trust. The rows reveal that most people in the sample never refuse to pay tax irrespective of the levels of trust as the percentages keep falling across the rows. The percentage of those who would never refuse to pay tax, as shown in column 1, increases with increasing levels of trust. Columns 2 to 5 show different levels of refusing to pay tax; overall lower levels of trust associate with increasing percentage of individuals refusing to pay tax.

Table 3.4 provides the distribution (in this case, a univariate analysis) of covariates used in the study by year. These are percentages calculated from respondents' perceptions. The percentage of corrupt government officials increased from 2012 to 2014 before slipping back slightly in 2018. Difficulty in accessing public services as proxied by accessibility to primary school enrolment has reduced over time from 2012 to 2018. Performance of the president and members of Parliament has consistently reduced over time. The remaining part of the table presents trends in the distribution of demographic and socioeconomic attributes of the respondents over the years. Moving away from the univariate and bivariate analysis presented in the aforementioned tables, we now go to the regression results, and these are shown in Tables 3.5 and 3.6.

Table 3.5 presents marginal effects of willingness to participate in demonstrations. These estimates control for all covariates presented in Table 5, but for brevity, we only present findings on the relationship between trust and willingness to demonstrate. Column 1 presents results for the year 2018. The reference category for the treatment is having no trust at all. The results show that having little trust increases the probability of non-participation in

Trust and Willingness to Demonstrate

Table 3.5: *The marginal effects for willingness to demonstrate*

Year	2018	2014	2012
Little trust			
Never demonstrate	0.082**	0.023	0.037
	[0.004,0.159]	[-0.078,0.124]	[-0.029,0.102]
Would demonstrate	-0.056**	-0.016	-0.025
	[-0.110,-0.002]	[-0.085,0.054]	[-0.070,0.020]
Once or twice	-0.014*	-0.003	-0.007
	[-0.029,0.000]	[-0.018,0.012]	[-0.021,0.006]
Several times	-0.006*	-0.002	-0.002
	[-0.013,0.000]	[-0.013,0.008]	[-0.006,0.002]
Often demonstrates	-0.005*	-0.002	-0.002
	[-0.011,0.000]	[-0.008,0.005]	[-0.006,0.002]
Somewhat trust			
Never demonstrate	0.082*	0.175***	0.025
	[-0.014,0.177]	[0.072,0.278]	[-0.041,0.091]
Would demonstrate	-0.056*	-0.121***	-0.017
	[-0.120,0.009]	[-0.188,-0.054]	[-0.063,0.029]
Once or twice	-0.014	-0.026***	-0.005
	[-0.031,0.003]	[-0.045,-0.008]	[-0.018,0.008]
Several times	-0.006	-0.016*	-0.001
	[-0.014,0.001]	[-0.035,0.002]	[-0.005,0.003]
Often demonstrates	-0.005	-0.012***	-0.001
	[-0.013,0.002]	[-0.019,-0.004]	[-0.005,0.002]
A lot of trust			
Never demonstrate	0.148***	0.077	0.100***
	[0.050,0.247]	[-0.017,0.170]	[0.040,0.160]
Would demonstrate	-0.101***	-0.053*	-0.069***
	[-0.169,-0.033]	[-0.115,0.009]	[-0.109,-0.028]
Once or twice	-0.026***	-0.012	-0.020***
	[-0.045,-0.007]	[-0.026,0.003]	[-0.034,-0.006]
Several times	-0.012**	-0.007	-0.006**
	[-0.021,-0.002]	[-0.020,0.005]	[-0.010,-0.001]
Often demonstrates	-0.010**	-0.005	-0.006**

	[-0.019,-0.001]	[-0.011,0.001]	[-0.010,-0.001]
Government corruption	Y	Y	Y
Public services access	Y	Y	Y
President performance	Y	Y	Y
MP performance	Y	Y	Y
Observations	1115	2246	2177

Notes: In these estimates we control for age, gender, employment status, religion, education, location and region. 95% confidence intervals in brackets $^{*}p < 0.10$, $^{**}p < 0.05$, $^{***}p < 0.01$.

demonstrations. Consistent with this finding we also observe that having little trust reduces the willingness to demonstrate once given a chance, once or twice, several times and often times, relative to when one has no trust at all. In support, the somewhat level of trust positively associates with never demonstrating and reduces the likelihood of demonstrating once given a chance. A lot of trust is positively associated with never demonstrating at all, negatively related to demonstrating once given a chance, reduces the likelihood of demonstrating once or twice, several times and often times. The level of significance for a lot of trust is higher relative to that observed for little trust and somewhat trust highlighting the increased strength of the relationship between trust and demonstrating at high levels of trust. In 2014 and 2012, as shown in column 2 and 3 respectively, we observe that increasing trust (even though at different levels) continues to reduce the likelihood of demonstrating.

Trust and willingness to pay taxes

Table 3.6: *Marginal effects for willingness to pay tax*

Year	2018	2014	2012
Little trust			
Never refuse	0.070*	-0.012	-0.006
	[-0.001,0.142]	[-0.091,0.067]	[-0.071,0.058]
Would refuse	-0.047*	0.008	0.004
	[-0.094,0.000]	[-0.046,0.062]	[-0.039,0.048]
Once or twice	-0.008*	0.001	0.001
	[-0.018,0.001]	[-0.007,0.009]	[-0.005,0.006]
Several times	-0.008*	0.001	0.001
	[-0.016,0.001]	[-0.008,0.011]	[-0.005,0.006]
Often refuses	-0.008*	0.001	0.001

	[-0.017,0.000]	[-0.007,0.009]	[-0.009,0.011]
Somewhat trust			
Never refuse	0.024	0.124***	0.041
	[-0.071,0.118]	[0.045,0.203]	[-0.027,0.109]
Would refuse	-0.016	-0.084***	-0.028
	[-0.078,0.047]	[-0.138, -0.030]	[-0.074,0.019]
Once or twice	-0.003	-0.012**	-0.003
	[-0.014,0.008]	[-0.023, -0.002]	[-0.009,0.003]
Several times	-0.003	-0.014**	-0.004
	[-0.013,0.008]	[-0.029, -0.000]	[-0.010,0.003]
Often refuses	-0.003	-0.013***	-0.006
	[-0.014,0.008]	[-0.022, -0.004]	[-0.017,0.004]
A lot of trust			
Never refuse	0.163***	0.055	-0.014
	[0.069,0.257]	[-0.024,0.134]	[-0.072,0.045]
Would refuse	-0.108***	-0.037	0.009
	[-0.171, -0.046]	[-0.092,0.017]	[-0.031,0.049]
Once or twice	-0.019**	-0.005	0.001
	[-0.034, -0.004]	[-0.014,0.003]	[-0.004,0.006]
Several times	-0.017***	-0.006	0.001
	[-0.030, -0.005]	[-0.016,0.003]	[-0.004,0.006]
Often refuses	-0.019***	-0.006	0.002
	[-0.030, -0.007]	[-0.014,0.003]	[-0.007,0.011]
Government corruption	Y	Y	You
Public services access	Y	Y	You
President performance	Y	Y	You
MP performance	Y	Y	You
Observations	1115	2246	2177

Notes: In these estimates we control for age, gender, employment status, religion, education, location and region. 95% confidence intervals in brackets $^{*}p < 0.10$, $^{**}p < 0.05$, $^{***}p < 0.01$.

Table 3.6 presents marginal effects on the willingness to pay taxes. Column 1 presents results for the year 2018. The reference treatment group is those who have no trust at all. Having little trust positively associates with never refusing to pay tax relative to when one has no trust at all. Consistent with this finding, we see that having little trust associates with reduced probability to refusing paying tax, refusing once or twice, refusing several times and refusing often times. The table also reveals that somewhat trust does not differ significantly with having no trust at all. Having a lot of trust increases the probability of never refusing to pay tax and reduces the probability of refusing to pay tax at all levels of trust. Noticeably, a lot of trust has the relatively higher levels of significance emphasizing the strength of the relationship between trust and willingness to pay taxes. In column 2 we present results for the year 2014. The results are consistent with those of 2018, even though they are significant at different levels of trust. In 2014 trust significantly associates with willingness to pay tax at somewhat levels of trust. In 2012 we find no significant relationship between trust and willingness to pay taxes.

Discussion

Malawi obtained its independence in 1964, and since then the country remained under one-party rule until 1994 when the country began its democratic era.[21] Democracy gave citizens the rights and freedoms including the privilege to choose their leaders through the ballot box. These visible advantages notwithstanding, the democratic dispensation brought its own challenges. One of these challenges is that the ruling government remained in power even under protest of the citizenry due to dissatisfaction with elections outcomes. The turnaround for this political trajectory was in 2014 when the ruling president lost elections.[22] The general election that followed in 2019 were marred by irregularities and its outcome met heavy protests through violent and non-violent demonstrations culminating in a court case. The greatest outcry from these demonstrations was that should the court rule against the results of the elections and order a re-run, then the electoral commission chair must resign as the people had lost trust in the commission to administer credible elections.

This study aimed at investigating if citizenry trust in national electoral commission relates to willingness to participate in demonstrations, and whether the trust also relates willingness to pay taxes using data from Malawi. The

21 Wiseman Chijere Chirwa, Nandini Patel and Fidelis Kanyongolo, "Democracy Report for Malawi", 2000.

22 Nandini Patel and Michael Wahman, "The Presidential, Parliamentary and Local Elections in Malawi, May 2014", *African Spectrum* 50/1 (2015), 79–92.

findings from this chapter confirm the hypothesis that indeed trust in national election commission associates with reduced citizenry willingness to participate in demonstrations and relates to increased citizenry willingness to pay taxes.

Trusted electoral commissions usher in governments that receive support from the citizens.[23] The support reduces tensions and minimises chances of protest. For instance, Gabriel and Trudinger showed that citizens that have higher levels of trust in their electoral bodies and other public institutions tend to be less dissatisfied with the tax burden, are more willing to support redistribution policies, and are less suspicious about welfare fraud.[24] These results support our findings. On the other hand, our study further shows that the relationship between trust in the national electoral commission and willingness to demonstrate is robust over time, at times leading to violent demonstrations. These negative outcomes of demonstrations disrupt economic activity through closure of businesses and could also lead to loss of jobs. The result is general depletion of overall welfare. Therefore, increasing trust in electoral bodies could be welfare-preserving.

In informal economies with poor tax collection mechanisms, people's lack of trust in electoral bodies increases willingness to evade tax.[25] For instance, in Malawi, most businesses are not registered and for those that are registered many underpay taxes due to bribes and corruption.[26] Previous studies showed that increased levels of trust in electoral commissions lead to less dissatisfaction with the tax burden, increased willingness to support redistribution policies, and reduced suspicion of welfare fraud. It has also been demonstrated that

---

23 Mwoya Byaro and Abel Kinyondo, "Citizens' Trust in Government and Their Greater Willingness to Pay Taxes in Tanzania: A Case Study of Mtwara, Lindini and Dar Es Salaam Regions", *Power & Public Policy* 12/1 (2019), 73–83.

24 Oscar W. Gabriel and Eva-Maria Trudinger, "Embellishing Welfare State Reforms? Political Trust and the Support for Welfare State Reforms in Germany", *German Politics* 20/2 (2011), 273–92; see also Bo Rothstein, Samanni Marcus and Teorell Jan, "Social Risks, Institutional Trust and the Welfare State Contract: Quality of Government Versus the Power Resource Theory", in *Equality and Personal Responsibility in the New Social Contract*, St Hugh's College, Oxford University, 2009; and Thomas J. Rudolph, "Political Trust, Ideology and Public Support for Tax Cuts". *Public Opinions Quarterly* 73/1 (2009), 144–58.

25 Anuradha Joshi, Wilson Prichard and Christopher Heady, "Taxing the Informal Economy: The Current State of Knowledge and Agendas for Future Research", *The Journal of Development Studies* 50/10 (2014), 1325–47.

26 Henry Kankwamba and Kornher Lukas, "Business Registration and Firm Performance: A Case of Maize Traders in Malawi", *Development in Practice* 30/7 (2020), 850–61.

higher trust in government improves tax compliance. Thus, perceptions about trust in the government translate into actual tax payments.

Further, our chapter shows that the relationship between trust in electoral bodies and willingness to pay taxes is only robust in the years close to general elections. These results are significant in 2018 close to the 2019 Malawi general election, and in 2014, a year of general elections, while being insignificant in 2012, a year not close to any elections. People become critical of the Electoral Commission's operations around the time the elections take place. Therefore, electoral management policy should aim at increasing the credibility of electoral commissions on one hand. On the other hand, public finance should consider finding short-term remedies to behaviour changes such as poor tax collection particularly around election years. This would ensure minimal disruptions in tax collection, hence, smoothening public service provision.

Conclusion

Our chapter aimed at examining the relationship between trust in the Electoral Commission and the willingness to demonstrate, and the link between the trust and willingness to pay taxes. We use Afrobarometer data obtained from Malawi to establish our findings. The results reveal that trust positively associates with the willingness to pay tax. Further, trust reduces the citizens' willingness to demonstrate. The results highlight the importance of credible electoral management systems in supporting public finance and reducing protests. These results appeal to research on democratic governance to include examination of people's behavioural responses as an important transmission mechanism through which citizens support or sabotage operations of government, depending on whether or not they trust electoral institutions. It is, however, important that these behavioural responses be observed within the same individuals over time to understand whether the outcomes change under different political environments. This is possible using panel data that interviews the same individuals across times. Since the current Afrobarometer surveys only provide repeated cross-sections of different people, we leave this to future research. Instead, our chapter provides conclusive evidence that trust in electoral bodies is critical in ensuring reduced demonstrations and increased willingness to pay taxes.

Chapter 4

Impunity versus Constitutional Legality in Malawi's 2019-20 Presidential Election Case

Garton S. Kamchedzera

> "...[T]he Commission is enjoined to ensure compliance with the provisions of the Constitution and Acts of Parliament in the performance of its duties and functions."[1]

Introduction

The case about the conduct of Malawi's 2019 presidential elections was indeed "the first time that the validity of presidential elections [had] been subjected to a full trial before the courts in this country".[2] In a very significant manner, after 26 years in operation, Malawi's Constitution[3] emerged as a potent yardstick for elections in a constitutional democracy. This chapter suggests that through the two judgments by the High Court sitting as a Constitutional Court[4] (Concourt) and the Malawi Supreme Court of Appeal[5] (MSCA), the law achieved significance because it resisted impunity and mediocrity.

The nullification of the results of the presidential election in 2019 and ordering of fresh elections within 150 days from 3 February 2020 is a unique rejection of "impunity with mediocrity". By "impunity with mediocrity", the chapter signifies two combined senses. The first is wanton decision-making and action-taking without respect for the law and its consequences. The second is paying little regard to professional standards or failing to attain average reasonableness in carrying out a duty. The premise in support of these two senses is rooted in an interpretation of Niklas Luhmann's perspective of the nature of the law, that it must be autopoietic in the results it produces and the conduct it seeks to

---

1 *Mutharika and Electoral Commission v Chilima and Chakwera*, MSCA Constitutional Appeal No. 1 of 2020 (in this chapter referred to as "*Mutharika and EC v Chilima and Chakwera*', at 3.

2 *Chilima and Chakwera v. Mutharika and EC*, High Court Constitutional Reference No. 1 of 2019 (in this chapter referred to as *"Chilima and Chakwera v. Mutharika and EC*").

3 Constitution of Malawi, Act No 20 of 1994 (in this chapter referred to as "Malawi Constitution").

4 In this Chapter referred to as "Concourt".

5 In this Chapter referred to as "MSCA".

establish.[6] In this regard, impunity with mediocrity is a negation of the key function of the law, to guide behaviour or decision- and action-taking.[7] By giving consequential directions to Parliament to pass necessary laws and inquire into the competence and capacity of the Electoral Commission, the two courts signalled that impunity with mediocrity is not tolerable under the law in governance and particularly in conducting elections.

This chapter focuses on and uses the two respective judgments of the MSCA and the Concourt. In doing so, the chapter explores two obvious inquiries about the proceedings and the two judgments. The first inquiry is about what was at stake conceptually in the electoral case. The second is about how the parties to the case and the two courts approached the court proceedings. The structure of the chapter follows these inquiries starting with this introduction. The chapter views the proceedings in the two judgments as a battle between impunity with mediocrity, on the one side, and constitutional legality, on the other side. In the second part, the chapter draws on the perspective of Pogge, Hardt and Negri, and Hutchinson, that sees a Constitution as a site of battle. In analysing the two judgments, the chapter uses Luhmann's autopoetic theory of law, that the law should be autopoietic. The argument is that by insisting on constitutional legality, the two courts underlined that the results of the law and its processes, including judgments, must be autopoietic to the goals and values espoused in a Constitution. The chapter discusses the battle between constitutional legality as a conceptual stand, with truth and justice as a binary code, on the one side, and attempts to use the law to frustrate constitutional purposes as revealed in statutory provisions. The third part of the chapter shows that the two courts' fidelity to constitutional legality and transformational constitutionalism determined the approach, procedure, and methods expected in the conduct of democratic elections and the case that was brought to court. The chapter ends with a conclusion that underlines the transformational implications of the two judgments in Malawi and beyond in safeguarding and advancing the use of elections to attain accountability and other values that are necessary in popular democracy.

---

6 Niklas Luhmann, "The Code of the Moral", *Cardozo Law Review* 14/3-4 (January 1993), 995-1010.

7 Lon L. Fuller, *The Morality of Law*, rev. ed., New Haven CT: Yale University Press, 1969; Joseph Raz, *The Authority of Law: Essays on Law and Morality*, Oxford: Oxford University Press, 1979, Chapter 9.

What was at Stake in the Proceedings in the Concourt and the MSCA

Superficially, the proceedings and the two judgments in the presidential election case were about the outcome of the 2019 presidential elections. Chakwera, Chilima, and many Malawians alleged that irregularities and possible fraud marred the conduct of the elections in favour of Mutharika. As remittance of results from polling centres to the National Tally Centre started to come out, it became apparent that Electoral Commission staff and agents had used Tippex, a correction fluid, to change numbers on a national scale. There were 147 complaints filed against the elections. Before all the complaints were resolved, the Electoral Commission declared that Peter Mutharika, the incumbent president, had won the elections, with Lazarus Chakwera and Saulos Chilima finishing second and third respectively. Chilima and Chakwera brought separate petitions disputing the conduct of the elections. In the end, the Concourt nullified the elections because the irregularities and anomalies were "so widespread, systematic and grave such that the integrity of the results [had] been seriously compromised".[8]

The Stand against Impunity and Mediocrity

The petitions brought by Chakwera and Chilima presented the Malawi judicial system with a fundamental case for the nation. In the words of the Concourt, "Upfront, the Court wishes to point out that it is alive to the enormous importance and the unprecedented nature of the present proceedings and of this judgment in particular, to the nation."[9] Earlier, Justice Mkandawire, noticing the similarities of the two cases, consolidated them into a single case,[10] with Chilima as first petitioner and Chakwera as the second.[11] Further, noticing the legal issues raised, Justice Mkandawire referred the case to the Chief Justice for certification that the matter was constitutional in nature.[12] The Chief Justice certified the case as constitutional[13] and empanelled Justices Healey Potani, Ivy

---

8 *Chilima and Chakwera v Mutharika and Electoral Commission*, *supra* note 2, at 416, para 1478.

9 *Chilima and Chakwera v Mutharika and Electoral Commission*, *supra* note 2, at 5.

10 Election Case No 16 of 2019 and Election Case No 26 of 2019, Order of Consolidations and Referring the Matters to the Constitutional Court.

11 Election Case No 16 of 2019 and Election Case No. 26 of 2019 Consolidated as Constitutional Reference No 1 of 2019, dated 4.

12 *Chilima v Electoral Commission High Court Election Case No 26 of 2019 and Chakwera v Electoral Commission*, High Court Election, Order of Consolidation and Referring the Matters to a Constitutional Court, dated 4 June 2019.

13 High Court of Malawi Reference No. 1, Certification by the Chief Justice., dated 5 June 2019.

Kamanga, Dingiswayo Madise, Mike Tembo, and Redson Kapindu to work as a Constitutional Court to adjudicate on the consolidated matter. The four issues[14] certified as Constitutional by the Courts were about the standards for the conduct of elections as expected by Malawi's Constitution. The issues were as follows:

1. Whether the Electoral Commission breached its duty under Section 76 of the Constitution of the Republic of Malawi;
2. Whether the Electoral Commission breached its duty under Section 77 of the Constitution of the Republic of Malawi; and,
3. Whether the Electoral Commission infringed on the Petitioners' and the citizen's political rights under Section 40 of the Constitution of the Republic of Malawi.

The two courts underlined that the Electoral Commission was a primary duty-bearer for the conduct of elections in Malawi under the Constitution,[15] the Electoral Commission Act,[16] and the Parliamentary and Presidential Elections (PPE) Act.[17] Constitutionally, the purpose of the Commission is for the country to ascertain "the authority to govern", which must derive "from the people of Malawi".[18] The Constitution adds that such authority should be "expressed through universal and equal suffrage in elections held in accordance with this Constitution in a manner prescribed by an Act of Parliament".[19] The PPE Act's standard for proper presidential election is whether the elections and its return are "due".[20] The Act adds that a court should declare void undue elections or undue election result.[21] The words "due" or "undue" invited the courts to examine the alleged impunity and mediocrity in the elections.

The Conceptual Stand for Constitutional Legality

What was at stake for the parties and the nation in the proceedings, however, was conceptual, with possible profound implications for future elections. Firstly, the two courts invoked the notion that elections are instrumental for

---

14 *Chilima and Chakwera v. Mutharika and EC, supra,* note 2, at 11.

15 Malawi Constitution, *supra,* note 7, *supra* 6, sections 75-76.

16 Electoral Commission Act, No 11 of 1998 (Chapter 2:03, *Laws of Malawi*), section 8(1).

17 Parliamentary and Presidential Elections Act, No. 31 of 1993 (Chapter 2:01, *Laws of Malawi*), in this chapter referred to as 'PPE Act', Long Title.

18 Malawi Constitution, *supra,* note 7, section 6.

19 Ibid.

20 PPE Act, *supra,* note 5, section 100(1).

21 PPE Act, *supra,* note 5, section 100(3)(b).

"popular sovereignty". The MSCA quoted Said Adejumohi's argument that elections have to be an expression of popular sovereignty as follows:

> Conceptually, elections symbolize popular sovereignty and the expression of the "social pact" between the state and the people which defines the basis of political authority', legitimacy and citizens' obligations. It is the kernel of political accountability and a means of ensuring reciprocity and exchange between the governors and the governed. ... Further, elections typify the representation of popular demands and a basis for leadership recruitment and socialisation. Renewal in democratic systems usually occurs via elections. Any political system which does not undergo such, will ultimately atrophise and suffer decay. In other words, elections constitute perhaps, the most important element in the conception and practice of liberal democracy.[22]

The court buttressed its argument and conceptual position on elections with Staffan Lindberg's work in which he argues that elections are an institutionnalised effort to realise the essence of democracy as rule of the people by the people.[23] Following the Universal Declaration of Human Rights[24] and African Charter on People and Human Rights,[25] the Concourt stated that it reckoned "that periodic and genuine elections are a key and indispensable element in ensuring the sustained trust of the governed in those who exercise the power of the State".[26] Thus, a judicial linkage was started, between elections and the authority to govern. Section 12(c) of Malawi's Constitution provides that "the authority to exercise power of State is conditional upon the sustained trust of the people of Malawi and that trust can only be maintained through open, accountable and transparent Government and informed democratic choice".[27]

The conceptual significance of the case, secondly, rested on the notion that actualisation of such aspiration comes with duties and duty-bearers must work under the Constitution and the law in general. Both the Concourt and the MSCA took it as a duty to ensure that "political disputes are resolved fairly and expeditiously with the Constitution as the supreme arbiter and the ultimate source of authority".[28] The Constitution is above all institutions, people, and

---

22 Said Adejumohi, "Elections in Africa: A Fading Shadow of Democracy?" *International Political Science Review* 21/1, 59-73, at 61.

23 *Mutharika and EC v Chilima and Chakwera*, *supra*, note 1, at page 4, quoting from Staffan I. Lindberg, *Democracy and Elections in Africa*, Baltimore: Johns Hopkins University Press, 2006.

24 Universal Declaration of Human Rights adopted by GA Res 217A (III) on 10 December 1948, UN Doc A/18/810, Article 21(3).

25 African Charter on Human and Peoples' Rights, 21 ILM 58 (adopted 27 June 1981, entered into force 21 October 1986) (1982), CABLE/LEG/67/ 3 rev 5, Article 13(1).

26 *Chilima and Chakwera v. Mutharika and EC*, *supra*, note 2, at 5, par 6.

27 Malawi Constitution, *supra*, note 7, section 12(c).

28 Malawi Constitution, *supra*, note 7, section 10(1).

laws. It states that the "[t]this Constitution shall bind all executive, legislative and judicial organs of the State at all levels of Government and all the peoples of Malawi are entitled to the equal protection of this Constitution, and laws made under it".[29] It further underlines that "[a]ny act of Government or any law that is inconsistent with the provisions of this Constitution shall, to the extent of such inconsistency, be invalid".[30] Hence, the MSCA stressed the legal consequences of having a constitutional democracy:

> [I]n a constitutional democracy, nothing perches itself above and beyond legal scrutiny, judicial review and such other relevant processes that are intended to ensure the supremacy of the very constitutions and laws upon which democratic values are affirmed. Thus, while aiming at protecting the sanctity of an election, it might become compelling that society be protected from what might be a semblance of an election. This will require a fine and yet delicate balance in protecting the ballot cast by the voter, the interest of the aggrieved candidates and those that they represent, as well as the integrity of the electoral system.[31]

The two courts therefore proceeded on the understanding that the Constitution demanded scrutiny of the legality of decisions and actions taken during the running of an election. The two courts were saying that constitutional legality is essential for "the authority to govern" in popular democracy.

The Stand for Transformational Constitutional Legality

The conceptual significance of the proceedings in the case is about the use of constitutional legality as an engine for transformation. The two petitioners invoked the Constitution in their case. When the Concourt issued its judgment, Mutharika said that it was against the Constitution and that it inaugurated "the death of Malawi's democracy".[32] During the proceedings, the two sides wrangled over the Constitution. The Constitution was not just a document that outlined essential elements, such as separation of powers, necessary for democratic constitutionalism.[33] When Constitutions become subjects of struggle, they are "ideological sites, providing a specific structure to society and

---

29 Malawi Constitution, *supra*, note 7, section 4.

30 Malawi Constitution, *supra* note 7, section 5.

31 *Mutharika and EC v Chilima and Chakwera*, *supra*, note 1, at 33, from line 3.

32 Peter Mutharika, Statement Broadcast on Malawi Broadcasting Corporation on 5 February 2020.

33 E.g., Louis Henkin, "Essentials of Constitutionalism", *ICJ Review*, 60 (1998), 11; Horst Dippel, "Modern Constitutionalism: An Introduction to History in the Need of Writing", *History Review* 73/1-2; *Unity Dow v Attorney General* 1992 BLR 119 (CA), at 130.

a justification for this structure".[34] This reflects more the view of those, such as Baxi and Ackerman, who regard a Constitution as a site for "state formative practices"[35] or symbol of identity.[36]

Further, the Constitution-based battles related to the proceedings reflect a view of democracy as a struggle advanced by thinkers such as Pogge,[37] Hardt and Negri,[38] and Hutchinson and Colon-Rios. Such a concept of a democracy and a Constitution places "a society's citizens, not its judicial or philosophical consuls, at the heart of the political process".[39] Hutchinson and Colon-Rios call for a move beyond liberal democracy's "anaemic and weak form and to engineer changes that bring it closer to its more full-bloodied potential."[40] As Hutchinson and Colon-Rios put it:

> Democracy ought not to be seen as a form of government embodied in a constitution because democracy always escapes constitutionalisation. Instead, democracy should be advanced as a substantive manifestation of popular sovereignty.[41]

The two judgments reflect this radical view of constitutionalism in at least three ways. First, the two judgments represent a stand that mirrors Habermas'[42] view that the law is an instrument to unify popular sovereignty and human rights, in that the individual needs to enjoy her or his human rights effectively and meaningfully to participate in popular sovereignty. The Concourt linked elections to the enjoyment of human rights in these terms:

> The Court recognises that the right of everyone to take part in the government of his or her country is an essential element in the effective enjoyment by all of their human rights. Holding genuine and regular elections ensures that those exercising

---

34 Peter A.J. Van Der Berg, "The Integrative Function of Constitutions: A Historical Perspective", in Peter Amtenbrink and A.J. van den Berg (eds), *The Constitutional Integrity of the European Union*, The Hague: T.M.C. Asser Press, 2010, 13-53, at 14.

35 Upendra Baxi, "Constitutionalism as a Site for State Formative Practices", *Cardozo Law Review* 21 (1999), 1183; Upendra Baxi et al. (eds), *Transformative Constitutionalism: Comparing the Apex Courts of Brazil, India and South Africa*, Pretoria: Pretoria University Law Press, 2013.

36 Bruce Ackerman, "Constitutional Politics/Constitutional Law", *Yale Law Journal* 99 (1989), 453.

37 Thomas Pogge, *World Poverty and Human Rights*, Cambridge: Polity, 2005, Chapter 6.

38 Michael Hardt and Antonio Negeri, *Multitude*, London: Penguin Books, 2006, Chapter 3.

39 Allan Hutchinson, and Joel I. Colón-Ríos, "What's Democracy Got to Do With It? A Critique of Liberal Constitutionalism", 2007, *Comparative Research in Law & Political Economy, Research Paper,* no. 29/2007, https://digitalcommons.osgoode.yorku.ca/clpe/245, accessed on 4 August 2020, at 49.

40 Ibid.

41 Ibid.

42 Jürgen Habermas, *Between Facts and Norms: Contributions to a Discourse Theory of Law and Democracy*, Cambridge, MA: MIT Press, 1996, Chapters 1 and 3.

> the power of the State remain electorally accountable and, in turn, maintaining an accountable government is a necessary precondition to the nurturing of an effective scheme for the respect, protection, promotion and fulfilment of human rights.[43]

Second, by insisting that accountability and transparency should characterise electoral processes, the two courts signalled a move away from the ideology of impunity with mediocrity. That ideology thrives on an "it's okay" culture, which expects people to move on when something is wrong. In other words, the courts were stressing that the conduct of an election must be, in Luhmann's words, autopoietic to the Constitution.[44] For an African country or a state in the "South", this was a radical departure from the norm: a situation where Constitutions infused with essentials of democracy would be allopoietic, producing results that are incompatible with the goals and values of the Constitution."[45] In countries of the South, as Neves notes, Constitutions or the law become an allopoietic system, where the "legal code" is kept in subordination to the interests and power of individuals and groups. Neves notes that "[t]this has grave [destructive] effects on the integration of society and is of course incompatible with the idea of autopoiesis law."[46] Unlike in allopoiesis, the concept taken by the two courts underlined an insistence to have an autopoietic electoral process, which complies with the Constitution and laws.

This shift was necessary because of the two courts' understanding of their roles in interpreting and applying a Constitution. Both the MSCA and the Concourt stressed the wording of section 9 of Malawi's Constitution in this regard. That section recognises that the responsibility of courts is to interpret, protect, and enforce the "Constitution and all laws and in accordance with this Constitution in an independent and impartial manner with regard only to legally relevant facts and the prescriptions of law". Within the concept of autopoietic law, the binary code of the law in electoral cases should be truth and justice, produced by compliance with the law.[47] Fidelity to such a binary code and constitutional

---

43 *Chilima and Chakwera v. Mutharika and EC, supra,* note 2, at 5-6, para 6.

44 Niklas Luhmann, "Operational Closure and Structural Coupling: The Differentiation of the Legal System", *Cardozo Law Review* 13 (1992), 1419–40; Niklas Luhmann, "Legal Argumentation: An Analysis of its Form", *Modern Law Review* 58 (1995), 285–98. Also, Gunther Teubner, *Law as an Autopoietic System*, trans. Anne Bankowska and Ruth Adler, ed. Zenon Bankowski, Oxford: Blackwell, 1993.

45 Marcelo Neves, "From the Autopoiesis to Allopoiesis of Law", *Journal of Law Society* 28/2 (2001), 242-64.

46 Ibid.

47 Niklas Luhmann, "The Code of the Moral", *Cardozo Law Review* 14/3-4 (January 1993): 995-1010; cf Norbert Altvater, "Another Quest for the Holy Grail of Law: Ius Generis – Law as a

legality can satisfy both the theories that judges should work as fiduciaries for the people[48] and as agents of the law.[49]

The Approach in the Proceedings

The ideological battle between impunity with mediocrity and constitutional legality affected the approaches taken by Mutharika and the Electoral Commission, on the one side, and the two courts and Chakwera and Chilima, on the other side. Impunity with mediocrity fought to perpetuate itself, while constitutional legality resisted and opted for transformation. Four battlelines are identifiable in the two judgments.

Expedition versus Attempts to End or Delay the Case

Firstly, the lawyers for Mutharika and the Commission fought with disdain to end and delay the case. The following table shows the many attempts by those lawyers to delay or end the case.

Table 4.1: *Attempts to Delay the End the Proceedings*

Stage	Examples of Attempts to End or Delay		Court's Response	
Preliminary	1	Application to dismiss the judicial review along with the lifting of the injunction not to declare the results.	1	Justice Mkandawire lifted the injunction but allowed the judicial review of the conduct of the elections to continue. [50]
Consolidation	2	Once the cases were consolidated, [51] there was an application to dismiss the petition on the ground that it was	2	The Concourt found no merit in the application. [53]

Countermovement to Human Cognition", *Washington University Jurisprudence Review* 12/2 (2020), 169-22

[48] Ethan J. Leib, David L. Ponet and Michael Serota, "A Fiduciary Theory of Judging", *California Law Review* 101 (2013), 699-753.

[49] Daniel Harris, "Judges as Agents of the Law", *Mitchell Hamline Law Journal of Public Policy and Practice* 41/2 (Spring 2020), 1-20.

[50] *State v Electoral Commission, Ex parte Malawi Congress Party and Others*, High Court Election Case No. 7 of 2019.

[51] *Election Case No 16 of 2019 and Election Case No. 26* of 2019 Consolidated as Constitutional Reference No 1 of 2019.

[53] *Chilima and Chakwera v Mutharika and Electoral Commission*, Election Case No. 1 of 1919, Application to Dismiss, decided on 22 June 2019.

		filed late and sworn improperly. [52]		
	3	Then there was an application for leave to appeal to the MSCA refusing to strike off the application.[54]	3	Concourt granted leave to appeal but stated that the case would proceed.
	4	Appeal to the MSCA.	4	MSCA dismissed the appeal. [55]
During Concourt Proceedings	5	Application to extend time by 14 days for getting sworn statements due to MCP disrupting the process suspecting attempts to buy witnesses[56]	5	The Concourt ordered MCP to issue a public retraction and granted a 5-day extension of the process to MEC and Mutharika. [57]
	6	Attempt to have many witnesses and examine them slowly in detail despite the fact that the case was largely to proceed on sworn statements	6	Court allowed the lawyers for Chakwera and Chilima to withdraw some witnesses remaining with 10 and not crossexamining some of Mutharika's and Electoral Commission's witnesses
Between Concourt and MSCA	7	Application to suspend Concourt judgment pending determination of appeal.[58]	7	Concourt refuses suspension.[59]

52 *Chilima and Chakwera v Mutharika and Electoral Commission*, Notice of 1st Respondent's Preliminary Applications, Filed on 12 June 2019.

54 *Chilima and Chakwera v Mutharika and Electoral Commission*, Constitutional Reference No 1 of 2019, Notice of Appeal, dated 24 June 2019.

55 *Mutharika and Electoral Commission v Chilima and Chakwera*, Constitutional Reference No 1 of 2019, Order, dated 15 August 2019.

56 *Chilima and Chakwera v Mutharika and Electoral Commission*, Constitutional Reference No 1 of 2019, Application for an Injunction and for an Order Extending Time within Which to Serve Sworn Statements. Filed on 18 July 2019.

57 *Chilima and Chakwera v Mutharika and Electoral Commission*, Order, dated 25 July 2019.

58 *Chilima and Chakwera v Mutharika and Electoral Commission*, Constitutional Reference No 1 of 2019, Application to Suspend Judgment Pending the Hearing and Determination of Appeal, filed on 7 February 2019.

59 *Mutharika and Electoral Commission v Chilima and Chakwera*, M.S.C.A. Appeal No. 7 of 2020, decided on 12 March 2020

	8	Appeal against refusal to suspend enforcement of judgment.	8	MSCA refuses to suspend judgment.
	9	Application to have foreign lawyers represent the Electoral Commission in the Appeal.	9	Application dismissed for failure of the foreign lawyers to appear before the Chief Justice.
	10	Appeal against the holding of the MSCA and consequential directions.[60]	10	Appeal dismissed in Concourt judgment in its entirety

This table shows that the applications to end the case implied that there was no need to answer the questions raised by the petitioners. This failure to respect the duty to account is a form of impunity in favour of public duty-bearers.

Conventional Burden and Standard of Proof versus Accountability

Secondly, the lawyers for Mutharika and the Commission fought to have Chilima and Chakwera prove the allegations they were making. Obstinately, their position was the old and general approach that "she or he who alleges must prove".[61] In contrast, the two courts stressed the importance of the public trust, accountability, and transparency enshrined in the Constitution.[62] Examining cases from various jurisdictions,[63] the two courts held that the burden for the petitioners was merely to raise a prima facie case for the Electoral Commission to prove that it had discharged its duties properly.

The lawyers for Mutharika and the Commission further argued for a quantitative test in proving whether the election and the result were due.[64] They

---

60 *Chilima and Chakwera v Mutharika and Electoral Commission, supra*, note 3.

61 Examples cited by the Malawi Supreme Court of Appeal: *Amanta Mbabazi v Yoweri Kaguta Museveni and Two Others*, Presidential Petition No. 01/2016; (2016) UGSC 3; *Abubakar v Yar'adua* [2009] ALL F WLR (PT. 457) ISC; *Raila Odinga and Five Others v Independent Electoral and Boundaries Commission and Three Others*, (Petitions 5,3 and 4 of 2013) [2013] e KLR; *Raila Amolo Odinga and Another v Independent Electoral and Boundaries Commission and Two Others*, Presidential Petition No. 1 of 2017 [2017] e KLR.

62 Malawi Constitution, *supra*, note 7, Preamble, section 12(c), and section 13(o).

63 E.g., in note 52 *supra*.

64 E.g., *Chamisa v Mnangagwa and 24 Others* 10 (CCZ 42/18) [2018] ZWCC; *Col (Rtd) Kizza Besigye v Yoweri Kaguta Museveni and Electoral Commission* 2001 Election Petition No. I of 2001.

insisted that Chakwera and Chilima had to show mathematically that any mistakes would have changed the eventual result. The two courts held that since an irregularity is non-compliance with the law,[65] there would be no result if non-compliance with the Constitution and supporting electoral laws compromised the elections. To arrive at this position, the two courts had to abandon an earlier position in the case of *Gondwe and Another v Gotani Nyahara*[66] in the following terms:

> A close analysis of the relevant statutory provisions reveals that the position taken in the *Gondwe and Another v Gotani Nyahara* is narrow and simplistic, especially in the context of a monumental event such as the election of a President. It may account for increased electoral malpractices over the years, where little attention is given to prescriptions of the law; the focus being on maximizing the numbers by whatever means, without complying with the law.[67]

Instead, the MSCA agreed with the Concourt, the High Court in *Ulemu Msungama v The Electoral Commission*,[68] and the Malawi Supreme Court in *Bentley Namasasu v Ulemu Msungama and The Electoral Commission* that "whether to apply the qualitative or quantitative test will largely depend on the manner the petition has been framed".[69] The court concluded, "If the petition is raising issues of both quality and quantity, then the Court should be able to use both."[70]

The lawyers for Mutharika and the Commission further advocated for a higher standard of proof than on a balance of probabilities, which is usual in civil cases. The reason was that elections are important and expensive and should not lightly be overturned. The court agreed that elections should not be overturned easily, but argued that cost should not be a determining factor. It then reasoned that "setting the standard too high for a petitioner to substantiate his [or her] grievance in such a matter might well impinge on the average Malawian's right to access justice when his [or her] constitutionally based rights have been violated".[71] This is within the context that Malawi's Constitution guarantees the right to access justice[72] and to have an effective remedy.[73] In the end, the court based the nullification of the elections and result "on a balance

65 PPE Act, section 3.

66 [2005] MLR 121 (SCA).

67 *Mutharika and Electoral Commission v Chilima and Chakwera*, *supra*, note 1, at 89.

68 Miscellaneous Case Number 8 of 2014 (HC).

69 MSCA Civil Appeal 8 of 2016, at 92.

70 Ibid.

71 *Mutharika and EC v Chilima and Chakwera, supra note 1*, at 39.

72 Malawi Constitution, *supra*, note, sections 41(3) and 46(3).

73 Malawi Constitution, *supra*, note, sections 46(3).

of probabilities", the appropriate standard of proof to apply in electoral petitions brought under section 100 of the PPE Act.[74]

Regularity and Substance v Irregularity

Thirdly, the lawyers for Mutharika and the Commission fought to disregard formality and regularity as long as there was express or implied agreement from others. It is true that undue regard to technicalities may lead to a failure to achieve a purpose. However, as Lon Fuller clarified, formalities perform an evidentiary, cautionary and channelling or labelling role.[75] In contrast, the lawyers for Mutharika and the Commission failed to appreciate that the quality of a process affects the nature and quality of a result. Five types of methods used by the lawyers for Mutharika and the Commission reveal that, if not resisted, impunity and mediocrity would be unchecked in elections.

First, the lawyers for Mutharika and the Commission made no distinction between general cases based on a petition and a Constitutional referral. Court procedures for petitions require that a case be based on pleadings or the statement of the case. Citing numerous cases,[76] the lawyers for Mutharika and the Commission argued that the courts should not allow non-pleaded claims and facts. This was despite the legal position that upon certification, the petition procedure "ceased to exist" though "the issues that were raised in the petitions survived".[77] The lawyers for Mutharika and the Commission further flouted rules on framing grounds of appeal. Grounds of appeal must be precise and concise, not argumentative, and state clearly whether they are based on law or fact. The following statement by the Malawi Supreme Court is telling about the mediocrity and impunity in framing the grounds of appeal:

> The second appellant filed 132 grounds of appeal, 15 of which are on pleadings, and many of these grounds of appeal are repetitive and argumentative. Some of the grounds split a point. Some of them are extremely confrontational and they make unwarranted and baseless allegations, including allegations of bias, against the Court below. Allegations of bias, especially against a court, should not be lightly made, but must be based on concrete and provable evidence. The second appellant did not point to any evidence of bias; on the contrary the record shows that the Court below bent backwards to accommodate the second appellant. We have to say some of the grounds were not just fictitious, but clearly unprofessional and distasteful. We have

---

74 *Chilima and Chakwera v. Mutharika and EC, supra,* note 2, at page 416, para 1479.

75 Lon Fuller, "Form and Consideration", *Columbia Law Review,* 1941, 799.

76 E.g., *Malawi Telecommunications Limited v. SR Nicholas Limited* [2014] MLR 218; and *Kamwendo v. Reunion Insurance* [2011] MLR 128.

77 *Mutharika and EC v Chilima and Chakwera, supra* note 1, at page 8.

> struggled to make sense out of the grounds of appeal in the second appellant's notice of appeal. We have found them to be unnecessarily numerous, convoluted and embarrassing.[78]

Second, the lawyers for Mutharika and the Commission argued for the methodological convenience of the Commission, including making agreements with electoral stakeholders and "making and implementing changes to the electoral systems as the election progressed".[79] Table 4.2 is a summary of the mismatch between the legal requirements and what the Electoral Commission actually did during the elections.

Table 4.2: *Legal Requirements, Rationales, and Examples of Electoral Commission's Non-Compliance*

Section	Summary of Key Requirements	Rationales	Examples of Electoral Commission's Implementation
90: Unused Ballot Papers	All unused ballot papers must be collected into an envelope that must be sealed, initialled, and stamped.	Elimination of the risks of unused ballot papers being abused through ballot stuffing.	The total number of ballots cast plus unused and cancelled/spoilt ballots exceeded the number of ballots provided.
90: Classification of votes	The election officials at the station must separate votes by type and candidate.	Easy and transparent counting at the polling station.	The EC introduced "valid votes cast" instead of "votes for candidates", and classified "null and void votes" as "null and void ballots".
92: Opening ballot boxes and counting	The election officials must announce the classification of each paper from the ballot box that was opened in the presence of other polling station officers and political party representatives present.	Transparency, accountability, and non-conflation during counting start.	Not all records showed who was present during opening and counting.

[78] *Mutharika and EC v Chilima and Chakwera, supra* note 1, at 42.

[79] *Mutharika and EC v Chilima and Chakwera, supra* note 1, at 57.

93: Polling station record and summary	The election officials must give political party representatives a copy of a summary posted at the polling station and based on a detailed record.	The requirements were safeguards against tampering and interfering with the results.	Prepared forms did not have space indicated for all the details required by the section and not all important occurrences were recorded.
94: District level record	The election officials must deliver the records and supporting papers to the District Commissioner's Office.	Have a district level compilation of results and key occurrences.	No such records were sent to the District Commissioner's Office, following an agreement with stakeholders.
95: District level records	Remit securely compiled district level records and all materials to the National Tally Centre.	Secure congregation of data for work flowing, transparency, and accountability.	Results from polling stations were sent to a constituency tally centre that was not provided for in the law.

Source: Chilima and Chakwera v Mutharika and Electoral Commission, supra note 2 and Mutharika and Electoral Commission, supra, note 1.

Third, the lawyers for Mutharika and the

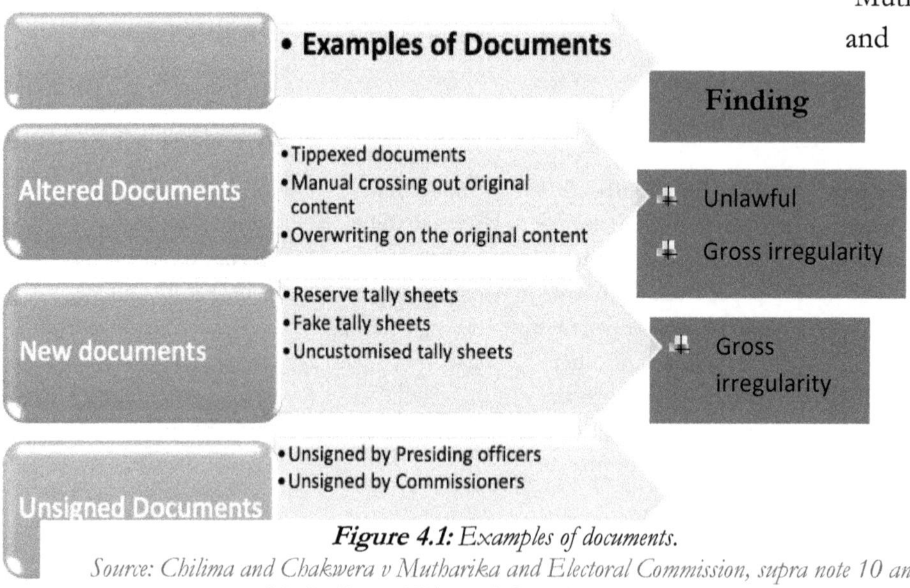

Figure 4.1: *Examples of documents.*

Source: Chilima and Chakwera v Mutharika and Electoral Commission, supra note 10 and Mutharika and Electoral Commission, supra, note 9.

Commission argued that the use of materials not prescribed by the law was acceptable as long as they served the purpose. The MSCA classified the documents that were in issue into three categories and made significant findings related to the eventual nullification of the presidential election. Figure 4.1 gives the examples and findings against each type.

The use of Tippex, introduction of new documents, and failure to sign key documents exemplified the unprofessional manner in which the Electoral Commission conducted the elections. The MSCA, in contrast, stated that:

> Not even the Commission itself can alter the results under section 113 of the Act under the guise of correcting and resolving complaints. The Commission must instead keep the original documents as received and resolve any complaints on a separate record.[80]

Fourth, a lax approach to the requirements of the PPA Act led the Electoral Commission to act without regard to the propriety of authority. In law, right people or institutions must take right actions. The Electoral Commission used constituency tally centres to receive and tally results from polling stations. In contrast, the Act requires the use of the District Commissioner's Office or any other properly designated Returning Office to consolidate results and records from polling stations by constituency into district level results. Both courts found the constituency tally centre unlawful, not being "a creature of statute". The Malawi Supreme Court put it in the following terms:

> This was not supposed to be. Results to the National Tally Centre, in accordance with section 95 (5) of the Act, come from the returning officer at the office of the District Commissioner. We also noted that returning officers delegated some of their functions to the Constituency Tally Centre. This was also illegal as no effectual delegation could have been made to an illegal entity. It is only the legislature that can change the structures in the electoral system. The consensus or agreement with stakeholders could not substitute the power and authority of Parliament.[81]

In a similar vein, the courts found as unlawful amendments of statutory forms by the Commission and its stakeholders.[82] Much as the Polling Station Voting Procedure Manual was "a good idea", the Commission and its stakeholders purported to change statutory contents, including the meaning of "null and void" in section 88.[83] Further, the MSCA observed that "the obligations which

---

80 *Mutharika and Electoral Commission v Chilima and Chakwera, supra* note 9, at 57.

81 *Mutharika and EC v Chilima and Chakwera, supra* note 1, at 59.

82 *Mutharika and EC v Chilima and Chakwera, supra* note 1, at 60.

83 Ibid.

the Act places on the Commission are necessitous, crucial and mandatory, and the Commission should therefore take these obligations seriously, especially the quasi-judicial obligations".[84] The Electoral Commission conveniently had used section 9 of the Electoral Commission Act as a defence for Commissioners "delegating" their powers to the Chief Elections Officer or a special committee.[85] To this effect, the government had passed subsidiary legislation.[86] The Concourt stated, "[S]uch delegation would amount to a blatant abdication and abrogation of functions and powers that are specifically vested in Commissioners under the Constitution."[87] The MSCA stated that the Commission "most certainly may not, and cannot, delegate its quasi-judicial powers and functions".[88]

Fifth, the lawyers for Mutharika and the Commission wanted to use precedent to entail that a previous error must continue to guide as long as a higher court made it. They relied on a decision of the MSCA in the case of *Gwanda Chakuamba v Attorney General*, where the MSCA refused to accept that majority means a minimum of 50%+1 vote, insisting that the word majority means the greatest number. The Constitution requires that a person must attain "a majority of the electorate through direct, universal and equal suffrage"[89] to win presidential elections. The PPE Act requires that "in any election the candidate who has obtained a majority of the votes at the poll shall be declared by the Commission to have been duly elected".[90] Both the Concourt and the MSCA held that "whether or not a particular candidate obtained a majority of the votes at the polls is a legal question that goes to the very heart of our political system regarding the election of a President".[91]

After deciding that the matter was properly before the Concourt, the MSCA noted two careless methods on the part of Mutharika and the Commission's lawyers. The first was that lawyers failed to appreciate that the Concourt had invoked the doctrine of *per incurium* to hold that majority should mean 50%+1

---

84 *Mutharika and EC v Chilima and Chakwera, supra* note 1, at 62.

85 Electoral Commission Act, No 11 of 1998 (Chapter 2:03, *Laws of Malawi*), section 8(1), section 9.

86 Parliamentary and Presidential Elections (Elections Complaints and Petitions Handling Procedures) Regulations, 2019, G.N.1 1/2019.

87 *Chilima and Chakwera v Mutharika and Electoral Commission, supra*, note 10, at 306, para 1116.

88 *Mutharika and EC v Chilima and Chakwera, supra,* note 1, at 71.

89 Malawi Constitution, *supra*, note, section 80(2).

90 PPE Act, supra, section 95(6).

91 *Mutharika and EC v Chilima and Chakwera, supram* note 1, at 100.

vote, despite the earlier MSCA case. *Per incurium*, meaning out of lack of care or inadvertently, is a doctrine invoked to show that a binding decision would have been different had it considered a certain existing legal position at the time. In this case, it was the legal definition of "majority vote", which *Blacks Dictionary* had defined as "vote by more than half of voters for candidate or other matter on ballot".[92] The second sloppy method on the part of Mutharika's and Commission's lawyers was failure to distinguish cases properly. Distinguishing cases is a basic skill employed to ensure that only like cases, according to the doctrine of precedent, are decided alike. Key in distinguishing is a comparison of the material facts and legal issues raised. The MSCA noted that the lawyers failed to distinguish the earlier MSCA case from the current one. The pertinent issue in *Gwanda Chakuamba v Attorney General* was whether the Commission had "unlawfully declared to have been elected President a candidate who obtained a majority of the votes at the poll instead of a majority of the electorate". In that regard, the Malawi Supreme Court clarified that the question was not about the meaning of the term "majority" in section 80(2) of the Constitution, but rather "'majority of what?' as a deciding factor in a presidential election".[93] In that regard the Malawi Supreme Court in *Gwanda Chakuamba v Attorney General* was right to hold that majority pertained to votes cast and not the whole electorate.

The Malawi Supreme Court departed from flawed reasoning on the part of the MSCA in the earlier case of *Gwanda Chakuamba v Attorney General* as far as it purported authoritatively to reject that majority vote in the context of Malawi's Constitution should mean 50%+1 vote. The MSCA observed that the earlier case had ignored the "real possibility that a Presidential contender may obtain the 50%+1 votes first time without the necessity for a run-off".[94] Further, the earlier case did not "consider a situation involving large numbers of Presidential contenders who share among them the votes at the polls, as has happened in the recent past".[95] Noting that there was a real possibility of a winning candidate obtaining as little as 10% of the votes, the court underlined its steadfastness to popular sovereignty:

It is an interpretation that would not lead to any absurdity in so far as presidential election under section 80 (2) of the Constitution is concerned. This

---

92 *Chilima and Chakwera v. Mutharika and EC, supra,* note 2, at 386, para 1442.

93 *Mutharika and EC v Chilima and Chakwera, supra* note 1, at 107.

94 *Mutharika and EC v Chilima and Chakwera, supra* note 1, at 109.

95 Ibid.

interpretation also safeguards principles of transparency, accountability, honesty and integrity in the conduct of elections to the high office of president. It would guard against the manipulation of the vote and the creation of numerous surrogate parties or presidential contenders designed to spread the vote to benefit a particular contender at the expense of other strong contenders.[96]

Self Interest v Duty-based Civic and Ethical Professionalism

Fourthly, the battle line was on insistence on self-interests at the expense of public duties. Mutharika was involved in the case as a candidate, an individual. As the case proceeded, he often used his presidential role publicly to fight the case and its results. The Electoral Commissioners, too, acted as contestant, not as a public duty-bearer. The Commission conflated its duties with the interests to protect Mutharika. Warning them that "any future wasteful and inappropriate conduct would entail that they pay their own costs for proceedings", the court found that the conduct of the Commissioners in the proceedings:

> [L]eft much to be desired, resulting in loss of colossal sums of money through litigation, to say nothing about the injury to our democratic processes as well as general and unquantifiable suffering of the people of this country. The truth of the matter is that all that loss and suffering could have been avoided had the second appellant conducted itself prudently as a duty bearer and assisted the Court early in the litigation of the matter rather than take sides.[97]

Such reprehensible impunity was also evident in the "inappropriate" conduct of the Attorney General, who claimed that section 20 of the Electoral Commission Act allowed the Commission to instruct him to represent it. However, the Attorney General could not distinguish his respective roles as a lawyer for a contestant in litigation, public duty-bearer employed to work as a principal legal advisor to the government,[98] legal officer, and Head of the Bar.[99] The Concourt reprimanded the Attorney General and eventually prevented him from arguing the appeal in the Malawi Supreme Court of Appeal.[100] The Electoral Commission and Mutharika appealed against this holding. The Malawi Supreme Court of Appeal stressed that the Concourt should have stopped the Attorney General representing the Commission and Mutharika

---

96 *Mutharika and EC v Chilima and Chakwera, supra* note 1, at 109-110.

97 *Mutharika and EC v Chilima and Chakwera, supra,* note 1, at 126.

98 Malawi Constitution, *supra*, note 7, section 98.

99 Legal Education and Legal Practitioners Act, No 31 of 2018, section 33.

100 *Chilima and Chakwera v Mutharika and Electoral Commission*, *supra*, note 2, at 428-431, paras 1484-1495.

even in the Concourt, once the matter had become a constitutional referral.[101] As a principal legal advisor to the whole of Government, he should have been assisting the Court in the interest of justice. The Court noted that the court record was "littered with instances of evidence that the Attorney General was conflicted and compromised".[102]

In contrast, the ethical professionalism of the five Concourt judges was exemplary. During the time the judges were working on the judgment, an allegation surfaced of an attempt by a businessperson in support of Mutharika to bribe them. The judges informed the Chief Justice who, in turn, reported the matter to the Anti-Corruption Bureau. Using a warrant issued by a magistrate in Lilongwe, the Bureau arrested the businessperson. However, a magistrate in Zomba released him in the night, although the warrant of arrest was still operational. Justice Dorothy nyaKaunda issued directions for the re-arrest of the businessperson and the disciplining of the judicial officer and lawyers involved.[103]

Conclusion

The proceedings in the 2019-20 presidential election case show resistance against impunity with mediocrity. The Concourt and the MSCA dismissed attempts to defend impunity and mediocrity in the conduct of elections. The two courts' linkage of elections with popular sovereignty towards progressive wellbeing in a constitutional democracy is novel in Malawi's legal system. The two courts steadfastly based this position on Malawi's Constitution. After 26 years in operation, Malawi's Constitution assumed potency to help deliver a nation from impunity and mediocrity. Such potency arose because the judges in both courts resisted impunity and mediocrity and demanded strict performance of duties, and accountability. Such a position on constitutional legality has the potential to transform societies through the realisation of aspirations of people as expressed in Constitutions. The nullification of the results of the 21 May 2019 presidential elections, the holding of fresh elections, and insistence that authority to govern for a president requires at least 50%+1 votes of those who vote in properly conducted elections, are results that manifest tremendous potential. The resilience of the law against impunity and mediocrity did not only bring the country to a profound crossroads, but also

---

101 *Mutharika and EC v Chilima and Chakwera, supra,* note 1, at 110-115.

102 *Mutharika and EC v Chilima and Chakwera, supra,* note 1, at 115.

103 *Mpinganjira v Anticorruption Bureau*, Criminal Review Case No. 3 of 2020, decided 28.1.2020.

signalled expected standards for public functionaries to work towards the aspirations envisaged in the country's Constitution.

If constitutional legality continues to challenge impunity and mediocrity, the potential towards progressive wellbeing or development can go beyond Malawi and the conduct of elections. This is because constitutional legality, in its insistence that duty-bearers must carry out their duties properly and account for their performance of such duties, may spur at least reasonableness in public service provision. For elections, the proceedings and the two judgments establish that although the expected standard is not excellence, it is certainly above average reasonableness.

Table of Statutes and International Instruments

African Charter on Human and Peoples' Rights, 21 ILM 58 (adopted 27 June 1981, entered into force 21 October 1986) (1982), CABLE/LEG/67/ 3 rev 5, Article 13(1)

Constitution of Malawi, Act No 20 of 1994

Constitution of Malawi, Act No. 20 of 1994, section 4

Constitution of Malawi, Act No. 20 of 1994, section 5

Constitution of Malawi, Act No. 20 of 1994, section 6

Constitution of Malawi, Act No. 20 of 1994, section 6

Constitution of Malawi, Act No. 20 of 1994, section 10(1)

Constitution of Malawi, Act No. 20 of 1994, section 12(c)

Constitution of Malawi, Act No. 20 of 1994, Preamble

Constitution of Malawi, Act No. 20 of 1994, section 13(o)

Constitution of Malawi, Act No. 20 of 1994, sections 41(3)

Constitution of Malawi, Act No. 20 of 1994, sections 46(3)

Constitution of Malawi, Act No. 20 of 1994, sections 46(3)

Constitution of Malawi, Act No. 20 of 1994, sections 75-76

Constitution of Malawi, Act No. 20 of 1994, section 80(2)

Electoral Commission Act, No 11 of 1998 (Chapter 2:03, *Laws of Malawi*), section 8(1)

Electoral Commission Act, No 11 of 1998 (Chapter 2:03, *Laws of Malawi*), section 9

Parliamentary and Presidential Elections (Elections Complaints and Petitions Handling Procedures) Regulations, 2019, G.N.1 1/2019

Parliamentary and Presidential Elections Act, No. 31 of 1993 (Chapter 2:01, *Laws of Malawi*), Long Title

Parliamentary and Presidential Elections Act, section 100(1)

Parliamentary and Presidential Elections Act, section 100(3)(b)

Parliamentary and Presidential Elections Act, section 3

Parliamentary and Presidential Elections Act, section 95(6)

Universal Declaration of Human Rights adopted by GA Res 217A (III) on 10 December 1948, UN Doc A/18/810, Article 21(3).

Table of Cases

Abubakar v Yar'adua [2009] ALL F WLR (PT. 457) ISC

Amanta Mbabazi v Yoweri Kaguta Museveni and Two Others, Presidential Petition No. 01/2016; (2016) UGSC 3

Chamisa v Mnangagwa and 24 Others 10 (CCZ 42/18) [2018] ZWCC

Chilima and Chakwera v Mutharika and Electoral Commission, Constitutional Reference No 1 of 2019, Notice of Appeal, dated 24 June 2019

Chilima and Chakwera v Mutharika and Electoral Commission, Constitutional Reference No 1 of 2019, Application for an Injunction and for an Order Extending Time within which to Serve Sworn Statements. Filed on 18 July 2019

Chilima and Chakwera v Mutharika and Electoral Commission, Constitutional Reference No 1 of 2019, Application to Suspend Judgment Pending the Hearing and Determination of Appeal, filed on 7 February 2019

Chilima and Chakwera v Mutharika and Electoral Commission, Election Case No. 1 of 1919, Application to Dismiss, decided on 22 June 2019

Chilima and Chakwera v Mutharika and Electoral Commission, Notice of 1st Respondent's Preliminary Applications, Filed on 12 June 2019

Chilima and Chakwera v. Mutharika and EC, High Court Constitutional Reference No. 1 of 2019

Chilima v Electoral Commission, High Court Election Case No 26 of 2019 and *Chakwera v Electoral Commission*, High Court Election, Order of Consolidation and Referring the Matters to a Constitutional Court, dated 4 June 2019.

Col (Rtd) Kizza Besigye v Yoweri Kaguta Museveni and Electoral Commission 2001 Election Petition No. I of 2001

Election Case No 16 of 2019 and Election Case No 26 of 2019, Order of Consolidations and Referring the Matters to the Constitutional Court

Election Case No 16 of 2019 and Election Case No. 26 of 2019 Consolidated as Constitutional Reference No 1 of 2019

High Court of Malawi Reference No. 1, Certification by the Chief Justice., dated 5 June 2019

Kamwendo v. Reunion Insurance [2011] MLR 128

Malawi Telecommunications Limited v. SR Nicholas Limited [2014] MLR 218

Mpinganjira v Anticorruption Bureau, Criminal Review Case No. 3 of 2020, decided 28 January 2020

Mutharika and Electoral Commission v Chilima and Chakwera, Constitutional Reference No 1 of 2019, Order, dated 15 August 2019

Mutharika and Electoral Commission v Chilima and Chakwera, M.S.C.A. Appeal No. 7 of 2020, decided on 12 March 2020

Mutharika and Electoral Commission v Chilima and Chakwera, MSCA Constitutional Appeal No. 1 of 2020

Raila Amolo Odinga and Another v Independent Electoral and Boundaries Commission and Two Others, Presidential Petition No. 1 of 2017 [2017] e KLR

Raila Odinga and Five Others v Independent Electoral and Boundaries Commission and Three Others, (Petitions 5,3 and 4 of 2013) [2013] e KLR

State v Electoral Commission, Ex parte Malawi Congress Party and Others, High Court Election Case No. 7 of 2019

Chapter 5

Legal Responses to Electoral Violence and Democratic Governance in Malawi: The Case of the 2019 and 2020 Elections

Fidelis Edge Kanyongolo

Introduction

This chapter explores the legal responses to violence related to elections conducted in Malawi in 2019 and 2020 and their implications for the country's democratic governance. The analysis addresses the nature and effects of the responses, identifies some of the contextual conditions that shape them and briefly outlines their effects on democratic governance institutions and processes. The analysis draws on insights from sociological jurisprudence and critical legal theory which in the broadest sense conceptualises the law as a projection of interests and power relations within given communities. Against this background, this chapter posits legal responses to violence as a function of the interplay of the various interests and power relations among key actors involved in generating electoral violence and those responsible for designing and implementing the legal responses.

The chapter seeks to understand the implications of legal responses to election violence in Malawi in 2019 and 2020. To this end, the chapter notes the paucity of legislative action to prevent or respond to election violence. It also discusses the perceived bias of the police in favour of the ruling party and its limiting effect on administrative and law enforcement responses to the violence. Finally, the chapter examines the limitation of judicial responses to violence caused by perceived political bias in the exercise of prosecutorial discretion. The chapter argues that limitations in the legal responses to electoral violence adversely affect democratic governance by undercutting the liberal democratic principle of equality before the law, which is guaranteed in the Constitution, and undermining the potential for the law to deter future acts of election violence and create a conducive environment for free and inclusive participation in elections.

Electoral Violence and Democratic Governance

There is no specific definition of election or election-related violence in Malawian law. The law views acts of violence perpetrated in connection to an election through the lens of the generic criminal offences such as assault, murder, malicious damage to property and arson. In this chapter, however, election violence will be used to denote a distinctive type of violence which is "levied by political actors to purposefully influence the process and outcome of elections, and it involves coercive acts against humans, property, and infrastructure".[1] The distinctiveness of electoral violence is reflected not only in its purpose, but also its institutional organisation which consists of election-specific actors, practices, and institutions.

The connection between a particular incident of violence and the electoral process may be direct, as in the cases in which some individuals assaulted officials of the Electoral Commission and damaged voting materials in Blantyre. In other cases, the relationship of particular acts of violence and elections is more remote, as is the case where a private argument over elections degenerates into a physical fight. The determining factor is whether violence is perpetrated for the benefit or to the detriment of a contesting candidate or his or her electoral interests.

Election violence adversely affects democratic governance in a number of distinct respects. Broadly, the prevalence of election violence creates an unfavourable environment for citizen participation,[2] especially by women[3] and youth,[4] and results in human rights violations. Apart from lowering participation in general, election violence is, therefore, likely to reinforce gender and age disparities in participation because women and the youth may be

---

1 Stephanie M. Burchard, "Get out the Vote–or Else: The Impact of Fear of Election Violence on Voters", *Democratization* 27/4 (2020), 588-604.

2 Dorina A. Bekoe and Stephanie M. Burchard, "The Contradictions of Pre-election Violence: The Effects of Violence on Voter Turnout in Sub-Saharan Africa", *African Studies Review* 60/2 (2017), 73-92; and Roxana Gutiérrez-Romero and Adrienne LeBas, "Does Electoral Violence Affect Vote Choice and Willingness to Vote? Conjoint Analysis of a Vignette Experiment", *Journal of Peace Research* 57/1 (2020), 77-92.

3 Gabrielle Bardall, "Towards a More Complete Understanding of Election Violence: Introducing a Gender Lens to Electoral Conflict Research", a paper presented at the European Conference on Politics and Gender, Uppsala, 2015, 11-13.

4 Dabesaki Mac-Ikemenjima, "Violence and Youth Voter Turnout in Sub-Saharan Africa", *Contemporary Social Science: Journal of the Academy of Social Sciences* 12/3-4 (2017), 215-226.

disproportionately deterred from participation due to their particular vulnerability to violence.

Election violence also undermines democratic governance because it results in violations of human rights, including the right to life, the right to human dignity and personal liberty, the right to non-discrimination, freedom of the press, freedom of expression and freedom of opinion, the right to property and the right to participate in elections. In addition, election violence also negatively affects democratic governance because it necessitates the re-deployment of public resources away from productive governance activities such as delivery of health and education services towards less socially beneficial activities such as funding security agencies and indemnifying victims of the violence for their material losses.[5]

Social responses to election violence include the enactment and enforcement of laws aimed at minimising or eliminating it. This aim has been pursued through the effective enforcement of laws which define the prohibited conduct which amounts to election violence and stipulate its punishment; establish and empower security and criminal justice institutions; and stipulate procedures for the conduct of criminal trials. Broadly, these legal responses to election violence are largely grounded in deterrence theories of law which essentially argue that human conduct can be inclined towards compliance with the law by dis-incentivising non-compliance. Effective deterrence is attained by ensuring certainty of the punishment of those who commit offences; swiftness in the conduct of investigations and trials; and severity in the punishments imposed by the courts. By deterring election violence, the law directly contributes to the creation of a conducive environment for democratic governance activities including the enjoyment of human rights and the effective and efficient administration of free, fair and credible elections.

The assessment of the contribution made by criminal law to any particular governance regime must take full account of the peculiarities of the social, economic and political context of that regime. This position is informed by

---

5 The Riot Damages Act entitles any person who suffers damage resulting from riotous conduct by members of the general public to claim compensation from the government. Disbursements under this Act have been very rare. In the most recent case on the matter, a business owner sued the government for failing to honour its obligations under the Act following substantial damage to his property during riots that occurred during anti-government demonstrations in Lilongwe. The few cases in which they have been effected have involved substantial sums of money: www.nyasatimes.com/mulli-demands-k11bn-pay-from-malaiw-government/.

sociological theories of law which argue that the law is a projection of the state and dynamics of private, public and state interests which constitute the society in which that law is made and applied.[6] On their part, critical legal theories identify the power relations underlying those interests as the most instrumental factor in determining the form and content of the law.[7]

Violence in the 2019 and 2020 Elections

Malawi conducted presidential, parliamentary and local government elections on 21 May 2019. The results of the presidential elections were challenged in a petition lodged with the High Court by two of the candidates who had contested in the elections. In the parliamentary elections, judicial challenges were mounted with respect to the results from less than 10 of the 193 constituencies, while out of the 462 wards in which local government polls had been conducted, judicial review was sought in relation to the results from less than five wards. The presidential election petitions essentially argued that the election had been characterised by irregularities which affected its outcome. On 3 February 2020, the court ruled in favour of the petitioners and ordered that a fresh presidential election be held by 3 July 2020. The election was held on 23 June 2020 and to date, its results have not been subject to any judicial challenge.

There are no comprehensive qualitative or quantitative data on the prevalence of violence and the legal responses that occurred in the run-up to, during and after the 2019 and 2020 elections.[8] However, a review of accounts in academic literature, election observer and monitor reports, media accounts, press releases issued by the police and the Malawi Human Rights Commission provides indicative evidence of the prevalence and character of the violence, and the legal responses it attracted. Among the notable characteristics was the geographic spread of the violence. In this respect, it was notable that the most

---

6 Roscoe Pound, "A Survey of Social Interests", *Harvard Law Review* 57/1 (1943), 1-39.

7 Roberto M. Unger, "The Critical Legal Studies Movement", *Harvard Law Review* 96/3 (1983), 561-675.

8 This paucity may be compared to other countries, such as Kenya, where, in the past, such data were generated and disseminated by the country's Ministry of Medical Services. See Mutuma Ruteere, "More than Political Tools: The Police and Post-election Violence in Kenya", *African Security Review* 20/4 (2011), 11-20. The data included the total number of people who had died as a result of the violence, the proportion of the fatalities who had died as a result of gunshot wounds and the geographic spread of the violence. See Report of the Commission of Inquiry into Post Election Violence, https://reliefweb.int/sites/reliefweb.int /files/ resources /15A00F569813F4D549257607001F459D-Full_Report.pdf, [16.10.2008].

serious incidents of violence—based on the severity of the injuries caused to people and value of property damaged or destroyed—occurred in the country's capital city, Lilongwe, and the city of Mzuzu in the Northern Region of the country.

In the capital city, Lilongwe, four people were killed in an arson attack on the office of an opposition political party,[9] one police officer was stoned to death by rioters,[10] more than a dozen women and girls were assaulted and raped,[11] several police officers were severely injured after being attacked by groups of stone-throwing rioters,[12] and rioters burned part of a government complex and offices of the Japan International Cooperation Agency.[13] In Mzuzu, reported incidents included the burning down of a number of government offices, a building belonging to the ruling party and a police unit.[14] In comparison, the violence reported in the country's second largest city, Blantyre, appears to have resulted in lower levels of personal injuries and damage to property than was the case in Lilongwe and Mzuzu. The most serious incidents reported in Blantyre included assaults of various actors perceived to be opposition supporters or sympathisers and included an assault on the leader of the non-governmental organisation responsible for organising nation-wide post-election protests against the Electoral Commission's declaration of Peter Mutharika as the winner of the presidential election.[15]

Although many reported incidents of violence were perpetrated in the country's urban centres, some of the country's smaller towns and settlements also experienced significant levels of violence at different stages of the 2019-2020 electoral cycle. In the eastern region town of Mangochi, for example, suspected ruling party supporters and sympathisers set on fire an opposition party's

---

9 Malawi Ensure Free, Fair and Safe Elections, www.hrw.org/news/2020/06/03/malawi-ensure-free-fair-safe-elections-0, [6.3.2020].

10 Malawi Protests Turn Violent After Disputed Election, www.africanews.com/2019/06/20/malawi-protests-turn-violent-after-disputed-election// [20.6.2019].

11 Malawi 2019 Human Rights Report, www.state.gov/wp-content/uploads/2020/02/MALAWI-2019-HUMAN-RIGHTS-REPORT.pdf [02.2020].

12 Malawi Protests Turn Violent After Disputed Election, www.africanews.com/2019/06/20/malawi-protests-turn-violent-after-disputed-election// [20.6.2019].

13 More violence in Malawi's post-election protests, http://www.xinhuanet.com/english/2019-07/26/c_138258383.htm [26.7.2019].

14 Ibid.

15 Malawi Protests Turn Violent After Disputed Election, www.africanews.com/2019/06/20/malawi-protests-turn-violent-after-disputed-election// [20.6.2019].

vehicles.[16] In the Northern Region town of Karonga, suspected opposition party supporters violently assaulted the driver of a ruling party vehicle and left him unconscious.[17] Another incident was reported in the Central Region district of Dowa, where a journalist working for the state-controlled Malawi Broadcasting Corporation was injured following an attack by a group of people, some of whom were using metal bars;[18] while in the country's southernmost district of Nsanje, a senior official of an opposition party and aspiring candidate in the parliamentary elections was physically assaulted,[19] and a ruling party candidate in the parliamentary elections was beaten up and undressed by suspected supporters of one of her rival contestants.[20]

The available evidence also suggests some variations in the demographic patterns in the identity of perpetrators and victims of the violence connected to the 2019 and 2020 elections. In the vast majority of the cases reported in the media and documented by election monitors, perpetrators were male, women were more likely to be victims than perpetrators,[21] and perpetrators tended to be young men. Available literature from elsewhere suggests that the gender and age profiles of perpetrators and victims of election violence may reflect pre-existing social structural realities, which may include structural gender inequalities in the access to public spaces, the patriarchal capture of information communication technology which results in the normalisation of election violence against women,[22] and economic discontentment caused by unemployment which disproportionately affects the youth.[23]

Some studies have also demonstrated correlations between the geographic location of election violence and the geographic spread of the political support

---

16 UTM Vehicles Set on Fire in Mangochi, https://malawi24.com/2018/08/19/utm-vehicles-set-on-fire-in-mangochi/ [19.8.2019].

17 EISA Pre-Election Assessment Mission Report, www.eisa.org/pdf/mal2019pam.pdf [17.5.2019].

18 Malawi Protests Turn Violent after Disputed Election, www.africanews.com/2019/06/20/malawi-protests-turn-violent-after-disputed-election// [20.6.2019].

19 Chidanti Lodges Formal Violence Complaint, www.mwnation.com/chidanti-formally-lodges-violence-complaint/ [8.4.2019].

20 MESN Condemns Assault, Public Humiliation on Hellen Buluma, www.nyasatimes.com/mesn-condemns-assault-public-humiliation-on-hellen-buluma-dpp-candidate-in-nsanje-south-west/ [22.5.2019].

21 The general profile of alleged perpetrators is evident in the age and gender of the 17 alleged rioters who were arrested during one of the biggest political protests in the country's history.

22 See Gabrielle Bardall, "Towards a More Complete Understanding of Election Violence".

23 Sebastian A. Paalo, "Political Party Youth Wings and Political Violence in Sub-Sahara Africa: A Case of Ghana", *International Journal of Peace and Development Studies* 8/1 (2017), 1-14.

of contestants in the election.[24] The correlation between the geographic distribution of violence in the 2019 and 2020 Malawian elections and the country's political geography requires more in-depth research. One area of particular interest would be to investigate any correlations between the geographic location of violence and the spatial spread of the support of the parties and candidates who contested in the elections. Another area of research interest would be the relationship between geographic location of specific forms, on the one hand, and the magnitude of the violence, the age and gender of its perpetrators and victims.

Research into any correlations between the spatial location of violence and the geography of political support for the contestants would use as a point of departure the apparent coincidence between the occurrence of the violent incidents in Lilongwe, Mzuzu, Dowa, Mangochi and Karonga, and the fact that in the elections, public support for the candidates appeared to be strongest in particular geographic locations, with Mangochi district being one of the strongholds of Atupele Muluzi, the running mate on the ruling party ticket in the presidential election, Phalombe district being where the ruling party has won more than 90% of the vote in the previous three presidential and parliamentary elections. In a similar vein, the research must investigate whether there is any significant correlation between the scale of violence in the cities of Lilongwe, Mzuzu and Blantyre as well as the other towns such as Dowa and the spatial distribution of political support for the opposition candidate in the presidential elections, Lazarus Chakwera, who drew most of his support from Lilongwe, Dowa and Ntchisi, and his running mate, Saulos Chilima, who drew the bulk of his support from residents of urban areas of Blantyre, Zomba, Lilongwe and Mzuzu.

The spatial distribution of poverty and youth unemployment, the geographic location and strength of police formations and other factors and their correlation to the spatial patterns of the violence that occurred in the 2019 and 2020 elections are additional areas in which future research can yield evidence-based insights into the nature of election violence in Malawi.

---

[24] For example, see Michael Wahman and Edward Goldring, "Pre-Election Violence and Territorial Control: Political Dominance and Subnational Election Violence in Polarized African Electoral Systems", *Journal of Peace Research* 57/1 (2020), 93-110; and D. Fielding, "The Geography of Violence During a Presidential Election: Evidence from Zimbabwe", *European Journal of Political Economy* 55 (2018), 538-558.

Legal Responses to Election Violence 2019-2020

In this chapter, legal responses to election violence refer to the totality of legislative, administrative and judicial actions which seek to prevent its commission and facilitate the prosecution and lawful punishment of its perpetrators and enablers. Legislative responses primarily consist of the enactment of laws by Parliament (or bodies with authority to pass subsidiary legislation) aimed at preventing election violence and establishing a legal framework for law enforcement and judicial action. The legislature also has the constitutional mandate to exercise oversight which empowers it to hold to account law enforcement agencies and the courts for their contribution to the reduction of election violence. On their part, administrative responses refer to the variety of measures which may be taken by law enforcement agencies to enforce the law and prosecute offenders, while judicial responses consist of actions taken by the courts to try cases and impose punishments on offenders.

There was no significant legislative response to election violence related to the 2019 and 2020 elections. A bill intended to introduce a range of electoral reforms which was passed by the National Assembly in February 2020 did not include any reforms related to election violence not incorporated into electoral law reforms. On its part, though, the Electoral Commission, which has the mandate to enact subsidiary legislation, published a code of conduct for the 2019 elections.[25] Among other things, the Code of Conduct reinforced the statutory prohibitions of violent conduct by prohibiting contesting political parties and candidates, as well as members of political parties, from engaging in any physical or psychological violence or intimidation "to demonstrate political party strength or prove supremacy",[26] using language that may promote or provoke violence,[27] or defacing or unlawfully destroying campaign material of a political party or candidate.[28]

In contrast to the paucity of legislative responses, law enforcement responses were more numerous and varied. They included the provision of protection to potential targets of violence and the arrest of its perpetrators. For the most

25 Electoral Code of Conduct for Political Parties and Candidates for the 2019 Tripartite Elections, http://mec.org.mw/wp-content/uploads/2019/03/Political-party-code-of-conduct-2019.pdf [March 2019].

26 Section 7(5).

27 Section 7(1).

28 Section 7(3).

part, protection was provided by the Malawi Police Service, whose constitutional mandate is "to provide for the protection of public safety and the rights of persons in Malawi according to the prescriptions of this Constitution and any other law". In the discharge of this mandate, the police provided security for campaigners and demonstrators, election officials and materials, voters and journalists involved in the elections.

However, due to a perception among a significant proportion of the public that the police force was "captured" by the party in government and biased against opposition and independent actors, the provision of security was increasingly undertaken by the country's military, the Malawi Defence Force. Although the most obvious form of bias was partisan in favour of the party in government, experience from elsewhere suggests that other biases may influence micro-level policing decisions. In Kenya, for example, the failure of the police to prevent post-election violence in 2007 and 2008 has been attributed to ethnic biases by security forces at the operational level.[29] The existence of bias at the operational level shows the limitation of the argument that police bias is the result of political "capture" of its leadership by the party in government. Local level biases also need to be factored into the analysis. After all, as Foucault and Ewald have observed, power at the micro-level does not slavishly follow instructions from above.[30] Establishing the incidence and nature of any micro-level bias in the context of the 2019 and 2020 elections requires research that was beyond the scope of this chapter. However, such research is essential for a fuller understanding of the factors that shape the dynamics of election violence at both local and national levels.

Bias may also be explained by the fact that the state itself has been implicated in much of the violence and cannot allow itself to permit processes that may lead to its own incrimination. It has even been suggested that in sub-Saharan Africa, most violence is perpetrated by incumbents.[31] There were numerous reports of election-related violence perpetrated by state agents, including members of the police and the Malawi Defence Force personnel, in relation to the 2019 and 2020 elections. The most widely reported incidents included one in which some police officers committed acts of violence against members of

---

29 Mutuma Ruteere, "More than Political Tools".

30 Michel Foucault and Francois Ewald, "Society Must Be Defended", *Lectures at the Collège de France, 1975-1976*, vol. 1, 2003.

31 Emilie M. Hafner-Burton, Susan D. Hyde and Ryan S. Jablonski, "When do Governments Resort to Election Violence?" *British Journal of Political Science* (2014) 149-179, 150 note 6.

a community as part of revenge for the death of a police officer killed by rioters during an earlier clash between the police and protesters. In a widely publicised aspect of the attack, some of the police officers allegedly raped a number of women and girls and following legal action undertaken by the women through the country's Women Lawyers Association, the High Court has since ordered expedition of the investigation into the criminal liability of individual officers and compensation for the victims.[32]

The perception that the state is biased also related to the exercise of its power to prosecute offenders. The Constitution vests this power in the Director of Public Prosecutions and any public official to whom the Director delegates it. In relation to the 2019 and 2020 elections the power was exercised to initiate prosecutions of people accused of responsibility for murder, assault and arson. Almost all people charged with election violence offences in the period prior to 23 June 2020 were associated with opposition parties, while very few prosecutions were initiated against members or supporters of the party in government who were alleged to have perpetrated violence. Following the change of the party in government in June 2020, all prosecutions targeted alleged perpetrators affiliated with the erstwhile party in government which had now become the opposition.

On their part, judicial responses to election violence are largely shaped by prosecutorial choices regarding the initiation and discontinuation of particular prosecutions and the selection of charges to proffer against particular suspects. In respect of the 2019 and 2020 elections, prosecutorial choices resulted in cases being tried mainly in magistrates' courts, courts trying only suspects who were affiliated to the opposition, discontinuing only a case involving a suspect affiliated to the party in government. In the performance of their functions Malawian courts are courts that were generally considered to be unaffected by the capture that appears to have affected the prosecution agencies. More pertinently, the majority of Malawians regard the courts as impartial and trustworthy in respect of their involvement in the 2019 election cases.[33]

Despite the constraints that prosecutorial choices place on courts' decision-making autonomy, the judiciary retains significant decisional discretion in

---

32 For the full text of the judgment, see *The State v Inspector General of Police et. al. ex. p. M.M. et. al.*, https://malawilii.org/mw/judgment/high-court-general-division/2020/24 [13 .8.2020].

33 Most Malawians see legal challenge to election results as justified, courts as impartial and trustworthy, http://afrobarometer.org/press/most-malawians-see-legal-challenge-election-results-justified-courts-impartial-and-trustworthy [4.2.2020].

determining the appropriate punishment to be imposed on any person convicted of acts of election violence. This autonomy empowers courts to impose sentences that deter further commission of crime, thereby promoting a conducive environment for democratic governance. Understanding the deterrent effects of sentencing decisions in election violence cases in Malawi depends on qualitative and quantitative assessments of the certainty, swiftness and severity of sentences that are beyond the scope of this paper. Suffice it to highlight a number of key indicators that emerged in relation to cases arising from the 2019 and 2010 elections.

Most incidents of election violence did not result in the trial and prosecution of offenders. Although this largely reflected investigative and prosecutorial inefficiencies and biases, some of the delays were attributable to delays in judicial proceedings. Although the judiciary has sought to improve the speed with which election cases are resolved by, among other things, adopting rules of procedure to expedite the hearing of civil election cases,[34] it has not done the same for criminal "election cases", including prosecutions for election violence. For example, at the time of writing, trials had been either not concluded or commenced with respect to the vast majority of reported incidents including some which occurred over four years ago. In the few criminal trials which were concluded, judges did not impose severe sentences that reflected the far-reaching negative effects of election violence on the country's democratic governance.

Legal Responses and Democratic Governance

The current normative framework on which legal responses to election violence are based consists of constitutional guarantees of human rights, including the right to life, personal security and property; the Penal Code, which defines a wide range of criminal offences, including those which involve violence; the Parliamentary and Presidential Elections Act, which criminalises the use of violence to prevent any person from registering as a voter, damaging campaign material which is lawfully displayed, using or threatening force to compel any person to sign or not sign any nomination paper and unlawfully destroying any official election document.

34 Civil Procedure Rules 2017. For the first time in the country's legal history procedural rules include a section dealing specifically with election cases.

The gaps in the legal definition of election violence, selective law enforcement and prosecutions and operational inefficiencies of legal institutions and processes in the legal responses to violence connected to the 2019 and 2020 elections undermined the constitutional principle of the rule of law, which is an essential element of democratic governance as provided for by section 12 of the Constitution. The gaps resulted in insufficient regard for the far-reaching political effects of electoral violence. Proportionality of legal actions is a key element of the principle of the rule of law which is itself one of the pillars of democratic governance.

On its part, selectivity and bias in legal responses to election violence affects democratic governance in Malawi in at least two respects. First, it undercut the liberal democratic principle of equality before the law which is guaranteed by the Constitution of Malawi. Among other things, the Constitution prohibits discrimination,[35] requires "all institutions and persons" to comply with the Constitution[36] and provides that "no institution or person shall stand above the law".[37] Secondly, selectivity of legal responses limits the potential deterrent effect of the law because offenders who are affiliated to the party in government are virtually certain that they will not be investigated, prosecuted or tried. Confident in their perceived *de facto* immunity, such actors perpetrate violence with impunity and thus continue to create an unfavourable environment for democratic governance.

On their part inefficiencies in investigative, prosecutorial and judicial processes are evident in the inordinate delays in the conclusion of cases. Delays in criminal justice processes are not peculiar to cases involving election-related violence. Institutions that are responsible for implementing the processes, such as the Malawi Police Service, the Director of Public Prosecutions and the courts, perennially face resource constraints on their capacity to perform their functions. However, in respect of election violence cases, delays may also be occasioned by the interests and power relations that influence investigative and prosecutorial decisions in favour of the party in government. Such delays limit the deterrent effect of the legal rules that prohibit election violence since swiftness of the criminal justice process is one of the three features of effective

35 Section 20.
36 Section 12(1)(f).
37 Ibid.

deterrence, the other two being certainty of apprehension, trial, conviction and sentence, and the severity of the punishment.

Conclusion

Legal responses to violence connected to the 2019 and 2020 Malawian elections were characterised by selective application of the law, inordinate delays in investigative and judicial processes and doctrinal limitations on the sentencing of offenders. These features reflected the capture of law enforcement agencies by the party in government, limited capacities of law enforcement and judicial agencies and the doctrinal gap in recognising election violence as a *sui generis* offence. The character of the legal responses limited their contribution to democratic governance and, in some cases, undermined some of its critical elements, including human rights, the rule of law and accountability. Further empirical research is required to facilitate deeper analysis of the interplay between violence, elections, democratic governance and law.

Chapter 6

Violence against Women in Elections in Malawi: The Role of Women Leaders as Game Changers

Anthony Jeckson Malunga,
Ngcimezile Mbano-Mweso
& Bernadette Wangisa Malunga

Introduction

This chapter investigates the role of women leaders in challenging violence against women in elections (VAWE) in Malawi during the May 2019 tripartite elections. We identify three main categories of women leaders for analysis. The first category is that of women in political leadership. The second category is of civil society women's rights activists. The last category is of women leaders in constitutional bodies with the legal mandate to act against VAWE, such as the Ombudsman and commissioners in the Malawi Human Rights Commission. The aim is to identify those women leaders who exercised agency to challenge or curb VAWE, what they did specifically and whether they can be regarded as game-changers or not.

VAWE is a global problem that negatively impacts democracy, human rights, gender equality and security.[1] During elections, violence against women is mainly used as a tool to undermine or prevent them from participating as candidates, voters, election officials, observers, activists, political party members and campaigners or organisers. The violence may be sexual, physical and psychological and may include misogynistic and sexist verbal attacks. Such violence can be perpetrated by a family member, community member, political opponent and/or by the state. In Malawi, women face inequality in their political participation including political violence.[2] For instance, there is evidence of VAWE during and after the May 2019 elections which thrived for

---

1 UN Women/United Nations Development Programme (UNDP), "Preventing Violence against Women in Elections: A Programming Guide", 2017, www.unwomen.org/en/digital-library/publications/2017/11/preventing-violence-againstwomen-in-elections.

2 Inge Amundsen and Happy Kayuni, *Women in Politics in Malawi*, Bergen, Norway: Chr. Michelsen Institute (CMI), 2016.

months due to street protests that followed the announcement of the election results. VAWE was mainly instigated by political parties especially by the then ruling Democratic Progressive Party (DPP).[3]

Addressing VAWE requires interventions from a host of actors and changes in individual and institutional discriminatory behaviours and attitudes.[4] Women leaders have a crucial role to play in providing force and influence in the effort to end VAWE. This is not to say that women are a homogeneous group; however, women's leadership presents an opportunity to uplift women's rights. Women leaders are "agents who have diverse valued goals and commitments on behalf both of themselves and of their society".[5] It is believed that women leaders are often more likely than their male colleagues to act for women or women's interests.[6] Efforts of women leaders to curb VAWE are essential because the reduction or elimination of any form of violence against women and girls requires concerted effort from a large body of committed and vocal leaders.[7] This notwithstanding, some women leaders—due to institutional, political and personal factors and interests—do not use their positions to contribute to curbing VAWE. For instance, some women may be coerced by 'real power' holders to undermine efforts in advocating for change or promotion of women's rights.[8] Women leadership, therefore, does not automatically translate to greater action or influence towards the promotion of women's rights. Other challenges for women leaders include institutional limitation regarding mandate and resources, but also competing discourses or demands of conflicting prescriptions such as self-interest and competitive push

---

3 OHCHR, "Press briefing notes on Malawi", 25 January 2019, spokesperson for the UN High Commissioner for Human Rights, Rupert Colville.

4 Mona Lena Krook, "Violence against Women in Politics", *Journal of Democracy*, 28/1 (2017), 74–88.

5 Amartya Sen, "Well-Being, Agency and Freedom: The Dewey Lectures", *The Journal of Philosophy* 82/4 (1985), 169-221 [203].

6 Sara Angevine, "Representing All Women: An Analysis of Congress, Foreign Policy, and the Boundaries of Women's Surrogate Representation", *Political Research Quarterly* 70/1 (2017), 98-110.

7 C. García-Moreno, C. Zimmerman, A. Morris-Gehring et al., "Addressing Violence against Women: A Call to Action", *Lancet*, 25/385 (2015), 1622.

8 K. Wollack, "Women as Agents of Change: Advancing the Role of Women in Politics and Civil Society", National Democratic Institute before the House Committee on Foreign Affairs Subcommittee on International Organizations, Human Rights and Oversight, June 9, 2010, www.ndi.org/sites/default/files/Women_As_Change_Agents_Testimony_090610_0.pdf. See also Candice D. Ortbals et al., *Gender and Political Violence: Women Changing the Politics of Terrorism*, Cham: Springer, 2018), 26.

for status.[9] Other studies have shown that sometimes the initial collective goal or focus can be to advance women's rights, but once in leadership, the interest to ensure re-appointment or re-election or retention in leadership position may divert attention from the initial goal of protecting women's rights.[10]

In interrogating the role of women leaders in challenging VAWE during the 2019 elections, the chapter will examine the kind of contribution made by the women leaders and whether any of the women leaders emerged as game-changers. Such examination is important because it highlights women leaders' experience and performance when they are in positions of power, including their substantive representation of other women. In order to answer these questions, the study employed qualitative methods of data collection. The study relied on key informant interviews to provide lived experiences for Malawian women leaders and this was complemented by a literature review. We identified 10 key informants purposively by mainly looking at the key informants' position with regard to VAWE. The interviews targeted women in political leadership (3), women who were heading NGOs dealing with VAWE (4) and women heading constitutionally constituted human rights organisations (3). The literature review involved reading and analysing books, journal articles, newspapers and research reports on VAWE and the role of women leaders as game-changers on the same. Due to limited literature on activities of women leaders as game-changers in the Malawian context, we relied on literature from elsewhere.

In the category of political or executive branch leaders, the chapter first identified three women leaders. Among them were the chairperson of the Parliamentary Women's Caucus, who, at the time, was leading the cross-party group of women parliamentarians from all political parties represented in the National Assembly. We also identified the Minister of Gender, Children, Disability and Social Welfare (Minister of Gender) as a potential game-changer. The ministry responsible for gender is particularly mandated to promote gender equality and protect the welfare of Malawian women, men, girls and boys to become self-reliant and active participants and beneficiaries of the national

9 Tyler G. Okimoto and Victoria L. Brescoll, "The Price of Power: Power Seeking and Backlash against Female Politicians", *Personality and Social Psychology Bulletin* 36/7 (2010), 923-936. See also Sandra Grey, "Numbers and Beyond: The Relevance of Critical Mass in Gender Research", *Politics & Gender* 2/4 (2006), 492– 502.

10 Chiweza, Wang and Maganga, "The Women's Parliamentary Caucus: Promoting Cross-Party Substantive Representation 2016", 33-40, www.cmi.no/publications/5820-acting-jointly-on-behalf-of-women

development agenda.[11] The Minister of Gender during the 2019 elections was a woman and her position and functions placed her as a potential game-changer in curbing VAWE.

Civil society women`s rights activists were the next to be identified as potential game-changers because of their power to influence change in society. Three women leaders in women's rights organisations were selected. These women belonged to NGO-Gender Coordination Network (NGO-GCN), Women Lawyers Association (WLA) and Women Legal Resources Centre (WORLEC) which leads the Women's Manifesto Movement (WMM). The NGO-GCN is also an umbrella body for 51 women's rights organisations. The WLA is made up of women lawyers in academia, law students, paralegals, some judicial officers and honorary male lawyers. The WMM is a grouping of various civic society organisations on women's rights and is led by a female executive director from WORLEC.

The last category of women leaders to be selected was those from constitutional bodies. This included the current Ombudsman and four female commissioners who are part of the Malawi Human Rights Commission, which has seven commissioners in total.

The chapter is organised into four main sections. The introductory section summarises the purpose of the paper, followed by a section on the conceptual framework to formulate what constitutes VAWE and how women leaders can exercise their agency to become game-changers in challenging VAWE. The third section details VAWE incidences that were reported in Malawi before, during and after May 2019 elections. This is followed by a final section that analyses and discusses women leaders' responses to the reported incidences of VAWE. The conclusion then follows.

Violence against Women in Elections (VAWE)

Elections are an important pillar of democratic governance. Significant advances have been made by women in democratic political life around the globe and in African countries. This notwithstanding, VAWE remains a global problem.[12] Violence against women in elections is a component of the broader

---

11 Government of Malawi, National Gender Policy, Lilongwe, 2015.

12 Mona Lena Krook and Juliana Restrepo Sanín, "Violence Against Women in Politics A Defense of the Concept", XXIII/2 (2016), *Política y Gobierno*, 459, 467. See also Mona Lena

concept of political violence against women and girls (PVAWG). PVAWG encompasses several distinct but related issues in the "exercise of political competition and governance in democratic states or democratisation process",[13] whilst VAWE focuses exclusively on the electoral dimension of PVAWG.[14] International Foundation for Election System (IFES) has defined VAWE as "any harm or threat of harm committed against women with the intent and/or impact of interfering with their free and equal participation in the electoral process during the electoral period."[15] VAWE therefore focuses on that violence that targets women during the entire electoral process including before, during and after electoral process.

VAWE is directed at a woman because she is a woman and is rooted in unequal power between men and women.[16] It is used to reinforce gender hierarchies. VAWE mainly manifests itself in three elements.[17] First, it consists of aggressive acts aimed largely or solely at women in politics. These aggressive acts may be physical, emotional and psychological in nature. Second, the violence is meted out to women because they are women and perpetrators often use gendered means of attack. Lastly, the violence is with the goal of deterring their participation in order to preserve traditional gender roles and undermine democratic institutions.[18] Efforts to impede women's political participation are not new as many societies around the world have long associated men with the "public sphere" of politics.[19] Women are thus often regarded as interlopers in the "male" space of politics, giving rise to various forms of hostility towards female leaders.[20] VAWE may be committed in the home or other private spaces as well as in public spaces. Acts of violence are directed at

---

Krook and Juliana Restrepo Sanín, "Gender and Political Violence in Latin America: Concepts, Debates, and Solutions", *Política y Gobierno*, XXIII/1 (2016), 125-157 [127].

13 See also Mona Lena Krook and Juliana Restrepo Sanin, "The Cost of Doing Politics? Analyzing Violence and Harassment against Female Politicians", *Perspectives of Politics* 18/3 (2019).

14 National Democratic Institute, "What Is Violence Against Women in Politics?", www.ndi.org/reporting-violence-against-women. See also Krook and Restrepo Sanin, "The Cost of Doing Politics?", 128.

15 IFES, Violence against Women in Elections: A Framework for Assessment, Monitoring and Response, 2017.

16 Krook and Restrepo Sanin, "The Cost of Doing Politics?".

17 Mona Lena Krook, "Violence Against Women in Politics", in M. Sawer, F. Jenkins, K. Downing (eds), *How Gender Can Transform the Social Sciences*, Cham: Palgrave Pivot, 2020.

18 Mona Lena Krook, "Violence against Women in Politics", 76.

19 Ibid.

20 Ibid.

women in any of their roles as electoral stakeholders such as voters, media, political actors, state actors, community leaders, and electoral officials.[21] The violence comes in six different forms. The violence may be physical, sexual, psychological, economic, verbal and symbolic. Physical violence involves harm inflicted on the body of female political actors or their family members and may comprise domestic abuse, beating, abduction, and even assassination. Sexual violence consists of sexual acts and attempts at sexual acts by coercion, including unwelcome sexual comments or advances. Examples of sexual violence include sexual harassment, rape, and sexual exploitation.[22] Psychological violence is that violence which entails hostile behaviour and abuse intended to cause emotional damage. Such violence includes threats of bodily harm, threats of rape, stalking, character assassination, and social boycotts among others. Economic violence refers to degradation and coercion through control over access to economic resources. Verbal violence is the use of offensive or sexist words with the intention to undermine women's political actions. Symbolic violence captures abuse and aggression at the level of portrayals that seek to deny women's competence as political actors. This may come in the form of highly sexualised images of women in media platforms.[23] According to Krook and Sanin, these are all aimed at making political engagement so difficult that female participants withdraw on their own accord.[24] We engage with all these types of violence and discuss how women leaders lacked agency or exercised agency to challenge these forms of violence as game-changers.

Game-Changers

According to Swilling, the notion of game-changer refers to "a structural determinant or social actor or anything else that implies some kind of inherent agency".[25] Structural determinants are the focus of transition studies and social innovation scholars that conceptualise game-changers as macro-phenomena (events, trends and developments) that change the "game" of societal

---

21 IFES, Violence against Women in Elections: A Framework for Assessment, Monitoring and Response. 2017.

22 Ibid.

23 Mona Lena Krook, "Violence against Women in Politics", 79.

24 Krook and Restrepo Sanin, "The Cost of Doing Politics?".

25 Mark Swilling, "Africa's Game Changers and the Catalysts of Social and System Innovation", *Ecology and Society* 21/1 (2016), 37.

interaction (the rules, fields and players).[26] For scholars like Tembo and Chapman, writing on social accountability, game-changers, also called interlocutors of change, are "the organisations or individuals with the 'game-changing' characteristics that are necessary to address, or contribute to a specific collective action problem".[27] Game-changers choose to act in a way that makes change possible by seizing opportunities that present themselves to them. Thus game-changing is the ability to make significant changes.[28] As such, game-changers are broadly conceptualised as societal actors who facilitate events and trends that are perceived to make a difference in understandings, values, institutions and social relationships.[29] The actions of game-changers may eventually lead to the emergence of (diverse) alternative narratives and practices, in response to the systemic framing of events. As catalysts of change, the game-changers do not work separately from social action but through collective action, based on alternative narratives that become aligned with one another through common criticism and shared values.[30] The game-changers "are able to bring together various other players to contribute to finding solutions to specific collective action problems".[31]

From the above conceptual definition, our understanding of women game-changers includes individuals and organisations led by women that initiated action against or in response to VAWE as a social problem. We, therefore, engage the concept of game-changer in this chapter to interrogate the kind of change that woman leaders brought to tackle VAWE in the 2019 elections. It must be noted, however, that women leaders may be limited in their game-changing role by both formal and informal institutions that shape and constrain institutional actors' behaviour, thus defining the parameters of what action is

---

26 Flor Avelinoa, Julia M. Wittmayer, Bonno Pel et al., "Transformative Social Innovation and (dis)Empowerment", *Technological Forecasting and Social Change* 145 (2019), 195.

27 Fletcher Tembo and Jenny Chapman, "In Search of the Game Changers: Rethinking Social Accountability", *Overseas Development Institute Discussion Paper*, 2014, 9, www.odi.org/sites/odi.org.uk/files/odi-assets/publications-opinion-files/9381.pdf, [20.2.2021].

28 Will Kenton, "Game Changer", *Investopedia*, August 2020, www.investopedia.com/terms/g/game-changer.asp.

29 Flor Avelino, Julia M. Wittmayer, René Kemp and Alex Haxeltine, "Game-changers and Transformative Social Innovation: The Case of the Economic Crisis and the New Economy", *Society* 22/4 (2014). See also C. Cipolla et al., "Coproduced Game-changing in Transformative Social Innovation: Reconnecting the "Broken City" of Rio de Janeiro", *Ecology and Society* 22(3) (2017), 3.

30 Avelino, Wittmayer, Kemp and Haxeltine, "Game-changers", 41.

31 Fletcher Tembo and Jenny Chapman, "In Search of the Game Changers: Rethinking Social Accountability", 11.

possible and intelligible.[32] Women leaders may, therefore, fail to be game-changers where there is no autonomy or necessary conditions and opportunities to enhance their ability to help themselves, and also to influence the world.[33] Further, merely having women in positions or bodies that offer opportunities to act and advance women's rights does not guarantee that they will represent fellow women's interest. Solidarity and consensus cannot be assumed.

The chapter pinpoints a range of actions that identifies women leaders as game-changers. Feminist activists find that identifying and naming a problem is a crucial first step in mobilising for change.[34] If a problem is not recognised, it will not receive the needed attention and effort for its resolution. Further, beyond identification of the problem, the actors must also map its manifestations, raise awareness and devise interventions.[35] There should also be campaigns and protests to stop the violence and adoption of legal reforms to prevent and respond to the violence.[36] The chapter, therefore, interrogates the commitment of women leaders to curb VAWE and further assesses the methods that these women leaders used to tackle this problem.

The next section discusses the types and forms of violence that women suffered during 2019 before, during and after the elections in Malawi, before looking at women leaders' potential game-changing activities.

Survey of Incidents of Violence against Women in the 2019 Elections

Malawi reported a number of cases of politically motivated violence prior to, during and after the disputed May 2019 tripartite elections. A survey by Afrobarometer revealed that more Malawians reported fearing and experiencing violence during protests or political rallies in 2019 than in 2017. The survey results indicated that 4 out of 10 (42%), 19% male and 23% female, said they had feared such violence during the previous two years, including 16% (17% male and 15% female) who said they had actually experienced the

32 Michael Chasukwa, "The Gender Machinery: Opportunities and Challenges for Women in Central Government", in Inge Amundsen and Happy Kayuni (eds), *Women in Politics in Malawi*, Blantyre: Political Administrative Studies and Chr. Michelsen Institute, 2016, 105-115.

33 Amartya Sen, *Development as Freedom*, New York: Alfred Knopf, 1999, 18–19.

34 Mona Lena Krook, "Global Feminist Collaborations and the Concept of Violence Against Women in Politics", *Journal of International Affairs* 72/2 (Spring/Summer 2019), 77-94.

35 Mona Lena Krook, "Violence against Women in Politics", 74-88.

36 J. Piscopo, "State Capacity, Criminal Justice, and Political Rights: Rethinking Violence against Women in Politics", *Politica y Gobierno* 23/2 (2016), 437–58.

violence.[37] The proportion of citizens experiencing violence at a political rally or protest doubled between 2017 and 2019.[38]

Violence targeting women was also reported where women were threatened, attacked and harassed. Generally, political violence seemed to have been normalised, as perpetrators of violence and their acts of violence were displayed and executed with the full knowledge of the public and law enforcement agencies and condoned by the authorities.[39] Acts of violence were mainly perpetrated by agents of the then ruling Democratic Progressive Party (DPP) against women who were their political opponents. It is reported that the DPP youth wing known as "cadets" enjoyed impunity as they considered themselves above the law. They were, thus, able to openly carry machetes and other types of dangerous weapons in full view of the police and public, while clad in party colours and emblems of their organisation.[40]

Before and during Election Violence

Malawi registered various forms of political violence against women before and during the May 2019 tripartite elections. The type of violence that women suffered was gender based aimed at silencing the individual women to whom violence was directed and other women who would witness or hear of the violence. Some incidences of political violence against women towards the 2019 tripartite elections occurred when political parties were conducting their party primary elections in the year 2018. Female candidates in the primary elections faced threats, harassment and intimidation.[41] Such violence mainly constituted physical and emotional or verbal violence. For instance, the 50-50 Management Agency reported to have received 30 complaints relating to primary elections disputes in the period from December 2018 to January 2019. Among others, the women reported facing verbal insults and derogatory remarks through songs. Female candidates also reported that their property was

---

37 Afrobarometer, Round 8 Survey in Malawi 2020, Centre for Social Research, University of Malawi.

38 Afrobarometer, "Malawians Support 2019 Post-Election Demonstrations but Split on Government Power to Limit Protests", April 2020, https://media.africaportal.org /documents/ab_r8_dispatchno354_malawians_support_postelection_protests_UPS9h65.pdf.

39 Moses Mphatso, "Aftermath of the Malawi General Election of May 2019 (Part 1) – Court Petitions and Large Protests", Sept, 2019, https://medium.com/@traffique/aftermath-of-the-malawi-general-election-of-may-2019-part-1-85f8363a97e3.

40 Ibid.

41 OHCR, "Press briefing notes on Malawi", 2019, www.ohchr.org/EN/NewsEvents /Pages/DisplayNews.aspx?NewsID=24119&LangID=E.

vandalised.[42] The European Union Election Observation Mission (EU Mission) also observed that women aspirants faced many hurdles in seeking candidacy, notably during primaries, and in the conduct of their campaigns, including being the targets of demeaning language.[43] The EU Mission report identified a case where the DPP Director for Elections and Cabinet Minister at the time, Ben Phiri, used defamatory language against former First Lady and the United Transformation Movement (UTM) founding member, Shanil Patricia Dzimbiri-Muluzi.[44]

Apart from attacking individual women politicians, family members of the women politicians were also attacked during the election period. For instance, a member of the then ruling party (DPP) whose wife had defected to another political party was humiliated at a political rally. At the rally, he was made to stand while a party official castigated his wife, calling her an idiot: "You know sometimes it happens that you are a good husband but it just happens that you married an idiot who drinks water used for shaving."[45]

The physical violence took the form of arson attacks, stripping women of clothes and barring women from participating in political and election activities such as campaigns. For instance, the local newspapers reported the torching of a vehicle belonging to a senior female party parliamentarian belonging to one of the opposition political parties called UTM.[46] Physical violence also took the form of assaults. In one incident, the ruling DPP cadets assaulted members of the opposition UTM, and forced a woman to take off a UTM-branded T-shirt leaving her in her underwear.[47]

---

42 Malawi Electoral Support Network (MESN), "Malawi Electoral Support Network (MESN) Pre-Election Statement on the 2019 Tripartite Elections", 2019, www.congoma.mw/wp-content/uploads/2019/05/MESN-Pre-Election-18-May-2019-Statement-vF-PDF.pdf.

43 European Union Election Observation Mission Malawi, "European Union Election Observation Mission Malawi", 2019, file:///C:/Users/User/Downloads/EUEOM%20Preliminary%20Statement%20-%20Malawi%202019%20-%20FINAL.pdf.

44 Ibid.

45 O. Khamula, June 2018, "Mchacha Faces Sharp Criticism for Insulting Kaliati Family", www.nyasatimes.com/mchacha-faces-sharp-criticism-for-insulting-the-kaliati-family/s.

46 *Nyasatimes*, "Hundreds March in Malawi to Oppose Violence against Women: submit Petition" 2019, www.nyasatimes.com/hundreds-march-in-malawi-to-oppose-political-violence-against-women-submit-petition.

47 OHCR, "Press briefing notes on Malawi", 2019, www.ohchr.org/EN/NewsEvents/Pages/DisplayNews.aspx?NewsID=24119&LangID=E.

Post-election Violence

In the aftermath of the 2019 general election, the country went through a series of protests mainly led by the Human Rights Defenders Coalition (HRDC), an umbrella body for civil society organisations focusing on human rights. The protests started soon after the results of the elections in May 2019 and did not stop until the elections were annulled by the High Court sitting as a Constitutional Court in February 2020. The objective of the protests was a relentless demand for the resignation of Malawi Electoral Commission (MEC) members and in particular its chairperson, Justice Dr Jane Ansah, on the grounds that they had mismanaged the election. The protests were popularly known as the Anti-Jane Ansah demonstrations. Some of the protests degenerated into deadly and destructive clashes with the police and ruling-party cadres.

The post-election violence against women targeted two categories of women. The first was the violence against female police officers who were part of the law enforcement team during the protests. These were seen to be agents of the then ruling party by the protesters. The second category was the violence experienced by women protesters or connected to the protesters at the hands of law enforcement agencies. In the first scenario, violence was perpetrated by protesters against law enforcement agents and female law enforcement officers were physically attacked. During the post-election period, militant factions formed; some broke out from the protesters to seek out property (homes, houses and businesses) of politically connected people to vandalise and burn. Police officials living in different communities were attacked in their homes, prompting some landlords in those communities to issue evictions without notice to police tenants for fear of having their houses attacked and burned.[48] The protesters are on record to have perpetrated violence against a female law enforcement officer during the protests. The female police officer was beaten and undressed while carrying out her duties during the Anti-Jane Ansah demonstrations.[49] It is worth noting that although male police officers experienced physical abuse, none of them were ever undressed. The female

---

48 Mphatso Moses Kaufulu, "Aftermath Of The Malawi General Election Of May 2019 (Part 1)", September 2019, https://iaffairscanada.com/2019/aftermath-of-the-malawi-general-election-of-may-2019-part-1.

49 *MBC Online*, "Worlec Denounces Undressing of Malawi Female Detective", August 2019, www.mbc.mw/opinion/item/8412-worlec-denounces-undressing-of-malawi-female-detective

police officer was targeted because she was a woman and the protesters chose the type of violence that would be most humiliating for women.

The second incident in the post-election violence concerns the violence which was experienced by female protesters or females connected to the protesters. One notable incident happened when, during one of the protests, demonstrators set up roadblocks in the capital city of Lilongwe, which led to the deployment of the police. In the pandemonium that followed, a male police officer was killed. Security officers stormed the area the following day, spraying teargas and attacking the public.[50] It was reported by the Malawi Human Rights Commission (MHRC), that several women were raped, sexually assaulted and harassed by the police during this operation. The report of the MHRC indicates that 18 women were sexually violated. Four of the survivors were children below the age of 18; one of these was defiled and the other three were indecently assaulted.[51] Sexual violence directed at women who were politically connected was therefore used to silence women in general and to punish their spouses and male relations who were taking part in the demonstrations. According to the Malawi Ombudsman, Martha Chizuma, the sexual assaults by the police were politically motivated: "From the time we did the investigations, we observed that, some of the women who were raped were targeted for being members of the then opposition party (Malawi Congress Party) as they were spotted in their party colors on the day of the ordeal."[52]

The above section has shown the types of violence that women faced during the May 2019 tripartite elections. It has been shown that the perpetrators of the VAWE employed types of violence that could only be felt by women in a profound way. The next section will analyse the response of women leaders to all the incidents of violence discussed above and answers the question as to whether their response would inscribe them as game-changers.

---

50 *The Guardian*, "Malawi Protesters Demand Inquiry into Allegations of Rape by Police Officers", 2019, www.theguardian.com/global-development/2019/oct/25/malawi-protesters-demand-inquiry-into-allegations-of-by-police-officers.

51 Malawi Human Rights Commission, "Investigation Report into the Alleged Rape, Defilement and Indecent Assault by Police Officers on Some Women and Girls in Lilongwe West (M'bwatalika, Kadziyo and Mpingu Areas)", Lilongwe, 2019.

52 Individual Interview with Malawi Ombudsman, Martha Chizuma, Lilongwe, July 2020.

Analysis of Responses of Women Leaders to VAWE in the 2019 Elections

There were a number of avenues women leaders explored in their response to VAWE. Overall findings identified from interviews point to the following measures categorised as: (i) education and mass awareness raising; (ii) documentation of violence cases and engagement of specific duty-bearers like leaders of political parties; (iii) organising and mobilising women and other interest groups to protest and march in solidarity against the violence and demand redress; (iv) seeking legal justice for the rights violations; (v) real-time recording and linking action on violence cases through the gender situation room and working with lawyers; (vi) media engagement to name and shame and vi) lobbying key duty bearers for action.[53] As already stated, the study focuses on three main categories of women leaders namely those in political leadership, civil society and constitutional bodies. The analysis will look at how these leaders responded during the different phases of the electoral process.

Pre-election and During Election Violence Response

As the physical, sexual, psychological and verbal abuses occurred during this period, some women leaders exercised agency to challenge this unfortunate state of affairs while others did nothing. We begin by looking at what civil society women did before looking at women leaders in politics and those in constitutional bodies. Civil society women leaders utilised several mechanisms to challenge or curb the violence. Firstly, they relied on education, mass awareness raising and media engagement both at local and national levels to prevent VAWE before and during the election period. Private media, such as Zodiak Radio and Television Stations, were used to raise awareness on the need to identify, report and shun any form of violence against women. The WMM led by WORLEC Executive Director Maggie Kathewera-Banda undertook the above initiative. The NGO-GCN led by Barbara Banda initiated engagement with the political party leaders, especially Secretary Generals and presidential candidates. The political party leaders signed undertakings to promote violence-free elections and the protection and respect of women's rights in general.

---

53 Key Informant Interviews with Malawi's Ombudsman, 5050 Management Agency Leader, NGO-Gender Coordination Network Leaders, Lilongwe, July 2020.

The civil society women leaders, together with other partners, also organised and mobilised women and other groups of interest to protest and march in solidarity against the violence that was happening. The marches happened in all the major cities, namely Lilongwe, Blantyre, Mzuzu and Zomba.[54] There were also marches and demonstration organised in other parts of the country, like Mangochi and Karonga. The civil society women leaders with support from different partners also made press statements besides presenting petitions to duty-bearers demanding the arrest and prosecution of the attackers and all others involved in VAWE. They also demanded redress for the victims and spoke of the negative impact of such acts in the pursuit of gender equality and women's participation in elections.

During the same period, a street protest was also organised by women leaders representing all major political parties (the cross party women leaders) under the leadership of the then chairperson of the Women Caucus in Parliament, Hon. Jessie Kabwila.[55] The street march was made under the theme "I refuse to be beaten and undressed for participating in politics." The street protest happened in the capital city, Lilongwe, where a petition was presented to relevant government officials. The petition made demands on the president, the Inspector General of Police and the Ministry of Gender, Children, Disability and Social Welfare. The protesters also demanded redress and a stop to violence against women politicians. The street protests were also an expression of disapproval and served to bring attention to the escalating political violence and impunity due to government inaction. At this point, no arrests were made even though there was a video regarding the case of the Mangochi UTM woman, who was stripped naked by perpetrators who were clearly identifiable. The protest was also a show of solidarity as senior female figures from all the five major political parties contesting in the elections came together to demand duty-bearers' responsiveness to the problem.[56] They each made

---

[54] Interviews with the Women's Rights Advocate under the 50:50 Management Campaign, Lilongwe, July 2020.

[55] *Nyasatimes*, "Hundreds March in Malawi to Oppose Political Violence against Women: Submit Petition", 29 January 2019, www.nyasatimes.com/hundreds-march-in-malawi-to-oppose-political-violence-against-women-submit-petition.

[56] J. Mphanda, "Women Protest against Political Violence", 23 January 2019, https://malawi24.com/2019/01/23/women-protest-against-political-violence/; see also Penelope Paliani-Kamanga, "Malawians Protest against Stripping of Women", 4 February 2019, https://southerntimesafrica.com/site/news/malawians-protest-against-stripping-of-women.

pledges to ensure that their respective political parties would contribute to ensuring the end of VAWE.

The coming together of the different organisations, senior female political figures from all the five major political parties and women from different walks of life was unprecedented.[57] As a result, there was an immediate response from the president and the Malawi Police Service. The president publicly condemned the perpetuation of VAWE while the Malawi Police Service effected arrests on some of the suspected perpetrators. This was a big win for the protestors and demonstrators.

For the women leaders in politics led by Jessie Kabwila, the protests were the only publicly recorded action in response to the violence, while the women civil society leaders and their organisations continued to pursue elimination of VAWE through other means. The women civil society leaders partnered with members of the legal fraternity including WLA, which was under the leadership of Tadala Chikwenzule. The initiative involved the creation of a gender situation room where there was real-time recording and linking action on political violence cases with lawyers. Cases of violence against women on election day were being received, recorded and referred to specific lawyers who were designated to follow up and take action.[58] This was an important aspect of redress to ongoing violence during the voting day. Women lawyers from WLA were also available for women candidates in the campaign period to help address any violence-related issues through legal services including litigation where necessary. Despite their availability, their service was not very adequate and did not bring any meaningful change as observed by NGO-GCN: "The women lawyers were offering their services, but this was not enough as some of the women politicians complained that they were not able to access their service when they needed them."[59] Although the initiative did not meet the expected goal, it was a good strategy and essential in ensuring justice for victims to access legal action on their complaints to curb the violence.

From the efforts analysed above, the two women civil society leaders from the WMM and NGO-GCN demonstrated great commitment and agency in tackling violence against women before and during elections. They emerged as

---

[57] Sarai Chisala "Insulting the Modesty of a Woman and the Push by the Woman's Movement in Malawi", available at https://africanfeminism.com/insulting-the-modesty-of-a-woman-and-the-push-by-the-womens-movement-in-malawi/.

[58] Interview, NGO-Gender Coordination Network Leader.

[59] Ibid.

game-changers through the multiple strategies used in tackling different aspects of VAWE. They utilised the opportunity presented to them to exercise agency and to make a difference. They provided awareness and knowledge to the masses, identified and named the problem, demanded accountability from duty-bearers and suggested means for redress for the victims. For WLA, although the leader did exercise agency, the action taken cannot be regarded as game-changing as it was not fully implemented to contribute to significant change at this point.

As regards the women political leaders, besides action by Jessie Kabwila, the others did not publicly react or respond to the VAWE. However, even with Jessie Kabwila, her action of organising a street march stopped at one of the repertoires of political action, namely protests, but did not go beyond. According to Dalton and others, although protests provide citizens with an avenue through which they express their interests and demands, it should be just one of the repertoires of political action.[60] We conclude that this cannot be regarded as game-changing as it did not contribute to significant change.

In the category of women leaders within constitutional bodies, there was limited opportunity to influence change because of lack of meaningful action towards addressing the problem of VAWE. For instance, the Ombudsman, Martha Chizuma, in an interview recalled that the issue of the woman who was undressed in Mangochi during pre-election period was brought to MHRC's attention (where she is a Commissioner) and it was recorded for possible follow-up.[61] Unfortunately, no action was made on the matter as other competing events came up and the complainants never followed up the matter with the commissioners or MHRC. Thus, the MHRC commissioners and the Ombudsman as female leaders failed in their role as potential game-changers by not following through their mandate to investigate cases of VAWE. This was as a result of institutional limitations. Overall, for the constitutional bodies, the Malawi Human Rights Commission and the Ombudsman at this point did not contribute much in addressing or condemning the pre-election political violence. This was because commissioners were only appointed on 25 March 2019 and were, thus, new in office and as such there are no statements or

---

60 R. Dalton et al., "The Individual-Institutional Nexus of Protest Behaviour", *British Journal of Political Science*, 40/1 (January 2010), 51-73.

61 Ombudsman, Martha Chizuma, Interview.

reports on their work dealing with pre-election violence.[62] Furthermore, there was a challenge in court on two newly appointed female commissioners as they had not been appointed from a prescribed list of names as per requirement of law.[63] As a result of this challenge, commissioners did not begin their work until after elections and hence could not have exercised game changing activities.

Women Leaders' Post-election Violence Response Analysis

Women leaders employed a number of responses to the post-election violence faced by women. The responses employed included administrative, civil and legal measures and tools. First, women leaders from state institutions and civil society organisations took administrative action by naming and shaming those perpetrating post-electoral violence against women. This was done through various media platforms, such as mass and print media. For example, the violence that was perpetrated on the female police officer by protesters was condemned collaboratively by various women leaders, including those from the NGO-GCN and WMM.[64] These women leaders deplored the undressing of a female police officer working in the Criminal Investigations Department (CID) who was carrying out her duties during the 6 August 2019 Anti-Jane Ansah demonstrations organised by HRDC.

The executive director from WOLREC demanded, for example, that the HRDC and political leaders who were part and parcel of the protests should put in place measures that would guarantee safety of women during protests. This female leader further demanded that the Malawi Police Service investigate and bring to book perpetrators of the violence. Similarly, the Minister of Gender also condemned the act and issued a statement indicating that the ministry had noted with great concern that a policewoman, who was in the line of duty, was beaten and undressed in Lilongwe on 6 August 2019.[65] Despite these efforts to condemn the post-electoral violence, its effectiveness depended on the goodwill of the perpetrators of violence or organisations that were in charge of the protests. More often, it was observed that protestors would listen

---

62 P. Kumbani, "New rights commissioners hired", *The Nation*, 2019, www.mwnation.com/new-rights-commissioners-hired/.

63 J. Mwale, "Court stops MHRC appointments", *The Nation*, 2019, www.mwnation.com/court-stops-mhrc-appointments.

64 NGO-Gender Coordination Network Leader, Interview.

65 MBC Online, "Worlec Denounces Undressing of Malawi Female Detective",' August 2019, www.mbc.mw/opinion/item/8412-worlec-denounces-undressing-of-malawi-female-detective

to women leaders from civil society organisations like WMM rather than female leaders from the Ministry of Gender. The female leaders from the Ministry of Gender were seen to be partisan and siding with women's issues that only affected victims belonging to the then ruling party, DPP. Thus, for the same action, the female leader from WMM would be deemed a game-changer while the Minister of Gender (Hon. Mary Navicha) could not be described as a game-changer.

For example, it is reported that the militant groups which arose from the protests had public sympathy despite inflicting political violence.[66] This was due to the fact that the Minister of Gender and indeed the law enforcement agencies, especially the Malawi Police Service, sided with the ruling DPP and MEC. Thus, the Minister of Gender, despite condemning the violence against women, lacked legitimacy to do the same. As one interviewee states, "The Minister responsible for Gender was conflicted, her perception of issues was biased and she did not provide guided leadership for tackling all forms of violence regardless of political inclinations."[67]

In further responding to post-election violence, the Ombudsman, Martha Chizuma, serving as a commissioner for MHRC, facilitated investigations on issues of VAWE and provided recommendations to duty-bearers. She investigated the sexual assault incidents perpetrated against women during the Anti-Jane Ansah demonstrations in Lilongwe. The investigation report made a number of recommendations to key government agencies. The Malawi Police was asked to institute criminal investigations into the matter and prosecute the perpetrators of the sexual assaults, which did not happen up to mid-2020 and no one had been arrested or prosecuted months after the allegations were made. Furthermore, the Chief Justice was tasked to have special arrangements for an expedited trial of the sexual assault cases. This recommendation depended on the conclusion of the investigations and the arrest of the perpetrators, which had not happened. The third recommendation was made to the Ministry of Gender, Children, Disability and Social Welfare to immediately facilitate counselling the survivors and their families and that the

---

66 M. Kaufulu, "Aftermath of the Malawi General Election of May 2019 (Part 1)" September 2019, https://iaffairscanada.com/2019/aftermath-of-the-malawi-general-election-of-may-2019-part-1.

67 Individual Interview with 5050 Management Agency Leader, Lilongwe, July 2020.

ministry should include survivors of sexual violence on the list of beneficiaries of social cash transfer.[68] The ministry is yet to abide by these recommendations.

The approach taken by the Ombudsman through MHRC to conduct a thorough investigation into the sexual violence emanating from political violence demonstrated a game-changer action and had a lot of merit. First, the investigations helped to unearth and document the happenings of the political violence and its particulars. Second, the investigations pointed out what went wrong, who was in the wrong and what needed to be done. As such, the investigations clearly identified the victims, the perpetrators, the duty-bearers and the remedies to the sexual assaults. However, from the reflections of the Ombudsman, the process of coming up with the report was very difficult on her part as she had to work less with MHRC secretariat which was not cooperative due to political influence and other vested interests against the process. She relied on technical support from Commissioner, Gertrude Hiwa and few female staff at the commission secretariat.[69] Further, the report only made recommendations but had no legal mandate of enforcing the recommendations which thwarted their game-changer role. At the same time, due to the inaction of the Malawi Police, there was no opportunity for the Ministry of Gender and Judiciary to demonstrate whether they were game-changers or not on this matter. It can be argued that on matters of VAWE, whose redress action depends on many players, the game-changer role depends on the sustained commitment of all institutions in the service chain.

Furthermore, there were civic action and solidarity marches organised by some of the women leaders in the post-election period. Women in Malawi, especially from the ruling DPP and the executive arm of government, marched in defence of the MEC Chairperson, Jane Ansah. The protesters were of the view that Ansah was being targeted with insults on social media and other platforms because she was a woman. For instance, a long-time prominent women's rights activist, Seodi White (then working in government as a Reforms Director under Office of President and Cabinet), formed a solidarity group named Forum for Concerned Women in Malawi, which organised the march supporting Ansah. White stated that the women were not protesting for Ansah alone but that they were also unhappy with the abuse that had spread to all women in the name of Dr Jane Ansah: "We are saying we are not tolerating it. It's enough. And we are

---

68 Malawi Human Rights Commission, 2019.

69 Ombudsman, Martha Chizuma, interview.

saying Jane Ansah should not fall nor resign, she is standing. She cannot dance to the whims and wishes of the people who are disgruntled."[70]

On observation, these protests were not effective given the organisers had seemingly taken a partisan narrative. As a result, the Anti-Jane Ansah protests continued in earnest after these demonstrations. The protests were also met with heavy criticism with critics accusing the organisers of selective advocacy for women's rights injustices. To that extent, while Forum for Concerned Women had an opportunity to bring a different point of view, they failed to become game-changers due to narrow partisan and selective advocacy on the plight of women.

In furthering action on the 18 women who were raped by the Malawi Police, women leaders from Women Lawyers Association also took a legal measure to deal with this political violence against women. They lodged a complaint with the court on behalf of the 18 women who were sexually assaulted by the police in Lilongwe.[71] The women lawyers accused the police of not investigating and prosecuting the sexual assaults. The women lawyers claimed compensation on behalf of the sexually assaulted women and asked the court to compel the state to investigate, arrest and prosecute the perpetrators. The court in this case delivered its judgment and ordered the state to compensate all 18 women and also to conduct investigations and prosecute perpetrators of the sexual assaults. As such, the women lawyers by their action and outcome are considered game-changers that facilitated change and enabled women victims of political violence to get much needed relief for their suffering.

Game-Changers

This far, the chapter has looked at the subject of violence against women in politics, the situations of violence before, during and after the 2019 elections in Malawi. Women in politics during the election experienced different forms of violence solely because they were women to deter them from participating in elections or to undermine democracy. The type of violence experienced was also gendered, portraying sexist thinking to undermine women's competence or exercise of their rights.

---

70 Cit. Masina, 2019.

71 *The State vs The Inspector General of Police and Others*, Judicial Review Cause No. 7 of 2020.

A key issue in this chapter was to interrogate the role of women leaders as game-changers by exercising agency to contribute to collective action against VAWE. Women leaders in political positions, civil society organisations and constitutional bodies all had opportunity to exercise agency against VAWE. However, only one category of women leaders emerged as game-changers. The women leaders in political positions did not emerge as game-changers. Their actions during the 2019 elections as regards VAWE were insignificant; they undertook only public protests and issuing of statements to condemn specific violence. They did not condemn all VAWE but focused on violence perpetuated against them or their parties or allies. They may be deemed to have failed to utilise their opportunity to make a difference due to the conflicts in political interests. The opportunity for women leaders from constitutional bodies to become game-changers was constrained due to institutional limitations but they did make a contribution by naming and investigating such violence as a human right violation. They too did not emerge as game-changers. The game-changers were the women leaders in civil society category who relied on several strategies to name, identify, condemn and respond to VAWE. They exercised agency collectively with others to contribute to curbing VAWE. There utilised their positions to exercise agency.

Conclusion

This chapter has reflected on the different situations of violence in the period from late 2018 to 2019 and the reactions of women leaders, women's rights organisations and the institutions led by women. We have shown that some women leaders qualified as game-changers, some did not. Thus, we conclude that to an extent some did represent women issues in such a way as to curb VAWE substantively while others did not. There were constraints that affected their opportunity to be game-changers due to conflicts in political interests, non-responsiveness of duty-bearers and institutional limitations among others. The women leaders used mixed methods to address VAWE with successes in some and failures in others. From this chapter, one can conclude that women's rights advocates, leaders and institutions can be game-changers to the extent of their action on VAWE. Their success hinges on personal choice, enabling environment and collective action in curbing VAWE.

Chapter 7

Malawi's Choice of Electoral System and Reform Agenda Quandary

Ernest Thindwa

Introduction

The use of simple plurality or first-past-the-post (FPTP) as the electoral system of choice for Malawi and the need for change have been fiercely contested over the years. Since the 1999 elections, when Gwanda Chakuamba of the Malawi Congress Party (MCP) unsuccessfully challenged the re-election of Bakili Muluzi on grounds that the declared winner did not attain the required majority as provided for by the Republican Constitution, calls for electoral reforms have been relentless. The drive to migrate from plurality to absolute majority (or 50%+1 vote) acquired new impetus after the 2014 general elections. In 2017, efforts to migrate to the 50%+1 vote electoral rules in readiness for the 21 May 2019 presidential election were thwarted in Parliament by the ruling Democratic Progressive Party (DPP). No sooner had Peter Mutharika of the DPP been declared the winner of the May 2019 presidential election with the narrowest of margins in Malawi's electoral history (38% against 36% for 2nd placed) than the legal challenge championed by opposition leaders, Saulos Chilima of United Transformation Movement (UTM) and Lazarus Chakwera of the MCP, began. The legal challenge was premised primarily on suspected electoral fraud and the legitimacy question.

The court and subsequent parliamentary proceedings were not without drama. A panel of five Constitutional Court judges nullified the 21 May 2019 presidential elections on 3 February 2020 on grounds of grave irregularities and failure to amass a majority vote. The Constitutional Court ordered not only Fresh Presidential Elections (FPE) within 150 days of the ruling but also the enactment of enabling legislation to operationalise use of the 50%+1 vote requirement.[1] Section 80(2) of the Constitution states that: "The President shall be elected by a majority of the electorate through direct, universal and equal

[1] *Daily Times*, 4 February 2020.

suffrage." The Presidential and Parliamentary Election Act (PPEA) 1994 section 96(5) states that: "The candidate who obtained a majority of the votes at the polls shall be declared by the commission to have been duly elected."

Mutharika of the DPP and the Malawi Electoral Commission (MEC) as first and second respondents respectively appealed against both the Constitutional Court nullification of the presidential election and the interpretation of the majority votes. A panel of seven Malawi Supreme Court of Appeal judges, sitting on 8 May 2020, upheld almost in its entirety the Constitutional Court ruling to nullify the presidential election, the interpretation of the constitutional provision of majority electorate, and the holding of FPE within 150 days of the Constitutional Court ruling.[2] In response to the Constitutional Court directive, Parliament tabled and passed the Presidential and Parliamentary Amendment Bill 2020 between 20 and 24 February 2020, which set the date for FPE and provided for the two-round system for presidential elections. The amendment bill was not assented to by President Peter Mutharika who alleged illegality in the bill process as he was still challenging, at the Supreme Court of Appeal, the Constitutional Court interpretation of majority provided for in section 80(2) of the Constitution.

When Malawians went to the polls for the FPE on 23 June 2020, there were genuine fears of a constitutional crisis in the event that none of the candidates amassed the required votes for outright victory. Lazarus Chakwera of MCP standing as a torch bearer for Tonse Alliance, an electoral alliance of nine parties, was declared the winner with 59.33% of votes against 39.92% for the second-placed, Peter Mutharika of the DPP who formed an electoral coalition with the former ruling party United Democratic Front (UDF). In spite of Malawi holding a successful FPE amidst glaring gaps in the legal framework, the threat of an electoral outcome related constitutional crisis had not been contained.

While recognising that the electoral reform agenda in Malawi has been multifaceted and a response to perceived credibility, legitimacy and representativeness challenges of electoral outcomes, this chapter focuses on the legitimacy question and raises key governance questions. For instance, what was the rationale for the choice of FPTP and what has been its effect on regime legitimacy? What was fuelling the attempt to move away from plurality and what kind of reforms have been suggested? Who was driving the reform agenda

2 *The Weekend Nation*, 9 May 2020.

and what were the motivations? What are the prospects for the reform agenda and implications?

The rest of the chapter is structured as follows. A review of literature on electoral reforms is presented to provide theoretical insights to understanding Malawi's experience with reforms. This is followed by a discussion on the rationale for Malawi's initial choice of FPTP and its effects on political legitimacy. Suggested electoral reforms, drivers of the electoral reform agenda and their motivations are discussed. The chapter concludes by evaluating prospects for the widely desired electoral reform outcomes and their implications.

Literature Survey

Whilst scholarship on democratisation and elections is unlimited, these studies have focused on effects of electoral rules on political stability and development rather than the justification for the establishment of electoral institutions.[3] Mehler laments the lack of systematic research on effects of different electoral systems on the quality of political regime, development of party system, civil liberties or political party organisation.[4] Mehler's concern is echoed by Hartmann who suggests limited understanding of African electoral institutions and claims authoritatively that scholarly inquiry on the justification for electoral system choice has only attracted scanty attention.[5] Hartmann shows further frustration when he observes that while electoral system reform has been a common feature of political and scientific debates in central and eastern Europe, and Southeast Asia, scholarly discourse on suitable electoral system typology for Africa has not only been a recent occurrence in few countries but also limited in scope and rarely leading to fully fledged change in the overall

3 See Christof Hartmann, "Paths of Electoral Reforms in Africa", in Andreas Mehler, Matthias Basedeu and Gero Erdmann (eds.), *Votes, Money and Violence: Political Parties and Elections in Sub-Saharan Africa*, Scottsville: University of KwaZulu-Natal Press, 2007, 144-67 [146]; Andreas Mehler "Political Parties and Violence in Africa: Systematic Reflections against Empirical Background", in Mehler, Basedeu and Erdmann (eds.), *Votes, Money and Violence*, 194-221 [196]; S.I. Lindberg, "Consequences of Electoral System in Africa: a Preliminary Inquiry", *Electoral Studies* 24 (2005), 41-69 [41]; Andrew Reynolds and Timothy D. Sisk, "Elections and Electoral Systems: Implications for Conflict Management", in Timothy D. Sisk and Andrew Reynolds (eds), *Elections and Conflict Management in Africa*, Washington: United States Institute of Peace Press, 1998, 9; Donald L. Horowitz, *South Africa: Constitutional Engineering in a Divided Society*, Berkeley: University of California Press, 1991, 115-27.

4 Andreas Mehler "Political Parties and Violence in Africa".

5 Christof Hartmann, "Paths of Electoral Reforms in Africa", 145.

electoral equation.[6] He warns that electoral reform in Africa tends to be both a thorny process and a hotly contested national discourse.

Examination of the types of electoral reforms can be a decisive springboard from which to dissect the nature of contestations on electoral reforms on the continent. The literature points to the existence of two distinct but equally important electoral rules which have been a target for reformists with varying success levels.[7] The first set is concerned with *electoral governance* and relates to the administrative process of registering voters and candidates, organising the ballot, regulating electoral campaigns and party financing, formulating a candidate and observer code of conduct, counting votes amid handling of electoral complaints. The second set, which relates to *electoral rules,* depicts the way in which voters express political preference for a party or a candidate and a method by which votes are translated into parliamentary seats or into governmental offices. Hartmann observed that whereas electoral governance reforms in Africa have been numerous and relatively successful, reforms on electoral rules have not just been few but also limited in scope and less successful in respect of intended outcomes.[8]

The work by Kaiser quoted in Hartmann distinguishes three types of possible institutional reform outcomes.[9] The first probable outcome reflects *institutional conservatism* which depicts reform initiatives as a confirmation of the status quo. The second probable outcome described as *path-dependent institutional reform* occurs when initiatives lead to changes which do not alter the logic of the existing set of rules. The third and last probable outcome is identified as *path-change institutional reform* and occurs when initiatives lead to adoption of institutions that depart significantly from the logic of the preceding set of rules. Whereas the second outcome highlights the tendency to learn from and build on the country's own institutional history, the third outcome shows the willingness to learn from foreign political systems. The most likely reform outcome is not so much dependent on its appropriateness for a given polity for the reform process. As Hartmann argues, electoral institution reform is not a technical and abstract initiative but largely a reflection of competing strategic

---

6 Ibid.

7 See Shaheen Mozaffer and Andreas Schedler, "The Comparative Study Electoral Governance", *International Political Science Review* 23/1 (2002), 5-24.

8 Christof Hartmann, "Paths of Electoral Reforms in Africa", 145-46.

9 Ibid.

interests of political actors involved in the reform process.[10] Most scholars concede that better electoral institutions do not necessarily secure the survival of democracy but consensus exists among institutionalists suggesting electoral rules are critically significant in shaping political strategies of the actors competing for the right to govern and representation, especially in emerging democracies.[11]

A number of scholars argue that analysis of an electoral system or reform of the same should not be limited to main types of electoral system (plurality, majority, proportional, mixed) and their variants, but extend to their effects on party system function, essentially because political parties are perceived as critical lynchpins between societies and their respective governments.[12] From a linking device perspective, three party system functions are distinctly identified.[13] These functions include a blockade of social cleavages, a translation of social cleavages into political cleavages and social cleavages aggregation. Work by the Institute for Democracy and Electoral Assistance (IDEA) published in 2008 shows that conscious design of electoral system in response to particular historical and social conditions of a country is a rarity. The question of interests is whether the electoral system choice and reform agenda in Malawi emanated from the desire to shape the political party system in a manner that secures and consolidates democratic gains.

Rationale for Electoral Choice in Malawi

The choice of simple plurality or FPTP as an electoral system in Malawi cannot be construed as resulting from a conscious effort to shape party system functions in a manner that enhances and sustains democratic governance in multi-ethnic Malawi. Indications suggest adoption of FPTP was a definitive outcome of both attitudes of institutional conservatism and path-dependent practices. Until the Constitutional Court ruling on 3 February 2020 which nullified the 21 May 2019 presidential elections, Malawi had employed FPTP as an electoral system in the first five rounds since political liberalisation in 1994. Like most former British colonies on the continent (see Table 7.1),

---

[10] Ibid.

[11] Ibid.

[12] Matthijs Bogaards, "Crafting Competitive Party Systems: Electoral Laws and the Opposition in Africa", *Democratization* 7/4 (2000), 163-190 [169].

[13] Ibid.

Nyasaland, as Malawi was then called, maintained the use of the plurality system.

Table 7.1: *Electoral systems in the first competitive elections in selected countries*

Electoral system	Former British Colony	Former French Colony	Former Portuguese Colony	Others
Plurality in MMC	Mauritius	Djibouti		
Plurality in SMC	Botswana, Gambia, Ghana, Kenya, Lesotho, Malawi, Swaziland, Tanzania, Uganda, Zambia, Zimbabwe	Côte d'Ivoire in 1961 when for the first time the black majority were granted the right to vote in electing a government owing to pressure for political independence.[14]		Ethiopia
Other majoritarian systems		Cameroon, Madagascar		
Absolute majority in SMC.MMC		CAR, Chad, Comoros, Gabon, Mali, Mauritania, Togo		Sudan
Segmented	Seychelles	Guinea, Senegal		
PR in small MMC		Burkina Faso, Niger	Cape Verde, Guinea Bissau, São Tomé	Burundi, Equatorial Guinea
PR in medium and large MMC		Benin	Angola, Mozambique	
Pure PR	Sierra Leone			Liberia, Namibia, South Africa

Source: *Nohlen, Krennerich and Thibaur (1999) modified by Hartmann.*

14 Edge Kanyongolo "The Constitution", in Nandini Patel and Lars Svasand (eds), *Government and Politics in Malawi*, Lilongwe: Capital Printing Press, 2013, 37-57 [41].

The process of decolonisation was concluded in 1964 with the adoption of a new Constitution declaring Nyasaland as the independent Republic of Malawi. Within two years of independence in 1964, the country moved from a parliamentary to presidential system of government and declared a one-party state in 1966.[15] The windows of opportunity to reform electoral institutions provided by the change of system of government in 1964 and the adoption of a relatively liberal Constitution in 1994 following the third wave of democratisation across the African continent and beyond were hardly exploited. The plurality system endured from 1961 until 2019 and could not attract attention in national discourse even during the constitutional review process of 1994.

When asked why the electoral system was not an issue in the constitutional redesign discourse in early 1990s given its significance in regulating political competition, an academician who was one of the facilitators of the constitutional review conference stated that: "Simple plurality was the only electoral system we knew as a country." His sentiments were echoed by the first chairperson of the Public Affairs Committee (PAC), a body established in 1993 to manage the transition from 30 years of one-party rule to political pluralism and facilitate constitutional redesign negotiations between MCP as an advocate of one-party state on one hand and the two pressure groups, Alliance for Democracy (AFORD) and United Democratic Front (UDF), which were advancing the cause of political liberalisation, on the other hand. Institutional conservatism reigned supreme during constitutional redesign negotiations.

Traces of electoral policy transfer from the European powers to their respective colonies on the continent are evident. Table 7.1 above shows that except for the Seychelles and Sierra Leone, all former British colonies opted for plurality as used for elections in the United Kingdom. Similarly, most former French colonies settled for absolute majority in keeping with French electoral tradition. While most British colonies including Malawi shifted from the parliamentary system obtaining in Britain to a presidential system soon after independence, plurality electoral systems endured. Electoral institutions transfer from Western powers to former colonies without regard for their effects on governance in societies with culturally diverse and historically competing groups, is a situation that has tended to threaten statehood in a number of ways as explained below.

---

15 Ibid.

Effects of Plurality Electoral System on Regime Legitimacy in Malawi

The use of plurality in Malawi has had a profound effect on the political legitimacy of various regimes. The political legitimacy of most administrations between 1994 and 2019 had been brought into question on a number of counts. First, the winning candidate for the presidential race in three electoral cycles (1994, 2004, 2014) out of five secured the right to govern with a narrow mandate, thereby bringing the legitimacy question to the fore (see tables 7.2 to 7.7).

Table 7.2: *1994 Presidential Election Results Summary*

Candidate name	Party	Region						National	
		North		*Centre*		*South*			
		Votes	%	*Votes*	%	*Votes*	%	*Votes*	%
Kamuzu Banda	MCP	33,650	7.3%	743,739	64.27%	218,964	16,09%	996,353	33.43%
Chakufwa Chihana	AFORD	404,837	87.8%	86,766	7.5%	71,259	5.23%	562,862	18.9%
Kamlepo Kalua	MDP	1,754	0.38%	5,161	0.44%	8,709	0.64%	15,624	0.52%
Bakili Muluzi	UDF	20,837	4.52%	321, 581	27.79%	1,062,336	78.04%	1,404,754	47.15%
Total		461,078	100%	1,157,247	100%	1,361,268	100%	2,979,593	100%
Region vote share		461,078	15.47%	1,157,247	38.84%	1,361,268	45.69%	2,979,593	100%

Table 7.3: *1999 Presidential Election Results Summary*

Candidate name	Party	Region						National	
		North		***Centre***		***South***			
		Votes	%	Votes	%	Votes	%	Votes	%
Gwanda Chakuamba	MCP	573,688	88.61%	1,124,359	62.42%	408,743	18.45%	2,106,790	45.17 %
Kamlepo Kalua	MDP	5,673	0.88%	27,240	1.51%	34,943	1.57%	67,856	1.45 %
Bakili Muluzi	UDF	61, 130	9.44%	634,912	35.25%	1,746,6 43	78.85%	2,442,685	52.38 %
Bingu wa Mutharika	UP	1,112	0.17%	6,701	0.37%	14,260	0.64%	22,073	0.47 %

Daniel Nkhumbwa	CONU	5,806	0.9%	8004	0.45%	10,537	0.48%	24,347	0.52%
Total		647,409	100%	1,801,216	100%	2,215,126	100%	4,663,751	100%
Region vote share		647,409	13.88%	1,801,216	38.62%	2,215,126	47.5%	4,663,751	100%

Source: Tabulation from MEC (1999) presidential election official results.

***Table 7.4**: 2004 Presidential Election Results Summary*

Candidate name	Party	Region						National	
		North		***Centre***		***South***			
		Votes	%	Votes	%	Votes	%	Votes	%
Gwanda Chakuamba	RP	373,539		98,407		363,972		835,918	24.95%
Justin Malewezi	Ind	5,240		36,399		26,173		67,812	2.02%
Brown Mpinganjira	NDA	18,472		41,721		226,127		286,320	8.55%
Bingu Mutharika	UDF	93,441		309,537		792,628		1,195,606	35.68%
John Tembo	MCP	17,776		915,283		31,906		964,965	28.8%
Total		508,468		1,401,347		1,440,806		3,350,621	100%
Region vote share		508,468	15.18%	1,401,347	41.82%	1,440,806	43.%	3,350,261	100%

Source: Tabulation from MEC (1999) presidential election official results.

***Table 7.5:** 2009 Presidential Election Results Summary*

Candidate name	Party	Region						National	
		North		*Centre*		*South*			
		Votes	%	Votes	%	Votes	%	Votes	%
Bingu Mutharika	DPP	634,973		853,073		1,256,664		2,744,710	66%
Kamuzu Chibambo	PETRA	2,435		13,301		17,077		32,813	0.78%
Loveness Gondwe	NARC	3,931		12,092		13.493		29,516	0.70%
Stanley Masauli	RP	2,081		14,070		15,209		31,360	0.75%
Dindi Gowa Nyasulu	AFORD	3,910		5,936		9,535		19,381	0.46%
James Nyondo	INP	1,951		11,493		12,292		25,736	0.61%
John Tembo	MCP	20,588		695,503		561,331		1,277,422	30.7%
Total		669,869		1,605,468		1,885,601		4,160,918	100%
Region vote share		669,869	16.1 %	1,605,468	38.58%	1,885,601	45.32 %	4,160,938	100%

Source: Tabulation from MEC (1999) presidential election official results.

***Table 7.6:** 2014 Presidential Elections Results Summary*

Candidate name	Party	Region						National	
		North		*Centre*		*South*			
		Votes	%	Votes	%	Votes	%	Votes	%
Joyce Banda	PP	445,551	56.25%	275,511	13.54 %	334,574	14.94%	1,055,636	20.83 %
L. Chakwera	MCP	136,737	17.26%	1,252,130	61.53 %	67,013	3%	1,455,880	28.73 %
K. Chibambo	PETRA	3,459	0.44%	8,229	0.40 %	7,672	0.34%	19,360	0.38%
John Chisi	UP	2,271	0.29%	4,435	0.22 %	5,369	0.24%	12,075	0.24%

F. Jumbe	NLP	1,041	0.13%	2,746	0.13%	5,032	0.22%	8,819	0.17%
A. Katsonga	CCF	674	0.09%	1,653	0.08%	5,077	0.23%	7,404	0.15%
Mark Phiri	PPM	1,521	0.19%	3,737	0.18%	15,722	0.70%	20,980	0.41%
Atupele Muluzi	UDF	21,264	2.68%	154,997	7.62%	540,987	24.16%	717,248	14.16%
P. Mutharika	DPP	173,119	21.86%	321,448	15.8%	1,242,913	55.51%	1,737,480	34.3%
George Nnesa	MAFUNDE	1,167	0.15%	3,337	0.16%	6,528	0.29%	11,032	0.22%
James Nyondo	NASAF	3,763	0.48%	3,812	0.19%	3,007	0.13%	10,582	0.21%
Helen Singh	UIP	1,469	0.19%	3,030	0.15%	5,169	0.23%	9,668	0.19%
National total		792,036	100%	2,035,065	100%	2,239,063	100%	5,066,164	100%
Region vote share		792,036	15.63%	2,035,065	40.17%	2,239,036	44.2%	5,066,164	100%

Source: Tabulation from MEC (2014) presidential election official results.

Table 7.7: *2020 Fresh Presidential Elections Results Summary*

Region	**Candidate name and party**						**Regional vote share**
	Lazarus Chakwera (MCP)		***Peter Kuwani (MMD)***		***Peter Mutharika (DPP)***		
	Votes	*% of total votes*	*Votes*	*% of total votes*	*Votes*	*% of total votes*	
Northern Region	516,515	87.05%	6,763	1.14%	1,751, 878	11.81%	13.52%
Central Region	1,711,887	89.07%	10,548	0.55%	199,465	10.38%	43.8%
Southern Region	375,641	20.05%	15,145	0.81%	1,482,356	79.14%	42.68%
National Total	2,604,043	59.33%	32,456	0.74%	1,751, 878	39.92%	100%

Source: Tabulation from MEC 2020 fresh presidential election official results

Tables 7.2 to 7.7 show that except for 1999 and 2009, winning presidents in the post-1994 period only amassed at the utmost 47% of the total votes, with the lowest percentage being 34.3% recorded in 2014. In the same year the narrowest of margins (5.64%) between the winner Peter Mutharika of DPP and the second-placed, Lazarus Chakwera of MCP, was recorded. The declining trend in percentage difference between the winner and the second-placed candidate when using the plurality system can be observed over the period (see tables 7.8 and 7.9).

***Table 7.8**: Presidential elections margins of victory (1994-2009)*

1994				
Candidate ranking		**Vote share %**	**% Difference from 50% mark**	**% Difference between 1st and 2nd**
1	Bakili Muluzi	47.15%	- 2.85%	13.72%
2	Kamuzu Banda	33.43%	- 16.57%	
3	Chakufwa Chihana	18.9%	- 31.1%	
4	Kamlepo Kalua	0.52%	- 49.48%	

1999				
Candidate ranking		**Vote share%**	**% Difference from 50% mark**	**% Difference between 1st and 2nd**
1	Bakili Muluzi	52.38%	2.38%	7.21%
2	Gwanda Chakuamba	45.17%	- 4.83%	
3	Kamlepo Kalua	1.45%	- 48.55%	
4	Daniel Nkhumbwa	0.52%	- 49.48%	
5	Bingu wa Mutharika	0.47%	- 49.53%	

2004				
Candidate ranking		**Vote share%**	**% Difference from 50% mark**	**% Difference between 1st and 2nd**
1	Bingu wa Mutharika	35.68%	-14.32%	6.88%
2	John Tembo	28.8%	- 21.2%	
3	Gwanda Chakuamba	24.94%	- 25.06%	
4	Brown Mpinganjira	8.55%	- 41.45%	
5	Justin Malewezi	2.02%	- 47.98%	

2009				
Candidate ranking		**Vote share%**	**% Difference from 50% mark**	**% Difference between 1st and 2nd**
1	Bingu wa Mutharika	66%	16%	35.3%
2	John Tembo	30. 7%	- 19.3%	
3	Kamuzu Chibambo	0.78%	- 49.22%	
4	Stanley Masauli	0.75%	- 49.25%	
5	Loveness Gondwe	0.7%	- 49.3%	
6	James Nyondo	0.61%	- 49.39%	
7	Dindi Nyasulu	0.46%	- 49.54%	

Source: Tabulation from MEC Presidential Elections summary results (1994-2009).

Table 7.9: *Presidential elections margins of victory (2014-2020)*

2014				
Candidate ranking		**Vote share**	**% Difference from 50% mark**	**% Difference between 1st and 2nd**
1	Peter Mutharika	34.37%	- 15.7%	5.64%
2	Lazarus Chakwera	28.73%	- 21.27%	
3	Joyce Banda	20.83%	- 29.17%	
4	Atupele Muluzi	14.16%	- 35.84%	
5	Mark Katsonga Phiri	0.41%	- 49.59%	
6	Kamuzu Chibambo	0.38%	- 49.62%	
7	John Chisi	0.24%	- 49.74%	
8	George Nnesa	0.22%	- 49.78%	
9	James Nyondo	0.21%	- 49.79%	
10	Helen Singh	0.19%	- 49.91%	
11	Friday Jumbe	0.17%	- 49. 83%	
12	Aaron Katsonga	0.15%	49.85%	

2020				
	Candidate ranking	Vote share	% Difference from 50% mark	% Difference between 1st and 2nd
1	Lazarus Chakwera	59.33%	+ 9.33%	19.41%
2	Peter Mutharika	39.92%	- 10.08%	
3	Peter Kuwani	0.75%	- 49.26%	

Source: Tabulation from MEC Presidential Elections summary results (2014-2020).

The shrinking margin of victory can be observed from 13.72% in 1994, when Bakili Muluzi of UDF edged out Kamuzu Banda of MCP, to 5.64% in 2014, being the difference between the winner Peter Mutharika of DPP and second-placed Lazarus Chakwera of MCP. The 2009 election stands out as an outlier, in which Bingu wa Mutharika of the DPP won with 66% registering a difference of 35.3% from the second-placed John Tembo of MCP.

The declining margin of victory in each successive election was associated with increasing post-election violence. Whilst protests against DPP's Peter Mutharika's victory in the nullified 21 May 2019 elections were fuelled by suspected massive electoral irregularities later confirmed by the Constitutional Court, the legitimacy question cannot be ignored in explaining rising political tension in each successive election. Mutharika was declared a winner with 38% of total votes as compared to 36% for second-placed MCP's Chakwera.[16] The slender margin of victory coupled with disproportionate support from one region out of three suggested the mandate of Mutharika and his DPP was not only narrow but also localised.

Secondly, political mobilisation in the absence of programme differentiation among political parties has tended to be along ethno-regional fault lines. Major parties in Malawi tend to attract disproportionate support from particular ethnic groups concentrated in a given geographic region, compelling scholars such as Karen Ferree, Donald Horowitz and Deborah Kaspin to conclude that elections in the country tend to be reduced to an ethnic and regional census.[17] Plurality provided the ethnic elite incentives to mobilise the electorate along ethno-regional frontiers. Tables 7.2 to 7.7 show regional-based voting patterns across all elections except that of 2009.

Thirdly and more significantly, the dominance of one region in politics has been evident when plurality is employed. Government alternation between regions was almost impossible as the region with numerical advantage was guaranteed victory. Since political liberalisation in 1994, five rounds of democratic elections (1994, 1999, 2004, 2009, 2014) produced a president from the most populous Southern region of Malawi (see tables 7.2 to 7.7 for regional vote share). In a country where political parties are used merely as instruments for political competition by ethno-regional political groupings, electoral victory or defeat has tended to be perceived largely as a win or loss for particular regions. Given the winner-takes-all character of plurality as an electoral system, political

---

16 Malawi Electoral Commission, 2019.

17 Karen Ferree and Jeremy Horowitz, *Identity Voting and Regional Census in Malawi*, Afrobarometer Working Paper No. 72, 2007; Deborah Kaspin, "The Politics of Ethnicity in Malawi's Democratic Transition", *Journal of Modern African Studies* 33/4 (1995), 595-620 [595].

liberalisation in 1994 created permanent winners and losers.[18] Except for 2009, when DPP's Bingu wa Mutharika secured a landslide victory, each electoral cycle has witnessed increasing levels of political tension and electoral violence tends to erupt immediately the winner of the presidential race is announced.

Close observation of the character of elections in Malawi suggests the country's democracy has been under increasing stress in each electoral cycle except for 2009. The scale of the strain on the country's democracy was revealed and reinforced during nine months of sustained violent electoral protests experienced between the 2019 nullified presidential elections and 2020 FPE. A survey of media coverage during the period demonstrated that protests were intense and widespread in the Northern and Central regions as opposed to the South, which experienced localised and less violent electoral protests limited to the metropolitan cities of Blantyre and Zomba. The variation in the character of electoral violence across regions mirrors deep-seated divisions along ethno-regional fault lines which continue to threaten the country's territorial integrity. The use of FPTP has not succeeded in either blocking mobilisation of the electorate along the ethno-regional divide or aggregating social cleavages in Malawi. Instead, it has not only produced administrations lacking a broad-based mandate but also reinforced ethnic and regional consciousness and polarisation, thereby threatening not only democracy as a desirable system of government but also the country's territorial integrity.

The Rationale for Electoral Reforms in Malawi

The rationale of electoral reforms in Malawi has been multifaceted. A look at both the 2015 report by the National Taskforce on Electoral Reforms (NTER) and the Law Commission Report (2017) suggests that electoral credibility, legitimacy of the elected government and societal representativeness of electoral outcomes have been the major concerns for reformists. The attention however is confined to reforms instigated by legitimacy concerns.

The first major challenge to plurality electoral rules was initiated by Gwanda Chakuamba of MCP who came second to the eventual winner Bakili Muluzi of UDF in the 1999 presidential elections. The legal challenge was premised primarily on the constitutional interpretation of "majority electorate". The electoral legislation (Constitution and Presidential and Parliamentary Elections

---

18 Earl Conteh-Morgan, *Democratization in Africa: The Theory and Dynamics of Political Transitions*, Westport: Praeger, 1997, 91-97.

Act) stated that the president shall be elected with a majority of votes but did not clarify whether it meant simple plurality or absolute majority. The interpretation by the Supreme Court of Appeal in the case of *Chakuamba and Others v the Attorney General and Others* (1999) was that majority votes meant simple plurality. The Supreme Court of Appeal in 1999 argued that the absence of legislation to provide for a two-round system lends credence to the view that framers of the Constitution settled on plurality electoral system.

The second major challenge to plurality emerged in the case of *Chilima and Chakwera v Mutharika and MEC* (2020), when the ruling by the Supreme Court of Appeal in 1999 was clarified by the Constitutional Court on 3 February 2020 with the latter interpreting the "majority electorate" provided for in section 80(2) of the Constitution to mean absolute majority or 50%+1 vote. The Constitutional Court argued that the 1999 Supreme Court of Appeal interpretation of majority electorate as simple majority was made *per incuriam* suggesting the determination did not take into account all critical factors. The Constitutional Court determination was upheld by the Supreme Court of Appeal on 8 May 2020. Both the Constitutional Court and Supreme Court of Appeal emphasised in their respective determinations the need for legitimacy of the elected government in securing democratic governance.

Review of the Law Commission Report (2017) and the 2015 report by the National Taskforce on Electoral Reforms suggests that legitimacy of the elected government had been the main theme that epitomised the voice of ardent advocates of electoral rules reform in Malawi. The agenda for reformists was primarily fuelled by presidential electoral outcomes often characterised by both a narrow mandate and disproportionate electoral support from a particular region.

Both the Law Commission and National Taskforce on Electoral Reforms reports stressed the dangers of exclusionary politics which were perceived to thrive on political party ascendancy to power through plurality without incentives for a broad-based mandate. In each electoral cycle incumbent regimes were viewed as dispensing disproportionate patronage to perceived loyal groups and regions to retain the right to rule at the expense of nation-building efforts, which partly explains increasing inter-ethnic and regional tensions.

However, the 2009 voting patterns for both the presidential and parliamentary elections suggested reducing the ethno-regional voting patterns to effects of the plurality electoral system, but this may be too simplistic. In 2009, Bingu wa Mutharika won the presidential election with 66%, with significant electoral support across all regions (see Table 7.8). An Afrobarometer survey (2009) and work by Ferree and Horowitz suggested that impressive economic performance coupled with a broad-based perception of regime inclusivity can significantly minimise ethno-regional voting patterns.[19] The trajectory to integrate social cleavages did not last long as ethnic and regional consciousness, which generally shape preference among electoral alternatives for majority voters, worsened in the subsequent election (see Table 7.9). Poor economic performance and widespread perception of exclusionary tendencies associated with the Peter Mutharika-led DPP regime may explain the resilience of ethno-regional voting patterns. Electoral reforms were seen as part of the solution to promote inclusivity and tame rising ethnic and regional tensions. Various actors have attempted to initiate electoral reforms in Malawi with limited success.

Drivers of Electoral Reforms in Malawi

Various actors with varying motivations and capacities have been instrumental in the progress of the electoral reform agenda or lack of it. Formal attempts to reform electoral institutions were first registered during the constitutional review championed by the Law Commission between 2004 and 2007. A more concerted effort on electoral reforms was observed after the 2014 tripartite elections when the initiative by the Malawi Electoral Support Network (MESN), a consortium of 29 local CSOs with an interest in electoral justice and the MEC, led to the formation of the National Taskforce on Electoral Reform to coordinate the electoral reform process (Law Commission Report, 2017).

Table 7.10: *Actors in electoral reforms in Malawi*

Nature	Actors
Political	Democratic Progressive Party (DPP), Malawi Congress Party (MCP), People's Party (PP), United Democratic Front (UDF)
CSOs	Malawi Electoral Support Network (MESN), National Initiative for Civic Education (NICE), Centre for Multiparty Democracy (CMD), NGO Gender Coordination Network, Public Affairs Committee (PAC)
Public	Law Commission, judiciary
Development partners	United Nations Development Programme (UNDP), National Democratic Institute (NDI)

Source: *Law Commission Report (2017).*

19 Karen Ferree and Jeremy Horowitz, *Identity Voting and Regional Census in Malawi*, 1t.

The taskforce attracted membership from the political parties, Civil Society Organisations (CSOs), development partners and the public sector (see Table 7.10 above).

The taskforce submitted its report to the Law Commission in January 2016, which in turn set up a Special Law Commission on the review of electoral laws. Specific actors, their roles and motivations in the reform agenda are discussed below.

Political Parties

Unlike CSOs, which proactively engaged in lobbying activities for electoral institutions reform, political parties assumed reactive and often competing roles. These political parties can be categorised into two. The first category relates to relevant (effective) parties. These parties include the DPP, MCP, UDF and People's Party (PP) on the basis of their performance in the presidential race and parliamentary strength in 2014 (see Table 7.9 and Table 7.11).

Table 7.11: *2014-2019 Party parliamentary strength and seat share*

Party	Northern Region		Central Region		Southern Region		National	
AFORD	1	3.03%	0	0%	0	0%	1	0.52%
CCF	0	0%	0	0%	1	1.4%	1	0.52%
DPP	6	18.18%	11	15.06%	32	45.07	49	25.52%
MCP	2	6.06%	46	63.01%	0	0%	48	25%
PP	15	45.45%	5	6.84%	8	11.26%	28	14.58%
UDF	0	0%	0	0%	15	21.12%	15	7.81%
Independents	9	27.27%	11	15.06%	30	42.25%	50	26.04%
Total	33		73		71		192	100%

Source: Tabulation from Malawi Electoral Commission (2019) official results.

The second category relates to smaller or ineffective parties which could neither win an election nor influence electoral outcomes; these include AFORD and CCF. Contrasting political parties' attitudes towards widely desirable migration from plurality to absolute majority were observed. Whereas minor or ineffective parties were unanimous in support of the intended reforms, relevant parties presented an objectionable position. Both the DPP and MCP, being the largest parties on the basis of presidential race performance and parliamentary strength in the last three electoral cycles (2009, 2014, 2019/2020), did not demonstrate keen interest to depart from the plurality electoral system during the period 2009 to 2019. Whilst the DPP was publicly opposed to migration from plurality to absolute majority, the MCP (according to CSO respondents) could only show publicly cautious support for such reforms under popular pressure. The adoption of absolute majority electoral system was rejected on two occasions. The first rejection was in November 2017 when the Constitution (Amendment) Bill no 27 was tabled. The amendment sought, among other matters, to provide for a second round of presidential elections in the event the first round did not produce an outright winner. The DPP- and MCP-dominated Parliament (see Table 7.11) rejected the amendment by 100 against 50 votes with 34 abstentions.[20] The second rejection was in February 2020 when in response to the Constitutional Court directive, Parliament passed the bill to adopt absolute majority only for it to be vetoed by President Peter Mutharika.

When asked about the DPP's position on the proposal to adopt absolute majority for the presidential elections, the party's Secretary General stated that: "It is not easy for the party to win an election with the 50%+1 vote requirement. Not only is it difficult to amass the required votes but also expensive for the party to run a two round campaign when required." This view, which was echoed by the Administrative Secretary of the MCP, was in sharp contrast to the position of minor parties, which placed their weight behind the proposed reforms. When asked why the PP would support the 50%+1 vote, the Publicity Secretary for the party responded that: "It gives us a chance to be in government," a position endorsed by the only legislator for another minor party, AFORD.

Whereas relevant parties, in pursuit of the mandate to govern, do not perceive political incentives beyond increased financial burden, minor parties view the 50%+1 vote requirement as providing a window of opportunity to make a claim on governmental powers whilst riding on the financial and political clout of the preferred relevant party for the electoral coalition.[21] In polities where absolute majority is employed and parties are clientelists as opposed to being programmatic, political entrepreneurs with a remote chance of victory compete

---

20 *Parliament of Malawi Hansard*, 2017.

21 Dieter Nohlen, *Elections and Electoral Systems*, New Delhi: Macmillan India Limited, 1996, 7.

in the first round with the view to sell their respective constituencies to the highest bidder between the two major parties competing in the second round. The contrasting incentive structure or lack of it for minor and relevant parties respectively reveals competing positions on the 50%+1 vote threshold.

Both rational and historical institutionalists contend that institutions such as electoral systems are not readily amenable to change. Rational institutionalists, for instance, assert that the normal state of politics is one in which the rules of the game are stable, actors learn the rules and adjust their strategies to maximise their utility (self-interest), consequently setting in motion an institutional equilibrium.[22] Changing rules is therefore resisted primarily because it entails enormous uncertainties, making calculation of the sum effect difficult. Historical institutionalists, however, explain the state of institutional inertia differently with less stress on self-interest as the primary causality. State capacities and path-dependent habits are viewed as chief determinants for policy choices or their redesign, with the latter perceived as a fertile ground for policy legacies.[23] When institutionalist lenses are employed, explaining the reluctance of relevant parties in Malawi to support reforms that alter the electoral formula becomes relatively obvious.

The widely desired change of electoral law was only secured in September 2020 during President Chakwera‘s administration. Parliament passed both the Constitution and Presidential and Parliamentary Elections Act Amendment Bills, which demanded that the president be elected by an absolute majority while maintaining plurality for parliamentary elections. The broad-based parliamentary support for the amendment bills this time around suggested both sides of the political aisle had sufficient incentives. Chakwera's administration was ushered in by the Constitutional Court, which ordered an absolute majority requirement, and legislators including those in opposition won seats through plurality, which was retained for parliamentary elections. Studies suggest politicians rarely change electoral institutions through which they secured the right to political office.[24]

---

22 Sven Steinmo, "The New Institutionalism", in Paul Barry Clark and Joe Foweracker (eds), *The Encyclopaedia of Democratic Thought*, London: Routledge, 2001.

23 Hall, P.A. and R.C. Taylor, Discussion paper presented to MPIFC Scientific Advisory Board, 1996.

24 J. Foweraker and T. Landmann, "Constitutional Design and Democratic Performance", *Democratization* 9/2 (2002), 43-66; Sven Steinmo, "The New Institutionalism"; Donald L. Horowitz, *South Africa*.

Civil Society Organisations

Civil Society Organisations (CSOs) have been the main sponsors of the electoral reform agenda. MESN championed the quest for electoral reforms when its 2014 post-election review necessitated a consultation meeting, which gave birth to the National Taskforce on Electoral Reform tasked to map out a collective plan of action to achieve desired electoral reforms. The taskforce was co-chaired by MESN and MEC. Analysis of the report reveals the taskforce was motivated primarily by the desire to enhance the credibility of the electoral process, legitimacy of the elected government and the societal representativeness of electoral outcomes. The reforms the CSOs were advancing can broadly be categorised into two.

The first category was the legal aspect, which sought to enhance the legitimacy of the elected government and increase the representation of women in Parliament. Whereas reforms for increased women representation were limited to amendment of the relevant legislation, the legitimacy question was seen at the time as requiring constitutional amendment. The second category of desired reforms was administrative in nature and aimed largely at enhancing electoral credibility. Improvement in electoral process from voter registration through vote count monitoring to the announcement of electoral results was the main objective.

The role of CSOs has generally been that of lobbying for reforms in both electoral governance necessary for electoral credibility and electoral institutions to secure legitimacy and gender representativeness. The main strength of CSOs has been the capacity to create collective desire and awareness for electoral reforms, but they are constrained by lack of voting and veto powers in reforms requiring legislative changes. Given the partisan and often competing interests in Parliament, none of the required legislative changes had occurred when Malawians went to the polls in the FPE in 2020. The chairperson of MEJN expressed his frustration when he stated that "We have done all the work. Unfortunately, any bill to adopt the 50%+1 vote requirement will be shot down by major parties."

Development Partners

The most visible development partners in the reform agenda have been the United Nations Development Programme (UNDP) and National Democratic Institute (NDI) whose key motivation has primarily been the quest for political stability. Political stability in Malawi has increasingly been strained after each election except in 2009. The intensity and scope of electoral violence has tended to increase in each successive election. The nine months of widespread and sustained violent electoral protests after the 2019 nullified presidential elections which had ethno-regional undertones epitomised the inherent threat to statehood in Malawi. It is this inherent threat that among other concerns attracted interest from development partners in electoral reforms perceived to hold the potential to recast rules for political competition in the manner that promotes political stability.

The UNDP and NDI have been major financiers of the consultations and lobbying process undertaken by CSOs in the reform agenda. For instance, the two organisations financed both stakeholders' consultation processes and the drafting of required legislative changes. A response from the representative of the UNDP revealed the interest of development partners when she was quoted saying, "We are prepared to support any initiative we believe strengthens mechanisms for political stability in the country." Devoid of both voting and veto powers, the financial prowess of the development partners, which often has been used to exert pressure for wider public service reforms among other concerns, did not succeed in incentivising major political parties to actualise migration from plurality to the desired absolute majority system before the Constitutional Court sanctioned FPE. An absolute majority electoral system is perceived generally to have the potential to secure a broad-based mandate for the elected government viewed as critical for political stability.

Public Institutions

The public organisations of interest are constitutional ones which enjoy relative autonomy from executive excesses but, like other public institutions, are devoid of voting and veto powers. The Law Society and judiciary have been key public institutions in the electoral reforms particularly in the push for the 50%+1 vote electoral threshold. For instance, the Law Commission reports both in 2007 and 2017 strongly recommended replacing the FPTP with the 50%+1 vote electoral rules. In both reports the Law Commission appealed without success for broad-based legitimacy for the elected government, which it observed was increasingly becoming elusive in each successive election using plurality. The Constitution (Amendment) Bill that the Law Commission drafted as part of its report in 2017 to provide for the 50%+1 vote requirement was defeated when tabled in the DPP- and MCP-dominated Parliament as the vote did not attain the two-thirds threshold for a constitutional amendment.

The judiciary has been the most influential among all actors in the pursuit for the adoption of absolute majority. The judiciary's game-changer status emanates from its constitutional independence which guarantees relative autonomy. Whereas other actors, such as CSOs, political parties, development partners and other public institutions, did not succeed in ensuring that the country adopted the 50%+1 vote electoral system between 2007 and 2019, the judiciary through court determinations effected the migration from plurality to absolute majority. The Constitutional Court in its ruling of 3 February 2020 and upheld by the Supreme Court of Appeal on 8 May 2020 interpreted "majority electorate" provided for in section 80(2) to mean "absolute majority", suggesting that a candidate can only be declared as duly elected as a president if he or she amasses at least 50%+1 of the vote. The determination made the requirement for the constitutional amendment to provide for absolute majority inconsequential. Meanwhile, the Constitutional Court had directed Parliament to address observed gaps in the country's electoral institutions by passing enabling legislation that provided for a two-round system in the event the first round of presidential election did not produce an outright winner.

Analysis of determinations by both the Constitutional Court and Supreme Court of Appeal suggests that the judiciary was motivated primarily by the quest to uphold the triple and mutually reinforcing values of constitutionalism, democracy and legitimacy. For instance, the Constitutional Court observed on page 378 of its determination of the case of *Chilima and Chakwera v MEC and Mutharika* that: "This is a matter of great constitutional importance for the country because the interpretation we give to this section will determine the correct procedure that must be followed in future presidential elections." The court reiterated its pursuit of constitutionalism when it stated that: "And in determining of that issue, we will have regard to the law and only to the law and to the relevant facts."

The advancement of democratic rule and legitimacy was evidently reinforced by the Supreme Court of Appeal's rejection of the continued use of plurality, arguing that it would not only undermine the very principle of majority rule in democratic governance but also raise questions of legitimacy of the elected government in a democratic set-up. It can be observed that the judiciary's edge over other actors lay in its constitutional mandate and independence.

Prospects for Electoral Reforms

The potential constitutional crisis as Malawi proceeded to hold FPE on 23 June 2020 without enabling legislation to provide for the ballotage was abated owing to Chakwera of the MCP standing as a torchbearer for the Tonse Alliance electoral coalition and winning with 59.3% against 39.9% for second-placed Mutharika of the DPP-UDF electoral coalition. Following the interpretive and adjudication role played by the judiciary, the use of FPTP in the 2020 FPE was deemed unconstitutional. Yet the glaring gap still existed in electoral institutions at the time Malawi went to the polls in the FPE. The Constitutional Court determination in the case of *Chilima and Chakwera v Mutharika and MEC* in 2020 and upheld by the Supreme Court of Appeal settled the legal contestations suggesting that "majority electorate" as referred to in section 80(2) of the Constitution provides for an absolute majority, rendering the need for constitutional amendment inconsequential. The Constitutional Court stressed that the Constitution had inherent provision for absolute majority but lacked a supporting legal instrument to operationalise the provision. The fundamental question then was whether major parties through collective action could work together to facilitate the enactment of enabling legislation providing for the run-off in the event the first round did not produce an outright winner in future presidential elections.

To the extent that use of FPTP in a presidential election is unconstitutional and that none of the relevant parties, on the basis of parliamentary configuration at the time, could alone amend the Constitution, the enactment of legislation providing for a run-off seemed more likely than ever before. Judicial intervention on the contestation of electoral rules through its interpretative constitutional duty should be perceived as a critical juncture in the electoral reform process in Malawi. The force of the law through court determination was sufficient to compel the competing partisan interests to reluctantly converge in support of passing enabling legislation to facilitate provision for a run-off in electoral institutions seen as critical for securing broad-based legitimacy of the elected government. The ushering into power of the MCP-led administration during the 2020 FPE coupled with popular pressure for electoral reforms could only brighten prospects for the enactment of enabling legislation designed to bridge the gap in electoral institutions. Suffice to say, the DPP as a symbol of resistance to the absolute majority was weakened by the loss in the 2020 FPE, which robbed the party of its unrestrained access to public resources it had effectively used for patronage to frustrate decisive electoral reform initiatives.

Accordingly, it came as no surprise when, within three months of President Chakwera's election, relevant sections of both the Constitution and Presidential and Parliamentary Elections Act were amended to provide clarity on the meaning of majority electorate and address gaps that existed in the electoral laws. The amended section 80(2) of the Constitution reads:

> (2) the president shall be elected by the majority of more than fifty percent of the valid votes cast through direct, universal and equal suffrage and where such majority is not obtained by any candidate in the first poll, a second poll shall be held within thirty days after the declaration of results in which the candidate who obtained the highest and second highest number of votes cast in the first poll shall be the only candidates.

The constitutional amendment was accompanied by the amendment to Section 96(5) of the Parliamentary and Presidential Elections Act, which now reads:

> (a) the candidate for the election of the president who obtains the majority of more than fifty percent of the valid votes cast at the poll and the candidate for election as a member of the National Assembly who obtains the greatest number of votes cast at the polls shall be declared by the commission to have been duly elected.

The amendments which provided for absolute majority for the election of the president and plurality for election of members of Parliament suggested both the executive and legislators had maintained electoral systems that ushered them into office.

The attitude exhibited by the political class suggests that political elites will be inclined to retain the electoral formulae that ushered them into power and fiercely contest any attempt to change the same. Given the veto powers of the elected, future attempts for electoral reforms such as initiatives to increase the number of women in Parliament should be designed in such a manner that incumbent holders of elective offices are not hugely disadvantaged if such reforms are to see the light of the day.

Conclusion

This chapter sought to explain not only the rationale for simple plurality as an electoral system of choice for Malawi and attempts to reform the same but also to analyse the roles and motivations of various actors in the electoral reform agenda and prospects for reforms. Whilst recognising that the electoral reform agenda has been broad with the aim of securing electoral credibility, regime legitimacy and representativeness of electoral outcomes, this chapter focused on the question of legitimacy paying particular attention to the quest for the 50%+1 vote provision in the country's electoral institutions.

The chapter suggests that the country's choice of FPTP was not a function of an attempt to structure the party system in a fashion that would disincentivise political actors to mobilise along the ethno-regional divide in heterogeneous Malawi. Adoption of FPTP was primarily a result of institutional conservatism fuelled by the colonial legacy without regard to its inherent effect on both the party system function and regime legitimacy in democratising multi-ethnic Malawi. The use of FPTP did not succeed in either blocking mobilisation of the electorate along the ethno-regional divide or in aggregating social cleavages. Instead, it not only produced administrations lacking a broad-based mandate but also reinforced ethnic and regional consciousness and polarisation. Such an effect threatened not only democracy as a desirable system of government but also the country's territorial integrity evidenced by escalating regional tension in each successive electoral cycle. To that end, the electoral institutions reform project should go beyond the quest for broad-based legitimacy, electoral credibility and representativeness and seek to make political mobilisation along ethno-regional fault lines a non-viable political enterprise. Qualified majority has the potential to fulfil the social cleavages aggregation in culturally heterogeneous Malawi.

It is the qualified absolute majority electoral system that presents huge potential to compel the largely ethnic-based parties to evolve not into regional political ventures but national parties. National parties are likely to emerge if the 50%+1 vote electoral threshold is reinforced by the requirement demanding that the winning candidate in presidential elections should secure a given minimum of percentage votes in each region of the country. The two conditions would not only render ethnic and regional parties less viable as electoral projects, but also incentivise parties in their quest to maximise votes to assume the social cleavage aggregation function vital for national cohesion in multi-ethnic Malawi.

Chapter 8

Awona Nyekhwe:[1] The Fate of Opposition in Multiparty Malawi (1994–2020)

John Chipembere Lwanda, George Chikondi Chipembere Lwanda & Raphael Mbwana

Introduction

This chapter contributes to the debates on the role and effectiveness of the opposition in Malawi.[2] We cover the period between 1994, when a multiparty dispensation was introduced to Malawi, to 2020, when the landmark Supreme Court of Appeal decision to overturn the 2019 presidential elections was made. Within the constraints of space, we examine the forms and effectiveness of the Malawi opposition between 1994 and 2020. Given that there were no opposition parties until the last few years of colonialism and that between 1964 and 1994 Malawi was a one-party state under a "strong man ruler", we consider the lack of prior experience to be important. Many of the current leading Malawi politicians came from or were mentored by a cohort that arose from the political culture of the one-party era. The ruling Malawi Congress Party (MCP) had been led by a "personality" who did not permit alternative political views to be heard. When Malawi became a multiparty state both the presidentialism and personality politics were retained within a hybrid multiparty context that combined strong presidentialism with a vibrant but often impotent Parliament.

---

1 "They will feel the heat", or they will sweat [after losing], implying political opponents will suffer social, economic or other consequences after losing elections.

2 For example: Lars Svåsand, "The Concept of Opposition and the Structure of Opposition in Malawi", *Commonwealth & Comparative Politics* 51/3 (2013), 307; Kings M. Phiri and Kenneth R. Ross (eds), *Democratization in Malawi: A Stocktaking*, Blantyre: CLAIM-Kachere, 1998; Martin Ott and Fidelis Kanyongolo (eds), *Democracy in Progress: Malawi's 2009 Parliamentary and Presidential Elections*, Zomba: Kachere, 2009, 115–152; Mustafa Kennedy Hussein, "Opposition Politics in Malawi: Hopeful Signs amid the Warnings", *South African Journal of International Affairs* 16:3 (2009), 347-369; Andrew Mpesi, "Political Parties and their Manifestos: Inferring Party Policy Positions in Malawi since 1994", *Forum for Development Studies* 38/1 (2011), 25–42; John Chipembere Lwanda, *Promises, Power, Politics and Poverty: the Democratic Transition in Malawi 1961–1999*, Glasgow: Dudu Nsomba Publications, 1996.

Thus, despite its post-Banda multiparty framework, Malawi's governance retained characteristics of elected autocracies rather than elected democracies.

Crucially, the president and the winning party could command vast amounts of patronage. Given that the biggest source of rent in Malawi is the government and its parastatals, this gives the "winner takes all" significant influence in Malawi politics. And there is, as we point out in this chapter, a long list of political losers in Malawi. Losers are associated with economic and social disadvantages and, sometimes, punishment. These disadvantages were called *maluzi* (losses), *mbwadza* (the unexpected) and *wina alira* (someone will cry), the last being commonly understood since it derived from losses at football games. During the intense 2018–2020 election campaigns, these Chewa words were suddenly replaced by the Lomwe phrase *awona nyekhwe* (they will [lose and] suffer the consequences).

Against this background, this chapter examines the fate of opposition parties and elements in Malawi, focusing on the *nyekhwe* factor. Some scholars have looked at other aspects of the opposition, like ideology, the powers and effects of incumbency on the opposition, funding, personalities and ethnicities, the role of religion, and the role of the judiciary. We will consider some of these factors in passing but our focus is on the effect of *nyekhwe* on opposition politics in Malawi.

The Concept of *Nyekhwe*

Nyekhwe, a Lomwe word, in one basic sense refers to sweat. In subsistence societies working in the heat of the sun makes one sweat. One explanation proffered is that the degree of sweating implied by *nyekhwe* is that which flows from the head, past the neck and lumbar spine, down to the natal cleft, making one extremely uncomfortable.[3] At a more philosophical level, various etymological derivations were advanced. *Nyekhwe,* derived from *nyekhwetha*,[4] for some means "the unexpected". For others, it means "the unpredictable" or "unforeseen". And yet for others it has the implication of the "shockingly unexpected, unprecedented and inappropriate".[5] Fluent in the Lomwe language or not, the meaning of the term is clear. Just as with an earlier chiNyanja battle

3 Cf. www.facebook.com/Malawinewsalert/posts/nyekhwe-ndi-chiyani-nyekhwe-ndi-ndi-liwu-la-chilomwe-lomwe-limatanthauza-thukuta/2820597724666411.

4 Informant TC, unattributable. *Nyekwetha*, the root word, implies experiencing the unexpected.

5 Paul Unyolo, a medical doctor's explanation.

cry "*Wina alira!*" (Someone will cry!) of the UDF days or the Chewa *Muona mbwadza* (You will see what you did not expect), it has ominous connotations of the loser massively regretting personally, (or as a group) politically, socially and economically. This is clear from its use in politics. *Awona nyekhwe* came into popular discourse during the 2019 election campaign and echoes *Wina alira* but in a more "ominous" way, much more than, say, *Awona mbwadza* (they will experience surprises, miracles).

Chewa society had "harsh punishments" which kept "theft, adultery and disobedience at a minimum".[6] People could be banished from villages or chiefly administrations for dissent. Mazrui argued that cultural factors do play a part in politics, politicians being part of the society.[7] He also argued that oral tradition, such as we largely have in Malawi, transmits from generation to generation, "mainly what is accepted and respected. It does not transmit heresies of the previous age… Oral tradition is a tradition of conformity, rather than heresy, a transmission of consensus rather than dissidence."[8]

Collective Political Memory

Pennebaker et al. posit that communities are "bound by shared beliefs, experiences and memories which act as a communal" binding force.[9] They argue that "collective memory is part of social psychology" from which the "health of a nation can be gauged". In their view these "powerful" memories can be real or imagined. Halbwachs situated collective memory in society, as opposed to individuals.[10] He also distinguished between autobiographical memory (personal experiences), historical memory (memories that are passed down through historical records), history (the remembered past) and collective memory, defining collective memory as "the active past that forms our identities".[11]

In the Malawi context we can exploit these and other psychological, political and cultural theories in efforts to examine the "national political psyche". The

---

6 Maxwell Marwick, *Sorcery in its Social Setting: A Study of the Northern Rhodesian Cewa*, Manchester: Manchester University Press, 1965.

7 Ali Mazrui, *Cultural Forces in World Politics*, Oxford: James Currey, 1990.

8 Ibid, 119.

9 James Pennebaker, Darjo Paez and Bernard Rime, *Collective Memory of Political Events*, Mahwah, NJ: Lawrence Erlbaum Associates, 1997, vii.

10 Maurice Halbwachs, *On Collective Memory*, translated and edited by L.A. Coser, Chicago: University of Chicago Press, 1992, 38.

11 Ibid, 23–29.

concept of *mnemo*history, which links group concepts with cultural modes of memory and transmission, "unlike history proper", is concerned not with the past as such, but only with the past as it is remembered.[12] This concept chimes with the concepts of the "invention of tradition in Malawi, where existing, constructed and remembered cultural memory was used to legitimise Dr Banda's one-party state".[13] It was no coincidence that Bingu wa Mutharika soon embraced the term *ngwazi* for himself. The argument is that acceptable collective versions of governance are transmitted *orally* and remembered in collective memory. We will further argue that re-invented oral traditional versions of governance, for example where presidents cease to be servants of the people but *amai* (mother) or *adadi* (dad) to their electors, appropriate traditional forms of governance, mix them with "democratic modern forms" and feed these to citizens to create contexts in which political *nyekhwe* intimidates the opposition.

With its brutality, the colonial experience did not provide a good example for future Malawi political losers.[14] John Chilembwe's rebellion was "ruthlessly" put down.[15] During the State of Emergency, Nyasaland was like a "police state".[16] Dr Banda, and other politicians, exploited/exploit the culture of orality to good effect.[17] Politicians' speeches may differ but their messages are usually an appeal to "our tradition" (*mwambo wathu*) of a remembered or constructed form of governance based on a mixture of constructed and invented traditions.

In these systems apologies from losers and dissidents often, but not always, led to rehabilitation into the system. The one-party system saw to it that punishments for dissidents were harsh. In 1964 a detention centre was created in Dowa, variously called among the Chewa "Dzaleka", the Nyanja "Dzeleka" or, among those in Mangochi, "Mdzaleka". *Mdzaleka* translates as "you will stop" [in this case transgressing the received rules]. Even chiefs like Mwase of

---

12 Cf. Marek Tamm, "History as Cultural Memory: Mnemohistory and the Construction of the Estonian Nation", *Journal of Baltic Studies* 39/4 (2008), 499-516.

13 Peter Forster, "Culture, Nationalism, and the Invention of Tradition in Malawi", *The Journal of Modern African Studies* 32/3 (1994), 477-497.

14 See John McCracken, *A History of Malawi 1859-1966*, Woodbridge: James Currey, 2012.

15 See George Shepperson and Thomas Price, *Independent African: John Chilembwe and the Origins, Setting and Significance of the Nyasaland Native Rising of 1915*, Edinburgh: Edinburgh University Press, 1958.

16 Colin Baker, "Nyasaland, 1959: A Police State?" *Society of Malawi Journal* 58/2 (1997), 17-25.

17 John Lwanda, "Poets, Culture and Orature: A Reappraisal of the Malawi Political Public Sphere, 1953–2006", *Journal of Contemporary African Studies* 26/1 (2008), 71-101.

Kasungu and errant prominent MCP leaders like Albert Muwalo and Gwanda Chakuamba experienced forms of *nyekhwe* under Dr Banda. Multiparty politicians have followed Dr Banda's tactics: nowadays a losing opposition figure may not be incarcerated in *Mdzaleka* but may experience *nyekhwe* while ruling party supporters chant: *wina alira*! And oral political power discourses continue to be dominated by the ruling leader's omnipotence and patronage.[18]

The Concept of "Opposition"

Malawi's colonial and postcolonial rulers were not, for the most part, very permissive or supportive of opposition parties or strong non-governmental organisations.[19] Opposition elements varied and included political parties, civil society organisations, religious groups, chiefs, labour organisations and individuals. In some cases, even academics and journalists, in their quest to publish what they saw as the truth, were regarded as opposition elements. Brack and Weinblum argue that: "The notion of opposition should be understood as a stance of disagreement expressed in the public sphere by mobilised actors, through different modes of action, the target of discontent being the government or its policies, the political elite, or the political regime as a whole."[20] Brack and Weinblum's definition allows a more inclusive view of the opposition in Malawi. Most "opposition discourses" in Malawi implicitly assume a legitimate state rather than a dominating state institution. Of course, when a non-parliamentary ruling party elite can exercise power over civil servants and parastatals, dispose of state assets with impunity and are seen as *boma ilo* ("the government"), this is inevitable.[21]

Viewing the postcolonial state as always being legitimate, even if that state does not arise from agreed electoral processes, perform effectively, provide security to its citizens and shares its vision with the majority of its citizens,[22] has roots

---

18 John Lwanda, "Poets, Culture and Orature".

19 See John McCracken, *A History of Malawi* and John Lwanda, *Kamuzu Banda of Malawi*.

20 Nathalie Brack and Sharon Weinblum, "'Political Opposition': Towards a Renewed Research Agenda", *Interdisciplinary Political Studies* 1/1 (2011), 74.

21 Mtemang'ombe, "Anti-corruption Drive Test of Chakwera's Character", *The Nation*, 8 August 2020, www.mwnation.com/anti-corruption-drive-test-of-chakweras-character/.

22 Cf. OECD, *The State's Legitimacy in Fragile Situations: Unpacking Complexity, Conflict and Fragility*, Paris: OECD Publishing, 2010, accessed 10/11/20 https://doi.org/10.1787/9789264083882-en. The 2020 High Court and Supreme Court rulings, which ruled that the Peter Mutharika DPP regime was, between 2019 and 2020, illegitimate, are relevant here. See at https://malawilii.org/system/files /judgment/high-court-general-division/2020/1/null.pdf.

in the colonial period.[23] Anyone opposing government is described as *chigawenga* (singular) or *zigawenga* (plural), which has mutated from meaning "thug" to "dissident".[24] As Pascal Kishindo observed:

> The word became semantically loaded [being] used to discredit and silence real or imagined political opponents … *chigawenga* is in class 7/8 in accordance with the classification of nouns in Bantu languages … [the same class as] *chirombo* (beast), … [rather than] class 1/2, the class of persons … [Then] calling someone a *chigawenga* was sentencing the person to either imprisonment or death.[25]

Opposing the views of the leadership was simply unacceptable. This concept continued the colonial model which prevented Africans from participating in legislative processes until the 1950s. However, Brack and Weinblum's concept enables the inclusion of disparate elements, like John Chilembwe "movement", the Nyasaland African Congress (NAC), Chipembere's movement, various 1990s pressure groups and those that followed, like the Human Rights Defenders Coalition (HRDC) of the 2020s, as opposition. Few African opposition groups survived past independence day. Most were either co-opted by ruling parties or "recalcitrant" opposition elements faced political, economic or social sanctions.

Opposition Parties and Politicians 1994–2020

Opposition parties existed in different forms over the 1994–2020 period with varying degrees of effectiveness. Between 2004 and 2020, four major parties existed: the Malawi Congress Party (MCP), the United Democratic Front (UDF), The Alliance for Democracy (AFORD) and the Democratic Progressive Party (DPP). The People's Party (PP) was formed in 2011 while the United Transformation Movement (UTM) was formed in 2018. Between 2004 and 2018 the MCP, UDF and DPP accounted for about 70% of all votes during each survey round. AFORD's fortunes dwindled from a high of 27% of national support in 1999, to 2% in 2005 and then to less than 1% in 2012 when the new People's Party then held 27% of national support.[26]

---

23 See John McCracken, *A History of Malawi.*

24 Pascal Kishindo, "Evolution of Political Terminology in Chichewa and the Changing Political Culture in Malawi", *Nordic Journal of African Studies* 9/1 (2000), 23.

25 Ibid.

26 Joseph J. Chunga "Examining the Relevance of Political Parties in Malawi", Afrobarometer Briefing Paper No. 125, January 2014, 9.

Although affiliated to the Liberal International until 2009, the UDF morphed into a Muluzi family-dominated dynastic party and, by 1999, it was difficult to determine its core ideology. Since 2014 *ung'ono* (youthfulness) has been, without elaboration, a major campaign feature. The Malawi Congress Party remains, at its core, a conservative party that, to some extent, still believes in the "four cornerstones" of unity, loyalty, obedience and discipline. It has, however, always been led by strong or charismatic personalities: Dr Banda, Gwanda Chakuamba, John Tembo and now Lazarus Chakwera. The DPP, which arose as a splinter from the UDF, initially attracted "progressive" but essentially conservative elements who were sympathetic to Bingu wa Mutharika's professed agricultural and economic reforms, like OVOP (itself a Nyerere-like socialist idea).[27] However, as the "petty" opposition from the UDF intensified, Mutharika used his presidential patronage powers to attract defectors from the UDF, diluting DPP ideology and making the party dependent on his personality.[28] The more personality-led parties became, the more patronage-dependent and hence less likely to tolerate criticism.

Bingu, and later Peter, Mutharika, manifested elements of Lomwe tribalism.[29] By 2009, a "DPP System" with a distinct "Lomwelisation" of the civil service was in train. Opposition to the DPP thus took on elements of anti-Lomwelisation rhetoric. Joyce Banda's People's Party started as a progressive move from Bingu's hegemony before losing ideological direction. It retained a small but significant female support base through its promotion of small-scale development policies. Joyce Banda was subjected to some criticism premised on misogyny.[30]

At their best, the Malawi opposition parties use parliamentary processes extremely well. But sometimes they "pull their punches", failing to call the executive to account. This is partly because personality leaders can make patronage deals with the ruling party. Once elections are done, opposition

---

27 "One Village, One Product".

28 Maurice Hutton, "A Dystopian Democracy: Discourses on Leadership Failure and National Transformation in Malawi's Urban Public Sphere", MA, Leiden University, 2013.

29 Cf. Mwayi Lusaka, "Dividing the Nation or Promoting Unity? Ethnic-based Associations and Production of Heritage in Malawi", in Kenneth R. Ross and Wapulumuka O. Mulwafu (eds), *Politics, Christianity and Society in Malawi: Essays in Honour of John McCracken,* Mzuzu: Mzuni Press, 2020, 394-395.

30 Edrinnie Kayambazinthu-Lora and Edith Kalilombe Shame, "A Different Yardstick Gender and Leadership in the Political Discourse", in Inge Amundsen and Happy Kayuni (eds), *Women in Politics in Malawi*, Zomba: CMI and University of Malawi, 2016.

leaders may negotiate for personal positions that benefit them and their kin; after all, *kukhala otsutsa ndi kowawa* (being in opposition is painful). Being in a position to negotiate, they protect their interests if they lose an election, without "bruising and upsetting the incumbent"" such is the fear of *nyekhwe*. Opposition leaders and family members do feature in patronage appointments.

Patronage silences constructive opposition even from traditional chiefs:

> There are ... MPs, chiefs and Malawians in general who ... believe that the only way to get *chitukuko* (development) in their areas is to support the government of the day. Sadly, their perceptions are justified for as long as successive administrations cynically [exploit this patronage].[31]

Until the events of 2019, political parties tended to use the judiciary for contesting electoral results or intra-party matters but rarely to call governments to account. The latter action is more likely to be initiated by CSOs. Malawi's opposition parties often render themselves inefficient, despite significant support, by not having effective internal mechanisms. For example, no Malawi political party has a programme of work that includes activities by MPs in their constituency and other systematic party programmes with clear deliverables and goals beyond narrow self or party interests.[32] Without these work programmes political parties offer a confusing array of promises, half-delivered promises and generalities from their manifestos, as well as copying other parties' maize or goat donation schemes.

Non-Party Actors

It is often forgotten that the Nyasaland African Congress arose from the activities of Civil Society Organisations in the 1920s, 1930s and early 1940s. However, under the one-party era CSOs were closely monitored, if they were allowed to operate at all, usually as service deliverers in famine relief, for example. During the transition to multiparty rule between 1989 and 1994, CSOs emerged and were involved in civic education and aspects of the transition like the drafting of the new Constitution. Once a multiparty regime was in power the inexperienced CSOs and their foreign partner NGOs found it difficult to call the Bakili Muluzi government to account. On the contrary, because they opposed the wasteful patronage associated with that regime and

31 A. Makonda-Ridley, personal communication, 21 May 2012.

32 Cf. Karim Fertikh, "The Political Programme as Genre: the Sociology of Producing Party Programmes. The Example of Bad Godesberg", *Revue française de science politique* 64/5 (2014), 905-928.

its failure to hold the 1998 local government elections, they were seen as opposition elements and not "development partners".[33]

Despite these impediments and the restrictive NGO Act of 2001, which was meant to give government a tool to control CSOs, they continued to take root and, despite financial constraints, thrive. They certainly played a significant role in opposing the Third Term project of Bakili Muluzi.[34] For many NGOs, a third term was a backward step towards an elected autocratic life-presidency. Without CSO opposition, Muluzi would have overcome opposition parties and achieved his third term.

When Bingu wa Mutharika abandoned the UDF in 2005 and formed the Democratic Progressive Party (DPP) he was initially supported by civil society, who wanted *chitukuko* (development) and "pro-poor" initiatives. Brown Mpinganjira of the National Democratic Alliance (NDA), Hetherwick Ntaba (MCP) and Gwanda Chakuamba (MCP) "joined forces" with Bingu, leaving the UDF, now riven with squabbles, as the main opposition. Bingu ensured they remained weak by poaching some UDF MPs. Politicians like Aleke Banda, though representing smaller parties, were more effective in playing the role of the opposition.

Mutharika's first term was an economic success and he was re-elected, winning 114 seats to John Tembo's 26 and Muluzi's 17, preserving the weakness of the opposition. Bingu's unrelenting patronage assault on MPs made them insensitive to "people's pain",[35] leaving CSOs and PAC to do the opposition's work. Mutharika turned Malawi into an elected autocracy but limited patronage to a few people, mostly within his party and ethnic group.[36] Mutharika also used the security apparatus and "Young Democrats" (YDs) to terrorise opponents, publicly declaring to his *ana adadi* (dad's children): "if someone comes to insult

---

33 Ollen Mwalubunju, "Civil Society", in Nandini Patel and Lars Svåsand (eds), *Government and Politics in Malawi*, Zomba: Kachere, 2007, 267-296.

34 See Kenneth R. Ross, "'Worrisome Trends': The Voice of the Churches in Malawi's Third Term Debate", *African Affairs* 103, no. 410 (2004), 91–107; and John Lwanda and Emmie Chanika, "Democracy, Donors and Dependency: The Rises and Falls of Non-Governmental and Civil Society Organisations' Agency in Malawi Opposition Politics, 1992 – 2017", *The Society of Malawi Journal* 70/1 (2017), 19-54.

35 See *Nation Opinion* 14/4/2012 "Why are DPP MPs speaking now?"

36 W.C. Chirwa, personal communication, July 2012. See also the leaflet by the Human Rights Defenders Coalition (HRDC) "Civil Society and Citizens petition embarrassing levels of executive thieving, corruption and impunity (Operation Chotsa Mbava): Time to restore our destiny", 21 September 2018.

your father, do you just stay quiet … I want to say starting from today that I am tired of it. Those that are insulting me should stop … I ask the DPP in the south, east, central and north if they start demonstrations you should know what to do."[37] This was an open Banda-esque appeal to visit *nyekhwe*-based violence on opposition demonstrators.

As the opposition faltered in their duties there was a tendency or trend, from 2004 onwards, for CSOs and PAC to do opposition work. Two events were critical and iconic in the conflict between Bingu wa Mutharika and his people: the Academic Freedom Debate of 2011 and the Diesel Petrol Palibe (There is no diesel or petrol) saga. "Guilt" played some part in CSO militancy; their "democrat and deliverer" had turned out to be an autocrat. Mutharika's political honeymoon was short-lived. But with the large majority he became selfish,[38] engaged in blatantly nepotistic appointments to key civil service positions and set about consolidating his power. He wanted his brother Peter to succeed him, ensuring a "peaceful Mwanawasa-free retirement".[39]

With rising import costs, poor exports and aid withheld, Malawi suffered foreign exchange shortages, leading to petrol and paraffin queues at filling stations. Mutharika would not devalue the kwacha. Civil society was further angered by his tribalistic patronage and appointment tendencies which favoured his own Lomwe people and DPP supporters with business contracts.[40] An educational quota system that favoured the Lomwe was introduced. The incumbent vice president, Joyce Banda, was vilified in an attempt to get her to resign.[41]

The national flag was changed at his insistence and "design". Bingu became a "table banger", dismissive of NGOs and CSOs.[42] By the first half of 2011,

---

37 Keith Somerville, "Malawi's democracy dips into recession", *African Arguments*, March 21, 2012, https://africanarguments.org/2012/03/21/malawis-democracy-dips-into-recession-by-keith-somerville/.

38 Mutharika bought himself a presidential jet costing about USD 22 million. Some donors became unhappy and withheld aid.

39 Personal communication, unattributable. President Mwanawasa of Zambia charged his predecessor Chiluba with corruption.

40 This explains why during the riots of July 2011 businesses associated with Vuwa Kaunda (a northern DPP die-hard loyalist) and the Mulli Brothers were attacked. See P. Pemba, "Mulli Implicated in July 20 Protests", http://www.mwnation.com/index.php?option=com_content&view=article&id=5802:mulli-implicated-in-july-20-protests&catid=87&Itemid=295.

41 E. Nyirongo, "DPP North Bashes Banda, Kachali: Support Peter Mutharika's 2014 Candidature Proposal", *The Nation,* 20 December 2010.

42 Personal communication unattributable.

NGO and CSO leaders and activists were openly complaining of Mutharika's "arrogance of power".[43] He dismissed and ridiculed dissenting NGO and CSO activists who saw themselves as well-educated Malawians with ideas to contribute.[44]

Mutharika's postponement of local government elections deprived CSOs and NGOs of political civil space, as well as sites of employment. Commodity shortages including fuel, fertiliser, "Fanta", and high transport costs, compounded by regular power outages, undermined Mutharika's "economic engineer" reputation. An angry civil society with multiple complaints against his regime was radicalised. But the formal opposition parties were relatively quiet. A more subtle phenomenon was the de facto "police state-isation" of Malawi, complete with numerous police traffic roadblocks ostensibly for traffic purposes.[45] A strong-man government requires adequate policing,[46] and he ordered that there be an accelerated training of police officers, at three-month intervals, to ensure a force of 20,000 by 2014 "to ensure peaceful elections".[47]

The Role of the Media

A feature of the political and human rights landscape in Malawi between 1994 and 2020 has been the large degree of freedom of speech. There has been, for most of the period a lively, mostly free media, if heavily supervised by the Malawi Communications and Regulatory Authority (MACRA), a government parastatal "media watch dog". The increase in independent radio and TV stations was critical in offering the population alternative viewpoints to the state-run MBC which, for most of this period, churned out a steady stream of state propaganda. The presence of independent commercial stations like MIJ FM, Zodiak, Power FM, Capital FM, Radio Maria, Radio Islam and, later, Joy Radio, made it possible for NGO, CSO and opposition politicians to have their voices heard, particularly on Zodiak and MIJ Radio. However, MACRA has

---

43 *Wamakani ngati Bingu* (as stubborn as Bingu) was a common insult among vendors.

44 John Lwanda and Emmie Chanika, "Democracy, Donors and Dependency".

45 The many un-roadworthy vehicles told a different story. In April 2012 there were six police roadblocks between Blantyre and Zomba.

46 Mutharika wanted a police force of 20,000 by 2014. This figure compares to an establishment of 16,000 in 2020.

47 See J. Mponda, "Half-Baked Police Officers Patrolling the Streets of Blantyre", *Malawi Voice,* http://www.malawivoice.com/2012/05/09/half-baked-police-officers-patrolling-blantyre-streets-16936/.

been a sometimes partial "political policeman", threatening to close any station that "goes too far" in the direction of government criticism.

The Academic Freedom Debate

One of the most visible tussles between government and civil society leaders was that involving the issue of academic freedom at the University of Malawi's Chancellor College. It started on 12 February 2011 when a Political and Administrative Studies associate professor, Blessings Chinsinga, was summoned by the Inspector General of the Malawi Police Service, Mr Peter Mukhito, to an interrogation over the contents of a lecture that he had delivered to one of his classes.[48] Though other NGOs and CSOs had been "weak" on previous issues, the Chancellor College CCASU and their supporters stood firm. There were a number of reasons for this: the leadership of the main activists Jessie Kabwila Kapasula, Garton Kamchedzera, Blessings Chinsinga, Franz Amin and Edge Kanyongolo; the desire to avoid going back to "Dr Banda's days", in terms of academic freedom, when some students and lecturers were detained;[49] the related fight against the educational quota system. Polytechnic students offered substantial support, Bunda slight, and the Kamuzu College of Nursing and the College of Medicine minimal. The support from the public was striking; the symbolic red cloths and Jessie Kabwila's "resolutely iconic"[50] leadership resonated with the public. Peter Mutharika, formerly a university professor, as Minister of Education did almost nothing, exposing the anti-intellectualism not only at the top the ruling DPP, but also in the country.

The DPP becomes "Diesel Petrol Palibe"

As Mutharika's arrogance helped send Malawi's economy into reverse, there was a convergence between this elite anger and that of peri-urban and rural people. Rural people were "used" to chronic shortages, but it was a testing time for the Malawi elite. "Impunity" played a part. Senior ministers were allowed

---

48 Jesse Kabwila-Kapasula, "The Challenge of Standing in Defence of Academic Freedom in Malawi", draft paper delivered at Codesria, 5-9 November 2011, Rabat, Morocco, www.general.assembly.codesria.org/IMG/pdf/Jessie_Kabwila_Kapasula.pdf [9.5.2012].

49 Among them was Dr Edge Kanyongolo.

50 See, for an overview of the period, Jessica Johnson, "Malawi: Taking Stock in Turbulent Times", *Journal of Southern African Studies* 46/2 (2020), 195-207. See also David Kerr and Jack Mapanje, "Academic Freedom and the University of Malawi", *African Studies Review* 45/2 (2002), 73–91.

to buy Malawi Housing Corporation houses cheaply.[51] "Expert NGOs" were ignored.[52] These factors affecting the elite, like the educational selection quota system, the academic freedom struggles at Chancellor College and economic difficulties, helped bring out the middle classes on to the streets. When donors suspended aid to Malawi in March 2011, Mutharika's "stressed" response was to "blast donors",[53] look east to China and promote a "zero deficit budget" agenda. In implementing this "Zero Deficit Budget" Mutharika began using the rhetoric of self-sufficiency. Coincidentally, tobacco sales in winter 2011 were poor and the government increased personal income taxes.

New laws restricting freedom of speech spurred civil society groups, particularly the HRCC, Rafiq Hajat's Institute for Policy Interaction (IPI) (whose premises were later petrol-bombed) and others, including an ecumenical collective of church leaders, to call for mass demonstrations against the government. Opposition parties were largely reactive to events. NGOs and CSOs, led by Undule Mwakasungula, Habiba Osman, Billy Mayaya and others, prepared a list of demands to be put to President Mutharika, otherwise a mass protest would be held on 20 July 2011. DPP "cadets" were sent out onto the streets to intimidate potential demonstrators but the demonstrations went ahead anyway on 20 July. The Malawi Police over-reacted and 19 people were killed, nationwide, before the Army was called out to restore order.[54]

A follow-up demonstration scheduled for August 2011 was cancelled. CSOs and NGOs agreed to talks with the government. A further "stay at home" demonstration arranged for 20-21 September was only moderately successful. The climate of fear, demonstrated by the death of a Polytechnic student "oppositional" activist, Robert Chasowa, allegedly killed by state operatives on 24 September 2011, added to the tension and climate of fear.[55] The lack of success of the second round of anti-government demonstrations is blamed on a number of factors. Some CSO and NGO activists, having gone "so far" did not want to "damage their CVs" given the chameleon nature of politics and employment prospects in Malawi and, like opposition politicians, sat on the

51 Anon, "ACB Revives MHC Houses Scam Case", *Nation Online*, 4 June 2013, www.mwnation.com/acb-revives-mhc-houses-scam-case/.

52 For example, on the safety of uranium mining.

53 Daniel Wroe, "Briefing: Donors, Dependency, and Political Crisis in Malawi", *African Affairs* 111, no. 442 (2012), 135-44 [135].

54 M. Thom, "Exposed: 15 die of gunshots, MHRC reveal", *Daily Times*, 16 August 2012.

55 See Human Rights Watch "World Report 2012: Malawi" at http//www.org/world-report-2012/Malawi.

fence.[56] Other NGO activists were perhaps "fed scones". Yet other activists placed their material belongings above principle. They did not want their own "foot soldiers"—the unemployed peri-urban youth, students, vendors and low paid workers—smashing shops and other middle-class feeding havens, like petrol stations.[57]

Between September 2011 and March 2012, as the NGO/CSO activists were "fed scones" and reduced to "barking dogs", Mutharika's DPP was in the ascendant. Any demonstrators were tear-gassed and arrested. The DPP "system"[58] prepared for a "certain" general election win in 2014. A number of covert activities were taking place: the extraction of funds from the MRA and commercial banks and business donors to ensure healthy 2014 DPP electoral funding. Further, Mutharika planned to buy targeted elements of civil society, establish a DPP TV station and rapidly train police officers to ensure "peaceful elections". Some informed observers consider that the roots of the significant electoral rigging that took place were planned during this period.[59]

Once the mass demonstrations had taken place, it became evident that opposition parties in Malawi rely on others to mobilise mass action. This suggests that leading opposition voices, both the political and civil, are not as effective without the masses responding with big protests or demonstrations. It has also been argued that after *kuwadyetsa mabanzi* (fed buns or being palm oiled), some leaders may be content to "sit in the office and read the paper", leaving ordinary Malawians voiceless.

Though eschewing violence, Malawi religious leaders often use the rhetoric of "Chilembwe's spirit" in social justice discourses.[60] In March 2012, this "spirit" moved PAC to organise a meeting where it declared that it wanted to "reclaim" people's rights. NGO, CSO and, significantly, opposition party representatives

---

56 Wapulumuka Mulwafu, personal conversation, July 2012.

57 John Lwanda and Emmie Chanika, "Democracy, Donors and Dependency", provides a more comprehensive account.

58 Wongani Chiuta, "Malawi: Chakwera Has 2 Choices - Format DPP System or Leave and Suffer Consequences", *Nyasa Times*, 6 November 2020 at www.nyasatimes.com/chakwera-has-2-choices-format-dpp-system-or-leave-and-suffer-consequences/

59 Cf. Baldwin Chiyamwaka, "Report Malawi's 2014 tripartite elections Electoral governance tested", Institute for Security Studies Southern Africa Report, Issue 1, September 2014, https://oldsite.issafrica.org/uploads/SAReport-Issue1.pdf and unattributable personal communications.

60 Cf. K. Msiska, "Clergy Defend their Role in Politics", *Daily Times*, 22 August 2012.

attended this meeting. The government was given another deadline.[61] By then Mutharika had boxed himself into a corner; civil society, in standing up for their rights, had been part of that pressure. He suffered a fatal cardiac arrest on 5 April 2012. After a two-day attempt by a group led by Peter Mutharika, Goodall Gondwe and others, to seize power, Joyce Banda, the vice president, assumed power.[62] Again, the formal opposition (including Joyce Banda herself) was seen to be hesitant over a four-day period, as if they were not aware of the Constitution.[63] The Army and CSOs were more proactive.

Joyce Banda, despite her previous experience in running an NGO, did not listen to CSO advice from the onset. She was not interested in delivering a two-year programme of work and de-constructing the excesses of the Mutharika regime. Instead of aligning with friendly civil society elements, she disappointed them from the start, pursuing a Bakili Muluzi-like ruling strategy. Unfortunately, her old party, the DPP, with the largest MP block in Parliament, became effectively her strongest (and most bitter) opposition. Using her political instincts, she tried to concentrate on building her political party through addressing meetings and giving goats to selected peasant farmers. In the process she surrounded herself with opportunistic fundraisers, some of whom were later implicated in the Cashgate affair.[64]

Cashgate aside, some analysts argue that her brief period delivered better economic performance than some of the other presidents, for example in terms of economic growth, security, forex and fuel availability. These issues should have brought most civil society on her side. It has been suggested that culture and gender played some significant part in explaining why some people viewed her as a "failed" president.[65] Another explanation is that the DPP opposition

---

61 K. Munthali, "CSOs Set March 28 Dialogue Deadline", *The Nation*, 20 February 2012.

62 K. Munthali, "How DPP panicked", *The Nation*,13 April 2012.

63 Edward Paice, "A 'Gang of Three', the 'Midnight Six' and the Death of 'Daniel Phiri': Anatomy of an Alleged Coup Attempt in Malawi", Africa Research Institute, 20 March 2013, www.africaresearchinstitute.org/newsite/blog/a-gang-of-three-the-midnight-six-and-the-death-of-daniel-phiri-anatomy-of-an-alleged-coup-attempt-in-malawi-2/.

64 See Baker Tilly, 2014 National Audit Office Malawi Report on Fraud and Mismanagement of Malawi Government Finances Covering transactions and controls in the six month period 1 April 2013 - 30 September 2013 Report dated 21 February 2014, www.gov.uk/government /uploads/system/uploads/attachment_data/file/285877/20140221_National_Audit_Office _ Malawi_-_Forensic_Audit_Report_-_FINAL_ISSUED.pdf, [18.8.2016].

65 See Edrinne Lora-Kayambazinthu and Edith Kalilombe Shame, "A Different Yardstick Gender", and Boniface Dulani, Lise Rakner, Lindsay Benstead and Vibeke Wang, "Do Women Face a Different Standard? The Gender and Corruption Factors in the 2014 Presidential

was, for once, too formidable to let a sitting president succeed and reportedly used every means at their disposal, including rigging the 2014 elections.[66]

The DPP System, State Capture, and its Dislodgement

Internal Opposition

On assuming power, Joyce Banda failed to prosecute the "Midnight Six".[67] Mutharika, then technically on bail, won the 2014 elections and proceeded to rebuild the DPP using the funds accumulated for this dynastic eventuality.[68] Saulos Klaus Chilima (SKC), then managing director at Airtel, in line with *ung'ono ung'ono* (an appeal to the youth vote) was head-hunted to partner Peter Mutharika. Those close to Chilima insist that both Bingu and Muluzi had been courting him as early as 2009. Apparently, although SKC had already decided to take up Peter's offer, his response to this courting was to say, as a devout Catholic, he wanted to consult the church. This was to buy time and reduce internal DPP opposition. It also highlights possible Catholic Church influence. The UDF then fielded young Atupele Muluzi, son of former President Bakili Muluzu, and Joyce Banda picked a youthful Sosten Gwengwe as running mate.

Within six months of becoming vice president, SKC's relationship with Mutharika was showing signs of strain. Once elected, SKC was apparently informed by DPP stalwarts that he was simply a ticket to court young people. On his part Chilima had made the mistake of not running as an MP as well, diluting his political clout. Chilima was also not of the generation to hide his presidential and political ambitions, ambitions clear from his days as president of the Chancellor College AFORD branch. Although technically well-suited and prepared for the job after rising through major corporate ladders,[69] he was insufficiently prepared for senior political party intrigues and ended up playing second fiddle.

Elections in Malawi", Programme on Governance and Local Development Working Paper No. 27.

66 Nandini Patel and Michael Wahman, "The Presidential, Parliamentary and Local Elections in Malawi, May 2014", *Africa Spectrum* 50/1 (April 2015), 79–92. Available at SSRN: https://ssrn.com/abstract=3676322.

67 K. Munthali, "How DPP panicked", *The Nation,*13 April 2012.

68 F. Chuma, "Malawi: a monarchy in the making?" *The Guardian*, 1 December 2010. www.theguardian.com/commentisfree/2010/dec/01/malawi-monarchy-making-mutharika.

69 W. Mijiga, "Hypocrisy of our Times", *The Nation*, 12 February 2018, https://mwnation.com /hypocrisy-of-our-times/.

Without the support of sympathetic party senior politicians, thrust into a party full of suspicious potential rivals, he was easy prey for DPP party and state house plotters. Chilima's temperament, particularity about dressing,[70] and his Dr Banda-style approach to civil service efficiency in the context of a very politicised environment, offered a very sharp weapon against him to his enemies. They accused him of seeking to centralise party power in his camp. An insecure Peter Mutharika swallowed these characterisations of his deputy. Mutharika's "Chilima insecurity" was not entirely unfounded according to insiders. Chilima and his group had planned to take over the DPP from within. They forgot that the DPP "Lomwe System" at the time was not going to allow a Ngoni, like Chilima, to lead it.

The rupture with Mutharika was the result of the inevitable *phwaka* (gossip) of the presidential hangers-on in search of patronage. Peter Mutharika was subject to a number of influences: financiers and party donors like Leston Mulli and quieter voices like the banker, Thom Mpinganjira;[71] the political advisers, like Goodall Gondwe, Bright Msaka, Ben Phiri and others; his wife Gertrude Maseko; and, finally and most crucially, his chief of security, Norman Chisale. Chisale controlled access to the president.[72] All these factions had their eye on the presidency, then seemingly intended for VP Chilima.

Chisale drove the final wedge between the president and his vice president by controlling traffic between them.[73] Chisale and Gertrude Mutharika groomed their own candidate for the 2024 presidency, Everton Chimulirenji. At one point, as the patronage cake seemed to slip from the president's hands, some DPP patriarchs like Leston Mulli became disgruntled. And when Leston Mulli, a major donor to the DPP asked for compensation for materials he lost during the 2011 riots,[74] and Peter Mutharika dithered, Mulli then backed a "SKC for president in 2019" move.[75]

---

70 www.nyasatimes.com/malawi-paper-backs-vp-chilima-sending-back-shabby-dressed-council-officials-late-comers/.

71 Frank Namangale, "My Life in Danger, says FDH's Mpinganjira", *The Nation,* 17 July 2019.

72 www.facebook.com/Malawinewsalert/photos/who-is-norman-chisaleintroductionlets-begin-by-introduction-norman-paulos-chisal/2482632468462940/.

73 AllAfrica.com 2020, "Malawi: Chisale Under Spotlight Over Wealth - Declares Luxury Cars Were "Gifts", No Business – Report", 7 August 2020, https://allafrica.com/stories/202008070842.html.

74 "DPP and Peter Mutharika acting like property grabbers", *Maravi Post,* 25 October 2018, http://www.maravipost.com/dpp-and-peter-mutharika-acting-like-property-grabbers/.

75 S. 3, "50 Members of Parliament back Peter Mutharika", 17 May 2018, www.times.mw/50-members-of-parliament-back-peter-mutharika.

After Mutharika was "fed advice" suggesting Chilima was disloyal for forming a proto-party within the DPP, he decided to fall in with Mulli.[76] This early pro-Chilima movement was attractive to some young DPP and non-party "transformative progressives" who sought to change the DPP from within. Some of the "transformative progressives" fell away when they perceived Chilima as acting precipitously and making common cause with DPP "conservatives and sinners". Patricia Kaliati and Callista Chimombo, both of whom played crucial roles in the new movement, have given their accounts of the beginnings of the United Transformation Movement,[77] as has Chilima.[78] The UTM was launched on 21 July 2018 as an opposition movement, just as Joyce Banda had done in 2011.

The Human Rights Defenders Coalition (HRDC)

The level of discontent in Malawi among civil society which was not being articulated by the formal opposition is shown by the fact that a year earlier, on 11 December 2017, the Human Rights Defenders Coalition (HRDC), a network of human rights organisations and "defenders", consisting of CHRR, the Centre for the Development of People (CEDEP) and the Malawi Law Society (MLS), was established following a UNDP-sponsored seminar on 13 December 2016. CSO activists and journalists had expressed concerns about the shrinking civil liberties space in Malawi. Of great concern were reports of attacks and harassment of journalists and activists, extrajudicial killings, arrests of people with dissenting views and further moves to restrict CSOs access to funding. The HRDC made efforts to be a nationwide body, establishing regional and district offices from the start. Three seasoned human rights activists led the coalition: Timothy Mtambo, Gift Trapence and MacDonald Sembereka.

When the DPP won the 21 May 2019 elections with what was seen as a biased Malawi Electoral Commission (MEC), civil society was energised against MEC and its Chair Justice Jane Ansah. Nationwide demonstrations were organised by the HRDC between June and October 2019. The government tried to stop

76 "Ngalande says Mulli was Silenced by K3.1 billion", *Malawi24,* 21 May 2018, https://malawi24.com/2018/05/21/ngalande-says-mulli-was-silenced-by-k3-1-billion/ and F. Namangale, "DPP trio rejects APM", 17 May 2018, https:// mwnation.com/dpp-trio-rejects-apm/.

77 For Patricia Kaliati"s version, see www.youtube.com/watch?v= hAlYm0kIGg. For a more detailed version see John Lwanda, *Malawi: the State We Are In?*

78 See Interview with Brian Banda, www.youtube.com/watch?v=o-GyZkrkTTg.

the demonstrations using city by-laws and other methods. DPP youths called *ana adadi* were recruited and behaved violently with "impunity" against anti-government demonstrators. On 25 September 2019, Billy Mayaya alongside four other CSO activists was brutally attacked by *ana adadi* in full view of the Blantyre police. The police merely stood by.

In the run-up to the 2019 elections, the voices of activism against the MEC and Mutharika grew louder, with the HRDC playing a major role. Later the activists called for both Jane Ansah and her "appointing authority" (the president) to resign. By initially targeting Ansah, rather than the "elected" president, HRDC somewhat blind-sided the DPP system, avoiding charges of "treason". Many Malawians perceived Jane Ansah's MEC as biased in favour of the ruling party, helping them to rig the elections with various methods, including the use of Tippex correction fluid on ballot return forms. The HRDC mobilised Malawians and gave them the confidence to believe that this time their voices would be heard.

Young unemployed people, urban and peri-urban youth, disillusioned with DPP governance, were the core of the demonstrators. The Malawi Army, led by General Vincent Nundwe, provided protection for the demonstrators from overzealous "tear-gas happy" riot police and *ana adadi* cadets. Army neutrality in the face of police partiality encouraged the HRDC-led anti-Ansah movement to morph into an anti-Mutharika "movement".

DPP cadets and their party machinery ran a counter movement, attempting to defuse and neutralise protests, using the motto *Awona Nyekhwe*! suggesting that anyone opposed to *adadi* (father) Mutharika's government would face stiff consequences. A number of casualties resulted among DPP and opposition supporters. The *nyekhwe* threats were real: frightened local councils tried to stop demonstrations; and the police, afraid of losing their jobs, looked the other way as people were assaulted. The HRDC emerged as agents of change in the face of opposition parties' hesitancy and apathy where they should have been challenging flawed governance. The HRDC leadership was confident. They succeeded, with good legal advice, by playing by the rules and following constitutionalism.

Another positive factor that contributed to change between 2019 and 2020 was the fact that three major opposition parties—MCP, UTM and PP—warily worked together in a serious attempt at opposing an incumbent party that was establishing a potentially long lasting "DPP system" of impunity. United, they were able to talk about concrete issues affecting their supporters: corruption, pensions, pay for chiefs, reduced fertiliser prices and job creation.

Third but more problematic was the rural factor. During the 2019 post-election protests, another group of protesters, in line with Afrobarometer predictions, came to prominence and was symbolised by villagers from Msundwe. Rural protests were problematic for the opposition parties due to their desperation, lawlessness, violence and use of traditional motifs, like *nyau.* Above all, they had their own agendas.

Another factor is that a generational change in political attitudes also contributed to the HRDC's support and Chilima fed into this demographic using his oratory and presentational skills.[79] The impatient insistence and willingness to fight "fire with fire" and Chilima's use of youth jargon resonated with a youth not afraid to stand for their rights against insensitive rule by *adadi* (patrimonialism or gerontocracy).

If the PAC "midwifed" the 1992–94 transition, then the Malawi Defence Force and the judicial system played guardian angel to events that pitted the opposition and youth-led pressure groups against a well-entrenched incumbent. The broad coalition between the opposition and civil society pressure groups and an activated rural and urban civil society willing to articulate its grievances seems, from the events of this period, to be the required minimum to call a ruling party to account.

A Promising Nyekhwe-Free Future?

The considerable work done by HRDC in objecting to, and subsequently achieving the removal of, the MEC chair Jane Ansah, and her replacement with Justice Chifundo Kachale, levelled the electoral field for the opposition. The Tonse Alliance government came in with an inbuilt tension between a "power consolidating" conservative MCP and some so-called "transformative" parties like the UTM, PETRA, Malawi Forum for Unity and National Development (MAFUNDE) and PPM, as well as the Citizens For Transformation (CFT) movement. Lazarus Chakwera declared that he wanted to "clear the swamp of corruption," indicating a desire for a clean old-fashioned corruption-free government based on "Hi Five" ideals of "Prospering Together, Uniting

79 Wellman Kondowe and Flemmings Fishani Ngwira, "Projecting Voice in Political Discourse: A Study of Saulos Klaus Chilima's Discursive Strategies, Malawi", *Theory and Practice in Language Studies* 9/5 (n.d.): 500.doi:10.17507/ TPLS.0905.03.

Malawi, Ending Corruption, following the Rule of Law, and practising Servant Leadership". That may not necessarily create jobs for the rural and urban working classes who marched with him. And commentators noted that Chakwera was no "pushover". He had been hard on internal MCP dissenters in the past, citing his handling of MCP "veterans" like Louis Chimango, Joseph Njobvuyalema, Lovemore Munlo, Jessie Kabwila, Nancy Tembo and Richard Msowoya.

On the other hand, the UTM and smaller parties' "transformative" agenda can only be actualised if there is indeed a clean united government, as their "Tonse" (All of us) motif suggested. However, Chakwera's first cabinet appointments pointed towards the "same old, same old" politics of neopatrimonial appeasement. Appointments reminded observers that, in Malawi, the biggest source of rent for rent-seeking political actors is the government.[80] What of the youth who marched with the HRDC?

Opposition movements are created out of discontent. Equally, solutions are usually, if not always, political. The underlying "swamp" in Malawi is economic poverty, both material and metaphorical. As Henry Chingaipe observed:

> political and economic institutions are products of politics and reflect temporal elite settlements. Thus, the road to understanding the formation, maintenance and change of institutions, especially of (SBRs) State Business Relationships, has to be a political one. A search for obstacles to broad-based economic, social and political development must concentrate on identifying the institutions that serve small groups of elites at the expense of broad access to opportunities by the non-elite majority. Reform of these institutions, however, will hardly be without controversy and can be expected to be slow.[81]

In 1992–94, Malawi had a transition from a one-party state to a democratic one. The workers who shook Dr Banda's regime in 1992 saw their efforts translate into a transfer of power from MCP elites to UDF *achikulire.* One does not have to be a Marxist theoretician to opine that there is a greater chance that the youth who braved *ana adadi* may see another elite transfer of power, with very little of the middle class "system" rubble being cleared.

---

80 Cf. J. Said and K. Singini, "The Political Economy Determinants of Economic Growth in Malawi", ESID Working Paper No. 40. Manchester, UK: University of Manchester, 2014, available at www.effective-states.org.

81 Henry G. Chingaipe Ng'oma, "Business and the State in Malawi the Politics of Institutional Formation, Maintenance and Change", PhD, University of York, 2010.

Conclusion

From a purely political science perspective people see winning and losing elections as only due to tangible factors, like funding, ethnicity and incumbency, and opposition parties as always being on full-throttle opposition duties. We have attempted to show that opposition parties and groups in Malawi, though often ill-funded, had periods of genuine measurable popularity and hence the ability to hold the government to account. And yet, there are periods when the formal opposition has performed perfunctorily, failing to use its full powers of opposition.

In an economy like Malawi's where the government is the main target for "rent-seekers", holding political power means having access to patronage, contracts, parastatal jobs, lucrative diplomatic postings, et cetera. But what we term "negative power" patronage also resides in opposition parties, even briefcase ones; they are potential troublemakers to be silenced or co-opted via *kudyetsedwa masikono* (being fed scones) or punished to *nyekhwe* proportions by having the liberties and economic wellbeing of their supporters curtailed.

Opposition parties can sometimes cruise along at that "negative power" rate for years. When they perceive an opportunity to win, gloves may come off. As Pascal Kishindo observes:

> … *ndale* is Chichewa for politics … [originally it had] no political connotations. [The original meaning of] *ndale* was "a mode of wrestling in which one [trips and] overthrows the other, […] tripping [here is called] *kupinga/kutchera. Kupinga/kutchera ndale*, then, is to "throw an obstacle in the path that your fellow may stumble" … Politics is concerned with the winning and holding of government power … winning political power entails not only that one's opponent "stumbles", but better still, disappears from the field of play completely. … […] to engage in politics is regarded as an instrument of settling scores and punishing those that hold opposing views.[82]

What Kishindo outlines here is a 1970s version of *nyekhwe*. *Nyekhwe*, like *wina alira,* feeds into the political discourses easily: if you lose you will cry, sweat and see the unexpected. Kayira et al. noted that "…these ethnic associations have the potential to be used for political mobilisation, especially when ethnic traditional authorities lack the capacity and autonomy to block the political manipulation of ethnic organisations".[83] *Nyekhwe* feeds seamlessly into

82 Pascal Kishindo, "Evolution of Political Terminology in Chichewa", 26.

83 Gift Wasambo Kayira, Paul Chiudza Banda and Amanda Lea Robinson, "Ethnic Associations and Politics in Contemporary Malawi", *Journal of Eastern African Studies* 13/4 (2019), 718.

ethnicised politics. In the 2020 elections Mulhako, Ngoni and *Nyau* discourses were recruited. Afrobarometer studies show an ethnicised rural DPP and MCP support pattern.

We highlight the dissonance between the very scientific and jurisprudential evidence in the Constitutional and Supreme Court cases in 2020 and the political discourses of the re-run 2020 elections. The latter recruited re-invented and ethnicised versions of flawed collective political memories of legitimation. For example, placing Peter Mutharika as the "father" of the nation and the younger politicians as "ungrateful, impatient" children. Using orality, Malawian and southern African politicians can create versions of a utopian political long and immediate past, replete with concepts of *ubuntu* (humanity) and *mwambo* (tradition). In 2019 and 2020 older Malawians were reminded of Dr Banda's *ngwazi* and *mbumba* theories as they heard about what would happen to those who crossed/opposed *adadi.* By utilising ethnic motifs, political discourses aimed at the rural population multiparty politics are reduced to "them and us, bypassing the socio-economic needs of the working classes, both rural and urban".[84]

We argue that the concept of *nyekhwe,* based on ancient and often flawed and re-invented political memories, hampers the Malawian opposition from acting as one that holds government to account and promotes opposition behaviour that is always reactionary and subservient to the dictates of the ruling party. This sometimes reduces the opposition to "briefcase party" managers,[85] collaborators and chameleon figures waiting to be "fed scones" rather than representing the interests of those sweating in the subsistence fields of Malawi.

---

84 Lumumba, PLO 2016 (interview in which he states "… yes he is a thief, but he is our thief") www.vanguardngr.com/2016/07/people-elected-public-offices-africa-thieves-lumumba/.

85 Refers to a party of one man or woman and his/her document-containing briefcase.

Chapter 9

Guarding the Guardians: Auditing Security Sector Governance in Malawi

Dan Kuwali

Introduction

The National Security Policy (NSP) in Malawi was launched on 6 March 2018 to ensure, among other things, the professionalism, coordination and interoperability of security organs in the country.[1] The primary aim of the Policy is to ensure the security of the population in Malawi, its citizens abroad, and the state in order to pursue by constitutional, democratic, just, sustainable and peaceful means, its national interests and national, regional and international objectives.[2] The NSP provides a national security structure that seeks to form an institutional framework including all stakeholders, such as the armed forces, law enforcement and co-opted civil institutions and private organisations. However, the security institutions in the country still operate more in silos, parallel to one another rather than in an integrated way. Politics, and not policy, seems to be at the heart of the disjointed operations of the security actors. In many instances, however, there has been poor co-ordination among security institutions, on the one hand, and between security institutions and other stakeholders, on the other hand, which has posed serious challenge in the provision of security in the country.

The existence of individuals and informal or semi-formal groups including political party cadres, engaged in security activities, poses a security risk to public authorities and other individuals. The NSP intends to promote effective regulation and control of private sector security companies, political party cadres, informal or semi-formal groups engaged in security activities. The question of democratic oversight and accountability of the security system goes to the heart of security sector governance. In Malawi, oversight exists at the executive, judiciary and legislature levels with the Committee of the National

---

1 Malawi Government, *National Security Policy*, Lilongwe, March 2018.

2 Ibid, 2.

Assembly on Defence and Security as a key oversight mechanism. In addition, there is also provision for extra-parliamentary oversight in the form of civil society agencies, the Anti-Corruption Bureau (ACB), the Office of the Ombudsman and other independent bodies such as the Malawi Human Rights Commission. Operational oversight is provided for by the security agencies themselves. Democratic oversight of the security sector is a key requirement for local ownership and public accountability. The NSP drafting implementation and multi-level monitoring frameworks should allow for the identification of the extent to which the activities and programme of the relevant statutory and non-statutory security providers comply with the objectives of the NSP.[3]

For example, while the Malawi Police Service (MPS) has been widely condemned as heavily politicised, mistrusted and seen as a threat to the public when, in fact, it is supposed to be the guarantor of public security, the military is trusted and commended for its professionalism.[4] Therefore, this chapter examines the challenges and opportunities to enhance security sector governance in Malawi. Among others, the discussion involves addressing the critical questions of how to arrest the perceived politicisation of security agencies and the militarisation of politics in Malawi. It does so by taking a juridical audit of the implementation of the notion of democratic control of the security sector in Malawi by examining the challenges faced by key security organs of the country. The chapter concludes by arguing that, to enhance security sector governance in Malawi, the key is to construct an institutional framework that nurtures professionalism and independence in the security sector by preventing direct political control of security organs. This could be done by, among others, enhancing the knowledge of politicians on the security sector; improving civil-military relations; periodic and transparent recruitment processes in the security sector; as well as provision of timely and appropriate training.

Overview of the National Security Policy

When Malawi adopted a progressive National Security Policy (NSP) in 2018 it embraced a paradigm shift from state security to human security and recognised the involvement of other non-tradition actors in the security sector such as the

---

3 Ibid, 22.

4 Afrobarometer, Malawi, http://afrobarometer.org/countries/malawi?page=1 [20.10.2020].

judiciary, the media and civil society. The NSP, which is a home-grown policy framework, has embraced a Whole of Government Approach (WGA) in addressing the various security challenges and threats facing the country.[5] The WGA or wholistic approach entails the involvement of all relevant sectors including economic, political, judicial and civil society to devise strategies to resolve the impasse within the spheres of their influence. The efforts in 2020 to respond to the novel Coronavirus Disease (Covid-19) pandemic have shown the need for a WGA in tackling contemporary threats to security. The traditional meaning of national security has been viewed in a rather narrow sense concentrating on the defence of sovereign state from physical attacks using conventional approaches. Recent trends have, however, unveiled a wide range of threats to the government and the people of Malawi, from threats to the economy and environment, and disasters, to organised crime, famine and health issues, among others. These new challenges require more innovative and coordinated responses from the government as well as civil stakeholders for the country to excel further. The NSP was drafted and adopted almost simultaneously with the National Peace Policy (NPP), which has also embraced human security.[6] The NPP established the National Peace Architecture, which is an overarching body that coordinates all initiatives to maintain peace and resolve conflicts in Malawi.

The NSP has clarified the institutional framework within which the Malawi Defence Force (MDF), the Malawi Police Service (MPS), Malawi Prisons Service (PS), National Intelligence Services (NIS), the Department of Immigration and Citizenship Services (Immigration Department), and civil institutions of the state will coordinate their activities to create an integrated and cohesive national security network to safeguard Malawi's national interests.[7] The NSP outlines that in identifying and responding to security challenges, the focus shall be on addressing the root causes of the problems and not only the symptoms. In so doing, relevant authorities are required to ensure inclusiveness of all stakeholders in all the various stages of public policy in order to facilitate effective responses in overcoming threats to national security and conflict resolution at the lowest level possible. The NSP further

---

5 Malawi Government, National Security Policy (NSP), paragraph 2. 3.

6 Malawi Government, National Peace Policy, Lilongwe, August 2017, www.undp.org/content/dam/malawi/docs/UNDP_Malawi_National%20Peace%20Policy.pdf [20.10.2020].

7 Malawi Government, National Security Policy (NSP), 1.

recognises that relevant authorities have clearly defined roles and responsibilities and division of labour in the implementation of the NSP.[8]

The NSP establishes the National Security Council (NSC), which is the custodian of the Policy and mandated to make recommendations to the Cabinet on matters relating to defence and security in Malawi.[9] The Secretariat of the NSC is headed by the National Security Adviser. The Defence Force Commander and the Inspector General (IG), who are members of the National Security Committee and the National Operations Committee, are the Military Advisor and Police Advisor to the Government, respectively. As a member of the National Security Committee, the Director General (DG) of NIS is required to provide relevant information to the National Operations Committee.[10] Subject to the directions of the NSC or the National Operations Committee, Regional and District Operations Committees are responsible for the policy to be followed regarding operations in their areas for the maintenance or restoration of law and order, and for giving directives on the relative priority of tasks, when necessary.[11] In this way, the police and the military are the instruments by which law and order is maintained or restored, and their respective commanders at the relevant level are responsible for orders, plans and executive action within the policy laid down by the relevant Operations Committees.[12] With the absence of principles of national policy on defence and security in section 13 of the Constitution, the NSP has closed the gap on guidelines for the security sector in Malawi. Like the NPP, the NSP does not necessarily have legal force, particularly due to the absence of a specific legal framework on national security.[13]

Auditing the Security Sector in Malawi

Since the NSP is an umbrella policy, the different organs in the security sector are supposed to formulate their own institutional policies which they have not yet done. Apart from a memorandum between the MDF and MPS on a code

---

8 Ibid, paragraph 2.4.

9 Ibid, 18.

10 Malawi Government, Instructions to the Malawi Administrative, Military and Police Officers on the Use of Armed Force in Case of Civil Disturbance paragraph 14.

11 Malawi Government, National Security Policy (NSP), paragraph 15.

12 Ibid, paragraph 16.

13 However, where applicable, reference can be made to institutional legislation such as the Defence Force Act, cap 12;01, the Police Act cap 13:01, National Intelligence Service Act, no 30 of 2018 as well as the Penal Code, cap 7:01 of the Laws of Malawi, among others.

of conduct, coordination and interoperability, there has generally been lack of centralised coordination of the security organs in Malawi mainly due to the inaction or passive approach of the office of the National Security Advisor.[14] For example, the skirmish between prison warders and police officers in April 2020 exposed how disjointed the security organs have become in Malawi. While both the NSP and the NPP have embraced human security in their approach the third Malawi Growth Development Strategy Paper (MGDSP III) only focuses on state security, particularly protection of sovereignty, territorial integrity and vital national interests against external and internal threats.[15] Below are some highlights of a juridical audit of the country's security organs.

The Challenge of Policing Protests

One of the challenges that has faced security organs in Malawi is how to strike a balance between the right to protest and prevention of riots. The challenges of policing the protests were manifested in the excessive use of force by the police on 20 July 2011.[16]

As underscored in *Malawi Law Society and Others* v. *The State and the President of Malawi and Others*, the only restrictions that can be justified to the exercise of this right are those prescribed by law, especially in the interest of national security, public order and safety, health and the enjoyment of rights and freedoms of others in line with section 44(1) of the Constitution.[17] As every person is guaranteed the freedom of peaceful assembly, it is the duty of the police to provide protection of public safety and the rights of all persons in question.[18] Where the police have reasonable grounds to believe that they will not be able to provide adequate protection for the persons participating in such assembly or demonstration, section 105 (1) of the Police Act requires that they should notify the convener in writing and may prevent persons participating in the assembly or demonstration from proceeding to a different place or

14 Malawi Defence Force and Malawi Police Service, Code of Conduct for Cooperation and Coordination between the Malawi Defence Force and the Malawi Police Service Lilongwe, November 2016.

15 Malawi Government, Malawi Growth and Development Strategy III (20-2022): Building a productive, competitive and resilient nation, Lilongwe, November 2017 p. 65, Malawi-Growth-_-Development-Strategy-MGDS-III-2017-2022-Final-Version-copy%20(1).pdf, [20.10.2020].

16 Malawi Human Rights Commission (MHRC), Final Report on 20 July 2011 Demonstrations, 5 April 2012.

17 Miscellaneous Civil Cause No. 78 of 2002 as per Justice Twea.

18 See section 38 of the Constitution of the Republic of Malawi (Constitution).

deviating from the route specified in the notice or from disobeying any condition to which the holding of the assembly or demonstration is subject.

The onus is, therefore, on the convenors of demonstrators that demonstrations should be peaceful and non-violent lest there will be restrictions on the right to freely assemble and demonstrate. Where the exercise of the freedom of assembly is not peaceful and becomes violent, it turns into an unlawful assembly and a riot and the police are mandated to use all reasonable force necessary including the use of firearms to prevent the commission of crime.[19]

To conduct law enforcement operations in accordance with the law, law enforcement personnel should possess relevant knowledge, skills and equipment. Law enforcement personnel are the guardians of the law, especially the police who are the first line of defence for human rights. The community depends on the police to protect the full range of rights through the effective enforcement of the country's criminal laws. Therefore, the effective training of law enforcement officers is an essential element in global efforts to promote and protect human rights.[20] In order to effectively protect human rights, law enforcement officers must first know and understand them. In the case of *National Consultative Council (NCC) v. The Attorney General (AG),* in a democracy, law enforcement personnel must sharpen their skills and competence and be familiar with the various international guidelines and bodies of principles and be able to use them as tools in their law enforcement operations such as riot control and crowd dispersal. Therefore, before deployment of law enforcement personnel for such operations, it is necessary to assess and ascertain that they have adequate personnel, requisite training, knowledge and skills as well as appropriate tactical equipment to overcome any resistance during crowd dispersal and riot control operations.[21]

There have also been questions with regard to the propensity of the MDF to deploy in internal security operations. The answer is found in section 160(1(b) of the Constitution which mandates the MDF to assist civilian authorities including the police in the proper exercise of their functions, where they are overstretched or overwhelmed, which is a decision that should be made by the president upon recommendation of the National Security Advisor. It is clear

---

19 See section 71 of the Penal Code.

20 *Human Rights and Law Enforcement: A Trainer's Guide on Human Rights for the Police*, New York and Geneva, 2002.

21 *Human Rights Standards and Practice for the Police: Expanded Pocket Book on Human Rights for the Police*, Professional Training Series No. 5/Add.3, New York and Geneva, 2004.

that the use of force including firearms to disperse a riotous assembly is a sensitive and delicate operation. To conduct such an operation in accordance with the law, it is necessary for law enforcement personnel to have the requisite training, knowledge and skill as well as appropriate tactical weapons. Such operations require clear and unambiguous orders with feasible rules on the use of force and firearms. Following the conviction of a Police Constable in the case of *Republic v. Stewart Lobo,* it is also important to sensitise law enforcement personnel that they are protected by law where they use reasonable force to quell a riot in order to enhance their morale, confidence, discipline and willingness to act.[22] Suffice to say that the Supreme Court of Appeal acquitted Constable Lobo on the grounds that he was not at the scene of the crime.[23] However, considering the apparent paucity of appropriate tactical weapons for crowd dispersal in law enforcement agencies in the country, it is imperative to contain and avert escalation of demonstrations. To do so, there is need to provide clarity on the distinction between peaceful assembly and unlawful assembly including riots.

Whither Professionalism of the Police

There has been a consistent cacophony about the lowering of professionalism in the MPS and a perception of politicisation of the police. The allegations against the police for rape and sexual assault when they raided villages of suspected law-breakers at Msundwe in Lilongwe in 2019 exacerbated the denting of the image of the police even further.[24] According to section 153 (1) of the Constitution the MPS is established as an independent organ of the executive to provide for the protection of public safety and the rights of persons in accordance with the law and subject to the direction of the courts.[25] The police enjoys immense powers, which must be controlled to prevent their misuse.[26] The political responsibility of the MPS for ensuring public safety and security lies with the minister responsible for Home Affairs and Internal

---

22 *Republic v. Stewart Lobo*, Criminal Case No. 24 of 2013. See also section 74 of the Penal Code, cap 7:01 of the Laws of Malawi.

23 *Stewart Lobo v The Republic,* Malawi Supreme Court of Appeal, Miscellaneous Criminal Appeal No. 24 of 2013.

24 See *The State and the Inspector General of Police, the Clerk of the National Assembly and the Minister of Finace (Ex Parte MM and others)*, Judicial Review Cause No. 7 of 2020).

25 Section 153(3) of the Constitution.

26 Human Rights Initiative, The Police-Politician Paradigm: The Executive Relationship, http://www.humanrightsinitiative.org/programs/aj/police/india/initiatives/police_executive_paradigm_stenning.pd> (accessed 24 June 2020), 13.

Security.[27] In this sense, the police are only implementers of policy. The Constitution also dictates that the IG "shall not be subject to the direction or control of any other person or authority" in the exercise of their duties and powers.[28] Law enforcement officials are required, at all times, to fulfil the duty imposed on them by law, by serving the community and by protecting all persons against illegal acts, consistent with the high degree of responsibility required by their profession.[29] Policing has intimate connections with social life, social progress, and social change.[30]

The constitutional roles of the MPS represent a shift from "policing the public" as it was during the one-party era, to "serving the public".[31] This transformation is also evidenced by the change of name of the police in Malawi, from the "Malawi Police Force" to the current "Malawi Police Service". The public plays a substantial role in policing and it is important to maintain the relationship between the public and the police. *The police are the only members of the public who are paid to give full-time attention to duties which are incumbent on every citizen, in the interests of community welfare and existence.*[32] This explains why the IG ought to steer the MPS clear of any political influence.[33]

The Constitution requires members of the MPS to discharge the functions, powers and duties as impartial civil servants of the general public and the government of the day.[34] For this reason, members of the MPS are not permitted to participate directly in political activities although this does not restrict their right to vote. Any police officer who wants to participate in active politics has the right to resign or retire in order to freely engage in political pursuits.[35] To facilitate the political independence for the MPS, the Consti-

---

27 Section 153(4) of the Constitution. See also Human Rights Initiative, above, 1.

28 Section 154(5) of the Constitution of the Republic of Malawi.

29 United Nations (UN), United Nations Blue Book, www.uncjin.org/Documents/Blue Book/BlueBook/english/bbepolrol.html (accessed 2 June 2020).

30 Bryan Vila and Cynthia Morris (eds), *The Role of Police in American Society: A Documentary History*, Westport, CT: Greenwood Press, 1999; see also The Role of the Police in Society, http://faculty.ncwc.edu/mstevens/205/205lect01.htm [0.6.2020].

31 C. Thomas Griffiths and Simon N. Verdun-Jones, *Canadian Criminal Justice*, Toronto: Harcourt Press, 1994, 70-71.

32 Robert Peel, Principle Seven in Policing Politics and Public Policy, http://menno zacharias.com/ [23.6.2020].

33 J. Mervyn Jones and J. T. Winkler, "Beyond the Beat: The Facts about Policing in a Riotous City", *Journal of Law and Society* 9/1 (Summer 1982), 103-114.

34 Section 158 of the Constitution of the Republic of Malawi.

35 Section 158 (1) and (2) of the Constitution.

tution also prohibits the government and any political party to cause any member of the MPS "to exercise functions, powers or duties for the purposes of promoting or undermining the interests or affairs of any political party or individual member of that party", and members of the MPS are also prohibited from acting that way.[36] Further, politicians are prohibited from causing members of the MPS to deploy any kind of support to promote or undermine any political party or members thereof as well as interest groups. Members of the MPS are also prohibited from deploying resources in such manner.[37]

Regarding law enforcement, the police must be independent in their decision-making with respect to enforcing the law in individual cases. This includes important decisions about whom to investigate, search, question, detain, arrest and prosecute in a particular case. Governments are not precluded from advising police of their views with respect to police decisions that may have significant public policy or public interest implications, for example, matters of national security, or matters that have repercussions for international relations. However, in all such cases the government must not seek to exert undue pressure on the police.[38] In *Malawi Law Society and Another v. The State and Others,* the then president issued a directive at a political rally to the police and the Defence Force not to allow and deal with any person who demonstrated against a proposed Constitutional Amendment Bill to allow for the third term for the presidency. In that case, Justice Twea underscored that section 158 of the Constitution, which provides for the political independence of the MPS, restricts police officers to professionalism and constitutionalism failing which they would be subject to disciplinary action.[39] Police officers are, therefore, obliged to stick to professionalism and constitutionalism failing which they would be subject to disciplinary action.[40] The buffer to ensure that politicians are not directly involved in the operational aspects of policing is the minister.

A classic instance of undue influence on the police is when the president of the Republic of Malawi ordered members of the MPS in 2011 to shoot to kill suspects of felonies in order to deter potential perpetrators. The president had

---

36 Section 158(3) of the Constitution.

37 Section 158 (4) of the Constitution.

38 Human Rights Initiative, above note 19, 3.

39 *Malawi Law Society and Episcopal Conference of Malawi and Council of Churches v. The State and the President of Malawi, Minister of Home Affairs, The Inspector General of Police and the Army General,* Miscellaneous Civil Cause No. 78 of 2000.

40 Per Justice Twea, *Malawi Law Society et al. v. The State et al., supra* note 23.

no mandate to give such direction to the MPS as the president does not have political control of the MPS.[41] On the other hand, the order is manifestly illegal as the Police Act in section 30(1) (c) (iv) explicitly abhors a policy of shoot to kill.[42] The weakness of this arrangement was noticed when the former president supported the then IG in an act that endangered academic freedom at the University of Malawi in 2011. The role of the then state president in the academic freedom saga from February 2011 to October 2011 exposed the lack of independence of, and the effect of political influence on, the police. The former president commended—as opposed to condemning—the miscalculation by the IG. Apparently, the said president weighed into the debate purportedly as the "Commander-in-Chief (C-I-C) of the MPS" and not necessarily as the Chancellor of the University of Malawi. It should be noted that the president is not, and should never be, the C-i-C of the MPS as it is supposed to be independent and insulated from political influence.

As noted above, the responsibility of intervening, if at all, lay with the Minister of Home Affairs who has the political responsibility for the MPS, and to an extent, the Police Service Commission (PSC) by virtue of their disciplinary mandate. The Parliamentary Committee on Defence and Security had the mandate to intervene by virtue of its oversight function. There is a significant distinction between appropriate political direction from the executive to the police, and inappropriate political interference in operational policing matters, both in terms of the way it is expressed in law and policy, as well as in practice. A careful balance should be struck between legitimate "supervision" of the police by the political executive and illegitimate interference and influence. Conversely, the police must always remain accountable to elected politicians—and therefore, the general public—for enforcing the law and to perform its duties in accordance with the law. The political executive must be able to craft policy and seek accountability for poor performance or wrongdoing by an essential public service paid for by taxpayer money. To avoid direct political control of the police by politicians, there is need to strengthen oversight mechanisms as well as the PSC, which should have powers to oversee operational aspects of policing as opposed to the current arrangement where the politicians seem to have direct political control.

---

41 Section 78 of the Constitution. See also section 154 of the Constitution.

42 Police Act, Cap. 13:01 of the Laws of Malawi.

Absence of Policy on Correction Services

Section 163 of the Constitution establishes the Malawi Prisons Service (PS), which consists of all penal institutions, labour camps, special and secure schools and other institutions that are used to house, detain and rehabilitate persons sentenced to imprisonment in whatever form such imprisonment may take. For the avoidance of doubt, these do not include holding cells in police stations. The PS is headed by a Commissioner for Prisons whose principal responsibility is to ensure the proper and efficient administration of the penal institutions.[43] Section 167 of the Constitution establishes the Prisons Service Commission whose powers are mainly administrative in nature, particularly appointment of persons to hold or act in offices in the PS, other than the Chief Commissioner for Prisons. The powers include confirmation of appointments and to remove such persons from office. Critical powers in relation to the PS are with the Inspectorate of Prisons, which, in section 169 (3) of the Constitution, include monitoring the conditions, administration and general functioning of penal institutions in line with international standards; and investigative powers; and the power to visit any institution within the PS with or without notice and without let or hindrance. Notwithstanding the impressive powers of the Inspectorate of Prisons, there have been consistent reports that inmates in Malawi prisons are confined in harsh and unsanitary conditions.[44] Most of these problems hinge on funding which requires Government to provide adequate resources to the PS.[45]

---

[43] Section 163 (2) of the Constitution.

[44] Mashable, "Life in prison: the prisons in Malawi are overcrowded, filthy and plagued by disease", https://mashable.com/2015/09/06/malawis-prisons-overcrowded/ (accessed 13 July 2020). See also Dr Vera Mlangazuwaa Chirwa, "Prisons in Malawi", Report of the Special Rapporteur on Prisons and Conditions of Detention on a visit from 17 to 28 June 2001, African Commission on Human and Peoples' Rights, www.achpr.org/public/Document/file/English/achpr30_misrep_specmec_priso_malawi_2001_eng.pdf, [13.7.2020].

[45] Malawi Inspectorate of Prisons, "Prisoners' Health and Staff Welfare", Report to Parliament, August 2014, p. iii. See also World Prison Brief, Malawi, https://prisonstudies.org/country/malawi [13.7.2020]. See also Michael Wines. "Wasting away, A Million Wait in African Jails", *New York Times*, 6 November 2005, Late Edition (East Coast): 1.1. Malawi Inspectorate of Prisons, as above. See also World Prison Brief, Malawi, https:// prisonstudies.org/country/malawi> [13.7.2020].

Loopholes in Migration Management Laws

The Immigration Department derives its mandate primarily from section 47 of the Constitution, the Malawi Citizenship Act[46] and the Immigration Act.[47] Although the Immigration Act accords Immigration Officers with powers of arrest, detention and search, its major weakness is the lack of an independent law providing for the establishment of the Immigration Department and its functions. This loophole seems to emanate from the history of the Immigration Department as it has for a long time been seen as a branch under the MPS. Immigration officers have been recruited together with police officers and undergo the same training at the Police Training School and Police Training College. Indeed, senior police officers have been appointed to head the Immigration Department. This arrangement has arguably led to lack of focus, stalled progress and development in the Immigration Department as a specialised institution on matters concerning citizenship and immigration. The apparent lack of linkage between the National Registration Bureau (NRB) and the Immigration Department, especially on registration of citizens and foreign-ners in the country is also a major weakness in the system.

Politicisation of the National Intelligence Services

Despite its inception in 1997, law regulating the NIS was only enacted in 2018 after the institution had time and again been changing names from being a "service" to a "bureau" back and forth depending on the taste of the government in power.[48] Section 5 of the National Intelligence Service Act (NIS Act) requires that the appointment of the DG of the NIS should be confirmed by the Public Affairs Committee of Parliament. One main challenge, however, has been circumventing of section 5 of the NIS Act and the recruitment of political party cadres who often are unskilled to perform such technical functions as collecting information, analysing and managing intelligence.[49] This requires involvement of professionals who are trained in the art of collecting, collating, evaluating, analysing, disseminating and preserving intelligence.[50]

---

46 Chapter 15:01 of the Laws of Malawi.
47 Chapter 15:03 of the Laws of Malawi.
48 National Intelligence Service Act, no 30 of 2018.
49 Section 4 of the National Intelligence Service Act, no 30 of 2018.
50 Ibid.

Although members of the NIS are prohibited from engaging in political activities in section 11 of the NIS Act, concerns have been raised over politicisation whereby the NIS has been used as a tool for the political party in power to profile individuals in the opposition. Such partisan use of the NIS creates cracks to miss out on critical intelligence for national security, including social, military or economic, as the focus has usually been on domestic politics which is not part of its mandate as explicitly stated in section 4 of the NIS Act. The Complaints Tribunal, which is supposed to be an oversight body for the NIS has not yet been established as required by section 26 of the NIS Act. Failure or delay to operationalise the Complaints Tribunal deprives the citizenry of a convenient forum to lodge their complaints relating to the operations of the NIS.

The Question of Upholding Constitutional Order

On a number of occasions, the MDF's professionalism has been put to the test. The most cited case is in April 2012 when the then state president died and his inner circle did not want the then vice president to take over as required by the Constitution. Section 83 of the Constitution as read with section 160(1) (b) of the Constitution mandates the MDF to uphold and protect the constitutional order in Malawi and assist the civil authorities in the proper exercise of their functions. Going by section 160(1)(b) of the Constitution together with regulations 5(2) and 7 of the Defence Force (Regular Force) (Officers) Regulations firstly, to uphold and protect the constitutional order implies that members of the MDF promise to stay loyal to the government of the day that is based on the Constitution; secondly, to support and defend the dictates of the Constitution as the supreme law of the land. The converse of this is that service members promise to oppose political manoeuvres that are outside the Constitution and that service members are not obliged to take orders that contravene the Constitution on the basis of section 160(2).

To decipher the meaning of the term "constitutional order", the key is in slicing the fundamental principles in section 12 of the Constitution, which include, (a) all legal and political authority of the state derives from the people of Malawi; (b) fiduciary duty of exercise of powers of state; (c) the principle of social contract (sustained trust maintained through democratic choice); protection of human rights and human dignity; (f) equality before the law; and (f) the rule of law and that no one is above the law (which underscores the need to take into account the interests, wishes and aspirations of the people of Malawi).

Borrowing the reasoning of Justice Tambala in *NCC v. AG*, upholding constitutional order entails performing constitutional functions without violating the rights and freedoms of the individuals and not frustrating the will of the people as guaranteed by the Constitution.[51]

The Challenges of Democratic Control of the Security Sector

The limits of civilian control of the security sector were tested between May 2019 and July 2020 when appointments and orders for deployment of senior military and police officers came from the State House and not the relevant oversight bodies. For example, in *The State (on application by Dr George Kainja) v. The President of the Republic of Malawi and the Acting Inspector General of Police*, the High Court set aside an order to deploy the Commissioner of Police to a diplomatic mission where the Applicant argued that the action was not taken in public interest but was a case of victimisation of a professional officer at the behest of persons interested to target such officials.[52] Similar orders were made for some General Officers in the MDF against the requirements of section 161(4)(b). The appointments were muted when the General Officers diplomatically challenged them for being unconstitutional, inappropriate and mala fide. The Constitution provides for the subordination of the armed forces to civilian control. The chapeau of section 160(1) of the Constitution dictates that the MDF shall operate at all times under the direction civil authorities entrusted with such power by the Constitution.[53]

To this end, the president has the ultimate responsibility of the MDF as the Commander-in-Chief (C-i-C).[54] The political responsibility of the Defence Force is vested in the Minister of Defence. The Defence Force Commander, who is appointed by the president, is accountable to the Minister of Defence in the day-to-day management of the Force.[55] As the C-i-C is also a leader of a political party in power, there is a thin line between objective control and political interest with regards to orders that the C-i-C may give to the Defence Force Commander. This arrangement may pose challenges where the C-i-C issues politically motivated orders as Defence Force Commanders may be compelled to obey such orders for fear of being seen to bite the finger that

51 *National Consultative Council* v. *The State,* [1994] MLR 243 (High Court of Malawi).

52 High Court, Lilongwe District Registry, Judicial Review Cause No. 38 of 2020.

53 Section 160 (1) of the Constitution of the Republic of Malawi.

54 Section 161(1) of the Constitution of the Republic of Malawi.

55 Section 161(2) and (3) of the Constitution of the Republic of Malawi.

feeds them. Illegal orders to the military by politicians are precursors to corruption, oppression and lack of professionalism.[56]

Mending Fences: Reconstituting the Security Sector in Malawi

In line with the country's NSP, the increasing complexity of contemporary and emerging threats requires an integrated and collaborative national security framework to address them. It is critical for key security agencies to work together in a fully integrated way to address the security interests of Malawians. To do this, the government should be committed to providing the leadership, resources and structures necessary to build a fully integrated and effective security system.[57] Below are some recommendations to enhance security sector governance in Malawi.

Incorporate Principles of National Policy on Defence and Security in the Constitution

This is further exacerbated by the fact that section 13 of the Constitution does not provide guidance for policy formulation and security sector governance in Malawi. For matters as important as defence and security of a nation, it is imperative that the guidelines governing approach to national security should be stipulated in the Constitution as opposed to leaving them at the whims of the political executive. As a way forward, it is necessary to incorporate the guiding principles of national police in section 13 of the Constitution to enable the political executive to craft policy that embodies the express wishes of the people of Malawi and which promote the principles of the Constitution, including human rights, rule of law and accountability for performance and operations by an essential public service paid for by taxpayer money.[58]

In order to implement the intention of the drafters of the Constitution on the professionalism, transparency and accountability of the security sector, the government should lay down policies and laws that protect the actors in the security sector from direct political control and enable the participation of the security sector towards the achievement of national security including human security. Further, improving managerial capacities of the authorities in the security sector is critical to the ownership and sustainability of good governance

---

56 Policy Studies Institute, *supra* note 19, 12.

57 NSP, note 1 above, 17.

58 Section 7 of the Constitution.

initiatives, national security strategies, defence policy and all other elements of security sector governance.[59]

Introducing an Oversight Role for the Police Service Commission (PSC)

There is a significant distinction between appropriate political direction from the executive branch of government to the police, and inappropriate political interference in operational policing matters, both in terms of the way it is expressed in law and policy, as well as in practice. Granted, the police must always remain accountable to elected politicians—and therefore, the general public—for enforcing the law and to perform its duties in accordance with the law. Therefore, a careful balance should be struck between legitimate "supervision" of the police by the executive and illegitimate interference and influence by politicians. The functions of the PSC are limited to disciplinary oversight thereby creating room for direct political control of the MPS by the politicians. This loophole can be closed by conferring a supervisory role on the PSC in order to make it more professional, transparent, accountable and, therefore, effective. This calls for rethinking and amending section 155 of the Constitution. As the PSC includes a judge and the ombudsman, it will be better placed to complement the oversight functions of the courts, the Human Rights Commission and the ombudsman in monitoring the performance of the MPS.[60]

Reforming the Correctional Services

What is certain is that the conditions in the prisons in Malawi are hard. What is not clear, however, is whether those conditions satisfy the principles of punishment, particularly the reformation of offenders. While such tough conditions may help deter potential offenders, they can equally harden habitual offenders. It is for this reason that the PS needs to reform and align itself to a correctional facility. The Inspectorate of Prisons has observed that in most prisons, inmates are generally kept idle without being equipped with vocational skills due to lack of resources. It is beyond dispute that equipping prisoners with vocational skills would contribute to their reformation and reintegration into society once they are released.[61] To supplement the funding to the PS,

---

[59] Dan Kuwali, "The End of Securocracy: The Future of Security Sector Governance in Malawi", *Malawi Law Journal* 6/1 (2012), 75-96.

[60] Dan Kuwali, "Addressing Contemporary Challenges to Security and Development in Malawi", Report of the Security Summit, 8-9 September 2015, Bingu International Conference Centre, Lilongwe, 11.

[61] Malawi Inspectorate of Prisons, above note 29, 2-3.

there should be an exemption on all revenue from the sale of agricultural products by the PS from being deposited into the Consolidated Fund in terms of section 172 of the Constitution but instead be reinvested in the farms and used to supplement the food budget for the prisons. There is need for a comprehensive policy to guide the operations of the PS including on education and provision of medical services for prisoners.[62] The link between the judiciary and the PS should be strengthened so that correctional facilities should actually serve to rehabilitate criminals and protect the public.

Reconciling Citizenship and Migration Management Legislation

The joint general training between police and immigration officers is commendable in terms of facilitating interoperability but this police-oriented programme should not overshadow the more specialised training of the latter. There should also be a deliberate policy for career immigration officers to lead the department, as imposing senior police officers on them may demoralise some immigration officers and erode the organisational culture and discipline. Section 47 of the Constitution is not adequate in describing who a citizen of Malawi is. It is also difficult to understand why the NRB, which is charged with the function of producing national identity cards in Malawi operates in parallel to the Immigration Department. A clear delineation and linkage of the roles of the two institutions will help to achieve one of the goals of the NSP to address migration management challenges, creation of a comprehensive national identification database for Malawian citizens, the creation of a system to be able to track immigrants in order to curb irregular migration and enhance border management processes.[63] Therefore, the Government should initiate a proper legislative and regulatory framework to govern citizenship and migration management in Malawi.[64]

Regulating the National Intelligence Services

The NIS Act is a comprehensive legislation which is frustrated by lack of implementation. The politicisation of the NIS at the expense of social, military and economic intelligence on domestic and international threats leads to poor policy decisions, inadequate protection of key national assets and interests and

---

62 Malawi Inspectorate of Prisons, "The Report of the Inspection of Prisons and Police Cells conducted by the Malawi Inspectorate of Prisons in March 2018", May 2018, ii-iii.

63 NSP, 11.

64 Kuwali, note 58 above, 15.

wastage of resources.[65] Section 4(2) of the NIS Act obliges the NIS to perform its functions at all times in the national interest and in compliance with Chapter IV of the Constitution. There are several steps that the NIS needs to take in order to live to up to its billing. First, there should be a sensitisation exercise for the members of the NIS on the NIS Act for them to understand their duties and functions and apolitical character. Secondly, recruitment of members of the NIS and appointment of the Director General and the Deputy Director General should be on merit and not politically motivated. Independence starts with recruitment of qualified personnel, and independence is sustained if there is no political influence in their course of their work.[66] Thirdly, the Complaints Tribunal should be operationalised in order to play its oversight role under section 26 of the NIS Act.

Arresting Politicisation of the Military

Section 160 (2) prohibits any person or authority from directing or deploying the MDF in contravention of the Constitution. However, the meaning and the extent of the term "uphold and protect the constitutional order" in the first limb of section 160(1)(b) has not been expounded in jurisprudence or military doctrine. In mundane terms, the martial aspects of the term "to uphold and protect the Constitutional order" entails that service members are obliged, to the best of their ability, to accomplish the missions given to them by the chain of command headed by the lawfully elected president, who is the constitutional C-i-C, in a manner consistent with the orders, laws, regulations and policies established by superior commanders, which are lawful and consistent with the Constitution. Simply put, the service members' oath is a promise that their loyalty is to the Constitution, the state and the people of Malawi, not a specific individual or political interest. This is why, in discharging their duties, service members are required to be professional, apolitical and patriotic, always acting with integrity.

Upholding Constitutional Order

The Constitution dictates that the powers of the president as the C-i-C shall only be exercised on the recommendation of the Defence Council, which is also mandated with, *inter alia,* the power to determine the operational use of the

65 NSP, note 1 above, 13.

66 NSP, note 1 above, 12.

MDF.[67] To ensure a system of checks and balances, the powers of the Defence Council and, by necessary implication, of the C-i-C, are exercised subject to the scrutiny of the Parliamentary Committee on Defence and Security.[68] The rationale of the doctrine of civilian control of the military is that "[w]ar is too important to be left to the generals".[69] The doctrine of "civilian control of the military", which is also referred to as "civil control of the armed forces" to cater for all arms bearing organs of the security sector, places ultimate responsibility for a country's strategic decision-making in the hands of the civilian political leadership, rather than professional military officers.[70]

Civil control is intended to ensure that decisions and risks affecting national defence and the employment of the MDF are taken by politicians who are accountable to the people rather than by military personnel who are not. As stated by Justice Tambala in the case of the *NCC v. AG*, the court held that law enforcement officials must be able to perform their functions of preserving peace, law and order without violating the rights and freedoms of the individuals. Matters of national security should not be used as an excuse for frustrating the will of the people expressed in the Constitution.[71] Sensitisation of politicians on defence and security issues is crucial in promoting effective civil-military relations for them to understand the rationale and limits of subordination of the armed forces to democratically elected political authorities, who are responsible for taking decisions concerning the defence of a country.[72] The relationship between the military and the political executive is critical to strengthening democracy, not limiting it.[73]

Minimising the Deployment of the MDF in Internal Security Operations

To reduce the involvement of the MDF in internal security operations, there is need to resuscitate and build the capacity of the MPS for it to be able to deal

---

67 Section 161 (4) of the Constitution of the Republic of Malawi as read with section 10 of the Defence Force Act, cap. 12:01 of the Laws of Malawi.

68 Section 45(2), 161(5) and 162(1) of the Constitution of the Republic of Malawi.

69 John Hampden Jackson, *Clemenceau and the Third Republic,* Westport, Connecticut: Hyperion Press, 1979, 228.

70 Peter D. Feaver, "The Civil-Military Problematique: Huntington, Janowitz and the Question of Civilian Control", *Armed Forces & Society* 23/2 (1996), 149-178.

71 *National Consultative Council v. The State,* note 47 above.

72 Levan Alapishvili, "The Civil-Military Relations and Democratic Control on Armed Forces in Caucasus - A Comparative Study", 9, http:/www.nato.int/acad/fellow/97-99/alapishvili.pdf [15.6.2020].

73 Human Rights Initiative, note 19, 13.

with internal security problems. In view of the interoperability of actors in the security sector, there is need for guidelines on interoperability to enhance proactivity and coordination of the stakeholders to ensure an effective and efficient response to humanitarian, peace and security concerns in Malawi. The goal is to improve professionalism and security sector governance in order to protect and enhance democracy and promote socio-economic development in Malawi. For the government to retain a hold on security there is need to enact laws that should govern the incorporation and registration of private security firms in the country. There is also need for legislation to regulate the activities of private security companies, including possession and use of firearms and such weapons by these private security firms. The government should also establish clear rules about the collaboration between private security companies and governmental security forces.[74]

Towards a Holistic Implementation of the NSP

The lacuna on guiding principles for national security policy in the Constitution has been partly closed by the adoption of the NSP, which has laid down an impressive array of principles that seek to ensure that the security sector is an instrument for protecting the safety and democratic rights of the people.[75] The NSP has embraced the paradigm shift from state security to human security, which points at the need for the country's security organs to reconfigure their roles in order to be more relevant by also playing roles that aim to achieve human security. This shift also introduces new actors in the security sector, such as the judiciary and civil society. The Whole-Of-Government approach adopted by the NSP has not been operationalised in part because of the inertia in activating the NSC. Most security organs still work in silos with little or no coordination. This points to the need to operationalise the NSC in earnest to coordinate the functions of the security organs in the country and to capitalise on the synergies in the NPP, which seeks to promote maintenance of peace and conflict prevention in the country.

There is a glaring disparity between the MGDSP III and the NSP in that the former only focuses on state security whereas the latter focuses on both state security and human security which is key for socio-economic development in

[74] Kuwali, note 56, 12.

[75] The Human Rights Initiative, *supra* note 19, 13.

the country.[76] To ensure effective security sector governance and cope with contemporary and emerging threats to security in Malawi, what is needed is an integrated and collaborative national security framework with a robust oversight mechanism.[77] The respective security organs, namely MDF, MPS, NIS, the Immigration Department and Prison Services should formulate institutional policies to facilitate implementation of the NSP. Some of the obvious challenges in security governance can be addressed by taking steps that incorporate principles of national policy on defence and security in section 13 of the Constitution. This enables the political executive to craft policy that embodies the express wishes of the people of Malawi and which promotes the principles of the Constitution, including human rights, rule of law and accountability for performance and operations by an essential public service paid for by taxpayer money.[78] It is also necessary to improve the managerial capacities of the authorities in the security sector as that is critical to the ownership and sustainability of good governance initiatives, national security strategies, defence policy and all other elements of security sector governance.[79] The other suggestion is to introduce an oversight role for the Police Service Commission to close the gap in monitoring the operational performance of the police to make it more professional, transparent, accountable and, therefore, effective.[80]

It is also suggested that there should be reformation of the correctional services to align itself with principles of punishment, particularly reformation of offenders by equipping prisoners with vocational skills.[81] The revenue from PS should also be exempted from being deposited into the Consolidated Fund in terms of section 172 of the Constitution but instead be reinvested to supplement the budget for running correctional facilities, especially improving education, health and nutritional services for prisoners.[82] It is also imperative that the link between the judiciary and the PS should be strengthened so that correctional facilities should actually serve to rehabilitate criminals and protect

76 See Malawi Government, MGDSP III, 65.

77 See http://www.osce.org/fsc/41355. See also the PA Resolution on the Democratic Control of the Private and Public Security Sectors of 2014, www.oscepa.org/meetings/annual-sessions/2014-baku-annual-session/2014-baku-final-declaration/1863-19.

78 Section 7 of the Constitution.

79 Kuwali, note 55, 75-96.

80 Kuwali, note 56, 11.

81 Malawi Inspectorate of Prisons, note 39, 2-3.

82 Malawi Inspectorate of Prisons, note 58, ii-iii.

the public. The success of security sector governance and reform is highly dependent on parallel advances in the area of the judicial system.[83] To this end, the NSP should support the coordination between law enforcement organisations and judicial action.

It also recommended that there should be a proper legislative and regulatory framework to govern citizenship and migration management in Malawi.[84] Further, there is need to reconcile the functions of the NRB, which is charged with producing national identity cards in Malawi and the Immigration Department, which produces passports to avoid duplication of effort.[85] In addition, it is necessary to professionalise the national intelligence services by insulating it from politics and implementation of the NIS Act to focus on matters of national interest including social, military and economic intelligence.[86] There is also need to activate the Complaints Tribunal to play its oversight role of the NIS under section 26 of the NIS Act.

Further, there is need to arrest the propensity of politicisation of the military and militarisation of politics by ensuring the professionalism of the MDF and its apolitical stance so that service members continue to discharge their duties in a professional, apolitical, patriotic manner and with utmost integrity. Furthermore, there is need for sensitisation of politicians on defence and security issues to promote their understanding of civil-military relations and the rationale and limits of subordination of the armed forces to democratically elected political authorities, who are responsible for taking decisions concerning the defence of a country.[87] Finally, there is also need to minimise the deployment of the MDF in internal security operations by building the capacity of the Malawi Police public order management arm.[88]

---

83 Organization for Security and Cooperation in Europe (OSCE), Security Sector Governance and Reform (SSG/R): Guidelines for OSCE Staff, Vienna, April 2016, On-going%20Publication/On-going%20Publication/Security%20Sector%20Governance/Literature/OSCE%20SSGR.pdf [21.10.2020].

84 Kuwali, note 56, 15.

85 National Security Policy, note 1, 11.

86 National Security Policy, note 1, 13.

87 Alapishvili, note 68 above, 9. See also Human Rights Initiative, note 19, 13.

88 Kuwali, note 56, 12.

Chapter 10

Executive Supremacy and the Armed Forces: A Case Study of Public Finance Management in Malawi

Mphatso Jones Boti Phiri

Introduction

The primary purpose of this chapter is to consider the extent to which public finance management in the Malawi Defence Force has adhered to principles of good governance. This is potentially a very significant contribution to both policy and academic literature for two reasons. First, public finance management is intrinsically related to good governance and democratic consolidation.[1] Second, very little has been written on governance and financial accountability of the military in Malawi. This research was conducted between February and November 2020 and incorporated 19 face-to-face interviews with 5 military officers, 6 members of Parliament, 3 parliamentary staff and 5 staff officers from the Ministry of Defence. The chapter utilises the concept of historical institutionalism to appreciate the broader policy trajectory and historical environment in which the military in Malawi has operated with regard to governance and financial accountability. Historical institutionalism primarily describes the reasons for the persistent trajectory of given policy decisions and how some occasional changes occur. [2] According to historical institutional theory, institutions survive due to self-reinforcing mechanisms. It is argued that

---

1 See Tom Pierre Najem, "Good Governance: The Definition and Application of the Concept", in Tom Pierre Najem and Martin Hetherington (eds), *Good Governance in the Middle East Oil Monarchies*, London: Routledge, 2003, 1-18. United Nations Development Programme, *Public Sector Management, Governance and Sustainable Human Development*, New York: UNDP, 1995; International Monetary Fund, "IMF Adopts Guidelines Regarding Governance Issues", Washington, DC: International Monetary Fund, 1997; British Council, "British Council, Good Governance, Law and Governance Briefing", *Issue 4,* London: British Council, 1997; Overseas Development Administration, "Good Government", *Technical Note*, no. 10, London: ODA, 1993. See also Rita Abrahamsen, *Disciplining Democracy: Development Discourse and Good Governance in Africa*, London: Zed Books, 2000, chapter 3.

2 Anika C. Leithner and Kyle M. Libby, "Path Dependency in Foreign Policy", in *Oxford Research Encyclopedia of Politics*, Oxford: Oxford University Press, 2017. See also Giovanni Capoccia and R. Daniel Kelemen, "The Study of Critical Junctures: Theory, Narrative, and Counterfactuals in Historical Institutionalism", *World Politics*, 59/3 (2007), 341-369.

"once a process has been initiated and invested in, it demonstrates benefits or returns because of coordination effects, diminishing marginal costs, learning effects or adaptive expectations".[3] Consequently, institutions will perpetually survive because of increasing returns and benefits.[4]

Malawi faces a myriad of challenges emanating from public finance management and corruption in ministries, departments and agencies (MDAs), that pose significant challenges to the successful implementation of its development agenda. Examining governance and public finance management in the armed forces is, therefore, essential for ensuring prudent use of public funds in institutions that are veiled in secrecy. The chapter consists of three sections. The first section briefly looks at the concept of good governance in order to locate accountability, as it provides the hallmark of sound public finance management. The second section analyses the institutional framework for security governance and financial oversight in the armed forces. The final section reviews the historical circumstances surrounding the management of the armed forces in Malawi, indicating how financial oversight has failed over time.

Good Governance and Public Finance Management

Most of the seminal documents of the World Bank have placed transparency and accountability among the most critical aspects of good governance.[5] Similarly, the transformation of public administration has endeavoured to provide mechanisms for careful stewardship of public money with its emphasis on the economic and efficient use of resources to achieve policy outputs.[6] The principles of good governance provide the space for democratically elected

---

3 Wouter Vandenabeele and Sylvia Horton, "The Evolution of the British Public Service Ethos: a Historical Institutional Approach to Explaining Continuity and Change", in *Ethics and Integrity of Governance*, ed. Leo W.J.C. Huberts, Jeroen Maesschalck and Carole L. Jurkiewicz, Edward Elgar Publishing Limited, 2008, 7-24.

4 Paul Pierson, "Increasing Returns, Path Dependence, and the Study of Politics", *American Political Science Review*, 94/2 (2000), 251–67.

5 World Bank, *Sub-Saharan Africa: From Crisis to Sustainable Growth*, Washington: World Bank, 1989; World Bank, *Governance and Development*, Washington: World Bank, 1992; World Bank, *Governance: The World Bank Experience*, Washington: World Bank, 1993; World Bank, *The World Bank and Participation*, Washington: World Bank, 1994.

6 See Cavin Drewry and Tony Butcher, *The Civil Service Today*, Oxford: Blackwell, 1988; Geoffry Fry, "The Development of the Thatcher Government's 'Grand Strategy' for the Civil Service: a Public Policy Perspective", *Public Administration* 62/3 (1984), 322–35. Sylvia Horton and David Farnham, *Public Management in Britain*, Basingstoke: Palgrave, 1999; Les Metcalfe and Sue Richards, *Improving Public Management*, London: Sage, 1990.

civilian leaders to have control over all policy decisions pertaining to the military, including the checks and balances between the executive and the legislature.[7] It is against this backdrop that public finance management (PFM) is located within good governance discourse. The main objective of the Malawi PFM Act 2003 is to foster and enhance effective and responsible management of public resources. The chapter, therefore, puts much emphasis on the content and extent of information on military revenue and expenditure that is made available to the public for scrutiny.

Institutional Framework for Security Governance and Financial Oversight in the Armed Forces

One of the most vital areas in security governance at a domestic level is the democratic civilian control of the military, where both the executive and the legislature play fundamental roles. It is through the Ministry of Defence that the executive performs its roles and functions.

The Ministry of Defence

Bruneau and Goetze suggest that the existence of a Ministry of Defence (MOD) is an important basic indicator of the quality of security governance in any country.[8] It serves to institutionalise civilian oversight of the military by structuring the power relations between democratically elected civilian leaders and the armed forces command. In this instance, civilians are empowered to formulate policy on defence-related issues and the military implements those policies by using public money and resources accordingly. Additionally, the MOD can help to prevent the military from being directly involved in politics and allow the selected civilian leaders to represent and negotiate for military needs and resources in the legislature. The MOD, therefore, enhances democracy and potentially removes the likelihood of introducing the military, which has a monopoly on violence and the potential to blackmail, into the political system.[9]

---

7 Mphatso Jones Boti Phiri, "Institutional Challenges to Viable Civil-military Relations in Malawi", MA, Naval Postgraduate School, 2008.

8 Some of these ministries are hardly more than façades, with no power whatsoever; however, an effective MOD is a core element in contemporary democratic civil-military relations. See Thomas C. Bruneau and Richard Goetze, "Ministries of Defense and Democratic Control", in *Who Guards the Guardians and How: Democratic Civil-Military Relations*, Austin: University of Texas Press, 2006, 71-100.

9 Bruneau and Goetze, "Ministries of Defense and Democratic Control", 71-98. If the armed forces are left to their own devices, which is most often the situation in authoritarian regimes,

In Malawi the MOD was established in 1994 to bridge the gap between the civil authorities and the armed forces.[10] It was designed to act as a central organisation for the strategic management of the Malawi Defence Force focusing on policy and control. Among its roles is formulation of National Defence Policy in liaison with the Defence Force and acting as a headquarters through which government policy decisions are translated into operational plans and orders. It is also responsible for formulating long-term plans, defence programmes and preparation of the defence budget.[11] The research findings, however, indicate that the Ministry of Defence has not been effective in its operations and most of its roles, including financial oversight, are performed by the military itself.[12] The research revealed that the MOD is exceptionally understaffed and lacks the necessary expertise in military issues to manage the armed forces effectively.[13] For instance, there are no personnel specialised in defence budgeting and analysis. In this light, the military has an extensive latitude in its budgeting and procurement process, thereby weakening any prudent public finance management. While MODs in developed countries like the United States of America and the United Kingdom are well staffed with military officers to provide the necessary expertise, the MOD in Malawi has only three military officers. In this light, the oversight functions of the MOD in the provision and distribution of military resources, including financial resources, are challenged. Additionally, the military regulates its own financial prudence through the office of Inspector General (IG)[14] and this arrangement is problematic as far as good governance is concerned. For example, the office of the Inspector General is responsible for military ethics and audit, however, the IG is appointed by the Defence Force Commander. Additionally, the IG office is not independent as it operates within the Office of the Commander of

---

they work out deals and understandings among themselves whereby they inflate their requirements to maximise the benefits of all services. And, as new democracies seek to bring their armed forces under control and to cut costs, an effective MOD appears to be the most appropriate institution for these purposes.

10 The MOD was introduced soon after Malawi transitioned from one-party rule to multiparty democracy.

11 James Kalilangwe, "The Roles of the Defense Ministry", *Msilikali Magazine* 1 (2003). See also the mission and objectives of the Ministry of Defense www.malawi.gov.mw/de fense/home [10 July 2020].

12 Interviews with senior staff in the Malawi Defence Force and Ministry of Defence and also personal experience in the Malawi Defence Force.

13 Personal experience. The author has sat in meetings with the MOD staff for more than twelve years and has in-depth knowledge of the MOD staff and expertise.

14 The Malawi Defence Force has within its establishment the office of the Inspector General that is not related to the Malawi Police Service.

the Defence Force. This institutional arrangement therefore weakens the regulatory role of the Inspector General's office. Although the MDF as an institution is audited by the Auditor General's office under the Public Audit Act, little has been revealed through such audits. Considering the acerbic media reports on rampant corruption and abuse of public money,[15] the MOD requires expertise to ensure military expenditures are within the Public Finance Act of 2003. The question of military accountability in public finance management is further addressed below.

Governance Dilemma and Financial Accountability Challenges within the MOD

The head of state in Malawi has on different occasions served as the Minister of Defence. This arrangement has been recurrent since 2004 when President Bingu wa Mutharika came to power and has continued up to the present. As the Defence Minister, the president is accountable to Parliament and cabinet, and is supposed to appear before the Defence and Security Committee of the National Assembly to present any significant military project and give an account of any business that might be of interest to the committee. However, procedurally the sitting president cannot appear before such a parliamentary committee. Section 3 of the Public Finance Act stipulates that

> the minister is responsible to cabinet and national assembly (b) ensuring adequate procedures, internal controls and guidelines exist for the use of public money and public resources; and (c) the compliance by the Ministry of Finance with its responsibilities under this Act.

Section 4 stipulates that

> the minister is responsible for (c) the supervision of the finances, assets and liabilities of the state so as to ensure that a full accounting is made to the National Assembly of all transactions involving public moneys or disposition of public resources; (d) the oversight of finances of the statutory bodies.

While the deputy minister appears in his stead, this is excessive delegation of authority, and section 5(c) of the PFM Act 2003 stipulates that the

---

15 Enelless Nyale "More rot as K3.2billion vanishes", *National News*, 26 March 2019; Ntchindi Meki, "K800million looters off the hook", *National News*, 6 January 2018; Enelless Nyale, "K7 billion kwacha vanishes", *National News*, 22 September 2017; Ntchindi Meki, "K9bn MDF utility bill worry committee", *National News*, 14 September 2019; Enelless Nyale, "MDF owes LWB K1bn, board moves to install prepaid meters", *National News*, 13 July 2017; "MDF, Police lead K21bn defaulters", *The Nation Online*, 11 March 2019.

responsibilities of the minister under this Act shall not be derogated merely by his having exercised his power of delegation under this section.

From this backdrop, the president, by heading the MOD, compromises both the cabinet and legislative accountability since he has the ultimate command of resources but is partially accountable for anything within the ministry. Thus, although the existence of the Ministry of Defence (MOD) is an important basic indicator for appropriate public finance management and security governance, the MOD in Malawi fails to meet the standard for effective financial oversight of the armed forces. Additionally, neither the MOD nor the Malawi Defence Force have operationalised the integrity committees that are aimed at improving public sector governance and adherence to the public finance management act.[16]

The Republic of Malawi Constitution stipulates that "the ultimate responsibility of the defence forces of Malawi shall vest in the president as commander in chief".[17] It further states that any power conferred on the president, by the Constitution, shall only be exercised on the recommendation of the Defence Force Council, which shall include the Minister of Defence, Secretary to the Office of the President and Cabinet and the high command of the Defence Force. These provisions imply that the president has the ultimate command when he also occupies the role of Minister of Defence. The Defence Force Act also gives the president responsibility for promotions and appointments of the military top command, including the commander-in-chief of the Malawi Defence Force. He can also fire them without giving any reason and without any involvement of the Legislative Committee on Defence and Security.[18] The combination of the presidential and ministerial roles, therefore, result in debilitating effects on the capacity of the MOD to cope with accountability requirements arising from the public finance management act.

The Legislature

The legislature is another institution that plays an important role in public finance management and security governance. Jeanne Giraldo argues that

---

16 Ministry of Finance and economic planning, "National Budget Statement for the year 2019-2020". The Ministry of Finance reminds all MDAs of the need to apportion resources towards the operationalisation of Integrity Committees within their institutions.

17 The Republic of Malawi Constitution, 1995, 71.

18 This has been the case since Malawi got its independence and has been the practice of all heads of state in Malawi. It is not only the case in Malawi, but also in Nigeria, Zambia, Zimbabwe and many other countries in Africa which were under British colonial rule.

legislative debates on defence issues can help contribute to the increased flow of information, thereby creating an informed public that will be able to participate constructively in future policy discussions. Additionally, this can help expose any abuse of power and public resources.[19] The legislative powers to make and oversee budgets, decisions, laws and policies and their implementation allow it to amend legislation and adjust the budget.[20] Parliamentary hearings on the military provide the legislature with the necessary means of getting feedback on the way resources have been used by the military and can be an effective means of evaluating the effectiveness and efficiency of the public purse. She further argues that meaningful parliamentary input into the budget process and expenditure of the military depends on whether the legislators have sufficient information about the contents of the budget and the policy implications of the fiscal decisions.[21] While the research revealed that most members of Parliament have little fiscal expertise, the challenge is even greater in scrutinising military expenditures due to both lack of specialised knowledge in defence budget and secrecy of military operations.

The Defence and Security Committee of the National Assembly is tasked to provide specialised oversight on national security expenditures that are secretive in nature. Research findings, however, reveal that the contributions of the Defence and Security Committee in establishing public finance oversight on secretive national security operations are absent due to lack of security clearance to handle such sensitive information.[22] Additionally, the committee lacks professional parliamentary staff with sufficient knowledge and expertise of the military's institutional requirements and expenditure of public money.[23]

Building the knowledge base in national security to provide the necessary financial oversight requires a considerable amount of time. Malawi, however, is challenged in this regard due to high turnover of members of Parliament. The Malawi Parliament has a turnover of over 40% of its members of Parliament in

---

19 Jeanne Giraldo, "Defense Budgets, Democratic Civilian Control, and Effective Governance", in Thomas Bruneau and Scott Tollefson (eds), *Who Guards the Guardians and How*, Austin: Texas University Press, 2006, 189-191.

20 Ibid. The power of the purse provides civilians with the key lever of control over the military and ensures its effectiveness and efficiency in the use of public resources.

21 Ibid.

22 This research reveals that the parliamentary committee has not demanded the requisite security clearance in order to handle the national security information.

23 Communications with inside sources on the parliamentary staff reveals that most parliamentary staff serving the Defence and Security Committee are involved in logistical and secretarial jobs rather than working as expert advisors to committees in the National Assembly.

every election cycle, thereby losing the institutional memory for parliamentarians in the defence and security committee.[24] The short tenure, especially considering the limited expertise regarding defence issues of most members of Parliament, is a fundamental obstacle to committee members developing the expertise they need to carry out the functions of the committee effectively. The combination of inexperienced members of Parliament and parliamentary staff with little or no expertise in defence and security has challenged the legislative oversight of military public finance management. Other than approving the military budget, which is usually passed without significant changes, rarely does any substantial discussion on military matters take place in either Parliament itself or its Defence and Security Committee. For instance, the Defence and Security Committee has been quick to find means of settling large bills of the armed forces without inquiring how such bills came about.[25]

The dismal performance of the MOD and the legislature in financial oversight of the armed forces in Malawi can further be explained by an historical account of security governance in the country. The research findings reveal that the policies adopted by all post-independence heads of state reduced legislative powers and created executive dominance, that resulted in lack of effective oversight of the military public finance management. The seeds of this executive dominance over the legislature were planted during the creation of the colonial state and nurtured by policies adopted by post-colonial Malawian leaders, thereby providing a persistent policy trajectory that is reflected in historical institutionalism.[26] As a result, this policy succession (the path dependency created) has not produced a system that ensures effectiveness and/or efficiency in the use of public money and resources in the armed forces.

---

[24] Malawi News Agency online, accessed 10 July 2020. In Malawi parliamentary elections the turnover is high but in 2019 elections it was even higher than usual with some people who had been in Parliament for decades being ousted. For example, the UDF party in 1994 won 85 seats while in the 1999 elections, the party got 91 seats, in 2004 it got 49 legislators, further dwindled to 17 in 2009, and in 2019 got 10. Meanwhile AFORD has dwindled from 1994's 33 to only one in the 2019 polls.

[25] Ntchindi Meki, "K9bn MDF Utility Bill Worry Committee", *National News*, 14 September 2019; "UN says Malawi was not Obliged to Buy Equipment", *The Nation News Online*, 15 March 2014.

[26] Leithner and Libby, "Path Dependency in Foreign Policy". See also Capoccia and Kelemen, "*The Study of Critical Junctures*", 341-369.

The Historical Context of Public Finance Management in the Armed Forces

As Nyasaland became independent Malawi, the first battalion of the British colonial Kings African Rifles became the Malawi Army in 1964. During the colonial era, the British authorities had used the military to suppress insurrections by the locals and to appropriate land from the native population within the Federation of Rhodesia and Nyasaland.[27] Consequently, the colonialists needed unwavering support of the military in order to fulfil their policy goals. The tight link between the military and political leadership persisted in post-colonial Malawi under President Dr Kamuzu Banda. Although the independence Constitution stipulated the existence of a Parliament with a regulatory role, this did not come into practical effect.[28] Soon after independence, Dr Kamuzu Banda succeeded in making Malawi a *de jure* single-party state and later made himself Life President of the country through legislation that was rubber stamped by Parliament.[29] Under Banda's authoritarian rule, the military was effectively a presidential preserve. This policy arrangement effectively isolated the military from any public scrutiny in its finance management and parliamentary oversight was non-existent. During the post-independence period, the army underwent significant restructuring and procurement of military assets in the quest to Africanise the institution. It is important to note, however, that the public expenditure was kept under wraps between the presidency and the military.[30] In this light, Banda maintained the status quo in the management of the armed forces that had been initiated, invested in, and demonstrated benefits or returns to the relevant actors (political leaders and

---

27 Bridglal Pachai, "Land Policies in Malawi: An Examination of the Colonial Legacy", *The Journal of African History* 14/4 (1973), 681-98. See also Bill H. Kinsey, "Land Reform, Growth and Equity: Emerging Evidence from Zimbabwe's Resettlement Programme", *Journal of Southern African Studies* 25/2 (1999). See also K. Elford, "Land Reform: Whites Biased", *Global Analysis*, 19 September 2007, www.glob.co.zw/homepage/land_reform.html [6.2020].

28 Boti Phiri, MA, 2008.

29 Harold Nelson, Margarita Dobert, Gordon C. McDonald, James McLaughlin, Barbara Marvin and Donald P. Whitaker, *Area Handbook for Malawi*, Washington DC: American University, 1975, 172-3. See also Wiseman Chirwa, Nandini Patel and Fidelis Kanyongolo, *Democracy Report for Malawi*, http://www.idea.int/publictions/sod [6.2020].

30 Malawi acquired its first aircraft and naval crafts in the 1970s, however, they were first assigned to the Malawi Young Pioneers (a Malawi Congress Party paramilitary wing) and later transferred to the Malawi Army without any involvement of the Parliament. Dr Banda had accumulated unquestionable powers through his dictatorial rule, so that he could regulate anything without any resistance from the military or from any government institution.

the army) and excluded public financial oversight.[31] As shall be seen in the subsequent pages, this policy has persisted even during Malawi's democratic era. This accords with the findings of Paul Pierson who argued that institutions will perpetually survive because of increasing returns.[32] Despite Banda's dictatorial regime, it is argued elsewhere that he pursued deliberate financial policies that favoured the military and made it uncritical of his authoritarian rule. For instance, on attainment of certain ranks, senior officers were given loans to acquire land for agriculture, and this was perceived as a means of buying military loyalty. Additionally, the military pay structure was also de-linked from the rest of the civil service and adjusted upwards.[33]

The first democratic elections in 1994 proved to be a "critical juncture", ending three decades of authoritarian rule.[34] This political change demanded subsequent changes in the institutional structure and accountability in the management of the armed forces. All government institutions, including Parliament, became more open to public scrutiny. Free media came with investigative journalism and became the primary source of information for the general public. However, as shown below, there was little progress in financial oversight of the military due to the sustained mode of security governance adopted by the British colonialists and Dr Kamuzu Banda. Additionally, the new democratic institutions and leaders failed to embrace the accountability policy changes accorded to them by the political change.

The legislative failure was to some extent attributed to the political choices made by the new president, Bakili Muluzi. The research findings reveal that he worked out a political manoeuvre and formed a coalition with the Alliance for Democracy (AFORD) party that resulted in an overwhelming majority in Parliament. He thus replicated Kamuzu Banda's control of both the executive and the legislature; hence there were no effective checks and balances on the executive powers over the military expenditure. Although Budget and Finance, and Defence and Security committees were established to provide active checks

---

31 Vandenabeele and Horton, "The Evolution of the British Public Service Ethos", 7-24.

32 Pierson, "Increasing Returns, Path Dependence, and the Study of Politics", 251–67.

33 E.I. Mandiza, "Civil-Military Relations in Malawi: A Historical Perspective", in Rocky Williams, G. Cawthra and D. Abrahams (eds), *Ourselves to Know: Civil-military Relations and Defence Transformation in Southern Africa,* Institute for Security Studies, 2002, 113-120.

34 Historical institutionalism is primarily linked to the concepts "path dependency" and "critical juncture". "Critical junctures" or disruption points occur to interrupt a policy path, resulting in disruptive change in the institutional make-up. See Leithner and Libby, "Path Dependency in Foreign Policy".

and balances, their work on military expenditure was minimal. For instance, Malawi deployed its first United Nations (UN) peacekeeping troops to Rwanda in 1994 without much involvement of Parliament.[35] Additionally, Malawi procured the necessary military equipment for peacekeeping and received UN equipment reimbursements that were kept under the wraps of the military command and the executive.[36] Although the 1994 Constitution provided for a Defence and Security Committee of Parliament, the committee did not perform its functions as stipulated by the law. As a result, the Muluzi government weakened the newly established institutional structure in military oversight and denied any learning opportunity for the new parliamentarians in a fledgling democracy.

Although the transition from authoritarian rule to democracy in 1993 and 1994 could be considered a critical juncture, it did not have any significant effect as regards institutional changes in security governance or public finance management in the armed forces in Malawi. President Muluzi further weakened the stability of the military command through frequent firing and hiring of Army commanders without any parliamentary involvement or oversight. Within a period of four years from 1994 to 1998, Muluzi changed the defence force commanders five times (one died in office) before he got one with whom he was satisfied, who remained in office until Muluzi handed over the presidency to his successor in 2004. President Muluzi, therefore, established personal links with the military commanders and controlled the military through a patron-client network rather than through legislative oversight.[37] It is argued in this chapter that the Muluzi patronage system in the appointment of military commanders allowed the armed forces to self-regulate their financial resources without any requirement to comply with transparency principles— (as evidenced by the management of the UN peacekeeping funds). Muluzi's control of the legislature and the military crippled any checks and balances in the financial oversight of the armed forces. The Muluzi term of office,

---

35 Interviews with parliamentary staff and military officers who deployed in Rwanda indicates that the Parliament was just informed about the deployment. The military officers did not recall any parliamentary debate on the deployment of troops.

36 For every UN peacekeeping deployment, the UN pays monthly reimbursements to the troops' contributing country for all the equipment and personnel. UN deployments are not classified operations and its expenditure is supposed to be within public domain.

37 The Retired Army Commander, General Chimbayo, later joined Muluzi's political party and contested in a parliamentary election on a UDF ticket, thereby substantiating the patronage argument in relation to Muluzi's security governance.

therefore, did not see security governance structure and public finance management evolve towards that expected in a democracy. The 1994 Constitution did not alter the executive powers over the management of the armed forces and the legislative oversight was minimal. It is important to note that the presidential powers to appoint and fire the Defence Force commanders without parliamentary approval has continued until the present day.

President Bingu wa Mutharika took over power as head of state following the general elections held in June 2004, having been hand-picked by Muluzi to succeed him.[38] Six months after being elected on the United Democratic Front party (UDF) ticket, Mutharika left the UDF and formed his own party, amidst public tensions with Muluzi, who was then UDF party chairman.[39] The UDF had performed poorly in the 2004 general elections and most parliamentary seats went to opposition parties and independent candidates. This was largely the result of an economic downturn and rampant corruption, which was attributed to the UDF government. In addition, some opposition parties protested against the presidential election results, claiming that they were rigged by the ruling party. This meant that Mutharika faced greater opposition in Parliament than Muluzi had, both from within his own party and from opposition parties. Although the legislature was dominated by opposition parties during the Mutharika era, there was no significant legislative oversight of the armed forces. The work of the Defence and Security Committee of the National Assembly was very minimal.[40] During President Bingu wa Mutharika's regime, the armed forces were deployed in several United Nations peacekeeping operations without any accountability for the public money spent and reimbursements from the UN missions. In this light, the president enjoyed overall control of the military and the legislature had largely been ignored. In the process, the military continued to be insulated from public accountability in its use of public money.

The regime of President Joyce Banda that took over after the sudden death of Bingu wa Mutharika in April 2012 continued on the same path in military

---

38 *BBC News*, "Malawi's President Rules 'his way'", September 1, 2004, www.bbc.co.uk/africa/html [6.2020].

39 United Democratic Front (UDF) is the political party led by Bakili Muluzi that sponsored Bingu wa Mutharika. Soon after taking office President Mutharika left the UDF and formed his own Democratic Progressive Party (DPP).

40 An assessment of the activities of the Defence and Security Committee indicates that it was not actively involved in its constitutional mandate apart from paying a routine visit to military cantonments.

governance and finance management. President Joyce Banda's administration utterly disregarded the Public Finance Management Act in the sale of the presidential jet (which was in the custody of the military) and the procurement of peacekeeping equipment for the armed forces.[41] The Joyce Banda administration used the MWK 6.3 billion (about USD 15 million) which government could have realised from the presidential jet sale to repay a loan of military equipment it procured for peacekeeping missions of MWK 8.2 billion (about USD 19 million). It is important to note that these transactions did not follow the public finance management act of 2003.[42] The peacekeeping transactions and related critical financial information were not duly revealed to the public, raising serious suspicions of corruption and fraud. Furthermore, the two-year presidency of Joyce Banda was marked by massive corruption in MDAs through the infamous Cashgate scandal that exposed widespread mismanagement of public money and flouting of the PFM Act.[43]

The election of Peter Mutharika as President in 2014 did not result in any change in the mode of security governance and public finance management of the military. President Peter Mutharika quickly adopted an ethnically inclined patronage approach in the appointment of senior military officers. Within a period of five years he fired four Defence Force Commanders (thereby adopting the Muluzi approach to the management of the armed forces) and the UN peacekeeping reimbursements were kept under the wraps of the presidency and the military. In other words, the policies adopted by his predecessors continued to define his approach to the management of the armed forces, resulting in lack of transparency and accountability in the management of public money in the military.

This historical analysis of security governance and public finance management in Malawi has shown extreme power imbalances between the executive and the legislature that can be traced back to the era of colonial government. This colonial legacy has been enjoyed by post-independence Malawian leaders and

---

41 "UN says Malawi was not Obliged to Buy Equipment", *The Nation News Online*, 15 March 2014.

42 Ibid. The former member of Parliament Jessie Kabwila had argued that Public Finance Management Act does not allow barter trade and the money should have first been deposited in Account Number One (government-consolidated account) before being used for procurement or settling a debt.

43 Cashgate is a financial scandal involving looting, theft and corruption that happened at Capitol Hill, the seat of government in Malawi. The scandal was uncovered during the administration of President Joyce Banda, though it is believed to have begun prior to her taking office. See "The $32m heist", *The Economist*, 27 February 2014.

has served their political interests. This policy trajectory is seemingly supported by a legislature that is uninterested in providing financial oversight on the use of public money by the military. The legislature has not been active in claiming its share of military oversight, even after the democratic transition of 1994.

Conclusion

The political history of Malawi indicates "executive supremacy" and unquestioned authority over all policy issues (including public finance management) related to the armed forces. The undisputed executive dominance that was created by the political elites in security governance resulted in an institutional imbalance that has weakened financial oversight of the military. The executive pre-eminence can be traced to the colonial government and then to Kamuzu Banda who accumulated unquestionable powers through his dictatorial rule, where he could regulate anything without any resistance from the military or any government institution. It is shown in this chapter that the post-independence heads of state have maintained this executive supremacy that has perpetuated lack of accountability and transparency in the procurement and expenditure of public resources in the armed forces. Although the formal institutions necessary for good governance are in place, such as the legislative committee on defence and security, these have been non-functional to a great extent. The historical policy trajectory in security governance and public finance management renders much credence to historical institutionalism in understanding politics and government in Malawi.

It has further been argued that both the legislature and the Ministry of Defence, have failed to embrace the powers accorded to them by the new democratic Constitution, leaving the control of the military in the hands of the president, thereby undermining good governance in the country. This chapter, therefore, reveals that the military in Malawi is not insulated from political manipulation and abuse of public money. Proactive steps by both the MOD and Parliament are, therefore, required to ensure that the security sector adheres to the public finance management act in Malawi.

Chapter 11

50-50 Campaigns: Lessons from 10 Years of Promoting Gender Equality and Women's Representation in Parliament

Asiyati Lorraine Chiweza

> I urge political parties to take affirmative steps to support the candidature of women since their election can make a difference in the number of female representatives in parliament and wards. Since May 2019, the Commission has conducted three by-elections but in all these areas there has never been a female candidate and only three political parties have participated. By-elections offer an opportunity to improve the statistics regarding women representation in parliament and councils. The Commission is expecting parties to come up with measures that will attract and protect women candidates when running for political office
>
> *Justice Chifundo Kachale, Chairperson of Malawi Electoral Commission, 11 September 2020).*

Introduction

Increasing the number of women in elected political office has emerged as a salient political issue in governance discourses across the globe.[1] Yet despite global pressure towards inclusive governance through the adoption of gender equitable regulations and funding schemes as incentives to increase the number of women elected into political office, gender parity in elected bodies remains an illusion in most countries. While women have made important inroads into political office across the world, their representation in national Parliaments, at 24.9%, is still far from parity.[2] In 46 countries, women now hold more than 30% of seats in national Parliament in at least one chamber.[3] The Inter-Parliamentary Union (IPU) notes that over a 25-year span, the largest progress in women's representation has been achieved by Rwanda (61.3%), Cuba

---

1 Ragnhild Muriaas, Vibeke Wang and Rainbow Murray, "Introducing the Concept of Gendered Electoral Financing", in R. Muriaas, V. Wang, and R. Murray (eds), *Gendered Electoral Financing: Money, Power, and Representation in Comparative Perspective*, Oxford: Routledge, 2020, 1-24.

2 United Nations, *UN Sustainable Development Goals, Goal 5: Achieve Gender Equality and Empower all Women and Girls.* Available at https://unstats.un.org/sdgs/repo rt/2020/goal-05.

3 Ibid.

(53.2%), Bolivia (53.1%), and United Arab Emirates (50.0%).[4] Within sub-Saharan Africa, on average 24.4% of the region's parliamentarians are women, a 14.6 percentage point increase since 1995.[5] In about 11 of these countries, women hold over 30% of seats in the lower or single house of Parliament. The share exceeds 40% of seats held by women in five of those countries: Rwanda (61.3%), South Africa (46.4%), Senegal (43.0%), Namibia (42.7%) and Mozambique (41.2%).[6]

The quest for inclusive governance through increased women's representation in elected bodies has been a feature of Malawi's governance landscape since democratisation in 1994 and it gained new impetus in 2009 when the government in collaboration with non-state actors introduced a fund for a gender parity scheme, popularly known as the 50-50 Campaign. While the campaign was initially deemed successful in 2009, the declining representation in Parliament in both 2014 and 2019 elections has triggered debate on the effectiveness of such schemes in improving gender parity in elected decision-making bodies at national level.[7] Using a review of existing literature, this chapter interrogates the source of this limited performance by focusing on the nature of actors who have been driving these campaigns and the congruency between the locus of the underrepresentation problem and the campaign interventions. While the 50-50 campaigns have targeted both parliamentary and local government candidates, this chapter focuses only on female representation in Parliament because there is comparable data for this group from 2009. Local government elections only took place in 2014 and 2019 and the campaign interventions for these two groups of women candidates have not been similar. Hence the discussion of local government councillors deserves separate attention.

The chapter begins by outlining the theory of women's political representation before going on to discuss the legal and policy framework guiding women representation in Malawi. It traces the genesis of the 50-50 campaigns and examines the nature of the actors who have been supporting it and the type of

---

4 Inter-Parliamentary Union, Women in Parliament 1995-2020: 25 Years in Review, IPU Report, 2020. Available at www.ipu.org/resources/publications /reports/2020-03/

5 Ibid.

6 Ibid.

7 Vibeke Wang, Happy Kayuni, Asiyati Chiweza and Samantha Soyiyo, "Relieving Women's Costs of Standing for Election: Malawi's 50/50 Campaigns", in Muriaas, Wang and Murray (eds), *Gendered Electoral Financing*, 113-32.

interventions they have been implementing under this campaign, with particular reference to the funding campaign and how this has had a bearing on descriptive representation of women in Parliament. The conclusion notes the implications and limits of relying exclusively on initiatives such as the 50-50 campaign to promote inclusive governance and increase descriptive female representation in electoral bodies in Malawi, and offers suggestions for the future.

The Theory of Women's Political Representation

Political representation solves the problem of democratic participation in large and populous nations through its practice of delegating or entrusting the advocacy of citizen interests to a smaller number of individuals who gather in assemblies and make decisions.[8] Most theorists of political representation identify its component elements and specify its core characteristics. The most influential was Hanna Pitkin's *The Concept of Representation,* published in 1967.[9] Her four types of representation are: (1) authorised, where a representative is legally empowered to act for another; (2) descriptive representation, where the representative stands for a group by virtue of sharing similar characteristics such as race, sex, ethnicity, or residence; (3) symbolic representation, where a leader stands for national ideas; and (4) substantive representation, where the representative seeks to advance a group's policy preferences and interests.[10] Issues of female representation emerged in the 20th century and the descriptive and substantive types of representation became the most commonly discussed dimensions of political representation of interest to gender and feminist scholars.[11] Descriptive representation is understood as representation by representatives who belong to the same societal group. Its focus is on being present in the political institutions while substantive representation is defined as the abilities of the women representatives to act for other women once they are in the political institutions.[12] The focus of this chapter is on descriptive

8 Karen Celis and Joni Lovenduski, "Power Struggles: Gender Equality in Political Representation", *European Journal of Politics and Gender* 1/1-2 (2018), 149-66.

9 Hanna Pitkin, *The Concept of Representation*, Berkeley: University of California Press, 1967.

10 Sarah Childs and Joni Lovenduski, "Political Representation", in Georgina Waylen, Karen Celis, Joanna Kantola and Laurel Weldon (eds), *The Oxford Handbook of Gender and Politics*, Oxford: Oxford University Press, 2013.

11 Ibid.

12 Petra Meier and Emanuela Lombardo, "Towards a New Theory on the Symbolic Representation of Women", Paper presented to APSA Annual meeting, Washington, D.C., September, 2010.

representation, understood broadly as the number of women elected to national elected bodies. In the Malawian context, support for women's representation has focused almost wholly on increasing numbers of women elected through the 50-50 campaigns, with limited attention to their performance while in Parliament.[13]

Theoretically there are three main arguments for why women should be representatives in elected political institutions. The first is the justice argument which contends that it is simply unfair for men to dominate descriptive representation. The second is the pragmatic argument which stresses the electoral advantage of increasing the numbers of female representatives, namely, that political parties will be perceived as more women friendly and, as a result, attract women's votes. The third is the transformative argument which suggests that women are a heterogeneous group who require equal descriptive representation if their diversity is to be reflected in decision-making. A key proponent of the transformative argument is Anne Phillips[14] whose idea of "the politics of presence" contends that political deliberation requires the participation of key groups if democratically representative decisions are to be made. Phillips reasoned that interests are realised in the course of deliberation and decision-making as various options and competing concerns are discussed. Only when present, may women benefit from such realisation and insert their interests. Thus, increasing the presence of women will change politics by improving the democratic functioning of legislatures.[15] Of course, this assumes that female representatives will behave in a more democratic fashion and that they will pay more attention to political inequalities than men.

The Legal and Policy Framework Guiding Women Representation in Malawi

Malawi had no specific policies on gender equality until the late 1980s when the country came under increasing international pressure to democratise. With democratisation in 1994 and the adoption of a new Constitution, issues of human rights, gender equality, and the rights of women became fundamental

---

13 Tam O'Neil, Ngeyi Kanyongolo and Joseph Wales, *Women and Power: Representation and Influence in Malawi's Parliament*, London: Overseas Development Institute, 2016.

14 Anne Phillips, *The Politics of Presence*, Oxford: Clarendon Press, 1995.

15 Anne Phillips, "Democracy and Representation: Why Should it Matter Who Our Representatives Are?" in Anne Phillips (ed), *Feminism and Politics,* Oxford: Oxford University Press, 1998.

components of Malawi's political discourse. The Constitution of the Republic of Malawi clearly stipulates that as a matter of national policy the state shall obtain gender equality for women through full participation of women in all spheres of Malawian society on the basis of equality with men.[16]

Since then, the government has committed itself to gender equality and promotion of women's representation and participation by signing and ratifying regional and international declarations and instruments. At the international level, Malawi signed the Convention on the Elimination of All Forms of Discrimination against Women (CEDAW) (1987) and its addendum (1999); the Vienna Declaration on Human Rights and Rights of Women (1993); the Beijing Declaration and Platform for Action which was adopted at the Fourth World Conference on Women (FWCW) held in 1995; and the Sustainable Development Goals (SDGs). For example, articles 1, 2 and 7 of the CEDAW ban all forms of discrimination and guarantee women to be eligible for election to all publicly elected bodies and to hold public office and perform all public functions at all the levels of government. The Beijing Declaration and Platform for Action proposes special measures and targets, review of electoral laws/systems and requires that all government-funded political parties should not discriminate against women. Sustainable Development Goal No. 5 seeks to achieve gender equality and equal opportunities for leadership by women and girls at all levels of decision-making in political, economic and public life.[17]

At the regional level, Malawi has been party to various human rights protocols and frameworks. For example, in 2004, the African Union (AU) Heads of State and Government adopted the AU Solemn Declaration on Gender Equality in Africa (SDGEA). This declaration is considered a critical milestone because it strengthened African ownership of the gender equality agenda at the highest political level in Africa.[18] In 2005, the AU also adopted the Protocol to the African Charter on Human and People's Rights (ACHPR) on the Rights of Women in Africa. Article 2 of the Protocol to the ACHPR states that parties shall combat all forms of discrimination through appropriate legislative, institutional and other measures and shall include in their national Consti-

---

16 Malawi Government, Constitution of the Republic of Malawi, Zomba: Government Press, 1994, article 13 (a).

17 United Nations, Agenda 2030: Sustainable Development Goals, New York, United Nations, 2015, www.undp.org/content/undp/en/home/sustainable-development-goals.html.

18 R. Sow, African Women's Decade 2010-2020: Mid-Term Review, A Research Report, Make Every Woman Count, 2016.

tutions or other legislative instruments, the principle of equality between men and women. This is meant to ensure its effective application; integrate a gender perspective in their policy decisions, legislation, development plans, programmes and activities and in all spheres of life; and take corrective and positive action in those areas where discrimination against women in law and in fact continues to exist.[19] The African Union Agenda 2063 supports gender parity in its provisions. Aspiration 6 is about "an Africa of 2063 that will have full gender parity, with women occupying at least 50% of elected public offices at all levels and half of managerial positions in the public and the private sectors".[20]

Malawi has also acceded to the Southern Africa Development Community (SADC) Protocol on Gender and Development (2008). The 2008 protocol builds on the 1997 SADC Declaration on Gender and Development which set a target of 30% representation of women in positions of power and decision-making by 2005. Heads of state upped this target to 50% through the 2009 declaration of 50-50 gender parity. Article 12 of the Protocol mandates state parties to achieve the 50% parity in political and other public decision-making positions and that affirmative action measures be taken to put that into effect. Malawi ratified the SADC Protocol on Gender and Development in 2012 which implies that the country is legally obliged to put in place mechanisms for ensuring gender equality at all levels, including electoral processes and political parties.

However, while the ratification of important international and regional instruments has served for lobbying and advocacy by various women's groups and other non-state actors, this alone does not translate into tangible practices and results on the ground. It has been observed that while most African countries have Constitutions and other laws that prohibit discrimination based on sex and recognise socio-economic rights, in Malawi there is a significant gap between the provisions for gender equality and the daily realities for women.[21] The government also adopted the Gender Policy in 2000 (updated in 2015) as a way of mainstreaming and institutionalizing gender in all government policies and plans. This policy is an advocacy tool for a wholistic approach for equitable

---

19 Article 2 of the African Charter on Human and People's Rights (ACHPR) on the Rights of Women in Africa.

20 Africa Union, Agenda 2063: The Africa We Want, Africa Union Commission, 2015, 8.

21 Africa Union, AU Strategy for Gender Equality and Women Empowerment (2018-2028). www.au.africa, 2018, 40.

participation of men, women, boys and girls in all domains of life including politics and decision-making structures.[22] Additionally, in 2013, the country enacted a Gender Equality Act which, among other things, obliges duty-bearers to ensure that in public decision-making structures, each gender constitutes at least 40% and at most 60%. Chikadza has aptly summarised this as a state in which the country has a comprehensive framework for women and politics at the global and constitutional level, but one that lacks teeth at the operational level.[23]

Trends in Women's Political Representation and the Genesis of the 50-50 Campaign

Prior to democratisation the number of women elected to Parliament was very low but improvements to women's representation in Parliament were made based on the goodwill of the president at the time.[24] Although this goodwill existed, the reality was that the then president, Dr H. Kamuzu Banda, never challenged the social-structural environment that impeded women's participa-

Table 11.1: *Women in Parliament during the One-Party State: 1966-1992*

Year	Total Composition	Elected members of Parliament		Nominated members of Parliament		Total Composition		Percentage of female members
		M	F	M	F	M	F	
1966	52	47	1	4	0	51	1	1.96%
1972	58	50	1	7	0	57	1	17%
1977	78	64	5	0	9	64	14	17.94%
1982	94	49	8	14	23	63	31	32.97%
1987	92	74	5	12	1	86	6	6.5%
1992	104	79	3	15	7	86	10	9.6%

Source: Malera, 2005

22 Henry Chingaipe and Francis Matita, Report on the Evaluation of the Gender Parity (50:50) Programme for the 2014 Tripartite Elections, evaluation report prepared for the NGO Gender Coordination Unit, Lilongwe: IPRSE, 2014.

23 Kondwani Chikadza, "Women in Political Parties: The Politics of Participation", in Inge Amundsen and Happy Kayuni (eds), *Women and Politics in Malawi*, 93-103.

24 Grace Malera, The Socio-Legal Status of Malawian Women in Politics: Opportunities and Challenges, A Research Paper, Denmark: Danish Institute for Human Rights, 2005.

tion in politics. Nonetheless using his prerogative, and later a constitutional amendment, he nominated additional members including women to Parliament. Thus, as shown in Table 11.1, from 1966 through to 1976, there was only one elected female Member of Parliament.

By 1977, five women had been elected to Parliament, and nine women were nominated as members of Parliament by Dr Banda. In 1981, a Constitutional amendment granted the president the right to appoint as many MPs as he wished.[25] As a result of this provision the membership of Parliament was increased from 87 to 101 in 1982. Of the 101 members, 38 members were singularly nominated by the president and 23 of them were women.[26] Together with the eight women who were elected this move resulted in a total female representation of 32.97%. This figure remains the highest ever representation of women in the Malawian Parliament as a result of the affirmative action taken by Dr Banda. For whatever reasons this form of affirmative action was not sustained in the subsequent years as the presidential appointment of women into Parliament drastically dropped to less than 10% after 1982. One thing that is clear is that the nature of the affirmative action that was introduced through a constitutional amendment in 1981 gave the president latitude to do as he saw fit. This explains why others have argued that the nomination of large numbers of women by the president in 1982 was strategically done to improve the image of his government's commitment to women empowerment, in preparation for the United Nations International Women's Conference, which was to take place in Kenya in 1984.[27]

Since democratisation in 1994, there has been a slow but steady increase in the number of women members of Parliament but huge imbalances between men and women remain evident. Although the absolute number of women candidates standing for elections have been increasing in successive elections, it has been much lower than that of men.

---

25 Henry Chingaipe, Analysis of the Contribution of First –Past the Post Electoral System to the Low Numbers of Women in the National Assembly and Local Authorities in Malawi and Options for Addressing the Gender Deficit, paper prepared for UN Malawi, Lilongwe, 2015.

26 Ibid, 30.

27 Grace Malera, "The Socio-Legal Status of Malawian Women in Politics: Opportunities and Challenges".

Table 11.2: *Women in Parliament after democratisation and before the onset of the 50:50 Campaign (1994-2004)*

	Candidates				Winners			
	Women	Men	Total	Female candidates	Women	Men	Total	Elected women
1994	46	541	587	7.8%	10	167	177	5.65%
1999	62	626	688	9.3%	16	177	193	8.29%
2004	154	944	1098	14.0%	27	166	193	13.99%

Source: Various Electoral Commission Reports 1994-2004.

Table 11.2 shows that in the first multiparty elections of 1994 only 10 women won seats out of a total of 177 parliamentarians. This gender balance did not improve significantly in the next two elections. In 1999, women won 8% of the seats while in 2004 the percentage rose slightly to 14%. The low numbers of women elected to political positions has received attention in Malawian governance debates concerning gender inclusivity. At the same time as a signatory to the SADC gender protocols, pressure was building up on Malawi government to speed up the process of getting more women elected into political offices and achieve gender parity (50-50) by 2015.[28] Thus ahead of the 2009 elections discussions ensued among state and non-state actors on possible interventions, but the funding for parity for women is the one that gained much ground in Malawi.[29] The funding for parity idea was inspired by UN Women studies that identified lack of economic resources as one of the main obstacles to women running for elections in developing countries with candidate-centered electoral systems.[30] Inspired by this idea, local civil society actors, particularly NGO-GCN, which was amongst the main advocates for strengthening women's political participation in Malawi lobbied government and development partners to set up a plan for funding women who wanted to run for election. This programme came to be popularly known as the 50-50

28 Vibeke Wang, Happy Kayuni, Asiyati Chiweza, and Samantha Soyiyo, "Relieving Women's Costs of Standing for Election: Malawi's 50/50 Campaigns".

29 Happy Kayuni and Ragnhild Muriaas, "Alternatives to Gender Quotas: Electoral Financing of Women Candidates in Malawi", *Representation* 50/3 (2014), 393–404.

30 Vibeke Wang, Happy Kayuni, Asiyati Chiweza and Samantha Soyiyo, "Relieving Women's Costs".

Campaign.[31] The argument was that providing financial support towards election campaign costs for female candidates would lead to an increase in descriptive representation of women in Parliament. Unlike gender quotas that require parties to find women to recruit into politics, funding support to women candidates was supposed to trigger the supply mechanism of political recruitment and it assumes that women will be more motivated to run for election.

Main Actors in the 50-50 Campaigns and their Strategies

Up to 2018, the main Malawian partners of the 50-50 Campaign were the Ministry of Gender and the NGO-Gender Coordination Network. Through the campaign, these two partners became the focal point for donor and civil society (CSO) efforts to support women's representation in the run-up to the 2009 and 2014 elections. For the 2019 elections, instead of relying on the NGO-GCN network the supporters of the campaign employed a new model by bringing in a management agency (MA) staffed with experts in various fields to run the campaign independent of the Ministry of Gender, donors and NGOs.

The Ministry of Gender and Social Welfare

The Ministry responsible for gender is the national gender policy-holder. In keeping with the SADC Protocol's target of equal representation of men and women in all electoral processes as well as other international commitments, the ministry launched the National Programme on Increasing Women's Representation in Parliament and Local Government in 2008. Through this the ministry sought to provide the political and policy leadership for the parity programme and to facilitate the coordination of all state and non-state actors' interventions towards the same. However, despite the ministry launching the programme and being the policy-holder, it has not been the key actor in designing and funding the 50-50 Campaign interventions. Indeed, other scholars have also noted that, worldwide, state responses to the Beijing commitments have fallen well short of expectations.[32] The Gender Department is the least funded and in the 2014 and 2019 elections there was literally no

---

31 Ibid.

32 Lina Abou-Habib, Valeria Esquivel, Anne Marie Goetz, Joanne Sandler and Caroline Sweetman, "Introduction: Gender, Development, and Beijing +25", *Gender & Development*, 28/2 (2020), 223-237.

budget allocation for the 50-50 Campaign.[33] This has been an enduring problem in the operation of the Ministry of Gender and as a result, throughout the implementation of the campaigns, the ministry's role has been limited to coordinating and supervising donor and CSO defined interventions.

Civil Society Organisations and Donors

Civil society actors along with international stakeholders have been the main advocates for strengthening women's political participation in Malawi. Countries dependent on development aid have looked to donors for sources of funding for their gender mainstreaming efforts and women's rights groups have lobbied donors to provide funding for governments to work on women's rights and to support women's and feminist activism in civil society.[34] Up to the 2014 elections, the parity programme was implemented by a number of civil society organisations under the coordination and managerial leadership of the NGO Gender Coordination Network (NGO-GCN).[35] The NGO-GCN is a loose network of civil society organisations (CSOs) working on women's rights and gender equality. Its 53-member organisations are organised into five permanent thematic committees. The network, through its Women in Politics and Decision-Making permanent committee, has been instrumental in the advocacy, design, and implementation the 50-50 Campaign in the run-up to the 2009 and 2014 elections.

In both the 2009 and 2014 elections, the bulk of funding was provided to the NGO-GCN by the Royal Norwegian Embassy, to the tune of MWK 600 million and MWK 400 million respectively. In collaboration with the donor, NGO-GCN designed the 50-50 parity campaign as a programme that was aimed at enhancing governance and coordination among different stakeholders, building the capacity of the female aspirants, advocacy and lobby-ing the opinion leaders to support the female candidates, raising community awareness and monitoring and observing the electoral process (see Table 11.3).[36] However, in 2009, the interventions targeted all aspiring female

---

33 Asiyati Chiweza and Tiyesere Chikapa, "Institutional Analysis of Gender Mainstreaming in the Malawian Public Sector", Research Report, Lilongwe: HIVOS, 2019.

34 Ibid, 361.

35 www.ngogcnmw.org.

36 Henry Chingaipe and Francis Matita, Report on the Evaluation of the Gender Parity (50:50) Programme for the 2014 Tripartite Elections.

candidates, but in 2014 the interventions concentrated only on nominated female candidates who had gone through the party primary election stage.

Table 3: *Summary of the 50-50 Campaign Interventions in the 2009 and 2014 Elections*

Category	Nature of Interventions
Direct support to candidates and capacity building	This included provision of campaign materials such as t-shirts, cloths, flyers, banners); cash payments to candidates (MWK 92,000 in 2009; MWK 200,000 (USD 276) in 2014 for parliamentary candidates and MWK 90,000 (about USD 124); support towards payment to monitors for women candidates (2 each, 2014 only). Capacity building was provided towards manifesto development, campaign management, public speaking skills, time management and overcoming challenges during campaign period.
Civic education	Print and radio civic education messages on the importance of voting for women and community sensitisation meetings with traditional and religious leaders
Media support	Media strategy to boost publicity of women candidates by paying for airtime for the candidates to talk about their manifestos on the major radio stations. Donor groups also organised training sessions with journalists on promoting female aspirants.
Political party engagement	Meetings with party leaders and development of cross-party communiqué to support women's leadership (2014).
Research	Several studies were commissioned: needs assessment of female parliamentarians (UN Women, 2015); study of voter behaviour after the 2014 election; (Nkuuhe and Kanyongolo, 2014); training needs assessment of women MPs (Mbilizi, 2011); needs assessment of female aspirants (Nawanga, 2008); factors and perceptions that affect women's political representation at national and local level in Malawi: A Political Economy Analysis (Chiweza and Kanyongolo, 2017).

For the 2019 elections, the architects of the parity campaign continued with a programme approach but adopted a different implementation modality based on lessons and challenges from previous experiences. Instead of relying on the NGO-GCN network, the main funder of the parity campaign, the Royal Norwegian Embassy in collaboration with the Ministry of Gender, employed a new model that saw the deployment of an independent civil society organisation called the Centre for Civil Society Strengthening as an independent management agency to run the main parity campaign. The nature of interventions implemented by the independent management agency under the 2019 parity programme was based on a theory of change that assumed that increased action and efforts to demystify negative social norms, practices and beliefs will deliver results for women. Even though this theory was different from the one used in the previous campaigns the nature of the activities did not significantly depart from the previous years. The management agency activities focused on the following: a) engaging political party leaders, opinion leaders and faith leaders to advocate against increased levels of discrimination against women in politics; b) building the capacity of female aspirants by enhancing self-esteem and reducing inferiority complex, and c) raising awareness through community campaigns to demystify negative social norms, beliefs, traditions and practices that hinder women participation in politics.

Table 11.4: *Support channelled through the Independent Management Agency - 2019 Elections*

Name of institution/funder	Nature of intervention	Amount of support	Time frame
Funding Support Channelled through the Independent Management Agency			
Royal Norwegian Embassy	Capacity building, Violence Against Women in Elections, and coordination of the campaign	MWK 1,100,000,000	2017-2020
OSISA	Capacity building for Young Women Politicians	USD 80,000	October 2018-June 2019
ICEIDA	Capacity building of Mangochi female candidates only	USD 90,000	October 2018 to June 2019
NBS Bank	IEC materials (baseball caps to the launch)	MWK 2,000,000	April 2018
First Discount House Bank	IEC materials (cloth)	MWK 6,000,000	April 2018
Commonwealth Secretariat	Capacity building of CSOs	Direct funding to service providers	January 2019

Perhaps what was different from previous interventions is that in 2019 the independent management agency package also provided some cost relief support to all candidates towards the refund of MEC registration fees.[37] Further, in the 2019 elections, there were also other international actors who worked separately with some independent CSOs to define and implement other activities related to the campaign. However, if we carefully look at the range of activities most CSOs were implementing, as in Table 11.5, it becomes evident that capacity building, community sensitisation, media support, campaign cloth, and engagement with political leaders were the most common interventions. project whose aim was to promote young women's participation in politics. Others such as Irish Aid and Oxfam focused on a retention component whose aim was to promote the visibility of incumbent candidates by producing documentaries of the 32 incumbent MPs and airing them on both television and radio. Yet others such as HIVOS focused on strengthening the women's agency and development of Women's Manifesto as a platform for women politicians across party lines to voice issues of interest.

Impact of Parity Funding Campaigns on Descriptive Representation of Women in Parliament in Malawi

The theory of change behind the 2009, 2014, and 2019 50-50 Campaign programmes assumed that by getting different actors together and having a coordinated effort in providing technical and financial support towards the campaign costs of female candidates, the women would be motivated to contest during elections, increase chances of getting elected and ultimately translate into increased descriptive representation in the legislature.[38] However, did the 50-50 funding campaigns really lead to improved descriptive representtation of women in Malawi Parliament in the three electoral periods? Several studies and evaluations show that there is no conclusive evidence that the 50-50 campaigns have had positive impacts in improving the descriptive representation of women in Parliament in Malawi.[39] An evaluation of the 2014

---

[37] Each parliamentary candidate was given 90 pieces of the 50-50 Campaign printed material, communication allowance of MWK 30,000 and transport allowance of MWK 80,000.

[38] Henry Chingaipe and Francis Matita, Report on the Evaluation of the Gender Parity (50:50) Programme for the 2014 Tripartite Elections.

[39] See for example: Henry Chingaipe and Francis Matita, Report on the Evaluation of the Gender Parity (50:50) Programme for the 2014 Tripartite Elections; Happy Kayuni and Ragnhild Muriaas, "Alternatives to Gender Quotas: Electoral Financing of Women Candidates in Malawi"; Vibeke Wang, Happy Kayuni, Asiyati Chiweza and Samantha Soyiyo, "Relieving Women's Costs of Standing for Election: Malawi's 50/50 Campaigns".

Some significant differences can be noted. For example, the European Union supported a number of CSOs to implement a Young Women in Active Politics

Table 11.5: *Support provided directly to other CSO implementing agencies - 2019 elections*

Name of institution/funder	Nature of intervention		Amount of support	Time frame
Oxfam with funding from Irish Aid (HQ) and Oxfam Ireland Oxfam with funding from Electric Aid through Oxfam Ireland	Profiling of 32 female sitting MPs through media-based campaign, engagement with community and chiefs to deconstruct stereotypes about women. Supply of branded campaign cloth and provision of bicycles to incumbent MPs.		USD 40,000 MWK 15 million	June 2018 - Feb 2019
Danish Church Aid with funding from European Union	Young Women in Active Politics projectai—rtime for radio campaigns, transport to campaign meetings, production of radio campaign programmes and provision of branded cloth for campaign		EUR 372,878.90	January 2018 to August 2021
HIVOS with funding from Dutch government working with WORLEC, GGJDC, Tovwi-rane, and Centre for Multiparty Democracy	Support towards the hosting of a Women's Assembly and development of Women's Assembly Manifesto, capacity building, community sensitisation, and engagement with political parties at the local level		EUR 440,000	2019
UN Women with funding from European Union, Royal Norwegian Embassy, Department for International Development and Irish Embassy	Engagement with political party structures at grassroots level, community awareness, women candidate profiling; training of monitors on violence against women, elections monitoring room during the polling day; and interactive dialogues with men on supporting female candidates, Refund of nomination fees, partial transport, communication support. Each candidate received a communication allowance of MWK 30,000 and transport allowance of MWK 80,000.		MWK 423,544,323 MWK 105,381,000	December 2017-June 2019 2019

50-50 Campaign by Chingaipe and Matita found that the campaign indeed energised the participation of women in electoral politics and also firmly put on the national agenda the need to open up spaces for meaningful women's participation in politics, but the programme did not achieve its target of getting 50% women into Parliament.[40] In fact, the percentage of women getting into Parliament dropped from 22% in 2009 to 16% in 2014. The 2014 50-50 funding campaign programme document explicitly stated that the aim was to increase the number of women elected to 50%, and the decrease in the number of female MPs was interpreted by many actors as a sign of failure. Although the number of elected women picked up again to 23% in 2019, it was still less than the required 50%. It may also be important to indicate that as of the first week of February 2021, the number of female parliamentarians had reduced further because two seats that were held by female parliamentarians were lost after a court nullification of the 2019 parliamentary election results due to irregularities in the respective constituencies.

The conclusion is that representation of women in both local government and national assembly has not changed much over the past three consecutive elections.[41] The studies also show that over the last three elections there has been a positive but fluctuating trend in the number of women standing as candidates in Malawi's parliamentary elections. In a study of the 50-50 Campaign in the 2009 Malawian elections, Muriaas and Kayuni[42] found that the campaign proved efficient in motivating women to compete in the elections, through seeking nominations in primaries or as independent candidates, but it did not efficiently address the obstacles women faced in the party primaries. As Table 11.6 illustrates, this trend continued between 2014 and 2019, but the actual increase in the number of women standing as candidates has been much lower than that between 2004 and 2009 and 2014 and 2019.

---

40 Henry Chingaipe and Francis Matita, Report on the Evaluation of the Gender Parity (50:50) Programme for the 2014 Tripartite Elections.

41 Emma Kaliya, "Malawi Women Political Participation Barometer", A Research Paper for the Annual Regional Barometer on Women Political Participation, 2021.

42 Muriaas and Kayuni, "Alternatives to Gender Quotas: Electoral Financing of Women Candidates in Malawi".

Table 11.6: *Trends in Women in Parliament after the implementation of the 50-50 Campaign (2004-2019)*

	Candidates			**Winners**		
	Women	All candidates	Female candidates	Women elected	All MPs	Women elected
2004	154	1,098	14.0%	27	193	13.99%
2009	237 (+83)	1,175	20.2%	42	193	22.27% (+8.28%)
2014	257 (+20)	1,292	20.0%	31	193	16% (-6.27%)
2019	304 (+47)	1,331	22.0%	45	192	23% (+7.00%)

Source: Various Electoral Commission Reports.

Why is this the case? One school of thought explains the low levels of women's descriptive representation on the basis of various contextual factors and conditions. For example, Mona Lena Krook's[43] analysis of women's descriptive representation in Western democracies and in sub-Saharan Africa finds that in the latter, low levels of representation in Parliament are associated with lack of quotas and women's low status, party systems and rules, including legal and electoral systems.[44] What this literature suggests is that the effectiveness of initiatives designed to improve descriptive representation of women depends on how those initiatives interact with existing institutional frameworks, including the electoral system, party systems, rules and political culture. Turning to the Malawi case, what are the plausible explanations behind the limited impact of the 50-50 parity campaign in inducing increased women's descriptive representation in Parliament?

I argue that the effort to promote gender equality through the 50-50 Campaign had limited success because the nature of the interventions that the non-state actors implemented did not challenge and dismantle the structural limitations that have contributed to Malawi's poor performance in terms of getting women

43 Mona Lena Krook, "Women's Representation in Parliament: A Qualitative Comparative Analysis", *Political Studies* 58/5 (2010), 886-908.

44 See Mona Lena Krook, *Quotas for Women in Politics: Gender and Candidate Selection Reform Worldwide*, Oxford: OUP, 2009; Meryl Kenney and Fiona MacKay, "Already doin' it for ourselves? Skeptical notes on Feminism and Institutionalism", *Politics & Gender* 5/2 (2009), 271-28.

into politics and key leadership positions. This relates to the historical legacy that characterised women as political party dancers with limited leadership roles, the patron-client relations emerging from the Banda era and neopatrimonialism, the absence of political transformation and the socio-cultural obstacles to women's participation.[45] These factors have been the key structural limitations towards any well-meaning civil society effort to promote gender equality. They are also the same factors that contributed to Malawi's inability to achieve the target of 30% women in Parliament recommended in 1997 by SADC.[46]

The first of these relate to the main incentives that shape the decisions of many political parties to field a candidate. At the policy level, the commitment of Malawian political parties to the cause of engendered political participation has been questioned repeatedly, owing to their purported failure to institutionalise gender-sensitive rules of candidate selection.[47] The Political Parties Registration and Regulation Act (1993), the Presidential and Parliamentary Elections Act (1993) and the Electoral Commission Act (1998) are the three pieces of legislation concerned with the regulation of political parties. None of these, however, explicitly spells out how they intend to protect, let alone promote, the participation of women in elected positions. None of these pieces of legislation provide for gender parity as a condition and none sets any minimum number of female members, for example, as a condition for the registration of a political party.[48] In contrast, political parties in some African countries such as Botswana, Cameroon, Mozambique, Namibia and South Africa have adopted internal rules on including a certain percentage of women among their parliamentary candidates.[49]

As a result of this formal institutional vacuum to guide political parties, the extent of women's participation through political parties has largely been at the mercy of political gatekeepers of the respective parties. Gatekeepers are individuals within a party who are able to influence the decisions of the party

---

45 Rebecca Tiessen, "Small Victories but Slow Progress", *International Feminist Journal of Politics* 10/2 (2008), 198-215.

46 Ibid.

47 Kondwani Chikadza, "Women in Political Parties: The Politics of Participation".

48 Ngeyi Kanyongolo and Bernadette Malunga, "Legal Empowerment; Laws Promoting Women's Participation in Politics", in Inge Amundsen and Happy Kayuni (eds), *Women in Politics in Malawi*, Bergen: CMI, 2016.

49 United Nations, UN Sustainable Development Goals, Goal 5: Achieve gender equality and empower all women and girls, https://unstats.un.org/sdgs/report/2020/goal-05/.

in terms of who should occupy party positions and stand for election on the party ticket.[50] In the absence of formal rules guiding primary elections—a written official and explicit set of internal rules on candidate selection—female aspirants have to contend with the stereotypes and sexist assumptions of local party elites at constituency and branch levels about the attributes of an "electable" candidate where women are perceived as belonging to the private rather than the public sphere.[51] Party politics has been observed to be a masculine domain and most of these gatekeepers are men who are imbued with cultural and male prejudices that work against women in party candidate selection processes.[52] In a study of local party gatekeepers that was done in 2016, Kayuni found that support for women was high for non-important positions within the party. He also found that political parties need women for local political mobilisation and the strengthening of the party structures at the grassroots level, but the parties are not interested in getting women for externally contested positions such as a member of Parliament or local government councillor. In such contexts, the more likely a party thinks it is to win a seat, the more likely it is to settle for a male candidate. Khembo also observed that gender is largely used as an electoral campaign rhetoric which is never seriously integrated into party structures.[53]

The new Political Parties Act of 2018 has not improved the situation either. While it provides for gender equality as a key guiding principle and encourages political parties to uphold the principles of gender equality when appointing members of party organs and nominating electoral candidates,[54] it does not oblige them to take specific affirmative measures to attract and protect women. Consequently, party nomination processes have proceeded in an informal manner. A survey of the 2018-2019 female aspirants' complaints compiled by the independent management agency revealed several areas of concern related

---

50 Happy Kayuni, "The Women's Parliamentary Caucus: Promoting Cross-Party Substantive Representation", in Inge Amundsen and Happy Kayuni (eds), *Women and Politics in Malawi*, 81-92.

51 Henry Chingaipe, Analysis of the Contribution of First Past the Post Electoral System to the Low Numbers of Women in the National Assembly and Local Authorities in Malawi and Options for Addressing the Gender Deficit, paper prepared for UN Malawi, Lilongwe, 2015.

52 Kondwani Chikadza, "Women in Political Parties: The Politics of Participation".

53 Nixon S. Khembo, "The Multi-Party Promise Betrayed: The Failure of Neo-Liberalism in Malawi", *Africa Development* 29/2 (2004), 80-105.

54 Political Parties Act No. 1 of 2018, section 3, 1 (d). Section 32 (I) also encourages parties to endeavour to achieve fair gender representation in the nomination of candidates to contest in presidential, parliamentary or local government elections.

to the administration of primary elections. For example, information on primaries such as access to candidate forms, venue, guidelines, delegates, and zones was kept as a secret and a privilege of a select few. The agency noted that:

> One has to have connections to the politburo who in most major parties are a 'boys club' in order to know the calendar of events. Unfortunately, where and time these 'boys' make these decisions are places where women embattled by patriarchy cannot step a foot. A case in point is a story of an aspirant who narrated how on the eve of a primary election she kept visiting the house of the constituency chairperson starting from morning and only to get the information on the venue at 10 in the evening when the wife of the constituency chairperson called him. Sadly, the information changed in the early morning hours of the next day. As compared to her male competitors, she had no resources to hire a vehicle to transport her supporters to the new venue.[55]

While these informal patriarchal political party practices have been prevalent since democratisation, the early years of the 50-50 Campaign concentrated on community sensitisation and engagement with opinion leaders such as chiefs and religious leaders with little influence on electoral processes while missing party primary nominations as important electoral decision-points.[56] Recent survey evidence shows that while it is common in Malawi for political leaders and individuals seeking political office to court the support of traditional leaders to persuade their subjects to vote for their candidature, a majority of Malawians (93%) say that they are very unlikely to be influenced by their traditional leaders in their voting choices.[57] In the 2014 and 2019 elections, the 50-50 Campaign intensified the lobbying meetings with party actors with an extra focus on appealing to the goodwill of the National Executive Committees (NECs) of the parties to field and support female candidates, but these efforts have largely been ignored. This explains why even though political party executive committees made commitments to field and support female candidates and signed a communiqué to that effect in 2014, the commitments were not followed or matched by any formal mechanisms or strategies within

[55] Viwemi Chavula, "Challenging Informality as a Patriarchal Dividend", policy brief, Lilongwe: Independent Management Agency, 2019.

[56] Henry Chingaipe and Francis Matita, Report on the Evaluation of the Gender Parity (50:50) Programme for the 2014 Tripartite Elections.

[57] Happy Kayuni, Michael Chasukwa, Boniface Dulani and Gift Sambo, "Perceptions on the Legitimacy of Traditional Leaders in Democratic Malawi", *Journal of Public Administration and Development Alternatives* 4/1 (2019), 42-54.

the political parties to influence local party selectors to support the 50-50 agenda.[58]

Connected to this is the ongoing structural process of neopatrimonialism in the state following the shift to a multiparty democracy in 1994 that has enabled a protracted patron-client relationship between the government and the population, thereby reinforcing women's marginal positions in all levels of society.[59] One of the special characteristics associated with neo-patrimonialism is a "zero-sum" approach to politics: the winner takes all. The prevalence of such attitudes among the political elite makes competition for power particularly critical in elections. Majoritarian electoral systems like the first past the post appear to raise the stakes by their winner-takes-all nature and by further clientelistic voting behaviour through the close personal relationship between voter and representative in single-member districts.[60] In Africa, clientelistic electoral campaigns associated with majoritarian systems are strongly biased towards men in two inter-related ways.[61] First, men are favoured by the distribution of patronage in those systems—men receive services, handouts, and other favours disproportionally—and hence, male political dominance tends to be reproduced.[62] For instance, some established political parties that have participated in previous general elections tend to have incumbent male members of Parliament (MPs) or shadow MPs who remain loyal and supportive of the parties and want to run for the party in their respective constituencies during the next election.[63] This further diminishes the chances of party elites to consider women of potential who would like to contest for the parliamentary seat. In these circumstances, to nominate a woman amounts to throwing out an incumbent male MP and snubbing loyal and supportive male members who may have previously sacrificed personal resources for the party. Hence in such situations, the party takes calculative moves to protect their preferred male candidates. As observed

58 Henry Chingaipe and Francis Matita, Report on the Evaluation of the Gender Parity (50:50) Programme for the 2014 Tripartite Elections.

59 Rebecca Tiessen, "Small Victories but Slow Progress", *International Feminist Journal of Politics* 10/2 (2008), 198-215.

60 Steffan Lindberg, "It's Our Time to 'Chop': Do Elections in Africa Feed Neo-patrimonialism rather than Counter-Act it?" *Democratization* 10/2 (2003), 121–140.

61 Leonard Wantchekron, "Clientelism and Voting Behaviour: A Field Experiment in Benin", *World Politics* 54 (2003), 399–422.

62 Ibid.

63 Henry Chingaipe, "Analysis of the Contribution of First Past the Post Electoral System to the Low Numbers of Women in the National Assembly and Local Authorities in Malawi and Options for Addressing the Gender Deficit", paper prepared for UN Malawi, Lilongwe, 2015.

by the independent management agency, in some cases female candidates who had a relatively good resource base had their names missing on the final party nomination list even when they had won the primary elections.[64] Other women were even given Malawi Electoral Commission nomination forms to fill only to be told at the District Commissioners Offices during submission that the party had submitted a different candidate. In many of these cases the women did not have any other avenues to have their grievances resolved.

Second, the FPTP electoral system puts the focus on the candidate and it compels him or her to engage in extravagant expenditures aimed at getting votes. In a context of minimal enforcement of campaign regulations, candidates try to outdo each other in all sorts of ways. In neopatrimonial systems, it takes great resources to sustain the "big man" politics of clientelism as copious funds must be expended to meet school fees, hand out small sums of money, contribute towards funerals, and cover similar outlays.[65] Election campaign costs in Malawi are very high because candidates seek to outdo each other on the basis of delivery of tangible public goods and provision of other materials of interest to voters. The expenses escalate because candidates have to travel long distances within the constituency; distribute party materials, such as t-shirts, caps, cloth; give cash handouts to chiefs and dancers during the campaign meetings; provide food and allowances to their campaign teams as long as they are on the campaign trail.[66] Men tend to have access to more resources, facilitating their participation in such activities. In a pre-elections statement released by the Technical Working Group on Political Empowerment of Women of the Ministry of Gender, Children, Community and Social Welfare, on 16 May 2019, the Ministry acknowledged this problem and the impact it has on women candidates as follows:

> We bemoan the many economic hardships most women candidates have been subjected to due to highly monetised politics in Malawi. It has become almost impossible to run a political campaign in Malawi, without spending huge amounts of money in order to garner support. This political culture has made voters prone to voter bribery as they become enticed by handouts from the political elites. The

64 Viwemi Chavula, "Challenging Informality as a Patriarchal Dividend".

65 Steffanie Lindberg, "It's Our Time to 'Chop'".

66 Vibeke Wang, Happy Kayuni, Asiyati Chiweza and Samantha Soyiyo, "Relieving Women's Costs of Standing for Election: Malawi's 50/50 Campaigns".

> persistence of 'money-politics' is unfortunate considering the many economic inequalities that exist in our society between men and women.[67]

Malawi ranks 142 out of 162 on the UN Gender Inequality Index (GII),[68] and women lag far behind men in their opportunities to access capital, markets, and leadership positions.[69] The 50–50 Campaign was introduced to address what was perceived to constitute the greatest barrier for women in politics, namely, a lack of personal funds and access to financial networks.[70] However, the funding support the 50–50 Campaign provided to individual women was far too little to make any significant difference. When compared to the total amount candidates needed to effectively campaign, the 2014 and 2019 cash support was perceived by the recipients to be insignificant.[71] Despite the cash support being a drop in the ocean, it was also given quite late in the process, after party nominations had already occurred. For example, in the 2019 election, the cash support and campaign materials were given to the women in April, a month before the actual day of elections. Thus, providing cash, capacity building support, t-shirts and other non-material support to female aspirants did not enable them to surmount huge electoral campaign costs and challenges.[72]

The cut-throat and personalised nature of majoritarian systems such as the FPTP electoral system has been shown to produce high-stakes electoral contests associated with greater levels of electoral violence.[73] Recent work has drawn attention to how intraparty competition can lead to violence in the

---

67 Independent Management Agency and Malawi Government, "Statement from the Technical Working Group on Political Empowerment of Women", 16 May 2019.

68 The Gender Inequality Index (GII) sheds new light on the position of women in 162 countries. It measures gender inequalities in three important aspects of human development—reproductive health, measured by maternal mortality ratio and adolescent birth rates; empowerment, measured by proportion of parliamentary seats occupied by females and proportion of adult females and males aged 25 years and older with at least some secondary education; and economic status, expressed as labour market participation and measured by labour force participation rate of female and male populations aged 15 years and older.

69 United Nations Development Programme, Human Development Report: Gender Inequality Index, 2020 Statistical Table, hdr.undp.org/en/composite/GII.

70 Ragnhild Muriaas, Vibeke Wang and Rainbow Murray, "Introducing the Concept of Gendered Electoral Financing", 4.

71 S. Chilundu, "Study Reveals High Cost of Elections".

72 Ibid.

73 Hanne Fjelde and Kristine Höglund, "Electoral Violence: The Emergence of a Research Field", *APSA Comparative Democratization Newsletter* 14/2 (2016), 8–11.

nomination process.[74] Women more often face acts of intimidation and psychological abuse.[75] The 2019 European Union Observation Mission noted that despite some measures and programmes to facilitate the participation of women in the elections, many faced hurdles in seeking candidacy, notably during primaries, and in the conduct of their campaigns, including being the targets of derogatory and demeaning language on occasion.[76] These tactics militate against women aspirants because many women in Malawi are culturally sensitive to flagrant personality attacks and innuendos that characterise political campaigns.

Finally, Malawi does not have any gender quotas in politics. Gender electoral quotas are the most commonly used means of correcting imbalances in gender representation in historically patriarchal contexts such as Malawi.[77] By 2020, electoral quotas for women had spread to all regions of the world with more than 130 countries adopting some form of quota to increase women's representation in politics up from 2 in 1995.[78] The 2020 Inter-Parliamentary Union report further observed that, on average, the share of women in parliamentary chambers without quotas is considerably lower and most sub-Saharan African countries that have achieved a high level of women's representation have done so through the use of various types of gender quotas. In Malawi, gender quotas have frequently been dismissed as discriminating against men.[79] This was clearly reflected in the legislature's reluctance to extend the Gender Equality Act (2013) quota provisions to cover electoral processes.[80] Consequently, the application of the Gender Equality Act (2013) technically

---

74 Merete B. Seeberg, Michael Wahman and Svend-Erik Skaaning, "Candidate Nomination, Intra-party Democracy, and Election Violence in Africa", *Democratization* 25/6 (2018), 959–977.

75 Elin Bjarnegård, "Making Gender Visible in Election Violence: Strategies for Data Collection", *Politics & Gender* 14/4 (2018), 690–695.

76 European Union Election Observation Mission Malawi, "European Union Election Observation Mission Malawi", 2019, EUEOM%20Preliminary%20Statement%20-%20Malawi %202019%20-%20FINAL.pdf

77 Ragnhild Muriaas, Vibeke Wang and Rainbow Murray, "Introducing the Concept of Gendered Electoral Financing", 1-24.

78 Inter-Parliamentary Union, Women in Parliament 1995-2020: 25 Years in Review, IPU Report, 2020. Available at www.ipu.org/resources/publications/reports/2020-03/.

79 Lindsay Benstead, Ragnhild Muriaas and Vibeke Wang, When do Donor Endorsements Help or Hurt? Policy Advocacy and Men's Interests in Malawi, Working Paper No. 16, the Programme on Governance and Local Development (GLD), Gothenburg, Sweden, 2018.

80 The initial gender quota proposals about the Gender Equality Act submitted to Parliament covered both electoral and non-electoral public service appointments.

leaves out elected bodies and political parties which are central to increasing numbers of women elected to political structures of governance in the country. Further, government's 2017 rejection of a proposal from the Malawi Law Commission to introduce 28 automatic seats for women through constituencies where only female candidates would be allowed to contest as members of Parliament further mirrors government's reluctance to adopt gender quotas. It is therefore not far-fetched to believe that government is caught up in a situation where it is ratifying a variety of progressive international and regional gender equality provisions and creating women-centred institutions, to "play the game", without necessarily shaking off the foundations that prevent high representation of women in public life.[81]

Conclusion

The 50-50 Campaign efforts to get more women into Parliament that Malawi has implemented since 2009 reflect a form of positive action aimed at promoting the supply side by encouraging women to stand as candidates through short-term material and technical support to individuals prior to an election. The campaign also tried to create a favourable environment for women by appealing to the goodwill of party duty-bearers and voters through advocacy and sensitisation. The campaign experience in Malawi illustrates the limits of employing technical approaches towards dealing with deep-seated patriarchal structures and institutions within the hybrid neopatrimonial characteristics of African societies. Without reforming the electoral rules or party institutions, and challenging the patriarchal gender norms and traditions that have historically constrained women's access to Parliament, there is a limit to what can reasonably be achieved. Results are mostly slow and, in the medium to long term, gender gains may be vulnerable to reversals as was the case in the 2014 elections.

However, there is strong evidence that electoral quotas have been important to increasing numbers of elected women in sub-Saharan Africa where a combination of gender norms, legal frameworks and informal political practices

---

[81] Michael Chasukwa, "The Central Government Administration Opportunities and Challenges for Women Representation", in Inge Amundsen and Happy Kayuni (eds), *Women and Politics in Malawi*, Bergen and Zomba: Chr. Michelsen Institute (CMI), Department of Political and Administrative Studies, 2016, 105-116.

have few incentives to select and support women candidates.[82] On average, once implemented, quotas dramatically increase women's representation, suggesting that when political opportunities exist, women take them.[83] A complementary strategy to positive action that is multi-pronged needs to be seriously considered. First, strengthening advocacy and lobbying to promote gender-sensitive electoral reforms and quotas for women's representation in political parties and elected bodies is needed if the quest towards inclusive governance is to be realised in Malawi. The appeal by the Chairperson of the Electoral Commission in the quotation at the beginning of the chapter attests to this point. Second, the reactive, short-term approach that has characterised previous campaigns where activities are set in motion before an election needs to be replaced with an on-going approach that seeks to support and build the capacity of incumbents to improve their constituency service and development performance overtime. This has potential to improve re-election chances of incumbent women in clientelistic electoral contexts such as Malawi. Other possible positive action may include introducing political education academies for women from across the political parties, covering several topics in a modular fashion; and creating and popularising positive narratives of women in politics and the notion of equality of outcomes.

---

[82] Tam O'Neil, Ngeyi Kanyongolo and Joseph Wales, "Women and Power: Representation and Influence in Malawi's Parliament".

[83] Amanda Clayton, Amanda Robinson, Martha Johnson and Ragnhild Muriaas, "(How) Do Voters Discriminate Against Women Candidates? Experimental and Qualitative Evidence from Malawi", *Comparative Political Studies*, 53/3 (2020), 601–630.

Chapter 12

Ethnicity, Regionalism, and Nation-Building Challenges in Post-1994 Malawi: Whither a Federal State System?

Gift Wasambo Kayira
& Paul Chiudza Banda

Introduction

On 26 September 2019, Yeremiah Chihana, a member of Parliament (MP) representing Mzimba North Constituency, moved a motion to replace the existing unitary governance system with a federated state system that would grant autonomy to each of the three regions of the country, one centred in the North and the other two in the Centre and South. For Chihana, federalism held the potential to promote equitable distribution of state resources and development programmes besides eradicating the "quota" system of selecting students to public universities.[1] If Chihana thought a federated state system would resolve the deep-seated historical problems of economic and social injustice in Malawi, others saw the proposal as dangerous and divisive to the Malawi nation. In his contribution to the parliamentary debate on the subject, Victor Musowa, MP for Mulanje Bale Constituency, dismissed the motion. He further argued that "even if Malawi were to adopt a federal system of government, the Northern Region, [which Chihana regarded as having a relatively unified identity], would still find it hard to identify a leader" because in the immediate past, two "sons", Enock Chihana and Frank Mwenifumbo, had fought for the presidency of a Northern Region-based political party.[2]

---

1 Malawi Government, Proceedings of the National Assembly, 48th Session, Thursday, 26 September 2019, 120. Under the quota system, the government selects secondary/high school students to public universities based on their districts of origin rather than strictly on merit on a nationwide basis. It was the government of Dr Hastings Kamuzu Banda, Malawi's first state president who ruled between 1964 and 1994, that first introduced the system. Although there is an element of merit at district level, many people from the northern region of the country condemn it as discriminatory because it leaves out some of the most gifted students.

2 Proceedings of the National Assembly, 48th Session, Thursday, 26 September 2019, 127; Also cited in *The Times*, "Federalism motion debate in Parliament", 27 September 2019, https://times.mw/federalism-motion-stirs-debate-in-parliament/. The political party in question was the Alliance for Democracy (AFORD).

The two positions are significant because they point to the merits and demerits of unitary and federal systems of governance. They also reflect the intersection of the themes of ethnicity, nation-building, regional identity, and development. Chihana's view challenges the existing governance model for promoting unified nationhood while failing to safeguard economic interests of all Malawians. On the other hand, Musowa's statement points to the question of whether there is a viable Northern Regional identity, touted as the basis for proposing a federated state system.[3] Both positions reflect an enduring scholarly debate on how pluralistic societies like that of Malawi can achieve the status of a nation-state and command citizens' confidence.

To what extent has the post-1994 Malawian state achieved the level of dynamism capable of resolving ethnic and regional cleavages while equitably spreading economic gains to its population? How relevant is a federated state system as a solution to Malawi's historical problems of ethnicity, regionalism, nation-building, and development? This chapter addresses these related questions.

We argue that the failure of the Malawian state to deliver on the promises of liberal democracy has nurtured the debate on federalism, forcing some quarters to turn to it as an alternative to what they perceive as the shortfalls of the unitary governance model. Despite considerable political publicity, however, the proposed federal governance structure is based on a false premise of unified ethno-regional identities whose existence in Malawi remain doubtful. Although studies by Deborah Kaspin and Wiseman Chirwa suggest the existence of some regional identities as significantly influencing the voting trend since 1994, the call for federalism based on such regional blocs is problematic because it masks ethnic differences within these regions.[4] In this way, the chapter contributes to the historiography on ethnicity, regionalism, development, and nation-building and how it intersects with the debate on federalism as an aspect of governance. These are not new themes in African scholarship. As regards Malawi, the works by Leroy Vail, Landeg White, Kaspin, and, to a limited extent, John McCracken,

---

3 A careful analysis of Chihana's arguments display a unified northern regional identity as the basis for proposing a federal state system.

4 See Debora Kaspin, "The Politics of Ethnicity in Malawi's Democratic Transition", *Journal of Modern African Studies* 33/4 (1995), 595-620; Wiseman C. Chirwa, "Democracy, Ethnicity, and Regionalism: The Malawian Experience, 1992-1996", in Kings M. Phiri and Kenneth R. Ross (eds), *Democratization in Malawi: A Stocktaking*, Zomba: CLAIM-Kachere, 1998, 52-69.

are pacesetters in the debate on ethnicity and regionalism and its relationship to nation-building.[5]

As early as the 1980s, Vail had already debunked the myth of primordialist and ascriptive ethnicities in southern Africa.[6] We now know that ethnic identities, for example, are fluid and historically constructed to serve specific interests. We also have a fair grasp of the multitude of culture brokers who helped to shape Malawi's ethnic identities. These range from Christian missionaries and African intellectuals educated in the Scottish missionary tradition, and colonial administrators, whose support of indirect rule further solidified ethnic groupings around chieftainships. Added to these is the role of post-colonial leaders particularly Dr Hastings Kamuzu Banda, whose bias towards the Chewa of the Central Region drew a backlash from other groups of the country who felt neglected and suppressed. In the 1990s, Kaspin and Chirwa documented the legacies of these constructed ethnicities by showing how ethnic and regional identities dictated the outcome of democratic elections.[7] Instead of making decisions based on sound understanding and analysis of campaign messages, the electorates mostly voted for co-ethnics during the 1994 elections. This trend has repeated itself in subsequent elections.

These works point to the view that ethnic and regional identities are a political problem because they frustrate the nation-building agenda; promote parochial economic interests that lead to inequalities in the distribution of state resources; and frustrate the gains of liberal democracy. One other legacy of these constructed identities that deserves greater scholarly emphasis because of its relevance to the future of Malawi is the more recent debate on the federal system of government, especially how it addresses the problems in question. The debate on federalism is significant because it centres on governance issues and the country's future unity. Therefore, it deserves a scholarly comment and

---

5 Leroy Vail (ed), *The Creation of Tribalism in Southern Africa*, Stanford: University of California Press, 1989; Leroy Vail and Landeg White, "Tribalism in the Political History of Malawi", in Leroy Vail (ed), *The Creation of Tribalism in Southern Africa*, 146-184; Kaspin, "The Politics of Ethnicity in Malawi's Democratic Transition", 595-620; John McCracken, "The Ambiguities of Nationalism: Flax Musopole and the Northern Factor in Malawian Politics, c. 1956-1966", *Journal of Southern African Studies* 28/1 (2002), 67-87.

6 Leroy Vail, "Introduction: Ethnicity in Southern African History", in Leroy Vail (ed), *The Creation of Tribalism in Southern Africa*, 1-50 [11-12].

7 Kaspin, "The Politics of Ethnicity in Malawi's Democratic Transition", 595-620; Chirwa, "Democracy, Ethnicity, and Regionalism", 52-69.

one that locates it within a broader framework of the politics of ethnicity, regionalism, and nation-building in the country.

The subsequent section examines at length the historiography of ethnicity and regionalism in Malawi and beyond. The idea is not to rehash the much-rehearsed subject of how Malawi's identities were constructed and how the process has complicated the nation-building agenda; instead, it highlights the most salient features in the literature relative to the questions at hand. The final section discusses the historical context of the empirical debate on a federal governance system, followed by an analysis of its merits and demerits. We argue that the problem confronting the country is not so much the existence of multiple ethnic and regional identities whose solution rests with a federal state system but rather that of unequal development and social injustice, which politicised ethnicities have helped to fuel rather than change. Although not prescriptive, Malawi will be better served by well-decentralised governance structures rather than by a federated state system. The Kenyan model for power devolution, we suggest, could provide some lessons for Malawi. We present our argument based on some primary sources from the print and online media, and other secondary sources, within the fields of both history and political science.

Nation-building in Multi-Ethnic Societies

Most African countries, Malawi included, have struggled to draw on anti-colonial nationalism in order to build unified nation-states.[8] Nation-building ranked among the cardinal objectives of new African states after independence. The other aims included the quest to achieve development, regional integration, and create democratic, open, and inclusive societies. The nation-building agenda aimed at achieving a national identity among diverse societies, which were either physically isolated because of colonial borders, or culturally separated owing to constructed ethnic identities that pitted them against each other. Besides, uneven regional economic development in most countries added another layer of pressure on politicians, who viewed it as a threat to nation-building. In most cases, history shows that societies were and remain multi-ethnic, multi-cultural, multi-linguistic, and multi-religious.

---

8 Although the nationalist movement constituted diverse interest groups, they were relatively united in their quest for political sovereignty.

The task of nation-building was by no means impossible. As Will Kymlicka has argued, almost all the dominant Western societies that serve as models of national unity, such as the USA, Britain, Germany, and Italy, are multi-cultural and some inherited colonial borders.[9] For African leaders, the nation-building agenda, and the opportunities it presented, proved almost impossible to attain. Instead, civil wars, military coups, and various forms of perennial instability dominated the histories of countries like Somalia, Sierra Leone, Eritrea, Sudan, Mali, Rwanda, Burundi, Kenya, and Nigeria.[10]

A combination of several factors helped to weaken African societies towards the end of the 20th century. These included the end of the Cold War, and the associated withdrawal of donor funding. Since the late 1970s, there were also a series of economic crises, some of which were presumed to have solutions in the Structural Adjustment Programmes (SAPs). Furthermore, limited democratisation created exclusive societies of political elites within the context of accelerated globalisation. The latter coincided with the spread and deepening of market forces, and relations on a global scale never witnessed before. These changes have had direct implications on both state capacity and legitimacy. They have also affected how various groups and individuals have redefined and repositioned themselves to meet the challenges posed by changing domestic and international dynamics. Failure to resolve these local and transnational challenges has also been a big part of the problem underlying the unending conflicts in Africa.[11]

In analysing the struggle for nation-building in Malawi, scholars often blame Dr Banda's regime (1964-1994) for failing to build on anti-colonial nationalism.[12] It is accepted that whatever role the missionaries, missionary educated intellectuals, and colonial administrators played in promoting ethnicities in Malawi, the immediate post-colonial government had the

---

9 Will Kymlicka, "Nation-building and Minority Rights: Comparing Africa and the West", in Bruce Berman, Dickson Eyoh and Will Kymlicka (eds), *Ethnicity and Democracy in Africa*, Athens, Ohio: Ohio University Press, 2004, 55.

10 Paul Tiyambe Zeleza, *Africa's Resurgence: Domestic, Global, and Diaspora Transformations*, Los Angeles, CA: Tsehai Publishers, 2014, 3-5; Ehiedu E.G. Iweriebor, "State and Nation-building since Independence", in Toyin Falola (ed), *Africa: Vol. 5: Contemporary Africa*, Durham, NC: Carolina Academic Press, 2003, 188-190.

11 See Liisa Laakso and Adebayo O. Olukoshi, "The Crisis of the Post-colonial Nation-state Project in Africa", in Adebayo O. Olukoshi and Liisa Laakso (eds), *Challenges to the Nation-State in Africa*, Helsinki: Institute of Development Studies, University of Helsinki, 1996, 7-39.

12 Although the anti-colonial struggle included different interest groups, these were united in their quest for political sovereignty.

responsibility to convert the anti-colonial unity into a strong sense of Malawian nationhood, a job that was poorly executed. Kings Phiri, Kaspin, and Chirwa have followed Vail's example by criticising Banda for pursuing parochial cultural interests that favoured the Chewa people of central Malawi, while parading a political language of national unity at his rallies.[13] These works have very clearly exposed the contradictions in Banda's language policy, where Chichewa was elevated to the position of a "national language", while downgrading other local languages. At fault here is not the strategy of using language as an avenue of securing national unity. In fact, it was common in the early 1960s for leaders to rely on a common language to achieve a national identity.[14] Besides, a common language has served some societies well, a case in point being the Western countries highlighted earlier. It is the idea of superimposing the Chichewa language of one region across the whole country that many have faulted in Banda's language policy.[15]

For instance, Bonaventure Mkandawire describes the declaration of Chichewa as a national language as a form of "cultural violence".[16] For him, the language policy helped to marginalise other indigenous languages, including ChiTumbuka, the predominant language in the country's Northern Region. Other local languages had no space on national radio, in print, public meetings, and in school curricula, on the pretext of adopting Chichewa as a unifying national language. Although the introduction of a national language was not unique to Malawi, the policy led to the marginalisation of ChiTumbuka, Chinyanja, and other languages spoken across the country. The policy denied these other languages a "national" profile, which Chichewa enjoyed between 1968 and 1994. Chirwa describes the resultant effects of Banda's policies as representing the "Chewa-isation" of the nation, which accounts for much of the current

---

13 Kings M. Phiri, "Dr. Banda's Cultural Legacy and its Implications for Democratic Malawi", in Kings M. Phiri and Kenneth R. Ross (eds), *Democratization in Malawi*, 149-167; Kaspin, "The Politics of Ethnicity in Malawi's Democratic Transition", 595-620; Chirwa, "Democracy, Ethnicity, and Regionalism", 52-69.

14 In Tanzania, for instance, Julius Nyerere declared Swahili a national language in 1967; earlier in 1943, Haile Selassie declared Amharic as Ethiopia's national language. See Sanghamitra Bandyopadhyay and Elliot Green, "Nation-building and Conflict in Modern Africa", *World Development* 45 (2013), 110-111.

15 Others saw Chinyanja and Chitumbuka, the two languages spoken in some parts of the South and North, respectively, as equally deserving languages.

16 Bonaventure Mkandawire, "Ethnicity, Language, and Cultural Violence: Dr. Hastings Kamuzu Banda's Malawi, 1964-1994", *Society of Malawi Journal* 63/1 (2010), 27-43. See also Themba Moyo, "Language Politics and National Identity in Malawi", *South African Journal of African Languages* 22/4 (2002), 264-269.

national unity crisis. Chewa-isation polarised the country along ethnic and regional lines and empowered some individuals to manipulate these divisions in their competition for political power and national resources.[17] But as Peter Forster has argued, although Chichewa became the national language, including adopting Banda's preferred dialect, it did not necessarily mean that Chewa cultural practices were imposed on other ethnic groups in the country.[18] The decision to elevate Chichewa as a national language, however, was enough to win the scorn of other groups in the country.

Another of Banda's nation-building strategies that has received scholarly condemnation is the transfer of the national capital from Zomba to Lilongwe, and the disproportional allocation of rural development resources to the Central Region. For Banda, Lilongwe was centrally located and would help to easily spread "development" to other parts of the country far removed from the South. In fact, moving national capitals was also a common trend after independence among African countries.[19] These arguments notwithstanding, Deborah Potts has argued that Banda might have harboured some political motives in shifting the capital to Lilongwe. Lilongwe is near Kasungu district, Banda's birthplace. Besides, Lilongwe is the district where the Chewa, Banda's ethnic group, are most dominant. Potts does not rule out other personal interests, noting that transferring the capital was personally glorifying to Banda as it identified him as a state president who restructured Malawi's space economy more equitably with a centrally positioned capital city.[20]

Centralising the state in Lilongwe, argues Kaspin, also enabled Banda to devote more funds to the development of the country's Central Region, where most of the Chewa are settled. Within a few years of capital relocation, Lilongwe acquired new and improved infrastructure, including banks, government offices, a college of agriculture, a college of nursing, and an international airport. All these helped to make Lilongwe the political hub of the "modernizing nation". The state also created economic opportunities for the population

---

17 Chirwa, "Democracy, Ethnicity, and Regionalism", 63.

18 Peter G. Forster, "Culture, Nationalism, and the Invention of Tradition in Malawi", *Journal of Modern African Studies,* 32/3 (1994), 292-293.

19 Other African countries that had their national capitals moved were Tanzania, Nigeria, Mauritania, and Botswana.

20 Potts, "Capital Relocation in Africa: The Case of Lilongwe in Malawi", 188.

living in and out of the new capital, including access to funds for rural development projects.[21]

While Lilongwe registered progress, the Northern Region stagnated, a trend that dates from the colonial era, when the region not favoured for European settler agriculture, experienced limited commercial and social development, and suffered from inadequate transport and communication facilities and lack of social services.[22] It became known as the "Dead North", because of its lack of economic opportunities. As a result, its people continued to migrate in search of better opportunities in mines and other forms of employment in South Africa and the Rhodesias. Although not as "underdeveloped" as the Northern Region, some parts of the Southern Region suffered a similar fate under Banda's rule. Areas such as the Lower Shire and other parts of the Shire Highlands (except for the urban areas of Blantyre and Zomba), experienced limited educational opportunities, little support for peasant production, and the persecution of politicians and others perceived to be critical of the regime. These forces combined to breed discontent among the people of the Southern Region.[23]

The 1964 Cabinet Crisis appears to have set the tone for the way Banda would treat people from other regions of the country.[24] Many of those who disagreed with Banda came either from the Yao- or Tumbuka-speaking areas of the country. As John McCracken has indicated elsewhere, the leaders of that crisis drew their support from their home region or districts. This included Banda on one side and Chiume, the Chisiza brothers, and Chipembere, on the other side. For instance, of the 54 supporters of the exiled cabinet ministers who received military training in Tanzania in 1965, 46 were reported to be from the Northern Region, while the remaining 12 were from the Southern Region. Furthermore,

---

21 Kaspin, "The Politics of Ethnicity in Malawi's Democratic Transition", 604-608.

22 One advantage the North enjoyed over the rest of the regions was the early presence of missionary education in the region which gave many northerners an upper hand in civil service recruitment. For many people, the "quota system" highlighted earlier served to reverse this advantage.

23 Kaspin, "Tribes, Regions, and Nationalism in Democratic Malawi", 484-488.

24 The "Cabinet Crisis" emanated from disagreements between Dr Banda and his cabinet colleagues over domestic and foreign policy directions for the then newly independent country. See for instance, Henry M.B. Chipembere, "Malawi in Crisis", *Ufahamu: A Journal of African Studies* 11/1 (1981), 80-95.

all of the 12 MPs who were expelled from the MCP during the crisis were from either the north or the south.[25]

Whatever the motives, imbalanced provision of state resources showed that the nation-building agenda had failed even before it started. A spate of events occurring during the 1980s further reinforced the ill feelings of the Northern and Southern regions against Banda's regime. One of them was the introduction of a quota system for selection of students to the University of Malawi, which seemed to have undermined the educational opportunities of gifted students from the north. The other centred on education policy that restricted teachers to their districts of origins, thereby confining some segments of the society to less-developed regions. Unsurprisingly, many people from the south and north welcomed the dawn of liberal democracy from 1994 with great anticipation. As it turned out, this optimism soon turned out to be a mirage. The post-1994 governments seem not to have fared any better in the nation-building exercise, and, as we show subsequently, their actions provided a space for the growth of contemporary feelings against a unitary government system.[26]

Right from the 1994 General Election, it became clear that ethnicity and regionalism would remain the enemy of the goals of nation-building and inclusive development. The voting pattern for both the 1994 and 1999 General Elections showed that the leading presidential candidates and their political parties won most votes and parliamentary seats in the "home regions" from where the party presidential candidates originated.[27] Moreover, one decade into liberal democracy, Malawian society remained far less inclusive than expected. As Edge Kanyongolo argued, even the 1994 Malawi Constitution did little to address the deep-seated historical problems—including those of lack of national unity, and inequitable distribution of national resources—that bother most Malawians. Besides, the country's Constitution failed to address the regional economic imbalances and the concerns of those who suffered under

---

25 John McCracken, *A History of Malawi, 1859-1966*, Woodbridge: James Currey, 2012, 448-449.

26 As we discuss below, members of Parliament from both the Northern and Central regions have been in the forefront supporting federalism.

27 For a detailed discussion of the regional or ethnic voting trend see Kaspin, "The Politics of Ethnicity in Malawi's Democratic Transition", 611-615; Chirwa, "Democracy, Ethnicity, and Regionalism", 52-69; Jonathan Mayuyuka Kaunda, "The State and Society in Malawi", *Journal of Commonwealth and Comparative Politics* 36/1 (1998), 58-63; H. Meinhardt, *Free at last! Malawi's Democratic Transition*, Lilongwe: NICE, 2004, 414-418; Alan Thorold, "Regionalism, Tribalism, and Multiparty Democracy: The Case of Malawi", *South African Journal of International Affairs* 7/2 (2000), 138-139.

the discriminatory policies of the distant colonial past and the immediate post-colonial present. Discriminatory land policies and power imbalances among diverse groups in the country rank among the significant aspects the Constitution left unchecked. For Kanyongolo, the solution to these challenges rests in a complete deconstruction of the existing Constitution because mere amendments to it would not address the problems in question, nor promote inclusive development and politics.[28] To what extent the proposed federalised state system can address these concerns is the subject to which we now turn. Before that, however, it is necessary to provide a historical context for the debate on federalism.

The Call for Federalism

In 2006, a special Consultation Paper, which the Malawi Law Commission prepared to facilitate a constitutional review conference, noted disappointment among people from the Northern Region:

> In the meetings in the North, it was strongly suggested that a system of rotating the presidency through the three regions of the country should be introduced in the Constitution. It was argued that the North is sparsely populated and, with the present arrangements, can never produce a president. This was seen as a disadvantage and a major contribution to the unequal distribution of national resources which has seen the North lagging behind. Hence, rotating presidents along regional lines was seen as the best solution.[29]

These ideas found a place in a paper that Peter Mutharika, the former President of Malawi, who had earlier been a law professor at Washington University in the USA, presented at the 2006 constitutional review conference. Organised by the Malawi Law Commission, the conference took place in Lilongwe between 28 and 31 March that year. Mutharika suggested "federalism, proportional representation, and rotational presidency" to address the problem of national unity in the country.[30] The constitutional amendments that came after 2006

---

28 Fidelis Edge Kanyongolo, "The Limits of Liberal Democratic Constitutionalism in Malawi", in Kings M. Phiri and Kenneth R. Ross (eds), *Democratization in Malawi,* 369-372. For Kanyongolo, deconstructing the Constitution would mean setting the existing one aside in favour of a new one that addresses the historical challenges highlighted here.

29 Malawi Law Commission, Constitutional Review Consultation Paper, Lilongwe, 2006, 47.

30 Peter A. Mutharika, "Towards a More Manageable Constitution", paper presented at the Constitution Review Conference, Lilongwe, 28-31 March 2006. Earlier, Mutharika expressed similar ideas through a paper he published for a scholarly audience. See his "The 1995 Democratic Constitution of Malawi", *Journal of African Law* 40/2 (1996), 205-220. See particularly 220.

stopped short of providing for these proposals. However, a few years later, after Mutharika became president in 2014, his admirers singled out federalism as a possible solution to the unitary system of governance and projected it to the Malawi society for debate.

The issue came to prominence following the victory of the Democratic Progressive Party (DPP) in the 2014 General Election. Christopher Mzomera Ngwira of Mzimba District, the Regional Governor of the losing People's Party (PP) in the North, drummed up support for federalism. Frank Mwenifumbo and Kamlepo Kalua, both of whom were MPs from the North joined him. "There is too much sectionalism in this country", charged Kalua, such that "when people today are calling for a federal government, it's because of the treatment the people of the North have faced in the past, and they are still facing today".[31] In calling for a referendum to decide the future of the unitary system, Kalua and Mwenifumbo reminded their colleagues of the 2006 paper Mutharika presented at the Constitutional Conference, which was in favour of federalism. Dr Lazarus Chakwera, now President of Malawi but at that time the leader of the opposition MCP, which equally lost the presidential election, also supported the call for federalism. Joyce Banda, the Malawi president under the PP-led government (2012-2014) and another victim of the May 2014 presidential election, rendered similar support.[32] However, the country's president, Peter Mutharika, seemed not keen on initiating his previous proposal for a federal system of government. Perhaps he felt that it could have weakened his grip on political power.

It is possible to dismiss support for a federal government system as representing recuperation from an election loss or, as one social commentator argued, a ploy on the part of political leaders to assume leadership of federal governments having failed to secure a national presidency. Moreover, none of the political parties in the 2014 elections featured federalism in their campaign manifestos.[33] Because the DPP had been in power since 2005, with a two-year interruption when Joyce Banda assumed the presidency following the death of

---

31 See "Malawi needs federalism, power sharing: MPs Kamlepo, Mwenifumbo", *Nyasa Times*, 24 September 2014, www.nyasatimes.com/malawi-needs-federalism-power-sharing-mps-kamlepo-mwenefumbo/.

32 "Growing Calls for Federalism", *The Economist*, 14 October 2014, http://country.eiu.com/article.aspx?articleid=782381262&Country=Malawi&topic=Politics&subtopic=Fo_3.

33 Such were the views of James Mwangali, "Federalism Masquarades", *Afriem*, 3 October 2014, https://www.afriem.org/2014/10/federalism-masquerades/.

President Bingu wa Mutharika (April 2012-May 2014), federalism promised power distribution to the losing leaders.[34] However, the arguments Ngwira and his Northern Region colleagues raised were not new. These date back to 2006 when the "quota system" ranked among the major sources of discontent in the North. Other arguments focused on the region's failure to produce a president since 1964. Without one, the economic development of the region seemed impossible to achieve. "There is a perception that other regions are favoured in terms of larger development projects", noted a commentary in *The Economist*, further adding that "government appointments [Mutharika made in June that year] are dominated by politicians from the Southern Region, the home region of the president".[35]

The debate on federalism soon became popular in some quarters in the North and gave birth to a Northern Region-based organisation, the Forum for the Advancement of Federal System of Government and Rural Development in Malawi (FAFESRUDEM), which agitated for a federated state. Led by Bina Shaba as its chairperson, the FAFESRUDEM won the support of such renowned individuals as Reverend Levi Nyondo, a notorious critic of the government. Nyondo was General Secretary of the Northern Region headquartered Livingstonia Synod of the Church of Central Africa Presbyterian (CCAP). FAFESRUDEM organised pro-federalism demonstrations in the North, one of which the government blocked in September 2014.[36] In rejecting the application to hold a demonstration, Mzuzu City Council Chief Executive Officer, Victor Chirwa, argued that the prospective demonstrators lacked legitimate intentions. Nevertheless, the decision did not prevent FAFESRUDEM from organising similar demonstrations, most of which featured placards displaying the socio-economic ills the Northern Region had suffered over time.

Worried about the direction the debate took, the Public Affairs Committee (PAC) stepped in and held a national stakeholders forum on inclusivity and federalism between 24 and 25 November 2014. PAC, established in 1992, is an organisation that comprises religious bodies and other civil society groups. It

---

34 Soon after assuming power, Joyce Banda ditched the DPP and formed her own political party, the People's Party (PP).

35 "Growing Calls for Federalism", *The Economist*, 14 October 2014, http://country.eiu.com/article.aspx?articleid=782381262&Country=Malawi&topic=Politics&subtopic=Fo_3.

36 Ibid.

promotes the socio-political and economic interests of Malawians through dialogue and civic education. The PAC led debates on the subject across the three regions of the country.[37] FAFESRUDEM, however, did not have confidence in the PAC's involvement in the debate. Its leadership accused the PAC of organising smokescreen debates whose intention was to frustrate the call to a federated state system. "We are completely of the view that such meetings [which are no more than education tours] are totally useless for the local people who are crying for change of the current unitary system of government to a federal system", protested Shaba, further adding that "we cannot be staying in this air-conditioned room debating issues that are obvious. These meetings [should] not have been done [because they will derail change]."[38]

Following the consultative meetings, the PAC dismissed calls for federalism, arguing that a proposal to adopt a federated state system was less popular among 64% of Malawians. In its recommendations, the PAC report advised the government to use the existing structures and address the concerns that proponents of federalism raised because they were legitimate.[39] FAFESRUDEM did not change its position, however. The organisation continued to criticise the PAC, further arguing that it did not have a legal mandate to preside over such an important national debate. In rejecting the PAC's findings, FAFESRUDEM argued that the PAC was a "mere interest group without [a] constitutional mandate, let alone legal powers to umpire, direct, regulate, and determine the debate on the need to introduce federal system of government in Malawi".[40] For some people in the North, the debate remained inconclusive, such that they looked to the future for an opportunity to reignite it.

One came on 14 June 2018 when Kamlepo Kalua, a People's Party MP for Rumphi East, raised the motion on federalism in Parliament. While Kalua's motion had the support of MPs from the opposition side, it did not win the

---

37 See "Federalism system advocates attend PAC debate", *The Times*, 24 June 2015, https://times.mw/federalism-system-advocates-attend-pac-debate/.

38 Ibid.

39 We have been unable to locate the PAC report and have had to rely on some media citations from it. See also "PAC says no to federalism in Malawi", *Malawi 24*, 10 December 2015, https://malawi24.com/2015/12/10/pac-says-no-to-federalism-in-malawi/.

40 FAFESRUDEM statement, cited in "Malawi federalism sea lots vow to fight on: PAC 'survey' trashed", *Nyasatimes*, 19 December 2015, www.nyasatimes.com/malawi-federalism-zealots-vow-to-fight-on-pac-survey-trashed/.

confidence of the government side such that it failed to pass.[41] It is against this background that one should understand Chihana's 2019 parliamentary motion on the subject, which was referred to the Legal Affairs Committee for its opinion.[42] This Committee is yet to release its report as Chihana awaits its findings with great anticipation.

Suffice to say, Chihana's 2019 motion on the subject was precise. He regarded a federal system of government as best suited "to resolve the tribal, nepotistic, and regional differences that tend to hinder progress as a nation".[43] For Chihana, a unitary government system was a weak framework because, in promoting the centralisation of power, it gives leeway to leaders bent on promoting regionalism and a skewed development agenda that favours some districts while leaving others in abject poverty. More significant was Chihana's conclusion. Federalism would encourage each region to raise policies for development based on their unique "economic and social fabric".[44] The "social fabric" in question, however, remained vague.

In his support of Chihana's motion, George Zulu, MCP MP for Lilongwe West Constituency, articulated what he perceived to be the benefits of a federal government system. First, such a system could promote inclusive development, as a regional state would direct allocated resources towards areas of its choice rather than waiting on the central government. Second, federated states could provide checks and balances to the central authority in ways not possible under the existing arrangements in which the executive branch of government controls the consolidated economic purse. Third, federalism could bring government closer to people, and finally, the reduced chain of command between the central government and district councils could help to arrest corruption.[45]

Whether Zulu's arguments have merit or not, the adoption of federalism in Malawi, we argue, should not be based on generic advantages associated with

---

41 From the opposition side, the following MPs supported the motion: Richard Chimwendo, Dowa East; Agness Longe, Mzimba North; Juliana Lunguzu, Dedza East, and Frank Mwenefumbo, Karonga Central. See *Malawi News Agency*, 15 June 2018, www.manaon line.gov.mw/index.php/national/politics/item/9402-mps-differ-on-federal-government.

42 Malawi Government, Proceedings of the National Assembly, 48th Session, Thursday, 26 September 2019, 142.

43 Ibid, 120.

44 Ibid, 121.

45 Ibid, 125-126.

the system elsewhere. The debate on federalism emerged as a solution to the unique challenges of ethnicity, regionalism, and unequal distribution of resources. An assessment of what such a governance system can achieve will depend on its potential to address these challenges before considering it for its generic utility. We argue that the projection of federalism as a solution to Malawi's unique nation-building and exclusive development challenges is a misplaced solution because it ignores the complexities of Malawian ethnicities and the fluidity of the regional identities. Moreover, experience elsewhere in Africa where federalism has been adopted does not commend confidence regarding its capacity to address the challenges of inequitable distribution of state resources.

Nigeria is a case in point. The country adopted a federal system of government following independence in 1960. The British-ruled colonial government put in place that system in 1954, to hold together that country's divided ethnic societies. In its ideal form, the federal system of government, as the one in Nigeria, which has 36 states, represents a reasonably viable and successful mechanism for managing inter-group conflict and preventing ethno-political disintegration. However, over the years, Nigerian politics have largely neglected or not prioritised the system's other roles of promoting democratic and economic development. Since independence, the country has experienced civil wars, military coups, and associated forms of authoritarian rule. Even civilian governments have often been dogged by political instability, misuse and lack of equitable distribution of government resources, massive electoral and monetary corruption, and limited socio-economic reforms at both state and federal levels.[46] In other words, there are still lingering cries of poor governance, ethno-political conflicts, and socio-economic underdevelopment. Among its only advantages, out of all the chaos associated with the federal system, have been enabling operations of ethnic minority states (other than the populous Yoruba, Hausa-Fulani, and Ibo-ruled states) to play an active role in the political system. Furthermore, it also serves as an instrument for equitable representation of groups and units in central government institutions. For instance, at Senate level, where each state sends three elected representatives.[47]

---

[46] Rotimi Suberu, "The Nigerian Federal System: Performance, Problems, and Prospects", *Journal of Contemporary African Studies*, 28/4 (2010), 459-462.

[47] Ibid, 463-466.

Writing on the ethnic-based federal system in Ethiopia, Siraw Megibaru Temesgen has argued that though established with good intentions, the system has had its attendant challenges or weaknesses. Established in 1994 to help end ethno-political conflicts and the domination of the majority ethnic groups (including the Oromo, Amhara, Somali, and Tigre), the system has planted divisions among that country's more than 80 ethnic groups. Ethiopia's Constitution recognises nine regional states and two city administrations. There have been several weaknesses associated with that model. For instance, the country is still ravaged by ethnic competition and conflicts. In 2013, Ethiopia ranked number 38 on the peace index out of the 46 sub-Saharan African countries. The conflicts in that country revolve around issues of claims to secede, the politics of resource-sharing, ascendancy to political power, political representation, citizenship, and ethnic and regional boundaries, among others. Over the years, the central government has also continued to monopolise policies and implementation strategies, thereby leaving state and regional governments aside.[48]

To illustrate this point, as of October and November 2020, the Ethiopian northern semi-autonomous federal state of Tigray has been involved in a war against troops from the central government. Tigray's government, led by the Tigray People's Liberation Front (TPLF), has long complained of being unfairly targeted in corruption prosecutions, of being removed from top government positions, of limited government funding, and of being scapegoated for some of that country's woes. When TPLF troops allegedly attacked army bases and government offices in the region, Prime Minister Abiy Ahmed responded by ordering the army to intervene, hence the ensuing civil war. Hundreds of people are reported to have been killed in this conflict, while many Ethiopians are trekking to neighbouring Sudan and Eritrea as refugees.[49] Although Malawi has had no history of such open violence, its cultural make-up is not very different from countries described here.

According to the most recent population census in Malawi, the country has 12 main ethnic groups and others that are not listed. The listed ethnic groups

---

[48] Siraw Megibaru Temesgen, "Weaknesses of Ethnic Federalism in Ethiopia", *International Journal of Humanities and Social Science Intervention*, 4/11 (Nov. 2015), 49-54.

[49] "Hundreds Dead as Conflict in Ethiopia's Tigray Worsens", www.aljazeera.com/news/2020/11/9/ethiopia-downplays-war-fears-while-attacking-tigray-region, [9.11.2020]. See also Cara Anna, "Ethiopia Reshuffles Top Officials as Tigray Conflict Grows", *Associated Press,* 8 November 2020. https://apnews.com/article/abiy-ahmed-africa-ethiopia-kenya-civil-wars-d8d6d6d2fdc993f5452b705ace378ff4.

include the Chewa, Ngoni, Tumbuka, Lomwe, Tonga, Yao and Ngonde. The Sena, Lambya, Sukwa, Mang'anja, and Nyanja also belong to this list. Of these main ethnic groups, the Chewa, making up 34.4% of the national population, is the largest, while that of the Nyanja is the smallest, contributing 1.9% to the national population. Malawians from these ethnic groups are spread across the country's three administrative regions, namely Northern, Central and Southern regions. It is worth highlighting that there are considerable cultural similarities linking clusters of these groups. For example, selected groups in the North (the Tumbuka, Ngoni, Ngonde and several others in Chitipa District) and some parts of the Southern Region's Lower Shire Valley are predominantly patrilineal societies. Those in the Central and Southern regions of the country, notably the Chewa, Yao, and Lhomwe, are predominantly matrilineal societies. These commonalities, however, should not conceal differences that often pull these groups apart. Based on a review of some selected secondary and primary sources, the subsequent section unmasks Malawi's ethnic and regional identities in ways that reveal the limits of current notions of federalism.

The False Prospects of Federalism

One consistent aspect of Chihana's 2019 parliamentary motion is the way in which he invoked the notion of regional identity to strengthen his proposal to promote regionally based federal states. As noted earlier, Kaspin and, to a limited extent, Chirwa's works have supported this thesis. They have shown the salience of a region as a significant determinant of electorates' voting behaviour in the post-1994 democratic elections. The 2020 presidential vote strengthens this position. The two major contenders, Lazarus Chakwera (from the Centre) and Peter Mutharika (from the South) got the most votes in the Central and Southern regions, respectively. Over 80% of the Northern Region vote went to Chakwera, probably because the North, like the Centre, was disillusioned with the DPP government. Chakwera's Northern Region vote could also reflect the previous voting trend in which one's region or ethnic label were important determinants. This is so because some leaders of the Tonse Alliance, which he represented, came from the North. This trend notwithstanding, we should not construe the regional identity as representing an ethno-regional identity.

John McCracken warns us not to treat these regional identities as fixed constructs but rather as fluid, tentative, and at best provisional forces that tend to mask rather than reveal internal divisions.[50] He does so by using the example of how the country adopted Chichewa as a national language in the late 1960s and how the debate leading to its adoption reveals cracks in the Northern Region identity. A crucial contributor to the language debate was Flax Musopole, a nationalist activist who organised the masses to resist colonial rule in the northern districts of Karonga in the late 1950s. Of Ndali/Sukwa ethnicity and with a political consciousness first shaped while working in South Africa, Musopole had misgivings about the dominance of ChiTumbuka language as a Northern Region lingua franca. For Musopole, ChiTumbuka rendered other groups in the region invisible. After independence, Musopole became an MP and moved with speed to agitate for a national and unifying language. Mckinley Qabaniso Chibambo of Ngoni ethnicity joined him with the intention to displace English from its status as a first language, all the while calling for "one flag, one nation, one language, one Party".[51] While contributing to the 1966 Malawi Broadcasting Corporation (Amendment) Bill, whose aim was to consolidate the power of the Minister of Development and Planning over the state broadcaster, Musopole proposed replacing ChiTumbuka language with Chinyanja. The latter was unfamiliar to the people of the Northern Region.[52] The suggestion won the attention of Dr Banda, who later replaced Chinyanja with Chichewa.

Vail and White have demonstrated how the Ngonde of Karonga district constantly challenged the Scottish missionaries for imposing ChiTumbuka language on the people of the north. The Ngonde despised the Tumbuka-speaking peoples who settled amongst them as refugees "and former allies of Swahili slavers".[53] Having their language imposed on them was the last thing they expected. There is little evidence to suggest that these cleavages remain a relic of the past with little influence on the present debate on federalism. More recently, when Chihana raised the motion on federalism in Parliament, Simon Vuwa Kaunda, of Tonga ethnicity and at the time serving as the Minister of Lands, Housing and Urban Development, challenged his colleagues from the North to avoid perceiving themselves as more northern than others.[54] The Northern Region identity brings together several ethnicities whose internal

---

50 John McCracken, "The Ambiguities of Nationalism", 68.

51 Ibid, 86.

52 Ibid.

53 Vail and White, "Tribalism in the Political History of Malawi", 154.

54 Proceedings of the National Assembly, 48th Session, Thursday, 26 September 2019, 130.

conflicts we cannot afford to overlook in contemporary debates on federalism. These complexities are not unique to the North and, in fact, play out at national level.

The post-2000 era presents another good illustration. When Chirwa and Kaspin undertook their studies in the 1990s, the voting trend in democratic elections was a significant marker of the country's ethnic and regional polarisation. The post-2000 proliferation of ethnic-based associations is another important indicator. The first to emerge was the Mzimba Heritage Association (MZIHA) in 2002. The group brings together the M'Mbelwa Ngoni in the country. MZIHA was joined later in 2008 by the Mulhako wa Alhomwe (MwA), another ethnic-based association that unites the Lhomwe in the country. The Chewa registered a similar association in 2009, the Chewa Heritage Foundation (CHEFO).[55]

More recently, several other associations have emerged in the ranks of Chiwanja Cha a Yao (formed 2019), Mdawuku wa aTonga (formed in 2017 as Nkhata Bay Tonga Heritage Association), and Karonga-Chitipa Heritage Group which was established in 2016. Among other aims, all these associations seek to promote cultural revival of their respective groups. They also aim at economically empowering their members by engaging in specific "development projects".[56] At present, there is no evidence of lack of co-existence between these associations. However, the geographical spread of these organisations challenges the idea of premising federalism on unified regional identities. Some associations have their branches or zones spread across the country. For example, although headquartered in Lilongwe, CHEFO has branches in the Southern and Northern regions of the country. The same applies to the Mulanje-based Mulhako wa Alhomwe and Mzimba-headquartered MZIHA, which have branches in other parts of the country.[57] This spatial distribution of these associations follows the uneven spread of members across the country and points to the limits of setting the debate on a federal state system on the

---

55 The years reflect registration dates. Plans to establish the associations were hatched between 2005 and 2008 for the Lhomwe and the Chewa and as early as 2000 for the Ngoni of Mzimba. For a detailed discussion see Gift Wasambo Kayira, Paul Chiudza Banda, and Amanda Lea Robinson, "Ethnic Associations and Politics in Contemporary Malawi", *Journal of Eastern African Studies* 14/4 (2019), 718-738.

56 Ibid.

57 Ibid.

premises of rather non-existent ethno-regional identities that problematically coincide with what Berman and colleagues describe as "moral ethnicity".[58]

Moral ethnicity is an ethnic identity that brings together people who are supposedly bound by "primordialist" ties. It is usually contrasted with amoral ethnicity, in which the distinctiveness of an ethnic group is built through what Wiseman Chirwa describes as politics of "putative we" versus "putative they".[59] The latter, which is a distinctive feature of the three regions of the country, is solidified externally in opposition to the state or other ethnic groups. As conceptualised, the proposal on the federal state system seeks to resolve the problem of amoral ethnicity for creating "political tribalism"—which describes the competition that emerges as diverse ethnic groups compete for control over state resources at the expense of others.[60] It is unclear whether these dynamics might not manifest under federalism. However, even if the three regions of the country displayed unified ethno-regional identities, and ones fitting the description of moral ethnicity, that is not a guarantee that federalism would work to the good of the country nor resolve its unique historical problems. This is so because moral ethnicity does not always give rise to ethnic homogenisation. There are divisions even among groups held together through moral ties.

Consider the recent divisions among the Chewa exemplified through the formation of a splinter group to CHEFO, the Bwalo la Achewa Foundation (BLAFO). CHEFO draws together the Chewa of Malawi, uniting them with those of Zambia and Mozambique under the leadership of Gawa Undi whose base is in Zambia. To ascertain their independence from Undi, some Chewa formed the BLAFO in 2019. Paramount Chief Lundu based in Malawi's Lower Shire Valley was named the patron of this splinter group. CHEFO leadership rejected this group and called upon the Chewa to preserve their unity.[61] During one of its press conferences, CHEFO Publicity Secretary, Henrix Chikuni, condemned the group as having a sinister agenda and that the group was

---

58 Bruce Berman et al., "Introduction and the Politics of Democratic Nation-building in Africa", in Bruce Berman, Dickson Eyoh, and Will Kymlicka (eds), *Ethnicity and Democracy in Africa,* 4.

59 Chirwa, "Democracy, Ethnicity, and Regionalism", 55.

60 Berman et al, "Introduction and the Politics of Democratic Nation-building in Africa", 5.

61 See "We are looking for our lost sheep", *The Nation Online,* 15 March 2019, www.mwnation.com/we-are-looking-for-our-lost-sheep/.

creating confusion and rebellion.[62] These divisions are not surprising. Some observers perceived Lundu as a DPP sympathiser who probably wanted to use the new group to garner support for the party. Others consider the Lilongwe headquartered CHEFO as a pro-MCP group.[63] Although such sentiments remain unsubstantiated, the divisions in CHEFO challenge the idea of premising the federalism debate on undifferentiated ethnicities. In this debate, we should not overlook that there are both inter- and intra-ethnic differences.

In any case, it is unrealistic to assume that federalism would iron out the ethnic differences highlighted here, nor should such be the goal of a nation-building agenda. However, a workable governance approach should consider the diversity and dynamism of the ethnic societies in the three regions and the potential threat they pose to building inclusive societies. At present, the debate on federalism ignores the ethnic polarisation we have highlighted here. In glossing over these ethnic differences, proponents of federalism ignore how individuals deploy ethnicity as a means with which to access state resources and the ways politicians mobilise it to access electoral votes. This is the problem to consider, and one we cannot easily resolve through a federal state system imposed on multicultural societies. The problem of Malawi is less the existence of the diverse ethnic groups than that of unequal development and social injustice, which, ironically, politicised ethnicities do nothing to change.

The call to federalism should not be dismissed, however. As noted, it speaks to the long-standing historical problems that the Malawian state has failed to address. The call also reflects the failure of liberal democracy to deliver and satisfy the expectations of some segments of Malawian society. Besides, the debate on federalism points to the need for radical constitutional reforms, taking into consideration, as Kanyongolo has argued, the social and historical pasts that continue to challenge the existence of a unified nation-state.[64]

More specifically, the debate represents the quest of the people from the North to develop a pan-ethnic base—albeit a problematic one—that is strong enough to demand services and inclusion in the state in ways that would reverse the

---

62 Cited in *Kulinji*, "Chewas Shun Splinter Grouping Bwalo la aChewa", 9 September 2019, www.kulinji.com/article/news/2019/chewas-shun-splinter-grouping-bwalo-la-achewa. [10.8.2020].

63 "The Uncustomary Paramount Chief Lundu", *Nyasatimes*, 4 March 2017, https://times.mw/the-uncustomary-paramount-chief-lundu/.

64 Fidelis Edge Kanyongolo, "The Limits of Liberal Democratic Constitutionalism in Malawi", 372.

historical problems of economic disparities and social injustice. The decentralisation of state power in ways that fully empower local and district assemblies can be a better solution. At present, the executive branch of the government appoints District Commissioners, making them function at the mercy of the appointing authority. Could a system that subjects qualified prospective District Commissioners to a popular local vote be empowering to the citizenry at the local level?

For instance, the 2010 amended Republican Constitution of Kenya provides for a fully "devolved" or "decentralised" system of government. This arrangement has led to the "devolution of two of the three government arms, namely, the Legislature and the Executive", in the 47 political and administrative counties. The leaders of these counties, titled "governors" since the 2013 General Elections, are elected alongside all other politicians, such as parliamentarians, senators, and state presidents. Devolution aimed at unlocking Kenya's economic potential by distributing responsibilities. The idea was to replace the monopolistic control of the national government over the country's purse and the development agenda. The change addresses previous concerns in which the citizenry accused governments of mismanaging state resources and promoting inequalities and marginalising others.[65]

The Kenyan model has not operated flawlessly. Firstly, the system has proven to be expensive. It is now costly to organise elections and pay, with all the associated benefits, the 47 county governors and members of the assemblies. Lack of proper accountability regarding management of resources, duplication of roles leading to both the national and county governments handling relatively similar responsibilities, rank among other problems.[66] These challenges notwithstanding, the changes have had some successes. First, there is an equitable distribution of national resources to the country's 47 counties.[67] Secondly, the creation of county governments, headed by a governor, has also helped to achieve growth both at national and county levels. County

---

65 Samuel Ngigi and Doreen Busolo, "Devolution in Kenya: The Good, The Bad, The Ugly", *Journal of Public Policy and Administration Research* 9/6 (2019), 9. See also The Constitution of Kenya, 2010: Chapter 2, Section 6: Devolution and access to services.

66 Ngigi and Busolo, "Devolution in Kenya", 14-15. See also Leah Kimathi, "Challenges of the Devolved Health Sector in Kenya: Teething Problems or Systemic Contradictions?" *African Development* XLII/1 (2017), 55-77.

67 This is based on a weighted formula calculated as follows: population, 45%; poverty rate, 20%; land area, 8%; fiscal responsibility, 2%; and a basic equal share of 25%. All the counties equally share 25% of the national revenue.

governments have helped to create new jobs and have overseen developments and investments at their level, the same way the central government has overseen developments under its jurisdiction. The county governments now oversee growth strategies in education, health, agriculture, mining, and other important sectors. They have also helped to improve people's participation in the affairs that directly affect them.

In the third place, the new governance system has allowed for the inclusion of previously marginalised communities. Since they now have local leadership, there is room for them to elect their own leaders and manage their developmental affairs and needs. Such communities can now determine which development programmes to pursue considering their immediate priorities. The devolved system has also helped to promote transparency, accountability, and democracy in Kenya. Since grassroots or local people now vote for their immediate leaders, it allows them to participate directly in decision-making processes that are central to modern democratic systems of governance.[68]

The Kenyan model, therefore, could address the problem of exclusive development and inequitable distribution of resources, which advocates of federalism highlight in Malawi. Adapting it to Malawi would help to weaken the advantage the central government has over the apportioning of development funding. It can also free the local and district assemblies, recognising them as fully fledged and fully funded centres with real oversight powers. In sum, the Kenyan model promises a better alternative in improving the existing governance system rather than replacing it with one that is already sowing seeds of division. Since the district commissioners or governors will be directly elected at local level, we argue, it will increase cases of accountability and equitable resource distribution. Instead of always being answerable to the central government, the immediate electorate will have a significant say over matters of governance. In that case, irrespective of the ethnic or religious makeup of a district, the person in charge will be compelled to deliver, including equitably sharing resources.

Conclusion

This chapter makes key contributions to modern Malawi's historiography, and socio-economic and political discourses. These pertain to notions of

---

[68] Ngigi and Busolo, "Devolution in Kenya", 10-13. See also Karuti Kanyinga, "Devolution and the New Politics of Development in Kenya", *African Studies Review* 59/3 (2016), 155-167.

regionalism, ethnicity, nation-building, and local and national development. In this case, the chapter has firstly assessed the extent to which the post-1994 Malawian state has responded to the problems of ethnicity, regionalism, and regional economic imbalances. Secondly, it has assessed how far a proposed federal state system can resolve the problems in question. We have also raised several other questions on the state of governance in Malawi. In general, we argue that the post-1994 Malawian state has lacked the level of dynamism capable of resolving these problems. The economic optimism that liberal democracy promised has not been sustained, a limitation that has forced some quarters of the society to turn to federalism as an answer. In doing so, they question the unitary state system, considering it a big part of the problem. However, the solution they present—federalism—has its own problems, not least of which is the idea of premising it on ethno-regional identities that, on examination, prove to be fraught with complexities.

Northern Region advocates of federalism assume that breaking the country into three federal states, one centered in the North, the other two in the South and Centre, would work for the good of society. While such a system could bring some economic results, it might not arrest the existing problem of politicised ethnicities, especially how politicians exploit them for personal interests. As noted, existing literature on the Northern Region identity shows cracks within it, and there is little evidence to suggest that ethnicity could cease to be a political problem under the new governance system. Rather than replacing the unitary state with federalism, we suggest decentralising state power in ways that would divorce district and local assemblies from the central government's control. Although still in its infancy, the Kenyan model seems more plausible than a fully fledged federal system.

Chapter 13

Rights Without Responsibility: Governance Crisis in the Management of Natural Resources in Malawi

Wapulumuka O. Mulwafu

Introduction

In November 2017, the Malawi government hired three heavy-duty, diesel-powered generators from Aggreko Power Solutions of India at a cost of MWK 57 billion (USD 80 million) to address the power supply crisis in the country. The official narrative attributed the problem of power shortage, which was not necessarily new at this time, to declining levels of water in Lake Malawi which empties into the Shire River where nearly 90% of the country's electricity is produced. At that time the procurement was viewed as an interim measure designed to improve power supply before a lasting solution could be found.[1] This decision came against the background of growing concerns by government that it was already losing a stunning MWK 26 billion (USD 58 million) annually due to environmental degradation.[2] From a broader perspective, this figure reflected quintessentially a deepening crisis that the country faced in its efforts to conserve the environment. At another level, it was symptomatic of the governance crisis which had paralysed the country's institutions and systems. In point of fact, both media and scholarly works have been replete with evidence of the dwindling trend of natural resources and the effects of which can be seen in the frequent occurrence of extreme events such as floods and droughts.[3] In October 2020, the UNDP reported that Malawi had lost an estimated MK707 billion (US $929) in five years due to natural disasters.

---

1 By August 2020, the generators were still being used although the circumstances surrounding their procurement and usage had become a highly charged political issue in the country. It was reported that the deal was mis-procured and the Anti-Corruption Bureau was investigating the matter.

2 Reported by Boniface Phiri, "Government Loses K26 billion in Nature Preservation", *Malawi Nation*, 10 June 2015.

3 A. Kerr, "Disappearing Forests in Malawi: Causes and Solutions", EEP; Ezekiel Kalipeni and Leo Zulu, "From Top-down to Bottom-up: The Difficult Case of the Blantyre City Fuelwood Project", *Journal of Southern African Studies* 28/1 (2002), 117-136.

During this period, three states of disaster had been declared with reconstruction works costing nearly USD 1.4 billion.[4] What do these costly interventions mean for the overall governance system of the country's natural resources? We demonstrate in this chapter that as citizens have assumed more rights and freedoms to access and use natural resources, there has been a corresponding lack of responsibility for the management of the same resources.[5]

The Environmental Crisis as a Governance Issue

During the administration of Peter Mutharika (May 2014 – June 2020), Malawi experienced one of the worst environmental crises in its recent post-colonial history. Between 2017 and 2019 more specifically, the country literally went dark as the main source of hydroelectric power could hardly generate enough power to meet demand. Electricity generation levels hovered around 250 megawatts, which represented about 60% of the national production capacity at the time. For nearly two years, households could access electricity for an average of eight hours a day under a centralised load shedding system. While the cause of the energy crisis was in itself contested, the strategy for dealing with it became even more politicised. Some critics and especially those in the opposition viewed government's response as far too weak to mitigate the magnitude of the crisis the country was experiencing.[6] The chapter argues that although shortages of energy, land and water supply became pronounced in the second half of the 2010s, the problem had been developing for many years. But faced with an inept political leadership, the situation worsened to the extent of further engendering a situation of crisis.

Malawi's environmental crisis manifests itself through the occurrence of prolonged shortages of energy, water and other ecosystem services. The contemporary crisis became a governance issue in two ways. First, when power and water shortages began to affect all sectors of the economy, government

---

4 Taonga Sabola, "Malawi Loses K707 billion to Natural Disasters", *The Daily Times*, 28 October 2020.

5 This chapter comes out of my long-term research on the history of natural resources in Malawi. See, for example, W.O. Mulwafu, "Is the Battle on Conservation of Natural Resources in Malawi Winnable? Perspectives from Historical Knowledge", *21st UNIMA Professorial Inaugural Lecture*, University of Malawi, Chancellor College, Zomba, 28 August 2015.

6 In the run up to the 2019 elections, the opposition revealed massive plunder of resources at ESCOM including fuel meant for emergency generators.

seemed unable to address the problem quickly. Hence, the shortages persisted for a long time while draining government resources. Second, citizens' values towards environmental conservation seem to have relaxed so much that they became agents of further degradation. As a result, environmental degradation has become a major public issue affecting many sections of society.

Explaining the Causes of Environmental Crisis

In order to understand the causes of the environmental crisis in Malawi, we should first take into account the role and influence of environmental narratives. As in other parts of the world, governance of environmental resources is driven by narratives which change over time. Narratives are a major driving force in decision-making as they can eventually feed into policies and practices. In fact, narratives exist for almost all of the country's environmental resources and they attempt to explain how resources are used or managed. For instance, there is a narrative about Malawi being a poor country that can hardly feed itself, or the narrative about the wood energy crisis, or indeed the narrative about Malawi having abundant water resources. There are also narratives about desertification, deforestation, disease, and about development and under-development. The purpose of narratives is as much about entrenching received wisdom as they are about struggles for power and social control.[7] They have the potential of placing our minds in comfort zones so that we believe orthodoxies and conventional wisdom unproblematically. But, if not carefully understood, they can blind one's thinking beyond existing narrative frameworks.

In the context of Malawi, we can identify at least three shifts in the narratives regarding environmental management. These will be discussed briefly and chronologically. First, there is a colonial narrative which blamed human beings as the main agents of environmental degradation. Through land use practices, this perspective justified strong state intervention through enforcement of laws and policies on exclusion, enclosures and dispossession of public goods and open access resources from Africans. For example, many of the protected game

---

7 Melissa Leach and Robin Mearns (eds), *The Lie of the Land: Challenging Received Wisdom on the African Environment*, Portsmouth, NH: Heinemann, 1996; D. Potts, "Environmental Myths and Narratives: Case Studies from Zimbabwe", in P. Stott and S. Sullivan (eds), *Political Ecology: Science, Myth and Power*, London: Edward Arnold, 2000, 45-65; William G. Mosely and P. Laris, "West African Environmental Narratives and Development-Volunteer Praxis", *Geographical Review* 98/1 (2008), 59-81; J. Pollini, "Environmental Degradation Narratives in Madagascar: From Colonial Hegemonies to Humanist Revisionism", *Geoforum* 41/5 (2010), 711-722; B.A. Beymer-Farris and Thomas J. Bassett, "Environmental Narratives and Politics in Tanzania's Rufiji Delta: A Reply to Burgess et al.", *Global Environmental Change* 23/5 (2013), 1355-1358.

and forest reserves created in colonial times subscribed to this narrative. Second, in the immediate post-independence period, the same narrative of degradation continued and, while anthropogenic factors were highlighted, the state minimised the use of draconian measures that had been applied in the colonial times. Environmental degradation was partly blamed on colonialism itself whose policies had created inequalities in access to natural resources such as land and forest products. A third narrative emerged in the post-liberalisation period where significant changes had taken place in the management of natural resources. Driven by the neoliberal economic theory, the narrative blamed resource degradation partly on weak and inefficient state policies. In particular, it looked at the state as being overbearing and yet not capable of addressing the enduring problems of poverty and population growth which have had adverse effects on the environment.[8] Hence, the state had to withdraw from management of public goods in order to create an opportunity for the entry of private capital and non-state actors. However, one of the perceived problems with this narrative is that state withdrawal can result in the potential loss of sovereignty and citizen control over natural resources such as land, water, minerals, and even oil.

Beyond the dominant narratives, other factors can be advanced to explain the causes of the environmental crisis. First, Malawi is part of the Rift Valley System and this physical position makes it vulnerable to natural disasters such that it requires a management regime that can prudently protect the resources. The country is perched on a catchment area connected by a network of rivers draining into Lake Malawi before emptying into the Shire and Zambezi rivers. This means that any activities done in the upland areas must be carefully monitored as they inevitably affect the water bodies. It is the same water bodies that are used by downstream population for their livelihoods as well as for other productive activities such as generation of electricity. For instance, there have been reports about the mining of uranium at Kayerekera in Karonga which could potentially affect water that ends up in Lake Malawi. Similarly, the deforestation of mountainous areas like Viphya, Dzalanyama and Zomba Plateau ultimately affects the livelihoods of downstream users.[9] In this context,

---

[8] See Adeniyi S. Basiru, "Neo-Liberal Globalization, The State and Conflicts: Some Remarks on Sub-Saharan Africa", *Global Journal of Human Social Science* 14/6 (2014), 37-42.

[9] S. Ngwira and T. Watanabe, "An Analysis of the Causes of Deforestation in Malawi: A Case of Mwazisi", *Land* 8 (2019), 48; https://doi.org/10.3390/land8030048.

human activities in the Shire River catchment have over time affected both the quality and quantity of its water resources.

Second, many people depend on the environment for their daily livelihoods. In fact, this dependence is so intricate that any disturbance to the ecosystem can negatively affect them. Both scholarly works and media reports are replete with stories of households that have suffered as a result of declining natural resource base.[10] It is also common knowledge that many of the natural resources which had earned Malawi a place in history as the one of the most beautiful places in Africa are rapidly disappearing. Many analysts have shown that the greatest decline has occurred since the dawn of multiparty democracy in 1994 for reasons that will be explained below.[11] But the consequence is that the country has experienced serious shortages in energy supply, potable water provision, deforestation and land degradation. For example, between 1990 and 2005, the forest cover reduced by 494,000 hectares (representing 12.7% of the forest cover) and it is continuing to disappear in many areas.[12] As far as water is concerned, the levels in the lake and some rivers have declined while the occurrence of floods has become more frequent and devastating. Extreme events tend to affect crop production, food security and can generally be a threat to promotion of sustainable management of natural resources.[13]

For many years, Africans have been steadily encroaching the watershed areas. Trees have been cut down and the land cleared for cultivation. These activities have resulted in serious erosion of soil from the catchment areas. The eroded soil has been taken down to the Shire river where it has silted up. The siltation of the river has, in turn, slowed down the movement of water to the waterfalls at Nkula which produces hydroelectric power for many parts of the country.

---

10 See P. Walker, "Roots of Crisis: Historical Narratives of Tree Planting in Malawi", *Historical Geography* 32 (2004), 89-109; A. Kerr, "Disappearing Forests in Malawi: Causes and Solutions" EEP; Ezekiel Kalipeni and Leo Zulu, "From Top-down to Bottom-up".

11 Daulos Mauambeta et al., "Status of Forests and Tree Management in Malawi", Unpublished Position Paper Prepared for the Coordination Union for Rehabilitation of the Environment (CURE), 2010; Rachel A. Bone et al., "Deforestation since Independence: A Quantitative Assessment of Four Decades of Land-Cover Change in Malawi", *Southern Forests: A Journal of Forest Science* 79/4 (2016), 269-275.

12 Rachel A. Bone et al., "Deforestation since Independence"; N. Katumbi, J Nyengere and E Mkandawire, "Drivers of Deforestation and Forest Degradation in Dzalanyama Forest Reserve in Malawi", *International Journal of Science Research* 6 (2015), 889-893.

13 C. Ngongondo et al., "Regional Frequency Analysis of Rainfall Extremes in Southern Malawi using the Index Rainfall and L-Moments Approaches", *Stochastic Environmental Research and Risk Assessment* 25/7 (2011), 939-955.

When the efficiency of the Nkula hydroelectric plant was reduced, the electrical output plummeted to such an extent that the plant could no longer supply power with the same regularity and effectiveness. As stated earlier on, this began to manifest itself in January of 1997 when power outages and inadequate pumping of water became a daily occurrence in the country.[14]

Governance Crisis in a Democratic Era

The transition from single-party state to multiparty democracy resulted in the introduction of a series of reforms in the governance system of the country. The old order was blamed for pursuing a top-down decision-making process and for muzzling the freedoms and rights of its citizens. Consequently, the new democratic dispensation sought to replace any policies, laws and institutions that stood in the way of promoting citizens' rights. Government operations were now expected to be conducted in a manner that promoted the principles of transparency, accountability and the rule of law. There is little doubt that both the state and non-state actors have made some appreciable efforts in developing policies and introducing measures for conserving the country's environmental resources. Indeed, over the years, significant investments have been made in policy formulation as well as development of some targeted interventions in different parts of the country. But while Malawi registered significant progress in developing the legal and institutional framework generally, implementation of these principles has left much to be desired.

The post-dictatorship democratic reforms were also extended to the management of environmental resources. In this section, we highlight a few of these changes in order to demonstrate the relationship between reforms and failure of governance. First, is the idea of unlocking the resources for economic use. This meant that policies and measures that had strict restrictions on access to and use of resources had to be loosened especially where such resources had economic benefits. Government monopoly over control of resources was reduced and, in some cases, removed altogether to allow the entry of new players. Second, there was need to reorganise resources so that they are used more efficiently. Hence, management systems fraught with wastefulness and destructive tendencies had to be replaced with those that promoted efficiency. Government civil service bureaucracy which had been central in the

---

[14] See Parliamentary Debates (Hansard) for 1997, and especially the Fourth Sitting, Thirty First Session held on Tuesday, 18 March 1997.

management of natural resources gave way to private interests and other stakeholders. Third, a call for review of rights of access to and use of natural resources was necessary. The policy and legal framework which had exclusionary rights to Africans and especially the poor had to be aligned with the new constitutional provisions. In the final analysis, the reforms entailed loosening up the grip on natural resources so that citizens and other players could find their way in.

Meanwhile, the environmental challenges of post-colonial Malawi are well documented.[15] While some of them have long historical roots, others are a product of post-colonial developments. For instance, in 1994, the National Environmental Action Plan (NEAP) identified the major problems to include the threat of climate change, deforestation, degradation of water resources, pollution and soil erosion.[16] The story of NEAP is not dissimilar to that of the Malawi Growth and Development Strategy (MGDS) which, although written almost 15 years later, also identified more or less the same challenges. These included weak management of the natural resources base, compounded by population growth, environmental degradation and encroachment of protected areas, and uncoordinated management of natural resources.[17] These are enduring issues which point to a governance crisis that has left environmental resources in a state of disarray where citizens and some unscrupulous business-people have had unbridled access to natural resources but without requisite responsibilities for their use.

Other aspects of the environmental sector have identified challenges which reflect a growing trend of degradation. The water and sanitation area illustrates perhaps one of the greatest challenges in the management of natural resources. Considering that availability of water resources is critical to the generation of electricity, we argue that its poor management has contributed to Malawi's current environmental crisis. The government's key development plan, the MGDS, did not mince words in decrying the following water-related chal-

---

15 Elton Laisi, "Water Resources in Malawi: An Assessment of the Critical Issues Affecting Water Resources in Malawi and a Call for Attention Towards their Sustainable Use and Management", Unpublished Paper Prepared for the Malawi Water Week, Lilongwe, May 2015; GOM, Malawi Growth and Development Strategy, Lilongwe: Ministry of Economic Planning and Development, 2006, 37-38.

16 GOM, National Environment Action Plan, Ministry of Environment and Climate Change, Vol. 1, 1994.

17 GOM, Malawi Growth and Development Strategy, Lilongwe: Ministry of Economic Planning and Development, 2006.

lenges: historic weak sectoral leadership and coordination; poor sustainability of existing water and sanitation services, coupled with financial poverty of the people, inadequate human capacity (including the impact of HIV/AIDS), and climatic, environmental and land tenure problems; lack of an integrated approach to water resources management and development; vandalism and theft of water supply and sanitation facilities; and degradation of water resources.[18] What comes out clearly is that reforms have so far not resulted in the expected improvement in the management of the country's water resources.

In addition to these challenges, urban landscapes have also been neglected to the extent that they have become an abetting factor in environmental degradation. There is so much littering of solid waste that in some cases parks and recreational facilities have been run down. The lack of adequate sanitation facilities contributes to pollution of water resources so that during the rainy season cesspools and gullies are not an uncommon feature. All these aspects point to failure at the level of governance. The general thrust of this chapter is that, while resources and programmes have been put in place, little progress has been made by way of averting the environmental crisis. If anything, the crisis deepened in the period after 2017 and reached its worst point in 2019.

The Relevance of Historical Experience

Before discussing the suggested measures for addressing the environmental crisis, we want to make a case for the value of historical experience if for no other reason than to glean from it the lessons that could be learnt. We emphasise that the battle for environmental conservation is not unique to Malawi; it has historically been fought with some degree of success in the USA, Germany and South Africa.[19] In these countries, conservation programmes were well supported with considerable amounts of investments accompanied with strict measures for implementation. A well-structured system of governance was instituted. In Malawi, a functional governance system had initially been put in place for implementation of conservation programmes but was later abandoned in the 1990s and thereby created room for unscrupulous individuals and companies to start abusing natural resources.

---

18 Ibid.

19 W.O. Mulwafu, *Conservation Song: A History of Peasant-State Relations and the Environment in Malawi, 1860-2000*, Cambridge: The White Horse Press, 2011.

Even before Malawi attained independence in 1964, a new approach to the management of environmental resources had been developed. First, it involved the abandonment of draconian policies which had characterised the colonial state on environmental conservation. Instead, African producers were to be taught conservation of natural resources through education, persuasion and demonstration. No longer was there to be uprooting of crops, payment of fines or imprisonment of offenders. The various colonial schemes designed in the 1940s and 1950s to promote environmental conservation such as the forest reserves, master farmer schemes and the village land improvement schemes were abandoned in favour of smallholder-based production systems. The

***Figure 13.1**: The environmental crisis model*

Banda regime did not push for any radical transformation of the environmental conservation strategy, probably because they knew full well that Africans still had fresh memories of the harsh colonial conservation campaigns. Second, the state established institutions across the country for the protection and management of the environment. One feature of the Banda regime was its success in instilling a sense of fear of state institutions among the population. Despite its negative implications for the promotion of democratic ideals, this aspect ironically helped to protect the country's environmental resources. Out of fear and respect for the law and state institutions, citizens generally tended to manage environmental resources in a manner that was relatively less destructive. State structures and agencies were strong enough to contain any perceived cases of degradation.

However, some scholars have challenged this view, arguing instead that it is the very same policies of the Banda regime that contributed to environmental degradation. Proponents of this view argue that from the late 1960s, the state began to promote estate agriculture whereby some members of the ruling elite acquired land for the production of tobacco. In particular, the production of fire-cured tobacco required significant quantities of firewood which in turn resulted in rising cases of deforestation. Thus, pursuit of this policy, which is believed to have characterised much of the early post-colonial period, explains the continued degradation taking place both in the African trust lands as well as in the privately owned estates.[20]

Thirdly, in addition to establishment of institutions for management and implementation of policies on natural resources, the post-colonial state created an environment for development of positive values. Through political campaigns, media and school-based programmes, people were persistently told about the need to conserve natural resources. The philosophy of environmental conservation was included in educational materials so that citizens were equipped with knowledge to appreciate not only the elements of agricultural practice but also environmental conservation in its widest sense. Citizens had to work towards conservation of all kinds of natural resources since they were all interlinked (see Figure 13.1). The change in attitude went beyond training provided by the existing educational systems. In addition, environmental conservation had to be adopted by all people across time and space. And this was not just the concern of rural communities. Urban people too had an equally important role to play through community-based programmes. While previously the colonial state had targeted the rural population, the post-colonial state viewed urban people as equally responsible for the misuse of environmental resources and hence the need for their involvement in conservation efforts.

Fourth, and related to the above point, is the issue of citizen participation in environmental conservation. Under the Banda regime, the National Youth Week programme became a vital strategy for implementing community-based projects including those in the environmental sector. As an aspect of community mobilisation, youth week became a key strategy for undertaking

---

20 See Alastair Orr, "'Green Gold'? Burley Tobacco, Smallholder Agriculture, and Poverty Alleviation in Malawi", *World Development* 28/2 (2000), 347-363; I.J. Minde, G. Kowero, D. Ngugi and J. Luhanga, "Agricultural Land Expansion and Deforestation in Malawi", *Forests, Trees, and Livelihoods* 11 (2001), 167-182.

broader development projects, including conservation works, across the country. In liaison with state authorities, citizens organised public works activities that needed to be implemented in their respective areas. This included maintenance of roads, planting trees in catchment areas, forest firebreaks, and building schools and clinics. The introduction of the National Tree Planting Day in the 1970s went a long way towards promoting the conservation drive as citizens participated in the annual afforestation programme. Between the 1970s and the early 1990s, a lot of environmental conservation projects were implemented under the aegis of both the National Youth Week and the Tree Planting Programme.[21]

Finally, the newly independent government identified land use as critical to the conservation of natural resources. It was further observed that most of the land use problems in the country were of social nature and required social change rather than technical solutions. Indeed, although physical factors such as rainfall intensity and terrain played a part, social problems were increasingly contributing to degradation of the environment. As the population of the country increased, so did the pressure on land which resulted in some people farming marginal areas, a process that accelerated soil erosion and other forms of environmental degradation. In a way, this created a dilemma for the state: the need to increase agricultural production to feed the growing population and the desire to promote exports against the declining quality of the land. Concern for environmental conservation was amplified at the time by the widely propagated neo-Malthusian views about an impending ecological crisis.[22] It was generally believed that the occurrence of droughts, floods, and water shortages were a clear sign of disasters that result from destruction or misuse of environmental resources. The government therefore launched various programmes through radio and print media where farmers were taught the benefits of managing land resources in the course of agricultural production. An assortment of land conservation activities such as contour ridging and building were emphasised.

---

21 P. Walker, "Roots of Crisis: Historical Narratives of Tree Planting in Malawi", *Historical Geography* 32 (2004), 89-109.

22 See the work of K. Otsuka and F. Place, "Land Tenure and Natural Resource Management: The Case of Customary Land Area in Malawi", *Journal of Environmental Economic Management* 41 (2001), 13-32; Melissa Leach and James Fairhead, "Challenging Neo-Malthusian Deforestation Analysis in West Africa's Dynamic Landscapes", *Population and Development Review* 26/1 (2000), 17-43; Betsy Hartmann, "Converging on Disorder: Climate Security and the Malthusian Anticipatory Regime for Africa", *Geopolitics* 19/4 (2014), 757-783.

The preceding section has shown that the post-colonial state made some significant investments in the management and conservation of environmental resources. Although by no means exhaustive, we have demonstrated how these strategies, including the promotion of positive conservation values, land use planning, and research helped to achieve a modicum of sound environmental management. These aspects are particularly worth noting in the context of the Banda regime between 1964 and 1994. We argue that it is the veracity of these key pillars of environmental governance which helped the country to avert or at least slow down the occurrence of an environmental crisis. It is also necessary to mention that while non-state actors were almost non-existent during this period, the state operated with greater latitude and authority in implementing its policies on the use of resources. The state may have undoubtedly used authoritarian means to push through its agenda but as far as the environment is concerned some positive values were inculcated among its citizens. We therefore hold that any attempt to achieve good governance of environmental resources in the country must of necessity take into account these critical pillars.

Suggestions for Addressing the Crisis

Environmental degradation has had serious effects on both society and the economy. But the process which is degenerating into a crisis cannot be allowed to continue indefinitely. Figure 13.2 presents a proposed strategy for dealing with the crisis. The strategy highlights key elements that could be considered in order to avert the further occurrence of the crisis: culture, state regulation, education and integrity of the ecosystem. The use of a holistic and integrated approach can help immensely to understand the interaction among different actors on the environment. But given the gravity of the current crisis, a laissez-faire approach is the least of options for mitigating its effects. We discuss each of these elements for whatever contribution they can make towards addressing the crisis.

The first element deals with existence of a strong policy and legal framework. In Malawi, significant changes have taken place in the structure and operations of government departments since the early 1990s. For instance, decentralisation has seen the transfer of some power from central government to lower levels of government. Although it is beyond the scope of this chapter to discuss the effectiveness of decentralisation, what cannot be disputed is that the process has resulted in some changes in the rights and responsibilities of various stakeholders. In general, the role of the state has been redefined and restricted to policy-making and regulation while stakeholders and beneficiary groups have assumed implementation roles of varying degrees. Although citizens are increasingly becoming aware of their rights, they sometimes do not go far enough in fighting to get duty-bearers to account for their actions on the environment.

For environmental resources in general, government has developed many laws and policies on various aspects of the sector such as forestry, water, wildlife and fisheries. Over the past years, Malawi has formulated very good policies and legislative frameworks. But, as many commentators have observed, the problem has often been that of implementation so that even before one cycle is completed, new policies are sometimes drafted. The promulgation of the Environmental Management Act of 2017 not only provides hope for the future but also fills many of the gaps identified in previous pieces of legislation including meting out tougher sanctions against destroyers of natural resources.[23] In addition to lack of enforcement, some policies contain inconsistent provisions. Sending mixed messages to the public does not reflect well in terms of citizen trust and political legitimacy. In addition, poor policy coordination can lead to improper utilisation of resources. During the apogee of the country's environmental crisis, conflicting sets of information were often received from the Electricity Supply Corporation (ESCOM) and Blantyre Water Board on the cause of frequent water and power shortages. ESCOM blamed its failure to supply power on low water levels in the Shire River while Blantyre Water Board attributed its inability to provide potable water to its customers to lack of power to pump the water. Such cases are an indication of poor governance in relation to management of natural resources.

The second issue concerns population growth. There is no doubt that the population of Malawi has increased significantly since independence. From four million people in 1966, it increased four times to 17 million in 2018, growing at an average rate of 2.8% per annum. In addition, average population density has gone up to 186 people per square kilometre in 2018 from 138 in

---

[23] Environment Management Act (www.climate-laws.org/geographies/malawi/laws/environ ment-management-act-no-19-of-2017

Figure 13.2: *Strategy for dealing with the environment*

2008.[24] This means that more and more of the country's resources are required to support the growing population. Population growth will continue to be a problem in Malawi and indeed Africa as a whole if it is not properly managed. So far, the discourse has tended to focus on population increase as being one of the factors contributing to environmental degradation. The strategy has been to try and control population increase. But placing too much emphasis on efforts to control population increase without making innovations which can spur development is in itself misleading and counterproductive. We contend that controlling population without transforming farming technology and household forms of energy use cannot in itself avert the environmental crisis. On the other hand, if the same kind of agriculture continues to be practised using the same type of technology, then population will surely remain a problem, as many neo-Malthusianists have argued.[25] Again, overdependence

---

[24] GOM, Malawi Population and Housing Census Report, 2018, Zomba: National Statistical Office, 2019.

[25] G. Carswell, "Continuities in Environmental Narratives: The Case of Kabale, Uganda, 1930-2000", *Environment and History* 9 (2003), 3-29; and D.E. Rocheleau et al., "Environment, Development, Crisis and Crusade: Ukambani, Kenya, 1890-1990", *World Development* 23/6 (1995), 1037-1051; M. Tiffen, M. Mortimore and F. Gichuki, *More People, Less Erosion: Environmental Recovery in Kenya*, London & New York: John Wiley, 1994.

on fuelwood for energy is another very significant factor in the destruction of environmental resources. There is need to ground arguments more adequately in historical contexts. In this respect, a lot of population-based arguments have been made without taking into account the specific cultural and socio-economic contexts. As far as the Malawian situation is concerned, population increase is just one of the drivers of environmental degradation that should be considered in relation to other drivers in a complex web of relationships.

The third issue deals with the knotty question of poverty. Poverty is often considered to be the antithesis of environmental conservation. It has become almost a cliché to posit that poverty causes environmental degradation especially in areas where the poor depend on environmental resources for their livelihoods. The Brundtland Report of 1987 clearly underscored this relationship and bemoaned the fact that economic policies were not adequately fighting poverty as one way of controlling environmental degradation.[26] In the case of Malawi, examples abound where the poor including small-scale charcoal makers, firewood fetchers, tobacco farmers, and timber loggers have been blamed for encouraging environmental degradation though felling and burning trees. Since the majority of the people live below the poverty line, it is necessary to develop strategies that would not only reduce poverty but also reverse the current trend of environmental degradation. One possibility is to develop a more diversified economic system which incorporates the interests of small-scale farmers and other poor people who might be incentivised to help in reducing environmental degradation.

Fourth, one of the aspects that has changed little in the post-independence history of Malawi relates to the form of energy used by the majority of its people for their livelihoods. Many Malawians continue to use traditional forms of energy, principally firewood and charcoal, for cooking and other domestic activities. It is estimated that about 90% of Malawians depend on fuelwood for energy. The use of electricity has generally been confined to urban and peri-urban areas, and the number of people on the grid accounts for a paltry 9% of the total population.[27] This means that the majority of the people use firewood whose continued extraction is a threat to environmental conservation. Whatever rationalisation one can make, it is simply self-deluding to think that

26 Brundtland Report of the World Commission on Environment and Development: Our Common Future (1987).

27 UNDP, Human Development Report, 2004; Kalipeni, Zulu, FAOSTAT.

environmental conservation can be promoted under such circumstances. Put bluntly, this scenario prepares a fertile ground for the continued occurrence of the crisis. Currently, electricity demand stands way above 400 megawatts which is the average production capacity.[28] Perhaps it may only be fair to state that since the introduction of multipartyism in 1994, the demand for electricity has always surpassed the supply and yet successive governments have made little investment to increase the generation capacity. Because of growing pressure to meet demand, government has been working towards increasing the generating capacity through investments in diesel and solar power as well as tapping electricity from neighbouring countries.

Another issue concerns the implications of human rights and democracy. Since liberalisation in the 1990s, space has opened up for private capital, the civil society and non-governmental organisations to operate in the country. Within the environmental sector, many of them are actively working in both rural and urban areas and tend to use predominantly the approach of trying to empower the grassroots and beneficiary communities in the utilisation and management of natural resources, pretty much in line with principles of decentralisation and stakeholder participation. The strategy of co-management of resources has also been widely encouraged. But, despite the great work being done by civil society organisations, at times the issue of asymmetrical power relations between providers of financial resources and their recipients tends to stand in the way of further progress. The project approach has seen many interventions fail to go beyond the life of the project itself. Usually conceived and funded by external agents, project implementers try to empower beneficiary communities but so far there is little evidence of successful programmes run by locally empowered communities. Apart from the NGOs, the private sector has also been brought in to complement the work being done in the management of environmental resources.[29] For instance, government recently granted licences to private entrepreneurs for production of electricity to add to the national grid. However, little progress has so far been made by way of reducing the impact of the energy crisis. Apart from the energy sector, the state has also liberalised the wildlife sector by granting concessions to private companies for the management of wildlife resources. For instance, the African Parks Network has

---

[28] World Bank, "Progress Towards Sustainable Energy: Global Tracking Framework", 2015.

[29] K.A. Wiyo, L. Fiwa and W. Mwase, "Solving Deforestation, Protecting and Managing Key Water Catchments in Malawi using Smart Public and Private Partnerships", *Journal of Sustainable Development* 8 (2015), 251-261.

since 2003 been given licences to manage the Majete and Liwonde National Parks and Nkhotakota Game Reserve. An interesting question one may ask is: Does this mean that the state together with the communities have failed to manage their natural resources? Is this the direction Malawi should take in order to achieve good governance of its natural resources?

Looking around the country's landscape, one gets the impression that citizens appear to have been given rights and freedoms not only to use but also to misuse natural resources with some degree of impunity. Some citizens think, wrongly for that matter, that they have the right to use the environmental resources without bearing the cost of degradation. A case in point is the caravan of citizens who trek to Zomba Plateau on a daily basis to collect poles and firewood. The same applies to other hills and mountains across the country. On a larger scale, the case of Chikangawa forest reserve in the north has become an example of a poorly managed natural resource. The governance system collapsed to the extent that different players have been competing to maximise their profits from the various forest products. Yet, the loggers and other forest product harvesters hardly participate in the replanting exercises; others have been accused of destroying the resources through bush fires and vandalism. Either the meaning and application of democracy may have been wrongly understood by citizens or the state is not doing enough to regulate the use and management of natural resources. The apparent lack of citizen responsibility in using resources and state failure to take to task individuals who degrade environmental resources are worrying trends in the battle for conservation.

Alongside the issue of citizen rights, changes have also taken place in perceptions and attitudes towards natural resources. Until the political and economic liberalisation of the early 1990s, the state had been the major and unrivalled player in the management of natural resources. But after this period, the role of the state changed in a manner that saw budgetary support being reduced and, in some cases, withdrawn. In the natural resources area, personnel responsible for conservation of a range of environmental resources such as forests and wildlife were retrenched and sometimes laid off in a rather disorganised manner. Increasingly, resources which were hitherto under the control of state agencies suddenly became orphaned or experienced a significant reduction of state presence. In the minds of some people, such resources were now open to use by anyone in society. On the other hand, natural resources that were viewed largely as social goods began to be considered as commodities for profit making. This transformation of attitudes and values contributed to the spread of reckless behaviours and practices whereby citizens have become agents of environmental destruction. While citizens and other players enjoy a significant degree of rights and freedoms, they have failed alongside the state in effectively managing the country's natural resources.

Conclusion

The message being advanced in this chapter is that lessons from history show a positive correlation between strong state intervention and effective governance of environmental resources. At the same time, creating space for active citizen participation is necessary to cultivate values for good governance. In the pre-1994 period, the state provided opportunities for citizen participation in the management of resources and this helped to minimise the effects of degradation. However, the period between 2017 and 2020 will go down in history as one of the worst so far as management of Malawi's environmental resources is concerned. It is a period that was marked by a legitimacy crisis, which in turn exposed deep-seated environmental problems in the country. Fighting environmental degradation cannot depend on sheer serendipity and cannot be achieved by a lukewarm approach as the post-liberalisation period has shown.

Chapter 14

Pandemics, Politics and Governance: Contestations over State Management of Covid-19 in Malawi

Bryson Gwiyani Nkhoma,
Gift Wasambo Kayira
& Paul Chiudza Banda

Introduction

On 11 March 2020, the World Health Organization (WHO) declared Covid-19 a global pandemic and called on countries to take aggressive action to contain the virus.[1] Nine days later, the former president of Malawi, Peter Mutharika, declared a State of Disaster in the country to contain the spread of the pandemic. Meanwhile, the Ministry of Health gazetted the public health (Corona Virus Prevention, Containment, and Management) rules under the Public Health Act.[2] On 15 April 2020, the government announced a country-wide lockdown to run between 18 April and 9 May.

Even before the lockdown took effect, the Human Rights Defenders Coalition (HRDC), a civil society organisation that fights for the rights of Malawians, obtained a court injunction, and applied for a judicial review of the lockdown decision. HRDC argued that although the pandemic required a swift response, the lockdown was insensitive to the plight of poor Malawians, most of whom live hand to mouth with an income of about a dollar per day. For HRDC, the government declared the lockdown without consulting other stakeholders, a position that won the support of some members of the opposition parties.[3]

---

1 World Health Organization (WHO), WHO Director-General's Opening Remarks at the Media Briefing on COVID-19, 11 March 2020, WHO, Geneva, 11 March 2020.

2 Malawi Government, Gazette Extraordinary: Public Health (Corona Virus Prevention, Containment and Management) Rules, 9 April 2020; Malawi Government, Measures for Prevention of COVID-19, Lilongwe: Ministry of Health, March 2020; *Al Jazeera,* "Malawi announces Corona Virus Lockdown", An Al Jazeera Report, https://perma.cc/9FZZ-WAWG.

3 *AllAfrica,* "HRDC says not against Lockdown: Malawi Government should first insulate the poor", https://allafrica.com/stories/202004200492.html.

What do these contestations over Covid-19 reveal about the Malawian state and matters of governance? This chapter examines the Covid-19 pandemic in Malawi to understand how public health interventions intersect with the socio-economic and political landscape to shape governance issues in the country. Like other pandemics in history, we argue that the Covid-19 pandemic in Malawi exposes the underlying social, economic and political tensions against which the citizenry makes claims on matters of governance and welfare. State failure to address the deep-seated political, economic, and social ills, most of which predate the current pandemic, created the Covid-19 impasse which civil society, opposition leaders, religious leaders, and ordinary Malawians exploited to their advantage. The contestations we highlight are significant in two ways. First, they complicate the notion of an overbearing and autonomous state and challenge what Dickson Ayoh describes as the self-assurance of the African political elites who seek to "dominate state power and national politics", while excluding the "not-so-privileged majorities in the societies".[4] The story we tell reminds us of Joel Migdal's, and many others, "State-in-Society approach", according to which the state, including government bureaucracy and the political regime presiding over it, contends with other interest groups within the society, such as the civil society and other private entities, which constantly make claims over matters of governance.[5]

Second, the contestations reveal the state of governance in the country, especially as this relates to the government's ability to contain a fast-spreading pandemic without sacrificing democratic ideals. Experience elsewhere shows that Covid-19 measures, like other public health interventions, potentially threaten both civil liberties and economic freedoms. As Klaus Dodd and colleagues have illustrated, countries that boast mature democracies such as the USA and Britain and those that are "politically closed" such as China and North Korea, have all adopted Covid-19 measures that have suppressed people's civil and political liberties, including the "right to move, to assemble, to demonstrate and to attend religious services".[6] What is unique in Malawi's case, we argue, is

---

4 Dickson Eyoh, "African Perspectives on Democracy and the Dilemmas of Postcolonial Intellectuals", *Africa Today* 45, 3/4 (1998), 291-304 [294].

5 Joel S. Migdal, *State in Society: Studying How States and Societies Transform and Constitute one Another*, Cambridge: Cambridge University Press, 2001, 3-23; See also Colin Leys, "The 'Overdeveloped' Post-colonial State: A Re-Evaluation", *Review of African Political Economy* 5 (1976), 41-42.

6 Klaus Dodds et al., "The Covid-19 Pandemic: Territorial, Political and Governance Dimensions of the Crisis", *Territory, Politics, Governance* 8/3 (2020), 292-293.

what Jürgen Habermas described as the power of "public opinion", which plays out within the "public sphere".[7] In summarising Habermas, Peter Probst defined the latter as a "particular social and communicative space [where] individuals excluded from the exercise of state power [publicly] express their needs and critique ... the state".[8] Such individuals form public opinion about issues that pertain to their welfare and how to address them. Evidence suggests that democratic countries that adopted strict measures did so with some level of public support.[9] Others, such as Malawi, failed to push through similar measures because they were against public opinion.

One reason explaining the absence of a strong public opinion in Malawi centered on the contradictions within the society when the lockdown measures were first announced. Diverse interest groups, ranging from street traders, religious leaders, students, parents and guardians, public health workers to politicians, presented contradictory concerns, in ways that made decision-making a daunting task to achieve.

In other words, while the chapter highlights the interaction between the state and other stakeholders in the face of Covid-19 pandemic, it also pays attention to the very composition of the stakeholders in question, pointing out the diverse views they expressed which are critical to understanding the state of governance in Africa amidst certain forms of pandemics. Evidence from Malawi shows that government response to pandemics like Covid-19, and that of opposing stakeholders, is complex, dynamic, varied and sometimes contradictory. While the demand for an inclusive and listening state is legitimate, conflicts and outright contradictions among the various responses to pandemics made it very hard for the 'state' to be 'inclusive' to everyone.

We begin by locating the study within the historiography of pandemics and how it relates to matters of governance in Malawi and beyond. Thereafter, we examine the onset of Covid-19 in Malawi and the measures the state introduced to curb its spread. We conclude with an analysis of various actors' responses to

7 Jürgen Habermas, *The Structural Transformation of the Public Sphere: An Inquiry into a Category of Bourgeois Society*, Cambridge: Polity Press, 1989, first published in 1962. Habermas conceptualised the public sphere in relation to the 18th- and 19th-century German bourgeois class which was critical of the state and its overbearing tendencies.

8 Peter Probst, "Mchape" '95, or, the Sudden Fame of Billy Goodson Chisupe: Healing, Social Memory and the Enigma of the Public Sphere in Post-Banda Malawi", *Journal of the International African Institute* 69/1 (1999), 132.

9 Dodds et al., "The Covid-19 Pandemic", 292.

the preventive measures the government introduced to contain the pandemic. We pay attention to how, confronted with the country's long-standing political, economic, and social ills, different actors used Covid-19 to confront the government on these aspects, albeit at the expense of life. We tell this story through an examination of both primary and secondary sources, drawn from several local and international libraries. The primary sources include newspaper articles (both print and online), presidential speeches and addresses, government documents, and press releases from Malawi and beyond. The secondary sources are in the form of books and journal articles. Qualitatively, the sources enabled us to capture the voices, opinions, and perceptions of different stakeholders with regard to the politics surrounding the response to Covid-19 in the country.

Pandemics and Governance in History

Experiences of pandemics like Covid-19 are not new in Malawian history and beyond. Noteworthy are the Spanish influenza of 1918 to 1920 and HIV and AIDS, which struck the country from the mid-1980s. The Spanish influenza entered the country through Malawian mineworkers returning from Southern Rhodesia in November 1918.[10] With a death toll of over 50,000 people within a year in Malawi, John McCracken argued that the influenza claimed more lives than the First World War.[11] Since its onset in 1985, HIV and AIDS spread from one case to a million cases by 2020, with an annual death rate of 29,000 in 2010 (currently down to 13,000 per annum).[12] Like Covid-19, the influenza and HIV and AIDS pandemics challenged the existing governance and health delivery systems, generating contestations with the locals who accused respective governments of negligence, complacency and apathy.

Due to their devastating effects, these pandemics and others have attracted scholarly attention. As early as the 1960s, scholars explored the struggles the Christian missionaries and the colonial state endured as they sought to contain the spread of diseases and encourage Africans to adopt western medicine.[13]

---

10 Terence Ranger, "The Influenza Pandemic in Southern Rhodesia: A Crisis of Comprehension", in David Arnold (ed.), *Imperial Medicine and Indigenous Societies*, Manchester: Manchester University Press, 1988, 173-5.

11 John McCracken, *A History of Malawi, 1859-1966*, Woodbridge: James Currey, 2011, 154.

12 UNAIDS, Malawi Country Report, 2020.

13 Michael Gelfand, *Lakeside Pioneer: A Social History of Medical Study of Nyasaland, 1875-1920*, Oxford: Basil Blackwell, 1964; Meghan Vaughan, *Curing their Ills: Colonial Power and African* Illness, Cambridge: Cambridge University Press, 1991; W. C. Chirwa, "Sexually Transmitted

Diseases and western medicine became an arena for political contestations between the state, missionaries, and Africans, as the last questioned the logic of new foreign medication. Luke Messac observed that the proposal to introduce payment of fees in government hospitals soon after Malawi attained independence became a cause of disagreement between the state and the country's citizens.[14] With the support of some cabinet ministers, most ordinary Malawians not only considered the proposal a betrayal of the newly won independence, but also a risky policy in a country that shared some history of widespread fatal pandemics such as Spanish influenza.[15]

Similarly, John Lwanda argued that until the late 1990s, politics and personal interests clouded the country's preparedness towards containing the spread of HIV and AIDS. For example, Hastings Kamuzu Banda, Malawi's first president, contested the presence of the pandemic among Malawians to sustain his political rhetoric of disciplined and morally upright Malawians under his leadership.[16] Banda renounced the use of condoms and banned family planning methods in the country, a position which affected the country's preparedness to contain the spread of the virus. Banda also denied that the Malawi army was the major culprit of the disease through its involvement in the Mozambican war between 1985 and 1995. Locally, the army, which previously found solace in Banda's apathy, vandalised the *Daily Times* office in 1996 for revealing that the war in Mozambique contributed to the spread of HIV and AIDS among Malawian soldiers.[17] Similarly, Banda refuted allegations that Malawian migrants comprised the largest number of people infected with HIV and AIDS

Diseases in Colonial Malawi", in P. W. Setel, M. Lewis and M. Lyons (eds), *Histories of Sexually Transmitted Diseases and HIV/AIDS in Sub-Saharan Africa*, London: Greenwood Press, 1999, 143-166; Markku Hokkanen, *Medicine and Scottish Missionaries in Northern Malawi, 1875-1930: Quests for Health in a Colonial Society*, Lampeter: Edwin Mellen Press, 2007; John McCracken, *A History of Malawi,* 116-121.

14 Luke Messac, "Moral hazards and Moral Economies: The Combustible Politics of Healthcare User Fees in Malawian History", *South African Historical Journal,* 2014, 4-15, http://dx.doi.org/10.1080/02582473.2014.903292. See also Luke Messac, "Birthing a Nation: Political Legitimacy and Health Policy in Hastings Kamuzu Banda's Malawi, 1962-1980", *Journal of Southern African Studies* 46/2 (2020), 212-216.

15 Colin Baker, *Revolt of the Ministers: The Malawi Cabinet Crisis, 1964-1965*, London: I.B. Tauris, 2001, 116-117 and 129-133.

16 John Lwanda, "Politics, Culture and Medicine: An Unholy Trinity? Historical Continuities and Raptures in the HIV/AIDS Story in Malawi", in E. Kalipeni, S. Craddock, L. Oppong and J. Ghish (eds), *HIV and AIDS in Africa*, Oxford: Blackwell, 2004, 29-42.

17 By that time Banda was no longer in power and was not in control of the HIV and AIDS narrative in the country.

in South Africa. The South African government and the mining sector cited cases of HIV and AIDS to reduce the recruitment of foreign workers, including those from Malawi. Banda rejected this narrative.[18]

Like Banda, Thabo Mbeki, the South African President (1999-2008), initially denied the existence of HIV and AIDS in that country, a decision that partly led to both loss of lives and his presidency to Jacob Zuma. Mbeki argued that HIV and AIDS was a Western narrative tactically framed to promote medical capitalism in South Africa, and to cover-up for the evils of apartheid.

Elsewhere, studies have shown how outbreaks and preventive measures of trypanosomiasis, bubonic plague, cholera, tuberculosis, Spanish influenza, and HIV and AIDS generated conflicts between the state and the local people.[19] What should also be emphasised is that these contestations also play out beyond the state-society binary, and often pit diverse interest groups within the society against each other. Richard Evans and Pule Phoofole, for instance, have used the example of European and southern African societies to show how pandemics revealed age-old political tensions and class conflicts, although not in ways that resulted in major political revolutions.[20]

Steven Feierman noted that the evolution of pandemics in African history, including the patterns of their spread, diagnosis and treatment, were intricately connected to broader social, economic and political aspects of societies.[21] He contends that for most African societies, these practices and the existence of multiple actors making claims to knowledge over health, healing, and death have been the primary cause of conflicts over matters of diseases. Such claims

---

18 W. Chirwa, "Aliens and Aids in Southern Africa: The Malawi-South Africa Debate", *African Affairs,* 97, 386 (1998), 53-70.

19 K.D. Patterson, "Disease and Medicine in African History", *History and Africa,* 1 (1974), 141-148; M. W. Swanson, "The 'Sanitation Syndrome': Bubonic Plague and Urban Native Policy in the Cape Colony, 1900-1909", *Journal of African History* 18/3 (1977), 387-410; R. Packard, "Maize, Cattle and Malaria: The Political Economy of Malaria Epidemics in Colonial Swaziland", *Journal of African History* 25/2 (1984), 189-212; R. Packard, *White Plague, Black Labour: Tuberculosis and The Political Economy of Health and Disease in South Africa*, Berkeley and Los Angeles: University of California Press, 1989; David Killingray, "A New 'Imperial Disease': The Spanish Influenza Pandemic of 1918-19 and Its Impact on the British Empire", *Caribbean Quarterly* 49/4 (2003), 30-49.

20 Richard Evans, "Epidemics and Revolutions: Cholera Outbreaks in Nineteenth-Century Europe", *Past and Present* 120 (1988), 123-146; Pule Phoofolo, "Epidemics and Revolutions: The Rinderpest Epidemic in Late Nineteenth-Century Southern Africa", *Past and Present* 138 (1993), 112-143.

21 Steven Feierman, "Struggles for Control: The Social Roots of Health and Healing in Modern Africa", *African Studies Review* 28, 2/3 (1985), 73-147.

were particularly true among government officials, traditional healers and religious leaders, as well as loose networks of patients' relatives and neighbours. Walima Kalusa and Megan Vaughan extended Feierman's thesis by exploring varied beliefs and practices around sickness, death, and burial in Zambia and Malawi.[22] For most African communities, these practices are as significant as official public health interventions. Failure to recognise specific roles that sickness, death, and burial serve in African societies often creates contestations as communities remind officials about the value they attach to these practices.

As others have done, we argue that matters of public health cannot be divorced from the socio-economic and political aspects of society. In Malawi's context, politics, culture, and concerns over people's livelihoods combined to undermine the fight against the Covid-19 pandemic that was rapidly spreading. More significantly, the response of various groups towards government measures to contain the pandemic further reveals how the parties involved used the pandemic to achieve their diverse interests. As we discuss in the subsequent sections, some stakeholders contested the imposed measures, thereby reminding the state about the need to support people's livelihoods and uphold inclusive governance principles in managing pandemics. More significantly, the interests of various groups often conflicted, thereby further complicating the state's interventions against the pandemic.

The 2019 General Election provided a political context in which to understand the contestations over the politics of Covid-19. The main contestants in the elections—which marked a quarter of a century since the country's return to multiparty democracy—were the Democratic Progressive Party (DPP), led by Peter Mutharika; the Malawi Congress Party (MCP), led by Lazarus Chakwera; and the United Transformation Movement (UTM), led by Saulos Chilima.[23] The former ruling party in the 1990s, the UDF, featured Atupele Muluzi as its candidate, but came in a distant fourth. Interestingly, Chilima who was still serving his constitutionally mandated term as the country's vice president, resigned from the DPP in July 2018 to establish his political party. The period leading to the polling day saw the opposition's campaign dominated by

[22] Walima T. Kalusa and Megan Vaughan, *Death, Belief and Politics in Central African History*, Lusaka: Lembani Trust, 2013.

[23] After the 1964 General Election, which also marked a former transfer of power from the colonial government to independent Malawi, the country became a de facto one-party state following the overwhelming victory of the Malawi Congress Party in the election. With time, the rest of the opposition parties were banned, and some leaders fled into exile.

messages denouncing the high levels of corruption involving the state president and some of his cabinet ministers, poverty, unemployment, poor economic performance, the controversial 2016 land reform programme (moving away from the predominant customary land tenure system to a registered land system), land scarcity in some parts of the country, and nepotism in government, among other issues.[24] Not satisfied with the outcome of the presidential elections, the opposition leaders, led by Chakwera and Chilima, went to court to challenge the final tally of national results announced by the Malawi Electoral Commission (MEC). On 3 February 2020, the Constitutional Court, comprising five judges of the High Court of Malawi nullified the May 2019 presidential results. Among other issues, the court cited poll irregularities and the fact that Mutharika who had been declared declared winner by MEC had not amassed the required 50% of the national vote. The court ordered a re-run of the presidential polls within 150 days of delivering its ruling.[25] The court battles, an unstable DPP-led administration, and anti-government demonstrations complicated responses to the spread of the Covid-19 pandemic.

Covid-19 and Earlier Government Responses

Covid-19, a respiratory syndrome which first appeared in the country on 2 April 2020, has affected Malawians in ways that expose the limits of state power. By the time of its onset in Malawi, the pandemic, which started in China in December 2019, had spread across the world claiming many lives. Italy, Spain and the USA were initially the most affected countries. But from mid-February, Africa began to register Covid-19 cases, with the first appearing in Egypt on 14 February; sub-Saharan Africa registered its first case in Nigeria on 28 February.[26] When South Africa confirmed its first case on 5 March 2020, it became clear to Malawi that the virus was within its vicinity.[27] Historically, Malawi had developed direct links with South Africa through labour migration,

[24] See Stephanie Regalia, "Malawi: The Road to the 2019 Tripartite Elections: Reflections on Corruption, Land, and Multiparty Politics", *Notes de l'Ifri* January 2019, 6-26.

[25] The Republic of Malawi: High Court of Malawi, Lilongwe District Registry, Constitutional Ref. no.1 of 2019. 3rd February 2020.

[26] *Egypt Today*, "Egypt Announces First Coronavirus Infection", 14 February 2020; *BBC News*, "Nigeria Confirms First Coronavirus Case", 28 February 2020.

[27] South African Government, "Minister Zweli Mkhize Reports First Case of Covid-19 Coronavirus", 5 March 2020.

education, and cross-border trade, and it was likely that Covid-19 would spread into the country through these networks.

Although the WHO declared Covid-19 a global disaster on 11 March, it was only when Malawi's immediate neighbours confirmed their first cases that the pandemic attracted serious public attention in the country. While Tanzania reported its first case on 16 March, with cases rising to six on 19 March, Zambia's first confirmed case appeared on 18 March 2020.[28] Alarmed by these cases in the neighbouring countries, the Malawian president declared the pandemic a national disaster on 20 March, a move the general public criticised as premature as the country had at the time registered no Covid-19 cases.[29] Through this declaration, government provided MWK 2.5 billion (USD 3.3 million) as immediate funding towards the Covid-19 response. Other measures included redeploying health personnel at all border posts to screen people entering the country, suspension of international meetings, and closure of all schools. Restrictions on public gatherings including weddings, funerals, church, political rallies, and government meetings to less than 100 people; banning of travel by foreign nationals from countries highly affected by coronavirus save for those from SADC region, were other significant measures.[30] Furthermore, to oversee the implementation of the preventive measures, Mutharika established a Special Cabinet Committee chaired by Jappie Mhango, the then Minister of Health.

Government announced more drastic measures after the country had confirmed the first four Covid-19 cases on 2 April. The measures included suspension of all formal meetings, gatherings and conferences, and release of prisoners with moderate crimes. On the economic front, government reduced fuel prices and encouraged financial institutions to temporarily halt repayment of large-scale loans by customers. Seven days after the country reported its first Covid-19 related death on 7 April, government announced a 21-day lockdown to commence midnight of 18 April, with the possibility of extension, depending on the results. In a televised address to the nation, Mutharika called on all

---

28 *Anadolu Agency*, "Somalia, Tanzania Confirm First Coronavirus Cases",16 March 2020; P. Vigija, "Covid-19: Tanzania Traces 112 Contacts as Cases Rises to Six", *The Star,* 19 March 2020; *News Diggers*, "Zambia Confirms 2 Covid-19 Cases, 18 March 2020.

29 *Quartz Africa,* "A Country with no Coronavirus Case has Declared a National Disaster and Shut Schools, Large Gatherings", 24 March 2020.

30 Office of President and Cabinet (OPC), Peter Mutharika's Presidential National Address on Covid-19, 20 March 2020.

Malawians to comply with the measures which prohibited people's movements except with written consent from authorities and only to access essential services such as medical care and food supplies.[31] During the proposed lockdown, the government would deploy security personnel to enforce compliance through border security patrols and mounting of emergency roadblocks.

These proposed measures did not go uncontested. As noted, the HRDC obtained a court injunction against the lockdown on 17 April, which the state had not yet lifted by the end of August 2020. It appears government agreed with some of the HRDC concerns. For example, there was criticism that the Covid-19 committee was too narrow and did not represent the interests of all sectors of the society. On 29 April, government announced a Presidential Taskforce on Covid-19, which replaced the Special Cabinet Committee Mutharika had instituted earlier.[32] The 21-member taskforce assumed responsibility on 6 May, with Dr John Phuka from the College of Medicine, and Joseph Mwanamveka, Minister of Finance, Economic Planning and Development, as co-chairs. Besides the taskforce, government opened institutional isolation and treatment centres in Blantyre, Lilongwe and Mzuzu. It also promised to recruit 2,000 nurses and 1,500 Health Surveillance Assistants. In addition, the government introduced an Emergency Cash Transfer Programme to financially support small businesspersons in the country's city markets. Under this intervention, individuals would receive a monthly stipend of MWK 35,000 (USD 47) for the next six months. But the government indefinitely suspended the programme even before the disbursement of funds apparently due to lack of trust in local level politicians who often abuse or misappropriate such funds. These interventions, even if carried out, were too little to contain resistance from some quarters of Malawi society. Several groups contested the government-recommended Covid-19 preventive measures.

Contesting Covid-19 Preventive Measures

When the state announced a total ban on formal gatherings on 7 April and later imposed a lockdown, some sections of Malawi society questioned government's logic in the fight against Covid-19. Although most people appreciated the need to take precautionary measures, they realised that Covid-19 preventive measures would infringe upon their religious freedom, livelihoods, political

31 OPC, Peter Mutharika's Presidential National Address, 14 April 2020.

32 Ibid, 29 April 2020.

rights and economic activities. Through the Malawi Council of Churches (MCC), religious leaders, for example, sought clarification on the ban on formal gatherings immediately after its announcement. The leaders were less disturbed by an earlier restriction that limited formal gatherings to a maximum of 100 people. Churches simply introduced more services of worship to comply with government regulations. However, they took issue with a total ban on formal gatherings, arguing that it was inappropriate. Some claimed that it was possible to eliminate the pandemic through prayers. They referred to Tanzanian President John Magufuli who allowed religious people to gather without restrictions and help the government deal with the pandemic through such prayers.[33]

The clergy from small churches also complained that a ban on religious gatherings would affect them economically as they earned their livelihoods from church offerings. For instance, Chikwawa Pastors Fraternal asked government to provide them with financial support if churches were to remain closed. Chair of the Fraternal, Pastor Wilson Kachenje, argued that most pastors were reluctant to close down churches because they depended on offerings and gifts for their survival.[34] After negotiations, government reversed the decision to impose a ban against church meetings, and only advised religious leaders to limit their gatherings to 100 people.

Following the religious leaders were street vendors or small-scale traders who ply their trades in cities and other urban areas. Vendors organised mass protests in Mzuzu, Blantyre, Mangochi, Karonga, Zomba and Lilongwe to challenge the planned 21-day lockdown. The vendors represented a large section of the Malawi population that was locked into a state of abject poverty due largely to the country's high unemployment rate. With a GNP per capita estimated at USD 381.40, Malawi is among the poorest countries ranking number 172 out of 185 countries on the UN human development index.[35] The private sector is also not fully developed and is not large enough to absorb those that cannot find jobs in government. This often leads many Malawians, including the street vendors, to find employment in the informal economic sector, which includes jobs such as car-washing, brickmaking, sand mining, street vending, bicycle and ox-cart taxiing. Others have continued to rely on clandestine labour migration to South Africa, a practice that has its historical roots in the colonial economy.

---

33 Abdi Latif Dahir, "Tanzania's President says Country is Virus Free – Others Warn of Disaster", *The New York Times,* 4 August 2020.

34 *Zodiak TV News,* 'Pastors Ask for Covid-19 Funding", 26 April 2020.

35 UNDP, Human Development Report, 2019, New York: UNDP, 2019, 302.

The resilience of labour migration despite the threat of deportation that migrants face in South Africa is a clear sign that the country's economy has been underperforming.[36] More recently, there has been growth of cross-border trade not only to South Africa, but also Tanzania and Zambia, with women being the dominant players.[37]

While the vendors appreciated the need to contain the spread of the pandemic, they feared that the lockdown would make their economic situation worse. Therefore, they staged protests to petition government to provide them with upkeep money to survive on during the lockdown. Most of them lived on a hand-to-mouth basis through daily petty casual work and feared that the lockdown would claim their lives more than Covid-19 itself. "Most of us rely on daily earnings to provide for our families", argued one protest leader in Mangochi, Madalitso Kalipinde, who further insisted that "without going out to sell our merchandise we cannot survive".[38] Not surprisingly, vendors welcomed the HRDC injunction against a lockdown that would have affected their economic activities.

Private school owners were another group that joined religious leaders and street traders in questioning government's lockdown that would potentially affect their livelihoods. Some of the private school owners complained that they were struggling to pay salaries to their employees following government's directive to close schools on 23 March 2020. At first, most schools were not very much affected by this closure since it coincided with the regular second term recess. But when the recess period ended, and the government appeared less committed to reopen schools, private school owners turned to the state for support. The indefinite closure affected cash flow, leaving them with inadequate resources to pay teachers' salaries.[39] Even with that, the government

---

36 M.M. Mtika, "Political Economy, Labour Migration, and the AIDS Epidemic in Rural Malawi", *Social Science and Medicine* 64 (2007), 2455-2457. See also Wiseman Chijere Chirwa, "The Malawi Government and South African Labor Recruiters, 1974-1992", *Journal of Modern African Studies* 34/4 (1996), 623-642; B. Nkhoma, "Competition for Malawian Labour: *Wenela* and *Mthandizi* in Ntcheu District, 1936-1956", *Malawi Journal of Social Sciences* 21 (2013), 28-46.

37 H.C. Banda, "Migration, Economy and Politics: Unprecedented Increase in Informal Labour Migration from Northern Malawi to South Africa in the 1990s", *African Renaissance* 15/4 (2018), 53-75

38 *Anadolu Agency,* Violent Protest in Malawi due to Covid-19 Lockdown-Opposition Blames Ruling DPP for 21-Day Lockdown to Delay Elections, 18 April 2020, www.aa.com.tr/en/africa/violent-protests-in-malawi-due-to-covid-19-lockdown/1809281.

39 *The Nation,* "Malawi: Covid-19 Hits Private Schools as Teachers Risk not Being Paid", 4 May 2020.

ignored their demands for financial support. Meanwhile, some schools resorted to offering part-time tutoring to learners for survival. Others embarked on online teaching, often charging high fees even where students were not physically present in schools, which also attracted government condemnation.

Private school owners continued to push for the reopening of schools. University students did the same, and on 12 May called upon government to reopen schools. In response, government formed a National Taskforce for the Possibility of Reopening of Malawi Schools, to provide guidance on school reopening amid the Covid-19 pandemic. Chaired by the Secretary for Education, the committee held its first meeting on 22 May, at which point it recommended 13 July as a possible date for reopening schools, colleges, and universities. With a surge in the number of Covid-19 cases during the months of April, May, and June, it became clear that schools would not open as proposed. As the committee remained silent on its earlier proposal, the Independent Schools Association of Malawi (ISAMA) advised its members to reopen schools on 13 July as earlier indicated, a call which the Ministry of Education dismissed. For the government, the Ministry of Health held a final say on school reopening. It was yet to advise the Taskforce regarding the new date. Here, the government also received support from some parents and guardians who threatened to sue those who opened schools under the prevailing circumstances.[40]

The position parents and guardians took shows the very contradictory interests that were at play in Malawi. University students' support towards reopening schools had less to do with loss of revenue than the long-term effects the closure of schools would have on their academic calendar. While acknowledging the economic concerns private school owners registered, parents and guardians were specifically concerned with the health of their wards. The contending interests of the groups discussed above provide a background which should help us to make sense of the concerns of the health personnel.

The health personnel, including medical doctors, nurses, pharmacists, laboratory technicians, and clinical officers, were another significant interest group. Their voices provide further insights into the politics of Covid-19. Unlike religious leaders who claimed that prayers would help to address the pandemic, this group feared that the country's health system was less prepared

---

40 *Zodiak Online,* 'Government, Private Schools Tussle over Date for Reopening of Schools", 7 July 2020.

to handle the pandemic. Under the Republican Constitution, the state is obliged "to provide adequate health care, commensurate with the health needs of the Malawian society and international standards of health care".[41] However, the health workers noted that the existing 509 health care centres had inadequate staff and funding, drug shortages, as well as lack of ambulances and personal protective equipment (PPE). Although already understaffed, the government pegged the risk allowance for health workers to as low as MWK 1,000 (USD 1.3) per month for the lowest paid and MWK 1,800 (USD 2.4) for the highest paid. With only 20 ventilators for a population of close to 18 million, 25 intensive care units (ICU) beds, 28 nurses and two physicians per 100,000 people, the country showed its ill-preparedness to confront the pandemic.[42]

While the 2001 Abuja Declaration recommended that African governments allocate 15% of the national budget towards the health sector, Malawi has consistently (over the past 20 years) allocated less than 10% of its annual budget to this sector.[43] A number of alternative private health care centres exist, but these mainly operate at clinic and dispensary levels. Besides, they are not completely accessible to most poor Malawians who cannot afford to pay the hospital fees charged. With a backdrop of continued spread of HIV, tuberculosis (TB), malaria, malnutrition, and diarrheal diseases, the Malawi population was in a vulnerable state at the dawn of Covid-19. High rates of perinatal conditions, hypertension, diabetes, reproductive and adolescent health, and unsafe abortions, have further challenged the capacity of existing health care facilities.[44]

The health risk that Covid-19 presented provoked health workers to act against government negligence. Health workers from all public health centres demanded that the government recruit more professionals in the sector. They also petitioned government to provide them with better working conditions

---

41 Malawi Government, "Health Sector Strategic Plan II, 2017-2022", (April 2017), 15-16.

42 United Nations Red Cross Malawi, "Malawi Emergency Appeal (May-October 2020), UN Malawi, 2 May 2020.

43 Martha T. Makwero, "Delivery of Primary Health Care in Malawi", *African Journal of Primary Health Care and Family Medicine* 10/1 (2018), 1-3. See also Eyob Zere et al., "Health Financing in Malawi: Evidence from National Health Accounts", *International Health and Human Rights* 10/27 (2010), 1-11. Note that the 2020-2021 Annual Budget which the new government of President Lazarus Chakwera shelved allocated 9.7% to the health sector. See "Malawi military hospital construction to start: Budget allocates MK195 billion for heath sector budget", by Paul Chandimba Nkhoma, www.nyasatimes.com, 15 June 2020.

44 Malawi Government, "Health Sector Strategic Plan", 18-20.

including risk allowances, adequate PPE such as face shields, full-body work suits, goggles, high-filter masks, and water-repellent long-sleeve gowns. "Most of our public hospitals are lacking protective wears, and … our frontline staff are exposed to the risk of contracting the virus", complained Collins Mitambo, the president of the Medical Doctors Union of Malawi (MDUM).[45] The placards demonstrators carried corroborated these concerns, with one stating that "we are not on [a] suicide mission", further reminding the government that "my family [should] not suffer because of my calling".[46]

When government agreed to address these concerns, including raising the risk allowance by 70%, the National Organisation of Nurses and Midwives (NONM) encouraged its members to return to work. However, the health workers continued with their strike, arguing that they could not resume work based on mere pledges. Disregarding NONM's appeal, the MDUM chair-person challenged the government to fulfil its commitment: "The Minister [of Health] says he will address our grievances within two weeks. As a Union, we feel like we do not have much time. We request government to expedite on the process of procuring equipment and the recruiting of the workers."[47]

It turned out that the health officers were right to be skeptical because during his visit to Kamuzu Central hospital on 19 April, the Minister of Health seemed to renege from the initial promises. He argued that workers' demands of MK150,000 risk allowance was unrealistic. The minister also wondered why the health workers also demanded payment of allowances when off duty and on isolation.[48] These sentiments did not go down well with the health workers, with one of their leaders stating: "If you think our demands are unrealistic, come and work. But if you think our demands are realistic come and hear us out."[49] This resilience paid off. The government raised the monthly risk allowance from MWK 1,000 to MWK 20,000 (USD 27) for the lowest-paid and MWK 1,800 to MWK 60,000 (USD 80) for the highest-paid worker.[50] On 23 April 2020, health workers agreed to return to work. Subsequently, the

---

45 *Al Jazeera,* "Malawi Health Workers Protest Against Lack of Protective Gear", 14 April 2020.

46 Ibid.

47 Ibid.

48 *Nation Online,* 20 April 2020.

49 Ibid.

50 Secretary to health, Revision of Risk Allowances for Health Workers, Memo, dated 19 April 2020.

government embarked on the recruitment process of 2,000 targeted healthcare workers and the distribution of PPE.[51]

That did not mark the end of their campaign, however. Some selected individuals, particularly medical doctors, continued to push for better ways of addressing the pandemic beyond the provision of allowances and medical equipment. One such individual is Adamson Muula, a professor in public health based at the College of Medicine. While others criticised the lockdown, Muula considered it as less restrictive than what was implemented in other countries. He doubted whether such "a loose lockdown", would yield positive results.[52] In keeping with his profession, he argued that the decision on the lockdown, whether it faced opposition or not, should be primarily based on public health grounds, with those in authority presented with enough statistical data to assist them make the right decision. Other interested parties such as religious and human rights groups should be consulted for purposes of implementing a lockdown that did not fundamentally conflict with other rights. Muula feared that the multiple and opposing voices would derail the most pressing need of saving life.

Health workers might have celebrated the lockdown as a step towards reducing the spread of the virus and hence allowing the country's weak health system to cope with the rising number of Covid-19 cases. Some quarters of Malawian society, however, saw the public health measures as potentially conflicting with traditional values. Of note is how some Covid-19 preventive measures conflicted with existing societal norms and practices affecting social relations such as care for the sick and funeral arrangements. Most Malawians, especially those from the remote villages, found norms to "stay home" and abstain from traditional handshake greeting as conflicting with their tradition. In a society where sickness management is a collective responsibility of the community, the requirement for patients' isolation at hospitals has been similarly hard for family members to adopt. They also took issue with limiting the number of funeral attendants, disallowance of face viewing, and prohibition of night funeral vigils. Communities have often argued against burying their loved ones away from their family graveyards.[53] For them, the practice defies cultural perceptions of

---

51 *The Times,* "Health Workers End their Strike", 26 April 2020.

52 *The Times*, Adamson Muula, "Are There Enough Grounds for a Lockdown?" 22 April 2020.

53 The social media was awash with these stories with video clips depicting some men and women, among others, venting their anger against public health officers for "snatching" the

belonging that regard home as the village from which a person comes and where his/her ancestors are buried. Thus, communities that have lost their loved ones have often disputed attributing the cause to Covid-19 when the patient suffered from other ailments such as diabetes, asthma, high blood pressure, HIV and AIDS and tuberculosis. With such denials, families have not appreciated the government decision to bury their loved ones under special public health conditions. Such communities often regarded those discouraging others from attending funeral ceremonies as social misfits. Not surprisingly, from the time the government announced the first Covid-19 death, there have been battles between family members and health officials regarding funeral send-offs. In some cases, family members have had to grab deceased bodies from health officials for burial in their home villages.

Conflicts over Covid-19-related deaths in Malawi affirm the scholarly call to treat funerals beyond notions of static social institutions but as arenas of contestations where matters of "communal identity and belonging are debated and expressed".[54] Studies have shown that funerals in Africa serve as public spaces, or as avenues of unity and reunion, drawing relations together to a village space where familial relations are rekindled.[55] When such aspects as sorrow, grief, or care for one another—what Deborah Durham and Frederick Klaits described as "sentimental dispositions"—are destabilised, social dislocation can result.[56] Moreover, beyond establishing a sense of belonging and identity among the living, death also serves a similar purpose for the deceased. Burial in one's home village, noted Durham and Klaits in their study among the Tswana, helped to establish the deceased's identity.[57] Covid-19 public health interventions that disrupted the significant social function funerals serve were likely to be resisted, as Malawi's case illustrates.

Apart from these cultural concerns, one other aspect that has generated controversy is the management of people who tested positive for Covid-19. To

---

bodies of their loved ones. Others verbally protested against public health measures for contradicting their traditions, as illustrated here.

54 Rebekah Lee and Meghan Vaughan, "Introduction: Themes in the Study of Death and Loss in Africa", *African Studies* 71/2 (2012), 167.

55 Deborah Durham and Frederick Klaits, "Funerals and the Public Space of Sentiment in Botswana", *Journal of Southern African Studies* 28/4 (2002), 777–795; Michael Jindra and Joël Noret, J. (eds), *Funerals in Africa: Explorations of a Social Phenomenon*, New York: Berghahn Books, 2013.

56 Durham and Klaits, "Funerals", 779.

57 Ibid, 780-781.

control domestic transmission, the government mounted quarantine facilities in selected areas, besides designated hospital spaces. These spaces accommodated those diagnosed with Covid-19 and those showing symptoms of the pandemic. But most Malawians blamed the government for its casual approach in dealing with asymptomatic people, especially those coming from outside the country. The government encouraged this group to self-isolate, thereby raising fears about the silent spread of the virus. In places where the government quarantined incoming citizens, the results were disappointing. For example, since the inception of the pandemic, the government welcomed back over 2,000 Malawian traders trapped in South Africa under lockdown measures. The first group of 800 arrived at Mwanza border post on 25 May 2020. Of these, 400 escaped from a Chichiri quarantine facility in Blantyre, citing improper accommodation arrangements, poor food and inadequate toilets. Others also cited the delay in receiving the results of the Covid-19 tests conducted at the Mwanza border. Ironically, the returnees left the isolation centres in full view of security officers, who feared contracting the virus while trying to arrest them.[58]

These factors combined with party political issues further complicated the fight against the pandemic. While fully acknowledging the threat Covid-19 posed to the Malawian society, opposition politicians interpreted government's intention to impose a lockdown as a ploy to prevent the country from holding fresh presidential elections scheduled to take place on 3 July. As noted earlier, the opposition leaders, Chakwera of the MCP and Chilima of the UTM, had on 3 February 2020 successfully won a court case to nullify the May 2019 presidential elections. The court directed the MEC to organise a Fresh Presidential Election within 150 days.[59] Meanwhile, the HRDC mobilised the masses in protests to force the chairperson of the MEC, Justice Dr Jane Ansah, to resign from her position. For logistical reasons, however, the MEC successfully negotiated with Parliament to extend the date of the election to 3 July, which was later shifted back to 23 June to accommodate the dictates of the Constitutional Court ruling. Meanwhile, together with Peter Mutharika, the MEC appealed, albeit unsuccessfully, against the Constitutional Court ruling.

---

[58] *Voice of America News,* "Malawi at Risk! 400 Returnees Escape from Covid-19 Test Centre in Blantyre", 28 May 2020, www.voanews.com/covid-19-pandemic/400-migrant-workers-escape-covid-19-screening-camp-malawi.

[59] Malawi Parliament, Proceedings of the National Assembly, Presidential and Parliamentary Elections Bill, 24 February, 2020.

Seeing the dilly-dallying by both the MEC and the DPP, opposition leaders contended that the government was using the threat of Covid-19 including the proposed lockdown to frustrate the fresh elections for which the ruling DPP was least prepared. "This is election fever", argued Patricia Kaliati, the UTM Secretary General: "If at all they [the DPP government] have passion for the people, they would have looked at what to do to give to the people.... They are shivering [sic] because of the elections."[60] Leaders of the opposition parties feared that the lockdown would prevent them from conducting political campaign rallies. They were also worried that the lockdown would halt voter registration, leading to a delay or cancellation of elections.[61]

Unsurprisingly, the opposition leaders supported the HRDC in its bid to seek relief from the High Court through an injunction against the lockdown. The court's decision did not please some individuals in government circles, chief among them being President Mutharika. When asked to comment on the lockdown, he declined, arguing that the matter was still in court. "On our part", he emphasised, "we will proceed to do what [is] necessary to [save] lives as circumstances warrant. For me, the right to life is supreme above all other rights."[62] As noted, the injunction was to take effect on 17 April, and with the possibility of an indefinite extension on 27 April, somewhat forced the government to introduce the Emergency Cash Transfer Programme. As highlighted above, this programme never came to fruition.

While the state grappled with these contending interests, confirmed cases of Covid-19 increased, with many of those diagnosed being Malawians returning from South Africa. On 8 June, the number of confirmed cases had risen to 455 from 203 recorded on 28 May, with 55 recoveries and four deaths.[63] And by the time the country went to the polls on 23 June, Malawi had 941 confirmed cases, of which 618 were diagnosed among Malawian returnees, while the other 303 cases were locally transmitted.[64]

Amidst the chaos, disagreements, and disorganisation surrounding the Covid-19 pandemic in the country, fresh presidential elections were held as

---

60 *Zodiak Malawi,* Patricia Kaliati, Interview with Radio Zodiak Malawi, 17 April 2020.

61 Later, the judgment of the Supreme Court of Appeal ruled against registering new voters for the fresh elections.

62 OPC, Peter Mutharika's Presidential Address, 29 April 2020.

63 United Nations Children Education Fund (UNICEF), Malawi Covid-19 Situation Report, 4-6 June 2020.

64 Malawi Government, Malawi Covid-19 Daily Situation Report, 23 June 2020.

rescheduled. Lazarus Chakwera and his running mate, Saulos Chilima, representing the Tonse Alliance, won with a clear majority, scooping over 59% of the national votes cast. In accounting for these electoral results, Paul Tiyambe Zeleza cited eight factors, one of which was the coronavirus pandemic. For him, the virus "exposed the glaring incapacities of the state and the depth of socioeconomic inequalities in the country".[65]

Under the leadership of President Lazarus Chakwera and his vice president, Saulos Chilima, the new government stepped up the campaign against the pandemic. For instance, the Chakwera-led administration abruptly cancelled the 6 July independence celebrations, which would have coincided with the inaugural ceremony of his presidency. The government did so in response to a surge in the numbers of Covid-19 cases, which had jumped to 1,742 by 5 July 2020. Instead, Chakwera channelled all the remaining finances for the celebration to the fight against Covid-19. Furthermore, the new government announced stricter measures such as banning public gatherings and street vending, while prescribing mask-wearing for those patronising religious gatherings.[66] However, the new Attorney General challenged the measures through a stop order which he issued on 13 July 2020. The Attorney General argued that government was yet to lift the injunction the HRDC had obtained against such measures akin to a lockdown.

Having taken office and come to fully appreciate the challenges the country was facing, the new government established a National Covid-19 Office under the Office of the President and Cabinet on 15 July 2020. The Office was tasked to oversee governance of the Covid-19 pandemic through a National Secretariat and the Covid-19 Presidential Taskforce that the government also reconstituted on the same day.[67] While the former had 21 members, the new taskforce had 12 members, with Dr John Phuka and the Minister of Health as co-chairs. This was the third time within a period of five months that government had changed the Covid-19 committee. The extent to which the government seeks to fight the pandemic and ensure that Malawians adhere to

---

65 Paul T. Zeleza, "Malawi Makes History: The Opposition Wins Presidential Election Re-run", www.linkedin.com/pulse/Malawi-makes-history-opposition-wins-presidential-election-zeleza.

66 Malawi Government, "Covid-19 Situation Update as of 10th July 2020", Malawi Government Press Statement, 10 July 2020.

67 Malawi Government, Establishment of Covid-19 Office in the Office of President and Cabinet, Press Release, 15 July 2020.

Covid-19 measures is a question to which we can only provide partial explanation.

What is immediately discernible is how these stories illustrate the difficulties encountered in trying to isolate matters of public health from the socio-economic and political milieu of the society. They also have broader implications in the way we understand the state of governance in democratic Malawi and the role of the state in entrenching inclusive politics. In declaring the lockdown without due consultations, and instituting an all-Cabinet member Covid-19 Taskforce, the government disregarded significant voices in society and the contribution of others to crisis management. The massive opposition it faced was a reminder that such a governance style did not have space in a democratic society. The contestations display the agency of the citizenry, an awareness of its rights, and how to enforce them each time government undermined them. Opposition politicians, on their part, seem to have taken advantage of this consciousness and projected the fresh elections as representing a defence of greater political rights, all the while compromising the fight against Covid-19. What the chapter illustrates, therefore, is a societal demand for inclusive governance that those in power will have to embrace to claim political successes. However, such an assignment becomes more complicated in the context of a pandemic that seems to threaten the very democratic principles the state should uphold.

As noted, even countries with mature democracies have pursued lockdowns, which seem to threaten other rights. Within the African continent, countries like South Africa and Zimbabwe have grappled with these same concerns and instituted similar measures. South Africa enforced a total lockdown, albeit one that did not have immediate positive results, at least in the short term. As of 23 August 2020, the country had the highest number of Covid-19 cases in Africa, with 607,045 confirmed cases, of which 12,987 had died.[68] Similarly, Zimbabwe had then registered 5,893 cases with 153 deaths, slightly above Malawi's 5,382 cases.[69] Critics condemned the Zimbabwean government for implementing ruthless lockdown measures that suppressed popular demand for freedom and

---

68 WHO, "WHO Covid-19 Africa Update", 23 August 2020. See also Channing Arndt, et al., "Covid-19 Lockdowns, Income Distribution, and Food Security: An Analysis for South Africa", *Global Food Security*, 26 (2020), 1-5.

69 Ibid.

economic liberty.[70] Besides, the Zimbabwean government had been notorious for suppressing and arresting civil society members who challenged lockdown measures through street protests.

On the other hand, neighbouring Tanzania to the north provided an example of a country that seemingly respected people's livelihood rights and shunned public health measures such as lockdowns. The government questioned the authenticity of the Chinese Covid-19 testing kits and argued that the social and economic effects of lockdown would be much worse than Covid-19 itself.[71] Since then, the government stopped testing its citizenry of Covid-19, and on 8 June, it declared the country free of the pandemic.[72] However, evidence suggests that the government restricted access to information regarding the number of Covid-19 cases and censored domestic and international media in ways that contradict the tenets of democracy.[73]

Failure to implement a lockdown in Malawi might symbolise a victory for society over government. But it also reveals cracks within the diverse interest groups of the society—divisions which prohibited the formation of strong public opinion in favour of such unpopular public health measures. The conflicts and outright contradictions among the various responses to serious pandemics like that of Covid-19 pointed out above makes it very hard for a state to be "inclusive" to everyone. As with many countries across the continent, there were distinct disagreements among various "stakeholders". Public health officials focused on protecting the health of as many people as possible; street vendors, private school owners and other related groups were concerned primarily with the loss of income. There were also class and income differences which one can only highlight in passing. The concerns of the street sellers were different from those of the top professionals who could work "from home" because of easy access to the Internet. Besides, local people were worried about the very erosion of their traditions. Although the state needed to respect the citizens' concerns, it was just difficult to cope with all these contradictions. The task was difficult because it demanded reconciling rather

---

70 BBC, "Military and Police Thwarted Anti-Government Protests in Zimbabwe", 31 July 2020.

71 Robson Kondowe, "Tanzania's President is Blaming the Sharp Rise of Coronavirus Cases on Faulty Testing Kits", *Quartz Africa,* 4 May 2020.

72 *BBC,* "Coronavirus: John Magufuli Declares Tanzania Free of Covid-19", 8 June 2020.

73 *BBC,* "Coronavirus in Tanzania: What Do We Know", by Peter Mwai and Christopher Giles, 19 June 2020.

complex priorities. But understanding such contradictions is a step towards achieving a better and more inclusive society.

Conclusion

This chapter has analysed the political economy of Covid-19 in Malawi in the first seven months of 2020. It has analysed the country's political and economic climate in the period prior to and during the outbreak of the pandemic. The pandemic hit Malawi at a time when the country was in political turmoil associated with the disputed May 2019 General Election. Furthermore, millions of Malawians were also suffering economic hardship. As such, when the pandemic arrived, it became a weapon which various players used to contest the state on several underlying social, economic, and political ills that have for several years affected ordinary Malawians. Different stakeholders, including politicians, street vendors, health workers, educationists, and religious leaders, took advantage of the pandemic to challenge the government on specific concerns. The Covid-19 pandemic is yet to be arrested, such that it is difficult to draw any conclusions with certainty. The events of the first few months, precisely from February to July 2020, allow us to comment on aspects regarding how the pandemic speaks to the broader theme of the state and governance in Malawi. The events of the period seem to suggest that stakeholders' contestations were dynamic, complex, and varied. Besides, although other scholars usually present the state as an all-powerful entity capable of imposing its will on the society, the politics of Covid-19 do not corroborate this view. Instead, various stakeholders forced the Malawian state to compromise its stand on lockdown, call for fresh presidential elections even against the risk of spreading Covid-19. In telling the story of Covid-19 and the politics it engendered, we have argued that the Malawian public made demands that centred on their livelihoods and cultural concerns, all of which point to the need to uphold principles of inclusive governance when handling pandemics that demand unpopular public health measures. Respecting societal contribution to the working of the state is a first step to cultivating inclusive societies that seek to serve the varied interests of the citizenry. However, as legitimate as holding the government accountable is, compliance was complicated by the politics of the time as well as the prevailing divergent opinions and interests of the stakeholders.

Chapter 15

Malawi's Governance Crisis in Theological Perspective: A Tale of Two Cultures

Mzee Hermann Yokoniah Mvula
& Kenneth R. Ross

This chapter seeks to explore the currents that shape political culture at the deep level that underlies the structures of democracy and the conduct of politics. It employs theological analysis to expose deep-lying flaws that have resulted in deficient governance in Malawi and to indicate resources that may be of value in terms of remedy. To demonstrate how enduring some of these flaws have been, it begins with a 25-year retrospect, reviewing a 1995 theological analysis of Malawi's political life. Having delineated a faulty political culture, it lays out some of the theological resources that can be of service at this level: the biblical text, global theological thinking and local contextual theology. Applying these to the question of governance in Malawi, it focuses on three particular issues: corruption and plunder, impunity and accountability, and the question of leadership. These are considered with specific reference to the Malawi context but lessons learned can be applicable in other African countries and indeed in the wider world where good governance is very much at stake even in some long-established democracies.

A 25-Year Retrospect

In the mid-1990s Malawi was emerging from 30 years of one-party dictatorship and seeking to build a new, democratic political culture. This proved to be harder to achieve than was first expected. Ways of thinking that had become engrained during the one-party era, and even the colonial period that preceded it, reasserted themselves. Even with democratic freedoms and a democratic Constitution there were a number of factors that inhibited the development of a democratic political culture. Among the first to take account of these from a theological perspective was Kenneth Ross, co-author of this chapter. In 1995 he wrote an essay titled, "A Practical Theology of Power for the New Malawi", that examined the emerging political landscape theologically.[1] We begin our attempt to offer theological perspectives on Malawi's political culture in 2020 by revisiting the 1995 essay and asking how far the issues raised have been resolved and how far they remain unfinished business.

The essay began by citing an observation by the historian Terry Ranger on the 1960-90 period in Africa: "The churches came to be seen as the only surviving institutions which ordinary people still trusted. Political institutions have lost all credibility, but ecclesiastical institutions have been gaining it."[2] At the time, this seemed a remarkable turnaround. In the 1960s, initiative lay with the nationalist movements that were forming the first independent governments in African countries and the churches seemed to be on the back foot. Malawi is a case in point where, after the politically hopeful days of the 1960s, many became disillusioned with the one-party regime of Kamuzu Banda and looked to the churches as the most likely agent of change.[3] In the subsequent period from the mid-1990s to 2020, though the churches have also had their problems, they have continued to enjoy greater credibility than political institutions.

At times of political crisis, people have looked to the churches. When the integrity of the Constitution was threatened by an attempt in 2002-03 to change it to allow President Bakili Muluzi to stand for a third term, it was the churches which were widely credited with defending the Constitution.[4] When there was widespread loss of confidence in the Bingu wa Mutharika Government in 2011-12 it was the church-led Public Affairs Committee that played a decisive role in addressing the crisis. In 2019-20 the courts and the judiciary took a leading role in addressing the political crisis that followed a flawed presidential election but the churches were also significant players, notably through the Catholic Bishops' Pastoral Letter, *A Further Call for a New Era in Malawi: Leadership at the*

---

1 Kenneth R. Ross, "A Practical Theology of Power for the New Malawi", in Kenneth R. Ross ed., *God, People and Power in Malawi: Democratization in Theological Perspective*, Blantyre: CLAIM-Kachere, 1996, 225-67.

2 Terence Ranger, "Conference Summary and Conclusion", in Paul Gifford ed., *The Christian Churches and the Democratisation of Africa*, Leiden: E.J. Brill, 1995, 19, cit. Kenneth R. Ross, "A Practical Theology of Power for the New Malawi", 225.

3 See Kenneth R. Ross, "Not Catalyst But Ferment: The Distinctive Contribution of the Churches to Political Reform in Malawi 1992-93", in Matembo S. Nzunda and Kenneth R. Ross eds., *Church, Law and Political Transition in Malawi 1992-94*, Blantyre: CLAIM-Kachere, 1995, 31-42.

4 Kenneth R. Ross, "'Worrisome Trends': The Voice of the Churches in Malawi's Third Term Debate", *African Affairs* 103 (2004), 91-107, republished in *Mission as God's Spiral of Renewal*, Mzuzu: Mzuni Press, 2019, 298-319.

Service of Citizens, issued on 23 May 2020.[5] Despite being politically compromised themselves at times and often disturbed by their own internal politics, Malawian churches have retained the credibility that Ranger identified as a surprising but unmistakeable feature of public life in sub-Saharan Africa in the early 1990s.

As regards salient issues identified in 1995, the essay turned first to the question of accountability for the abuses perpetrated during the one-party period. Could a new era begin without settling the ghosts of the old one? This was the time when South Africa was embarking on its Truth and Reconciliation Commission and the question was asked whether something similar was needed in Malawi. In the event, apart from a few cases like the Mwanza murders, there was never any comprehensive reckoning with the injustice and suffering that was inflicted on many thousands during the one-party era. The most serious attempt was the work of the National Compensation Tribunal but it was limited in its range and effectiveness.[6] Thankfully the democratic era has been free of such injustices as detention without trial while, notwithstanding the activities of the UDF Young Democrats and the DPP Cadets, political violence has been reduced in scale. Government impunity, however, remains an issue. Government tends to find ways to avoid scrutiny and has successfully resisted the development of a culture of accountability. As a result, government misdemeanours remain unaddressed and, as John de Gruchy observed, "to repress the demons of the past inevitably means the bedevilment of the future".[7]

The essay's next topic, the "spectre of regionalism", does not require any lengthy discussion to demonstrate that it is still a determining factor in Malawi's political culture. If anything, regionalism is more deeply entrenched in 2020 than in 1995. Political parties continue to rely on a particular ethnic and regional base, depending on its support to propel them to power and then governing for its benefit. The CCAP, which was singled out as a church whose structure is regionalist, has become less of a national body and more of a regional one.[8] Far from achieving the "closer cooperation and unity among the Synods" for

5 Episcopal Conference of Malawi, *A Further Call for a New Era in Malawi: Leadership at the Service of Citizens*, Pastoral Letter, 23 May 2020.

6 See *History and Hope in Malawi: Repression, Suffering and Human Rights under Dr Kamuzu Banda, 1964-1994*, Blantyre: Government of Malawi, 2005.

7 John W. de Gruchy, *Christianity and Democracy*, Cambridge: Cambridge University Press, 1995, 217, cit. Kenneth R. Ross, "A Practical Theology of Power for the New Malawi", 234.

8 See further Rhodian Munyenyembe, *Pursuing an Elusive Unity: A History of the Church of Central Africa Presbyterian as a Federative Denomination (1924-2018)*, Carlisle: Langham, 2019.

which the World Alliance of Reformed Churches called in 1995, it has moved in the opposite direction.[9] The long-running border dispute between Nkhoma and Livingstonia synods has effectively disabled the General Assembly that is intended to unite the synods. They have been more inclined to identify with the political party that represents their region than with their fellow synods in the CCAP. The Catholic bishops are better placed to point out that: "Malawi is now departing from the unifying spirit of our forefathers and going towards fragmentation and tribalism … This is a very dangerous road we are taking as a nation."[10] The spectre of regionalism still hangs heavily over Malawi.

Regionalism is all the more damaging when it is allied to corruption and nepotism. Already in 1995 it was noted that, "Much popular concern has been focused on the conspicuous consumption and suspected corruption of government ministers and others entrusted with high office. Democratisation has evidently done little to challenge the 'gravy train' mentality inherited from the colonial and one-party periods in which access to resources was centrally controlled and political involvement a matter of bettering oneself through the patronage of the powerful..[11]

During the subsequent years Malawi has continued to suffer from various types of corruption—from high-level political corruption to petty bribery that impedes service delivery. Patronage and nepotism exacerbate inequality and poverty. Corruption is seen to be particularly severe in the police, registry and permit services, customs and the judiciary. There are also reports of widespread corruption and extortion by public officials in procurement and it is widely understood that this extends to the highest levels of government. Matters came to a head with the Cashgate scandal of 2013 when it was estimated that some 35% of government funds had been stolen over the previous decade.[12] This goes a long way to explain why a tiny elite has prospered financially while the great majority of the population have seen services deteriorate and living standards diminish. At the same time, during the democratic era questions have

9 World Alliance of Reformed Churches, "Report of Pastoral Team Visit to the Church of Central Africa Presbyterian (CCAP), Malawi, 30 June–3 July 1995", Geneva, 1995, 3, cit. Kenneth R. Ross, "A Practical Theology of Power for the New Malawi", 238.

10 Episcopal Conference of Malawi, *A Further Call for a New Era in Malawi*, 3.

11 Kenneth R. Ross, "A Practical Theology of Power for the New Malawi", 245.

12 Baker Tilly, Report on Fraud and Mismanagement of Malawi Government Finances from April to September 2013, Lilongwe: NAO, 2014.

arisen over whether the churches have proved resistant to the culture of corruption or can they too be bought?

Sections of the essay on "A Re-definition of Politics" and "The Drive for Popular Participation" highlighted how, despite the introduction of the structures and institutions of democracy, there was a stubborn tendency for politics to remain the preserve of the elite. As John Minnis observed, "The party tends to be seen as *the* site of politics, the source of political truth and wisdom; the people, on the other hand, are viewed as being politically immature and in need of 'education'."[13] By 2020, while such attitudes remain ingrained in the minds of many political leaders, there was increasing agency on the part of the people. The large-scale protests that followed the flawed presidential election of May 2019 demonstrated that ordinary people were ready to take political responsibility and action.

When journalist Susan Dalgety interviewed Rev Maxwell Mezuwa Banda, retired Synod of Livingstonia minister and former Electoral Commissioner, in late 2019, he remarked: "Malawi has always been peaceful, with people accepting their lot. But there comes a time when people say enough is enough, we cannot go on like this. I think that time has come."[14] It may be that the popular mobilisation that marked the post-election situation in 2019 was a signal from the people of Malawi that they can no longer be taken for granted by their politicians. However, given the acceptance of domination by the elite that pervades public consciousness, there remains a long way to go before there will be a political culture marked by popular participation.[15]

A related issue, possibly still more intractable, is the polarisation between rich and poor that was highlighted in the 1995 essay. Already at that time there were signs that, far from addressing the inequalities in society that played a big part in provoking the movement for political change, the democratic dispensation might be further entrenching them. This has continued to be the trend up until 2020. A popular play in 1995, *Tisaiwale*, had a bishop tell his people that if you

---

13 J.R. Minnis, "Prospects and Problems for Civil Society in Malawi", in Kings M. Phiri and Kenneth R. Ross (eds), *Democratization in Malawi: A Stocktaking*, Blantyre: CLAIM-Kachere, 1998, 145-65 [163].

14 Int. Maxwell Mezuwa Banda, October 2019, cit. Susan Dalgety, *Spirit of Malawi*, Edinburgh: Luath Press, forthcoming 2021.

15 Perhaps one reason for political participation taking long could be patronage where the elites act in ways that show that they are the ones that matter and not the electorate or the masses. John Lwanda calls this "the Achukulire syndrome". See John L. Lwanda, *Kamuzu Banda of Malawi*, Zomba: Kachere, 2010.

were married to a husband who was constantly beating you and you decided to remarry only to find that you could not eat or clothe yourself, you would think twice about whether or not the change had been worth it.[16] This has turned out to be prophetic. Economic hardship during the democratic era has prompted many to look back nostalgically to the supposedly better times of the Banda dictatorship. The beatings have been forgotten and what is remembered is a better standard of living. Meanwhile, a minority has flourished economically during the democratic era, causing the gap between the rich and the poor to grow wider and wider. The polarisation that was already an issue in 1995 is even more serious in 2020.

A Question of Political Culture

What was already becoming apparent in 1995 and is even clearer in 2020 is that there are deep-lying flaws in Malawi's political culture that have inhibited the successful development of good governance.[17] The democratic Constitution of 1994[18] provided the structures that could support a successful democracy. However, an underlying political culture carried forward from periods of authoritarian and exploitative rule has proved to be a stronger influence in determining the direction of governance, much to Malawi's detriment.[19] Such pervasive issues as government impunity, regionalism, patrimonialism, nepotism, corruption, elitism and inequality are yet to be resolved.

Another feature of the past 25 years in Malawi has been the continuing growth of Christianity, with more than 80% of the population now professing to be Christians. The churches that emerged from the missions established in the late 19th and early 20th centuries have been augmented by new movements and a proliferation of churches and ministries. The spirituality, thinking and daily behaviour of many Malawians are much influenced by their participation in church life. The question being addressed in this chapter is whether this faith dimension of Malawian life can yield resources that are relevant to the renewal

16 Cit. Kenneth R. Ross, "A Practical Theology of Power for the New Malawi", 255.

17 For a revealing study of an earlier period in Malawi's political history see Joey Power, *Political Culture and Nationalism in Malawi: Building Kwacha*, Rochester: University of Rochester Press, 2010.

18 The Constitution was adopted in 1994, but there were some revisions in 1995.

19 See Harri Englund, "Introduction: The Culture of Chameleon Politics", in Harri Englund ed., *A Democracy of Chameleons: Politics and Culture in the New Malawi*, Stockholm: Nordiska Afrikainstitutet and Blantyre: CLAIM-Kachere, 2002, 11-24.

of Malawian political culture. In other words, are there theological perspectives that can add value in Malawi's quest for good governance?

In pursuing this question, we recognise that in the Malawi context, besides theological resources drawn from Christianity, Islamic theological perspectives offer a necessary and significant contribution to the discussion—which requires consideration in its own right. We are also aware that Christianity is by no means monolithic. It includes different expressions of faith and different forms of theology. During the past 25 years, a rising force in Malawi has been a fundamentalist "moral majority" kind of Christianity that envisages extending its influence through assertive political engagement, with the aim of creating a confessional Christian state.[20] This too is a subject that deserves attention in its own right. Within the limitations of this one chapter, however, we confine ourselves to an attempt to mine some Christian theological resources that might be of service when it comes to resolving current issues that lie at the heart of Malawi's crisis of governance.

The importance of this question lies in the fact that Malawi's failures in governance are derived more from a faulty political culture than from any shortcomings in the constitutional and political structures of the country. It is the way people think, their motivations and ambitions that are in need of transformation. Here religious and theological considerations can be formative. This is not to say that theology can automatically hand down ready-made solutions to deep-lying political problems. Indeed, bad theology can have the opposite effect. But it is to recognise that, especially in a country where a large majority are active in the life of faith, there is a theological resource available that can be brought to bear on the issues at stake. Fundamental attitudes to such matters as the exercise of power, accountability, identity, democratic participation and social justice can be significantly shaped by theological considerations. It is at the fundamental level of understanding the nature and purpose of institutions of government that Malawi has struggled to build firm foundations. This means that reforms at the institutional level, however well-designed, only have limited effect. There is need for a more fundamental guiding vision to be established and this is where theological perspectives can be relevant.

---

[20] See James Tengatenga, "*Moral Majority* redivivus: Assertive religious politics and the threat to religious freedom and citizenship in Malawi", *Stellenbosch Theological Journal* 5/3 (2019), 165-82.

This chapter will indicate three sources of such theological perspectives and suggest how these might be deployed in addressing challenges of governance in Malawi. The first is the biblical text. The Bible is a constant point of reference in Malawian life but perhaps its value in regard to the political context has not yet been fully exploited. The second is global theological thinking. Malawi is not an island and many of the governance issues it faces are not unique. Therefore, there can be value in tuning in to global theological discourse. The third is local contextual theology. Malawian theologians have been active in addressing governance issues, particularly during the democratic era. Surveying their work can yield resources relevant to current challenges. Having mined these different resources, the chapter will conclude by drawing out theological perspectives that are urgently needed in relation to the crisis of governance in Malawi revealed by the events of 2019-20.

The Biblical Text

It would be hard to overestimate the reach and resonance of the biblical text in the Malawian context. For many households, the Bible is the only book they possess. Moreover, its stories and teachings are constantly recounted orally—at home, at church, in popular music, in public discourse and in everyday conversations. For many, it functions as a sacred and authoritative text—one to which they pay attention as they seek direction in their lives. It can have application in many different dimensions of life, including the political. To illustrate how it might have value in relation to political culture, we take just one text: Deuteronomy 17:14-20, a passage that concerns political processes and the conduct of political leaders.

> When you enter the land the LORD your God is giving you and have taken possession of it and settled in it, and you say, 'Let us set a king over us like all the nations around us' be sure to appoint over you the king the LORD your God chooses. He must be from among your own brothers.... The king, moreover, must not acquire great numbers of horses for himself or make the people return to Egypt... he must not take many wives or his heart will be led astray. He must not accumulate large amounts of silver and gold. When he takes the throne of his kingdom, he is to write for himself on a scroll a copy of this law, taken from that of the priests, who are the Levites. It is to be with him, and he is to read it all the days of his life so that he may learn to revere the LORD his God and follow carefully all the words of this law and these decrees and consider himself better than his brothers and turn from the law to the right or to the left....[21]

[21] Our italics showing emphasis.

This remarkable text of Deuteronomy argues that Israelite kings must differentiate themselves from all other kings who enjoy *mass weapons* (military prestige), *much wealth* (silver and gold), and *many wives* (harem). J.A Thomson states, "Only the study of this law could preserve him from the temptations which beset a king. Military aggrandisement, an enlarged harem and the pursuit of wealth would turn his heart away from Yahweh and his commandments and cause him to lift up his heart above his brothers."[22] In the context of the day, it might have been wondered whether it was worth being king at all on such terms, but this was the case with the kings of Israel. The requirements were deliberate, i.e., to place kings on equal footing with the citizens so that they would not feel super-human, an attitude that has characterised most political leaders in Malawi. Consequently, the passage demonstrates the authentic biblical concept of political leadership and governance as mutual servanthood as explicitly stated in 1 Kings 12:7: "If today you will be a *servant* to these people and *serve* them, they will always be your *servants*."[23]

The passage in Deuteronomy presents a concept of servant leadership where the leader/king is a servant of both God and the people. Leadership and/or governance principles are given in form of requirements and restrictions thereby allowing the law to permeate the leader's behavior in every sphere, whether political, administrative, judicial or military.[24] Therefore, the passage shows "a radically different, consciously distinct and counter-cultural model of political leadership and governance altogether. It is a model that limits power, prestige and private gain—hence it puts all political executive authority firmly under the authority of the law itself."[25]

Based on this passage, therefore, a number of crucial theological motifs and ethical trajectories for contemporary Malawi's governance and political culture can be drawn:

1. Political leaders are like any other citizen—hence they should not feel special;
2. Political leaders are the people's servants—they must serve them;
3. Political leaders are to be democratically elected—since power belongs to the people to choose who they want to lead and serve them;

22 J.A. Thomson, *Deuteronomy: An Introduction and Commentary*, edited by D.J. Wiseman, Leicester: Inter-Varsity Press, 1974, 206.

23 Our italics. This is the pattern of political leadership in Israel, nowhere more succinctly expressed than in the advice given to Rehoboam by his older advisors.

24 Christopher Wright, *Deuteronomy*, Grand Rapids, MI: Baker Books, 1996, 207.

25 Ibid, 210.

4. Political leaders are to uphold and enforce the law—they must be the first to practise constitutionalism to set an example and demand the same from the people;
5. Political leaders are accountable first and foremost to God, then to the electorate;
6. God must be involved in our governance affairs, notably in our political processes.[26]

The passage in Deuteronomy shows that, while the term democracy[27] does not appear in the Bible, the concept is implied and is as old as the time of Moses or even further back to the times described in the Book of Genesis, a time usually referred to as the Primeval Period. While at a popular level the Bible may seem as if it does not directly talk about democracy, it can be argued that biblical moral values show us that the best form of government is democracy, where the intrinsic worth of human beings is fundamental.[28] Therefore, democracy as a system of governance has its foundations in biblical ethical principles of goodness, fairness and justice.[29] Theologically, the values on which democracy depends must be promoted by all because scripturally that is what God desires for all peoples.[30] Hence, political leaders must be accountable on these values, and practise such values and principles as they seek to consolidate democracy in Malawi. Such an exercise of biblical moral principles can help repudiate the hegemonic demagoguery evident among some political leaders in Malawi which has brought in bad governance tendencies. Therefore, by a brief examination of the Deuteronomy passage, it is demonstrable that the Bible carries potential to inform, challenge and inspire the healthy political culture that is needed if Malawi is to build a strong foundation in terms of democracy and good governance.[31]

---

26 See ibid.

27 For further discussion on democracy see Bernard Joinet, *Step by Step Towards Democracy*, Nairobi: Paulines Publications Africa, 2000; Bernard Joinet, *The Challenge of Modernity in Africa*, Nairobi: Paulines Publications Africa, 2000; Oskar Wermter, *Politics for Everyone and By Everyone: A Christian Approach*, Nairobi: Paulines Publications Africa, 2003.

28 See e.g. Hans Haselbarth, Christian Ethics in the African Context, Nairobi: Uzima Press, 1978.

29 See Afrifa Gitonga, "The Meaning of and Foundations of Democracy", in W.O Oyugi and A Gitonga (eds), *Democratic Theory and Practice in Africa*, Nairobi: East African Educational Publishers, 1987.

30 See Christopher Wright, *Deuteronomy*, Grand Rapids: Baker Books, 1996.

31 See Wright, *Deuteronomy*, 210. Wright argues that the Deuteronomic law for the king should be included in any attempt to derive ethical principles for the political life from the OT.

Global Theological Thinking

One way to get the measure of global theological thinking is to tune in to the major conferences of the World Council of Churches. Its 2018 World Mission Conference, hosted at Arusha in Tanzania, was the latest in a series held on a roughly decennial basis since 1910.[32] Under the heading "Moving in the Spirit: Called to Transforming Discipleship", the Conference took account of the global context. It recognised that, "we are living in times when our shared life is volatile, uncertain, fragile and fragmented".[33] It lamented the ascendancy of death-dealing forces: "the nationalism and fundamentalism that foment hatred, the militarism that stokes conflict, the greed that concentrates resources in the hands of the few at the expense of the many, and a new type of colonialism associated with the despotic reach of the culture of money". It highlighted "issues such as forced migration, disease and its effects on the population, ecological degradation, war and conflict, gender inequalities, exclusion and marginalisation, appropriation of land, poverty and unemployment, and a reduction of social welfare and security".[34]

As the Conference probed the reasons for such a troubled global context it put its finger on one issue above all: "the shocking accumulation of wealth due to one global financial system, which enriches few and impoverishes many. This is at the root of many of today's wars, conflicts, ecological devastation, and suffering. This global imperial system has made the financial market one of the idols of our time."[35] Faced with gross injustice on a global scale it seems that politics has been eviscerated and rendered impotent. The neoliberal global economic order exercises such hegemony that neither national governments nor international institutions can challenge its injustices and excesses. A powerful economic order has been imposed and all are expected to comply. This is, in the trenchant words of the Call issued by the Arusha Conference, "the false god of the market system". Social injustice and political failure in Malawi are set in context by these global realities.

---

32 See Risto Jukko and Jooseop Keum eds., Moving in the Spirit: Report of the World Council of Churches Conference on World Mission and Evangelism, 8-13 March 2018, Arusha, Tanzania, Geneva: WCC, 2019.

33 Ibid, 8.

34 Ibid.

35 Ibid, 2.

The task at Arusha, however, was not simply to lament destructive global trends but to discern the meaning of Christian mission in today's world. The Conference did so by returning to a fundamental theme of the Gospels—Jesus' call to discipleship, defined as: "a Christ-connected way of life".[36] In the vision cast at Arusha, discipleship is a very wide-ranging commitment stretching from personal spirituality to communal commitment to action for justice in the world at large. The Conference was particularly alert to the dynamics of exclusion and set a course that contrasts with prevailing conditions in many contexts today: "We are called as disciples to belong together in just and inclusive communities, in our quest for unity and on our ecumenical journey, in a world that is based upon marginalisation and exclusion."[37] Malawi is not spared from this reality of exclusion as many feel that they are not being given any chance. The Arusha Conference was responding to their experience.

Another sharp contrast was drawn by the Conference when it affirmed that, "We are called to worship the one triune God—the God of justice, love and grace—at a time when many worship the false god of the market system."[38] The economic realities that are so determinative for human life today were interrogated in theological terms to expose an idolatry no less destructive than that which called for human sacrifice in ancient times. It is against the all-encompassing reality of the market system that the meaning of faith and discipleship have to be negotiated. This also involves a reckoning with the exercise of power.

In all of this the Conference set a premium on the question of leadership: "We are called to be formed as servant leaders who demonstrate the way of Christ in a world that privileges power, wealth, and the culture of money."[39] In line with its central theme, the Arusha Call set the question of leadership in the context of discipleship. It recognised that a call to *servant* leadership very much goes against the grain so far as today's prevailing culture is concerned. In place of domination and exclusion it called for a form of leadership that is marked by "mutuality, reciprocity, humility and interdependence".[40] It echoed the Lausanne Movement 2010 Cape Town Conference's assertion that "authentic Christian leaders must be like Christ in having a servant heart, humility,

---

36 Ibid.
37 Ibid, 3.
38 Ibid.
39 Ibid, 3.
40 Ibid.

integrity, purity, lack of greed, prayerfulness, dependence on God's Spirit, and a deep love for people".[41] In a global context where leadership is often being moulded by destructive forces, the Conference pointed to the way of Christ.

Local Contextual Theology

As well as an ancient text and a global community to inform theological thinking, a third resource to be considered is the local context. Malawi has produced her own theologians who have attempted to think through the meaning of the faith in relation to the local situation. An important pioneer in this respect was Patrick Kalilombe, Catholic Bishop of Lilongwe (1972-76). As he sought to reorganise the Diocese around the concept of base Christian communities, giving greater initiative to the church at local level, he was exposed to the suspicion that he was attempting to create a rival political movement and was ultimately forced to go into exile. At one level this reflects no more than the paranoia of the one-party regime since Kalilombe had no intention of starting a rival political party. At a deeper level, however, the Banda regime might well have been right in perceiving that Kalilombe's work represented a kind of theology that invited political application and that might present a significant challenge to the prevailing system.

He reflected later that the approach he was developing carried a critical and disturbing quality: "that type of theology is neither neutral nor merely theoretical. It is a theology that aims at transforming society by constantly questionning the *status quo* and working to change it. It uses the SEE-JUDGE-ACT methodology."[42] Such questioning was not welcome in Banda's Malawi of the 1970s. Nonetheless Kalilombe continued to champion a grassroots theology that, in his words, "is capable of unleashing a power among those who hitherto have been powerless, so that they can begin to change the *status quo*".[43] In this way he did much to set the scene for a Malawian contextual theology.

Another theologian who took on the mantle of contextual theologian is Augustine Musopole, particularly during the first two decades of Malawi's democratic era when he brought theological thinking to bear on current issues. He was alert to the fact that there were issues of political culture that needed

---

[41] Lausanne Movement, Cape Town Commitment, 2010, §3.

[42] Patrick A. Kalilombe, *Doing Theology at the Grassroots: Theological Essays from Malawi*, Gweru: Mambo-Kachere, 1999, 173.

[43] Ibid, 189.

to be addressed: "While the country may have a reputation of being a democracy, it is not run in a democratic manner. The very parties that are governing the country are themselves not democratic in their operation. What seems to be the case is that Malawi is being treated by the leadership as if it were a personal estate and its people as if they were exploited tenants."[44] He was forthright in pointing out how, despite the introduction of a democratic Constitution, governance continued to be autocratic: "using fear, violence, women, youth, chiefs, the state apparatus, namely police, MBC, now MTV etc., the tactics of divide and rule, claims of invincibility, ill-gotten wealth, job patronage, … lies, and manipulative politics".[45]

As Musopole searched for a philosophical and theological basis on which to challenge a faulty political culture, he proposed that the home-grown concept of *uMunthu* could be a guiding light, always remembering that *uMunthu* finds its ultimate expression in Jesus Christ.[46] On his analysis, it was a recovery of true humanity that was needed to bring renewal to Malawian political life. Such a recovery would counter the culture of violence and foster a participatory and consensual democracy.[47] It would cultivate a vital symbiosis between the human community and the environment. It would counter regionalism and nepotism and demonstrate a preferential option for the poor, the weak and the marginalised.[48] Corruption was a theme to which he often returned, lamenting the fact that corruption (loosely translated as *katangale*—"stealing") had become the order of the day: "The government is being impoverished by the day in this way and those involved are the very people given the responsibility to guard public property."[49] Again, Musopole traced the malaise back to a failure to properly understand and appreciate the nature of our humanity. As human beings we cannot flourish so long as we depend on craftiness, cheating and theft.[50]

---

44 Augustine Musopole, "Politics: Malawi's Privatisation", *The Lamp* 47 (May-June 2004), 18-19 [18].

45 Augustine Musopole, "A Theology of Governance", *The Lamp* 40 (November-December 2003) 6-7, at 6.

46 See further Augustine Chingwala Musopole, *uMunthu Theology: An Introduction*, Mzuzu: Mzuni Press, 2021.

47 Ibid, 7.

48 Ibid, 7.

49 See e.g. Augustine Musopole, "Honest Men and Women, Honest Pay and Honest Work", *The Lamp* 27 (January-February 2001), 6-7, at 6.

50 Ibid, 7.

In more recent years Qeko Jere has stepped into this role, mining theological resources to offer critical perspectives on issues in the public realm. [51] On the deeply entrenched issue of corruption, for example, he assesses the public role of the church in anti-corruption work and argues that the defeat of corruption requires not only secular mechanisms but theologically based approaches where biblical teaching on moral and ethical conduct can inform and inspire the effort. He indicates some of the resources that are available to bring theological perspectives into play: using the pulpit for advocacy against corruption, pastoral empowerment to generate prophetic critique, promoting collaboration for effective governance and integrating gender for effective collaboration in anti-corruption work.[52]

One outstanding example of contextual theology, highlighted by Jere, is the pastoral letters through which the churches have addressed public life in Malawi. [53] Since the Catholic Bishops' Pastoral Letter of Lent 1992, *Living our Faith*, reshaped the socio-political landscape, this form of action from the churches has gained a special place in the popular imagination. The bishops themselves have capitalised on this by issuing pastoral letters at moments when there seemed to be much at stake in national life, often on the eve of elections. The democratic era in Malawi has therefore been punctuated by a series of such letters, with the efforts of the Catholic bishops sometimes complemented by letters from the CCAP. These represent contextual theology, bringing biblical teaching to bear on such social issues as corruption, poverty, abortion, same sex marriage, nepotism, regionalism and tribalism. The fact that pastoral letters have become an accepted part of Malawian public life demonstrates the value that is accorded to contextual theology. The churches are regarded as both watchdog and guide dog, protecting Malawi's democracy from danger and bringing theological vision to the politics of the day.[54]

---

51 See Qeko Jere, "Public Role of the Church in Anti-corruption: An Assessment of the CCAP Livingstonia Synod in Malawi from a Kenosis Perspective", *Verbum et Ecclesia* 39/1 (2018); Qeko Jere, "Pastoral Letters and the Church in the Public Square: An Assessment of the Role of Pastoral Letters in Influencing Democratic Processes in Malawi", *Verbum et Ecclesia* 39/1 (2018); Qeko Jere, "Perichoretic Interaction within the Trinity as a Paradigm for Fostering Unity in the Public Affairs Committee (PAC) in Malawi", *Stellenbosch Theological Journal* 4/2 (2018), 553-578.

52 See Jere, "Public Role of the Church in Anti-corruption".

53 Jere, "Pastoral Letters and the Church in the Public Square".

54 There is, of course, variety in the approach of churches to public life but this is a topic that merits dedicated consideration, which space cannot allow in this present chapter.

Malawi in Crisis 2019-20: Theological Perspectives

The crisis of 2019-2020 has shed much light on issues of governance in Malawi. It became clear that the prevailing political order was not serving Malawi well. The Tonse Alliance Government was elected in June 2020 on a prospectus of addressing its deficiencies. When examined from a theological perspective, at least three issues stand out in clear relief: corruption, impunity and leadership.

Corruption and Plunder

If there is one issue above all others that demonstrates the decisive role of the prevailing political culture it is that of corruption. No government ever takes office with a pro-corruption policy. On the contrary, invariably the government professes to be highly committed to eradicating corruption. In Malawi's case there is also a statutory Anti-Corruption Bureau. Nonetheless corruption has remained a running sore throughout Malawi's democratic era, with the 2013 Cashgate scandal turning out to be only the tip of the iceberg. Regardless of the systems in place to resist corruption, regardless of the rhetoric that unreservedly condemns it, corruption continues since it is supported by a political culture of treating public office as an opportunity for personal enrichment. As Harri Englund observed in 2002: "The shallowness of the democratic reform has become evident in tandem with the new leaders' demonstrated capacity to continue with corruption and plunder. The 'paraphernalia of democracy'—multipartyism, regular Parliamentary and Presidential elections, new Constitutions, freedom of expression, a non-governmental sector—have ensured the flow of development aid that leaders may appropriate for their locally and regionally-defined orbits of power."[55]

This culture of corruption has become so engrained that it is expected and accepted by the general public. How can it ever be dislodged? Another contributing factor is that after 26 years of multiparty democracy, governance in Malawi remains heavily centralised. The president makes even the smallest of decisions and undertakes mundane tasks that should be reserved for line ministries. This encourages a system of patronage. Government contracts, tenders and board memberships all go to sympathisers of the party in power and not necessarily to the best bidder or the most competent applicant. Government sympathisers or ruling party members get contracts regardless of

---

55 Englund, "Introduction: The Culture of Chameleon Politics", 19.

their levels of competence. Such neopatrimonialism has become so much a way of life that it has become difficult to imagine anything else.

All the evidence suggests that there needs to be some deep reformation if corruption is to be eliminated from public life in Malawi. A theology of humanity and a theology of community could have a part to play. Prevalence of corruption indicates that there has been a loss of true understanding of the meaning of our humanity. A theology that recovers the dignity and responsibility of living a human life can become an assault force combatting the prevalence of corruption by undercutting it at the profound level of what it means to be human. At this juncture, the biblical text is a critical resource as it condemns all forms of graft. Old Testament scholar Christopher Wright observes: "Bribery is singled out as the worst form of corruption because it blinds the eyes of the wise, that is, it makes those who should have the wisdom to act with insight and understanding behave as if they were foolish and uninformed."[56] Alert to such dangers, ethical political leadership will avoid indulging in any form of graft so as to serve God faithfully and people diligently. Likewise, a theology of community that emphasises what we owe to one another and counters greed and self-interest can help to dissolve the wrong motivations that drive corruption. A theology of *uMunthu*, as Augustine Musopole has argued, can draw deeply both on Malawian tradition and biblical faith to retrieve a sense of the dignity and interdependence of human life that will act as a powerful antidote to corruption.

Impunity and Accountability

Underlying government impunity is the entitlement culture of the ruling elite that allows them to imagine that they can take the masses of the people for granted, fooling (*kupusitsa*) them into allowing themselves to be exploited for the benefit of the powerful few. Confidence that they will never be called to account allows almost unlimited abuse of power. Events of 2019-20 suggest that time is up for such complacency. The flawed presidential election of 2019 seems to have been the last straw for many Malawians. After waiting patiently to exercise their democratic choice they felt after the 2019 election that they had once again been cheated by the ruling elite. They took to the streets in their tens of thousands, the vast majority protesting peacefully but determined not to be denied. Their determination was vindicated by the Constitutional Court as its judgment exposed just how widespread were the irregularities in the 2019

---

[56] Wright, *Deuteronomy*, 211.

election, leading the judges to declare it "invalid, null and void". Prevarication by the government as it sought a way to avoid the court-ordered Fresh Presidential Election, was met by unyielding determination on the part of the people at large to ensure that constitutional order was followed.

From the perspective of *uMunthu* theology there has been a recovery of the dignity and initiative that are essential to a true humanity. The impunity and arrogance with which governments have conducted themselves could easily have crushed the human spirit. However, the resilience and recovery of the people have created a moment of hope for Malawi. The challenge ahead is to foster true humanity in the relations between government and people. The Tonse Alliance government that took office in June 2020 faces strong popular expectation that firm action will be taken against those who have perpetrated corruption, ensuring that they face the full force of the law. In line with the principles set out in Deuteronomy 17, those entrusted with political office are subject to the authority of the law. Should they fail to meet the demands of the law they must expect to be called to account. Politicians who use threats, fear, intimidation, divide and rule tactics, or promised rewards to ensure compliance cannot promote the common good.[57] Popular mobilisation in Malawi is now insisting on transparency, accountability and responsibility in the management of state resources. In his inauguration speech President Chakwera called for an end to government secrets, suggesting that the Access to Information law might now come into effect.[58]

Malawi's leaders have traded on a tendency in the African tradition to sacralise authority and political power. The tragedy is that when the Presidency is treated as sacred and beyond critique or accountability, its all-too-human capacity for corruption and impunity has free rein. Here a Christian theology of power, with its capacity to expose pretensions and cut authoritarian leaders down to size, potentially has a highly significant role to play. As Ghanaian theologian Kwame Bediako remarked: "The recognition that power truly belongs to God, rooted in the Christian theology of power as non-dominating, liberates politicians and rulers to be humans among fellow humans, and ennobles politics and the business of government into the business of God and the service of God in the service of fellow humans."[59] It may be that only such a theological vision can

---

57 Ibid.

58 See Dr Lazarus Chakwera's Inauguration speech for his presidency, Monday 6 July 2020.

59 Kwame Bediako, *Jesus in Africa: The Christian Gospel in African History and Experience*, Yaoundé: Editions Clé and Akropong-Akuapem: Regnum Africa, 2000, 105.

cut through the culture of impunity that has been allowed to prevail in Malawi. It provides the possibility to discover the true meaning and purpose of political power as something that can be exercised to the glory of God and the blessing of the people, especially the deprived and the vulnerable.

Leadership: Lions Led by Donkeys

Leadership has emerged as a key issue for Malawi. The phrase "lions led by donkeys" was coined after the First World War to describe the British infantry and the generals who led them into combat. Its intention was to contrast the strength and bravery of the ordinary soldiers with the ineptitude and ineffectiveness of the leaders whose decisions often cost many lives. It might be an apt phrase too for the Malawi context where ordinary people often heroically engage with difficult circumstances but are let down by the national leadership. This may not necessarily be primarily the fault of the individual leaders. It may be that they are forced into a mould not of their own making, which proves to be their undoing. Of course, it is a truism that every political career ends in failure but after a series of leaders who have ended up losing the confidence of the population at large, is it not time to ask if there are deeper, systematic issues at stake rather than simply the flaws of a given individual? Some of these issues can be addressed by constitutional reform, including the new president's commitment to reduce the power of the Presidency. Others need to be addressed at a more cultural level.

The issue of leadership was highlighted by the Catholic Bishops pre-election pastoral letter in 2020 when they set out the characteristics required of an effective leader: "honesty, democratic, transformational leadership, visionary, selflessness, servant leadership (*Mark 10:44*), good stewardship, exemplary, decisiveness, respect for the Constitution and the rule of law, willingness to step down (*Luke 17:10*), being above tribal/regional/political interests, accountable and God-fearing".[60] This was the first point they made, suggesting both that such leadership has been lacking and that it is highly important. It is by no means an entirely original point. Indeed, President Lazarus Chakwera, an Assemblies of God pastor, made it part of his electoral pitch that he would offer "servant leadership". There is some risk that this can become a cliché that is of little practical effect. Nonetheless its currency demonstrates its importance

---

60 Episcopal Conference of Malawi, *A Further Call for a New Era in Malawi*, 1.

and its sustainability might depend on how far it can be strengthened and deepened through the application of appropriate theological resources.

Given the capacity of political life to wear down moral aspiration and the resilience of an unhealthy political culture that has proved resistant to many attempts at reform, biblical and theological resources can help empower an entirely different form of leadership, modelled on the words of Jesus: "But I am among you as the one who serves" (Luke 22:27). It can draw too on the teaching of the Book of Deuteronomy that leadership is servanthood, deriving its mandate from the governed, accountable to both God and the electorate, subjecting itself to the rule of law, and stewarding the national resources for the benefit of all. When such a biblical and theological vision of leadership takes hold, Malawians can bid farewell to the deeply engrained political culture of corruption, impunity and leadership mediocrity. This is what Malawians were looking for when they chose to introduce a multiparty democracy in 1993, and voted in the first democratically elected government in 1994 with hopes of good governance, which unfortunately have not been realised even 26 years later.

A Tale of Two Cultures

A political culture has been allowed to develop in Malawi that includes some deeply unhealthy and self-destructive features. A key question is how such a culture can be challenged, replaced and renewed. One potential answer to the question lies in the fact that the country also has a deeply religious culture. The two cultures intersect at certain points but there is more to be done in the application of theological perspectives to the political realm.

One point of intersection is the national anthem, which features on all significant political occasions and takes the form of a prayer. The anthem includes a prayer specifically for the political leadership.

> O God bless our land of Malawi,
> Keep it a land of peace.
> Put down each and every enemy,
> Hunger, disease, envy.
> Join together all our hearts as one,
> That we be free from fear.
> Bless our leaders, each and every one,
> And Mother Malawi.

The anthem includes theological affirmations about the existence of God, the power of God and the blessings of God. It also features a vision of a flourishing humanity while recognising threats and flaws that imperil such flourishing. It is sung often, including at the opening and closing of daily broadcasting on national TV and radio. This fundamentally religious vision also finds expression in the prayers with which all social occasions, including political ones, are expected to begin. In the Malawi context, it would be a mistake to imagine that there is a political realm that operates entirely separately from the realm of faith. The two are constantly intersecting.

As Winston Kawale has argued: "Surely, if Malawi is not a God-fearing nation, or if it is secular state, why is God invoked in virtually everything including the national anthem? This means that the state orders the president and other public figures to seek help from God as they discharge their national duties. How can it be justified that Malawi and the Constitution itself are secular?"[61] The salience of the religious was further indicated when Malawi set out its national vision for 2020: "By the year 2020, Malawi *as a God-fearing nation* will be secure, democratically mature, environmentally sustainable, self-reliant with equal opportunities for active participation by all, having social services, vibrant cultural and religious values, and being a technologically-driven middle-income country."[62]

Nonetheless, a question still to be answered is how religious identity and religious values can be deployed so as to have a critical and constructive role in the reform and renewal of Malawi's political culture. A convincing answer will take account of religious plurality in Malawi, recognising the need to uphold religious freedom and foster inter-communal harmony. Meanwhile this chapter has set out a range of theological resources that are available to help address some pressing contemporary governance challenges. As Malawi seeks to take a new direction in regard to such matters as corruption, impunity and leadership, among the resources at its disposal are theological perspectives. In the Malawi context, these may have deeper reach than anything found at a merely structural or political level. The roots of culture lie deep and it is at this profound level that theology must do its work. Here too governance must find its foundations

---

61 See Winston Kawale, "Malawi Resists Secularism", *The Lamp* 99 (November-December, 2012), 18-19.

62 See further Lewis B. Dzimbiri, *Industrial Relations in a Developing Society: The Case of Colonial, Independent, One-Party and Multiparty Malawi,* Zomba: Academic Books Publications, 2016; our italics.

and it will be missing an important opportunity if it fails to call theology into service.

Bibliography

Unpublished Sources

Chingaipe, Henry, "Business and the State in Malawi: The Politics of Institutional Formation, Maintenance and Change", PhD, University of York, 2010.

Hutton, Maurice, "A Dystopian Democracy: Discourses on Leadership Failure and National Transformation in Malawi's Urban Public Sphere", MA, Leiden University, 2013.

Kameme, Siame, "Politics, Democracy and Governance in Independent Malawi: The dichotomy between promises and reality ", MPhil, University of Birmingham, 2011.

Mauambeta, Daulos et al., "Status of Forests and Tree Management in Malawi", unpublished position paper prepared for the Coordination Union for Rehabilitation of the Environment (CURE), 2010.

Boti Phiri, J. Mphatso, "Institutional Challenges to Viable Civil-military Relations in Malawi", MA, Naval Postgraduate School, Monterey, 2008.

Published Sources

Abou-Habib, Lina, Valeria Esquivel, Anne Marie Goetz, Joanne Sandler and Caroline Sweetman, "Introduction: Gender, Development, and Beijing +25", *Gender & Development* 28/2 (2020), 223-237.

Abrahamsen Rita, *Disciplining Democracy: Development Discourse and Good Governance in Africa*, London: Zed Books, 2000.

Ackerman, Bruce, "Constitutional Politics/Constitutional Law", *Yale Law Journal* 99 (1989), 453-547.

Adejumohi, Said, "Elections in Africa: A Fading Shadow of Democracy?" *International Political Science Review* 21/1 (2000), 59-73.

Africa Union, *Agenda 2063: The Africa We Want,* The Africa Union Commission, 2015.

Africa Union, *AU Strategy for Gender Equality and Women Empowerment (2018-2028)*, www.au.africa, 2018.

Altvater, Norbert, "Another Quest for the Holy Grail of Law: Ius Generis—Law as a Countermovement to Human Cognition", *Washington University Jurisprudence Review* 12/2 (2020), 169-219.

Angevine, Sara, "Representing All Women: An Analysis of Congress, Foreign Policy, and the Boundaries of Women's Surrogate Representation", *Political Research Quarterly* 70/1 (2017), 98-110.

Arndt, Channing et al., "Covid-19 Lockdowns, Income Distribution, and Food Security: An Analysis for South Africa", *Global Food Security* 26 (2020), 1-5.

Asaduzzaman, Mohammed and Petri Virtanen, "Governance Theories and Models", in Ali Farazmand (ed), *Global Encyclopedia of Public Administration, Public Policy, and Governance*, Cham: Springer, 2016.

Avelino, F. et al., "Game-changers and Transformative Social Innovation: The Case of the Economic Crisis and the New Economy", transit working paper 1, (2014).

Baker, Colin, "Michael Hill Blackwood—Obituary", *Society of Malawi Journal* 58/2 (2005), 42.

Baker, Colin, "Nyasaland, 1959: A Police State?" *Society of Malawi Journal* 50/2 (1997), 17-25.

Baker, Colin, *Revolt of the Ministers: the Malawi Cabinet Crisis, 1964 – 1965*, London: I.B Tauris, 2001.

Banda, H. C., "Migration, Economy and Politics: Unprecedented Increase in Informal Labour Migration from Northern Malawi to South Africa in the 1990s", *African Renaissance* 15/4 (2018), 53-75.

Bandyopadhyay, Sanghamitra and Elliot Green, "Nation-building and Conflict in Modern Africa", *World Development* 45 (2013), 108-118.

Bardall, Gabrielle, "Towards a More Complete Understanding of Election Violence: Introducing a Gender Lens to Electoral Conflict Research", paper presented at the European Conference on Politics and Gender, Uppsala, 2015.

Barker, Paul, "Deuteronomy", *ESV Study Bible*, ed. Dennis Lane, Wayne Grudem, et al., Wheaton, IL: Crossway, 2008.

Barzilai-Nahon, Karine, "Toward a Theory of Network Gatekeeping: A Framework for Exploring Information Control", *Jasist —Journal of the American Society for Information Science and Technology*, 2007.

Basiru, A.S., "Neo-Liberal Globalisation, The State and Conflicts: Some Remarks on Sub-Sahara Africa", *Global Journal of Human Social Science* 14/6 (2014), 37-42.

Baxi, Upendra, "Constitutionalism as a Site for State Formative Practices", *Cardozo Law Review* 21 (1999), 1183-1210.

Baxi, Upendra et. al. (eds), *Transformative Constitutionalism: Comparing the Apex Courts of Brazil, India and South Africa*, Pretoria: Pretoria University Law Press, 2013Bayart, Jean-Francois, Stephen Ellis and Beatrice Hibou, *The Criminalisation of the State in Africa*, Oxford: James Currey, 1999.

Bediako, Kwame, *Jesus in Africa: The Christian Gospel in African History and Experience*, Yaoundé: Editions Clé and Akropong-Akuapem: Regnum Africa, 2000.

Beinart, William and Lotte Hughes, *Environment and Empire*, Oxford: Oxford University Press, 2007.

Bekoe, Dorina A. and Stephanie M. Burchard, "The Contradictions of Pre-election Violence: the Effects of Violence on Voter Turnout in Sub-Saharan Africa", *African Studies Review* 60/2 (2017), 73-92.

Benstead, Lindsay, Ragnhild Muriaas and Vibeke Wang, When do Donor Endorsements Help or Hurt? Policy Advocacy and Men's Interests in Malawi, Working Paper No. 16, the Programme on Governance and Local Development (GLD), Gothenburg, Sweden, 2018.

Berman, Bruce, Dickson Eyoh and Will Kymlicka, "Introduction and the Politics of Democratic Nation-building in Africa", in Bruce Berman, Dickson Eyoh and Will Kymlicka (eds), *Ethnicity and Democracy in Africa*, Athens, Ohio: Ohio University Press, 2004, 1-21.

Bertelsmann Stiftung, *BTI 2020 Country Report—Malawi*, Gütersloh: Bertelsmann, 2020.

Beymer-Farris, B.A. and Thomas J. Bassett, "Environmental Narratives and Politics in Tanzania's Rufiji Delta: A Reply to Burgess et al.", *Global Environmental Change* 23/5 (2013), 1355-1358.

Bjarnegård, Elin, "Making Gender Visible in Election Violence: Strategies for Data Collection", *Politics & Gender* 14/4 (2018), 690-695.

Bogaards, Matthijs, "Crafting Competitive Party Systems: Electoral Laws and the Opposition in Africa", *Democratisation* 7/4 (2000), 163-190.

Bogaards, Matthijs, "Electoral Systems, Party Systems and Ethnicity in Africa", in Andreas Mehler, Matthias Basedeu and Gero Erdmann (eds), *Votes, Money and Violence: Political Parties and Elections in Sub-Saharan Africa*, Scottsville: University of KwaZulu Natal Press, 2007.

Bone, Rachel A. et al, "Deforestation since Independence: A Quantitative Assessment of Four Decades of Land-Cover Change in Malawi", *Southern Forests: A Journal of Forest Science*, 79/4 (2016), 269-275.

Brack, Nathalie and Sharon Weinblum, "'Political Opposition': Towards a Renewed Research Agenda", *Interdisciplinary Political Studies* 1/1 (2011), 69-79.

Bridges, Katherine Marguerite, and Michael Woolcock, "How (Not) to Fix Problems that Matter: Assessing and Responding to Malawi's History of Institutional Reform", Policy Research Working Paper, No. WPS 8289, Washington: World Bank Group, 2017.

Brown, R. and C. Saunders, "Malawi: Recent History", in Katharine Murison (ed), *Africa: South of the Sahara 2002,* 31st edition, London: Europa Publications, 2002.

Brundtland, Our Common Future: Report of the World Commission on Environment and Development, 1987.

Bruneau, Thomas C. and Richard Goetze, "Ministries of Defense and Democratic Control", in Thomas Bruneau and Scott Tollefson (eds), *Who Guards the Guardians and How: Democratic Civil-Military Relations*, Austin: University of Texas Press, (2006), 71-100.

Burchard, Stephanie M., "Get out the Vote—or else: the Impact of Fear of Election Violence on Voters", *Democratisation* 27/4 (2020), 588-604.

Camargo, Claudia Baez, *Social Accountability: A Practitioner's Handbook,* Basel: Basel Institute on Governance, 2016.

Cammack, Diana, "The Politics of Chameleons Revisited: The Burden of Malawi's Political Culture", in Martin Ott and Edge Kanyongolo (eds), *Malawi's 2009 Parliamentary and Presidential Elections*, Balaka: Montfort Media, 2010.

Cammack, Diana, Fred Golooba-Mutebi, Fidelis Kanyongolo and Tam O'Neil, *Neopatrimonial Politics, Decentralisation and Local Government: Uganda and Malawi in 2006*, Good Governance, Aid Modalities and Poverty Reduction Working Paper Series, London: ODI, 2007.

Capoccia, Giovanni, "When Do Institutions 'Bite'? Historical Institutionalism and the Politics of Change", *Comparative Political Studies* 49/8 (2016), 1095-1127.

Capoccia, Giovanni and R. Daniel Kelemen, "The Study of Critical Junctures: Theory, Narrative, and Counterfactuals in Historical Institutionalism", *World Politics*, 59/3 (2007), 341-369.

Carswell, G., "Continuities in Environmental Narratives: The Case of Kabale, Uganda, 1930-2000", *Environment and History* 9 (2003), 3-29.

Catt, Helena et al., *Electoral Management Design*, International IDEA Handbook, 2014.

Celis, Karen and Joni Lovenduski, "Power Struggles: Gender Equality in Political Representation", *European Journal of Politics and Gender* 1/1-2 (2018), 149-66.

Chasukwa, Michael, "The Central Government Administration Opportunities and Challenges for Women Representation", in Inge Amundsen and Happy Kayuni (eds), *Women and Politics in Malawi*, Bergen and Zomba: Chr. Michelsen Institute (CMI), Department of Political and Administrative Studies, 2016, 105-116.

Chavula, Viwemi, "Challenging Informality as a Patriarchal Dividend", policy brief, Lilongwe: Independent Management Agency, 2019.

Chikadza, Kondwani, "Women in Political Parties: The Politics of Participation", in Inge Amundsen and Happy Kayuni (eds), *Women and Politics in Malawi*, Bergen and Zomba: Chr. Michelsen Institute (CMI), Department of Political and Administrative Studies, 2016, 93-103.

Childs, Sarah and Joni Lovenduski, "Political Representation", in Georgina Waylen, Karen Celis, Joanna Kantola and Laurel Weldon (eds), *The Oxford Handbook of Gender and Politics*, Oxford: Oxford University Press, 2013.

Chingaipe, Henry, "Analysis of the Contribution of First Past the Post Electoral System to the Low Numbers of Women in the National Assembly and Local Authorities in Malawi and Options for Addressing the Gender Deficit", paper prepared for UN Malawi, Lilongwe, 2015.

Chingaipe, Henry and Francis Matita, "Report on the Evaluation of the Gender Parity (50:50) Programme for the 2014 Tripartite Elections", An evaluation report prepared for the NGO-Gender Coordination Unit, IPRSE: Lilongwe, 2014.

Chingaipe, Henry, Austin Zvoma and Roosevelt Gondwe, *Political Economy Analysis of the Malawi Parliament: Determinants of Performance and Prospects for Improved Effectiveness*, Lilongwe: Institute for Policy Research & Social Empowerment, 2016.

Chingaipe, Henry et al., "The Political Economy of the Performance and Effectiveness of the Malawi Parliament", Lilongwe: RNE, 2016.

Chingaipe, Henry, "Effectiveness of the Malawi Anti-Corruption Bureau", in Open Society Initiative for Southern Africa (OSISA), *Effectiveness of Anti-Corruption Agencies in Southern Africa*, Johannesburg: OSISA, 2017, 132-66.

Chingaipe, Henry, "Regulatory Threats to the Civic Space in Malawi and their Impact on the Functioning of CSOs/NGOs", Lilongwe: Economic Justice Network, 2020.

Chinsinga, Blessings and Colin Poulton, "Beyond Technocratic Debates: The Significance of Transience of Political Incentives in the Malawi Farm Input Subsidy Program (FISP)", *Development Policy Review* 32/52 (2014), 5123-5150.

Chinsinga, Blessings and Mirriam Matita, *The Political Economy of the Groundnut Value Chain in Malawi: its re-emergence amidst policy chaos, strategic neglect, and opportunism*, APRA working paper series no. 56, Brighton, UK: Institute of Development Studies, 2021.

Chinsinga, Blessings, "The Green Belt Initiative, Politics and Sugar Production in Malawi,' *Journal of Southern African Studies* 43/3 (2017), 501-15.

Chinsinga, Blessings, "The Political Economy Context", in Nandini Patel and Michael Wahman (eds), *The Malawi 2014 Tripartite Elections: Is Democracy Maturing?* Lilongwe: National Initiative for Civic Education, 2015.

Chinsinga, Blessings, "The Political Economy of Agricultural Commercialisation in Malawi", Agricultural Policy Research in Africa, Working Paper No. 17, 2018.

Chinsinga, Blessings, Happy Kayuni and Sidon Konyani, *Governance and Corruption Survey 2010*, Zomba: Centre for Social Research, 2010.

Chipembere, Henry M.B., "Malawi in Crisis", *Ufahamu: A Journal of African Studies* 11/1 (1981), 80-95.

Chirwa, Ephraim and Andrew Dorward, *Agricultural Input Subsidies: The Recent Malawi Experience*, Oxford: Oxford University Press, 2013.

Chirwa, W.C., "The Malawi Government and South African Labor Recruiters, 1974-1992", *Journal of Modern African Studies* 34/4 (1996), 623-642.

Chirwa, W.C. "Sexually Transmitted Diseases in Colonial Malawi", in P. W. Setel, M. Lewis and M. Lyons (eds.), *Histories of Sexually Transmitted Diseases and HIV/AIDS in Sub-Saharan Africa*, London: Greenwood Press, 1999, 143-166.

Chirwa, Wiseman C., "Aliens and Aids in Southern Africa: The Malawi-South Africa Debate", *African Affairs* 97, 386 (1998), 53-70.

Chirwa, Wiseman C., "Democracy, Ethnicity, and Regionalism: The Malawian Experience, 1992-1996", in Kings M. Phiri and Kenneth R. Ross (eds), *Democratisation in Malawi: A Stocktaking*, Blantyre: CLAIM-Kachere, 1998, 52-69.

Chisiza, Dunduzu, *Africa: What Lies Ahead?* New Delhi: Indian Council for Africa, 1961.

Chiweza, Asiyati and Tiyesere Chikapa, "Institutional Analysis of Gender Mainstreaming in the Malawian Public Sector", Research Report, Lilongwe: HIVOS, 2019.

Chunga, Joseph J., "Examining the Relevance of Political Parties in Malawi", Afrobarometer Briefing Paper No. 125, January 2014.

Chunga, Joseph and Arne Tostensen, "Clergy in Politics: The Opportunistic Engagement of Faith-Based Organisations in Malawi's Politics", *Journal of Religion in Africa* 49 (2019), 1-33.

Cipolla, C. et al., "Coproduced Game-changing in Transformative Social Innovation: Reconnecting the 'Broken City' of Rio de Janeiro", *Ecology and Society* 22/3 (2017).

Clayton, Amanda, Amanda Robinson, Martha Johnson and Ragnhild Muriaas, "(How) Do Voters Discriminate Against Women Candidates? Experimental and Qualitative Evidence from Malawi", *Comparative Political Studies*, 53/3 (2020), 601-630.

Conteh-Morgan, Earl, *Democratisation in Africa: The Theory and Dynamics of Political Transitions,* Westport: Praeger, 1997.

Cortell, P. Andrew and Susan Peterson, "Altered States: Explaining Domestic Institutional Change", *British Journal of Political Science* (1999), 177-203.

Daase, Christopher and Cornelius Friesendorf, "Introduction: Security Governance and the Problem of Unintended Consequences", in Christopher Daase and Cornelius Friesendorf (eds), *Rethinking Security Governance: The Problem of Unintended Consequences*, Abingdon: Routledge, 2010, 1-20.

Dahl, Robert, "Patterns of Opposition", in Robert A. Dahl (ed), *Political Oppositions in Western Democracies*, New Haven: Yale University Press, 1966.

Dalgety, Susan, *Spirit of Malawi*, Edinburgh: Luath Press, 2021.

Dalton, R. et al., "The Individual-Institutional Nexus of Protest Behaviour", *British Journal of Political Science* 40/1 (January 2010), 51-73

Daniel Harris, "Judges as Agents of the Law", *Mitchell Hamline Law Journal of Public Policy and Practice* 41/2 (Spring 2020), 1-20.

De Gruchy, John W., *Christianity and Democracy*, Cambridge: Cambridge University Press, 1995.

Dionne, Kim Yi and Jeremy Horowitz, "The Political Effects of Agricultural Subsidies in Africa: Evidence from Malawi", *World Development* 87 (2016), 215-226.

Dippel, Horst, "Modern Constitutionalism: An Introduction to History in the Need of Writing", *History Review* 73/1-2, 153-69.

Dodds, Klaus, V.C. Broto, K.D.M. Jones, V. Mamadouh, M. Ramutsindela, M. Varsanyi, D. Wachsmuth and C. Y. Woon, "The Covid-19 Pandemic: Territorial, Political and Governance Dimensions of the Crisis", *Territory, Politics, Governance* 8/3 (2020), 289-298

Drewry, Cavin and Tony Butcher, *The Civil Service Today*, Oxford: Blackwell, 1988.

Dulani, Boniface, "Progress or Stagnation? Twenty Years of Democracy", in Dan Banik and Blessings Chinsinga (eds), *Political Transition and Inclusive Development in Malawi: The Democratic Dividend*, Abingdon: Routledge, 2016, 15-34.

Durham, D. and F. Klaits, "Funerals and the Public Space of Sentiment in Botswana", *Journal of Southern African Studies* 28/4 (2002), 777-95.

Dzimbiri, Lewis B., *Industrial Relations in a Developing Society: The Case of Colonial, Independent, One-Party and Multiparty Malawi*, Zomba: Academic Books Publications, 2001.

Dzimbiri, Lewis, "Politics and the Public Service", in Dan Banik and Blessings Chinsinga (eds), *Political Transition and Inclusive Development in Malawi: The Democratic Dividend*, Abingdon: Routledge, 2016, 75-94.

Easton, David, *A Framework for Political Analysis*, Englewood Cliffs, NJ: Prentice Hall, 1965.

El-Ojeili, Chamsy and Patrick Hayden, *Critical Theories of Globalisation*, New York: Palgrave Macmillan, 2006.

Ellett, Rachel, *Politics of Judicial Independence in Malawi*, Washington D.C.: Freed, 2014.

Englund, Harri, "Introduction: The Culture of Chameleon Politics", in Harri Englund (ed), *A Democracy of Chameleons: Politics and Culture in the New Malawi*, Stockholm: Nordiska Afrikainstitutet and Blantyre: CLAIM-Kachere, 2002, 11-24.

Episcopal Conference of Malawi, "A Further Call for a New Era in Malawi: Leadership at the Service of Citizens", *Pastoral Letter*, 23 May 2020.

Erdmann, Gero, "Party Research: Western European Bias and the African Labyrinth", Democratisation 11/3 (2004), 63-87.

Evans, Peter, *Embedded Autonomy: States and Industrial Transformation*, Princeton: Princeton University Press, 1995.

Evans, Richard J., "Epidemics and Revolutions: Cholera Outbreaks in Nineteenth-Century Europe", *Past and Present* 120 (1988), 123-146.

Eyoh, D., "African Perspectives on Democracy and the Dilemmas of Postcolonial Intellectuals", *Africa Today* 45, 3/4 (1998), 281-306.

Falola, Toyin (ed), *Africa: Vol. 5: Contemporary Africa*, Durham, NC: Carolina Academic Press, 2003.

Feaver, Peter D., "The Civil-Military Problematique: Huntington, Janowitz and the Question of Civilian Control", *Armed Forces & Society* 23/2 (1996), 149-178.

Feder, D.R., "The Political Ecology of Deforestation in Malawi", *East African Geographical Review* 19/2 (1997) and published online in 2012, 23-28.

Feierman, Steven, "Struggles for Control: The Social Roots of Health and Healing in Modern Africa", *African Studies Review* 28, 2/3 (1985), 73-147.

Ferree, Karen and Jeremy Horowitz, *Identity Voting and Regional Census in Malawi*, Afrobarometer Working Paper No. 72, 2007.

Ferree, Karen and Jeremy Horowitz, "Ties that Bind? The Rise and Decline of Ethno-regional Patterns in Malawi, 1994–2009", *Democratisation* 17/3 (2010), 532-63.

Fielding, David, "The Geography of Violence During a Presidential Election: Evidence from Zimbabwe", *European Journal of Political Economy* 55 (2018), 538-558.

Fioretos, Orfeo, Tulia G. Falleti and Adam Sheingate, "Historical Institutionalism in Political Science", in *The Oxford Handbook of Historical Institutionalism*, Oxford: Oxford University Press, 2016, 3-30.

Fjelde, Hanne and Kristine Höglund, "Electoral Violence: The Emergence of a Research Field", *APSA Comparative Democratisation Newsletter* 14/2 (2016), 8-11.

Forster, Peter G., "Culture, Nationalism, and the Invention of Tradition in Malawi", *Journal of Modern African Studies* 32/3 (1994), 477-497.

Foucault, Michel and Francois Ewald, "Society Must Be Defended", *Lectures at the Collège de France, 1975-1976*, vol. 1, (2003).

Foweraker, J. and T. Landmann, "Constitutional Design and Democratic Performance", *Democratisation* 9/2 (2002), 43-66.

Fry, Geoffrey, "The Development of the Thatcher Government's 'Grand Strategy' for the Civil Service: A Public Policy Perspective", *Public Administration*, 62/33 (1984), 322-35.

Fuller, Lon L., *The Morality of Law*, rev. ed., New Haven CT: Yale University Press, 1969.

García-Moreno C., C. Zimmerman, A. Morris-Gehring et al., "Addressing Violence against Women: A Call to Action", *Lancet*, 25;385 (2015), 1685-95.

Giraldo Jeanne, "Defense Budgets, Democratic Civilian Control, and Effective Governance", in Thomas Bruneau and Scott Tollefson (eds), *Who Guards the Guardians and How*, Austin: Texas University Press, 2006, 189-191.

Gisselquist, Rachel M., "Good Governance as a Concept, and Why This Matters for Development Policy", Working Paper No. 2012/30. UNU-Wider, 2012.

Gitonga, Afrifa, "The Meaning of and Foundations of Democracy", in W.O. Oyugi and A Gitonga (eds), *Democratic Theory and Practice in Africa*, Nairobi: East African Educational Publishers, 1987.

Government of Malawi, Malawi Growth and Development Strategy, 2017-2020, Lilongwe: Ministry of Economic Planning and Development, 2017.

Government of Malawi, National Energy Policy for Malawi, Lilongwe: Ministry of Natural Resources, Energy and Mining, 2018.

Government of Malawi, National Environment Action Plan, Ministry of Environment and Climate Change, Vol. 1, 1994.

Government of Malawi, Population and Housing Census Report, 2018, Zomba: National Statistical Office, 2019.

Government of Malawi, *Rapid: Population and Development in Malawi*, Lilongwe: Ministry of Development Planning and Cooperation, 2010.

Government of Malawi, *Vision 2020: National Long-Term Development Perspective for Malawi*, National Economic Council, 1998.

Grey, Sandra, "Numbers and Beyond: The Relevance of Critical Mass in Gender Research", *Politics & Gender* 2/4 (2006), 492-502.

Griffiths, C. Thomas and Simon N. Verdun-Jones, *Canadian Criminal Justice*, Toronto: Harcourt Press, 1994.

Gutiérrez-Romero, Roxana and Adrienne LeBas, "Does Electoral Violence Affect Vote Choice and Willingness to Vote? Conjoint Analysis of a Vignette Experiment", *Journal of Peace Research* 57/1 (2020), 77-92.

Habermas, Jürgen, *The Structural Transformation of the Public Sphere: An Inquiry into a Category of Bourgeois* Society, Cambridge: Polity Press, 1989.

Habermas, Jürgen, *Between Facts and Norms: Contributions to a Discourse Theory of Law and Democracy*, Cambridge, MA: MIT Press, 1996.

Hafner-Burton, Emilie M., Susan D. Hyde and Ryan S. Jablonski, "When do Governments Resort to Election Violence?" *British Journal of Political Science* 44/1 (2014), 149-179.

Halbwachs, Maurice, *On Collective Memory*, translated and edited by L.A. Coser, Chicago: University of Chicago Press, 1992.

Hall, A. Peter, *Governing the Economy: The Politics of State Intervention in Britain and France*, New York: Oxford University Press, 1986.

Hall A. Peter "Policy Paradigms, Social Learning, and the State: The Case of Economic Policymaking in Britain", *Comparative Politics*, 25/3 (1993), 275-96.

Hall, A. Peter and Rosemary C.R. Taylor, "Political Science and the Three New Institutionalisms", *Political Studies* 44/5 (1996), 936-957.

Hardt, Michael and Antonio Negeri, *Multitude*, London: Penguin Books, 2006.

Hartmann, Christof, "Paths of Electoral Reforms in Africa", in Andreas Mehler, Matthias Basedeu and Gero Erdmann (eds.), *Votes, Money and Violence: Political Parties and Elections in Sub-Saharan Africa*, Scottsville: University of KwaZulu-Natal Press, 2007.

Haselbarth, Hans, *Christian Ethics in the African Context*, Nairobi: Uzima Press, 1978.

Held, David (ed), *States and Societies*, New York: New York University Press, 1983.

Helmke, Gretchen and Steven Levistky (eds), *Informal Institutions and Democracy: Lessons from Latin America*, Baltimore: Johns Hopkins University Press, 2006.

Henkin, Louis, "Essentials of Constitutionalism", *ICJ Review* 60 (1998).

Hetherington, Marc and Jason Husser, "How Trust Matters: The Changing Political Relevance of Political Trust", *American Journal of Political Science* 56/2 (2012), 312-25.

Hetherington, Marc J., "The Political Relevance of Political Trust", *American Political Science Review* 92/4 (1998), 791-808.

Hokkanen, Markku, *Medicine and Scottish Missionaries in Northern Malawi, 1875-1930: Quests for Health in a Colonial* Society, Lampeter: Edwin Mellen Press, 2007.

Horowitz, Donald L., *South Africa: Constitutional Engineering in a Divided Society*, Berkeley: University of California Press, 1991.

Horowitz, Donald L., "Electoral Systems: A Prime for Decision-Makers", *Journal of Democracy* 14/4 (2003), 115-27.

Horton, Sylvia and David Farnham, *Public Management in Britain*, Basingstoke: Palgrave, 1999.

Hussein, Mustafa Kennedy, "Opposition Politics in Malawi: Hopeful Signs amid the Warnings", *South African Journal of International Affairs* 16/3 (2009), 347-369.

Husu, Liisa, "Gate-keeping, Gender Equality and Scientific Excellence", in M. Brouns and E. Addis (eds), *Gender and Excellence in the Making* Brussels: Directorate General for Research, European Commission, 2004, 69-76.

Hyden, Goran, *African Politics in Comparative Perspectives*, Cambridge: Cambridge University Press, 2005.

International Monetary Fund, "IMF Adopts Guidelines Regarding Governance Issues", Washington, DC: International Monetary Fund, 1997.

Jackson, John Hampden, *Clemenceau and the Third Republic,* Westport, Connecticut: Hyperion Press, 1979.

Jere, Qeko, "Pastoral Letters and the Church in the Public Square: An Assessment of the Role of Pastoral Letters in Influencing Democratic Processes in Malawi", *Verbum et Ecclesia* 39/1 (2018).

Jere, Qeko, "Perichoretic Interaction within the Trinity as a Paradigm for Fostering Unity in the Public Affairs Committee (PAC) in Malawi", *Stellenbosch Theological Journal* 4/2 (2018), 553-578.

Jere, Qeko, "Public Role of the Church in anti-corruption: An Assessment of the CCAP Livingstonia Synod in Malawi from a Kenosis Perspective", *Verbum et Ecclesia* 39/1 (2018).

Jindra, Michael and Joël Noret (eds), *Funerals in Africa: Explorations of a Social Phenomenon*, New York: Berghahn Books, 2013.

Joinet, Bernard, *Step by Step Towards Democracy*, Nairobi: Paulines Publications Africa, 2000.

Joinet, Bernard, *The Challenge of Modernity in Africa*, Nairobi: Paulines Publications Africa, 2000.

Jones, J. Mervyn and J.T. Winkler, "Beyond the Beat: The Facts about Policing in a Riotous City", *Journal of Law and Society* 9/1 (Summer 1982), 103-14.

Jukko, Risto and Jooseop Keum (eds), *Moving in the Spirit: Report of the World Council of Churches Conference on World Mission and Evangelism*, 8-13 March 2018, Arusha, Tanzania, Geneva: WCC, 2019.

Kalilangwe, James, "The Roles of the Defence Ministry", *Msilikali* 1 (2003).

Kalilombe, Patrick A., *Doing Theology at the Grassroots: Theological Essays from Malawi*, Gweru: Mambo-Kachere, 1999.

Kalipeni, Ezekiel and Leo Zulu, "From Top-down to Bottom-up: the Difficult Case of the Blantyre City Fuelwood Project", *Journal of Southern African Studies* 28 (2002), 117-36.

Kaliya, Emma, "Malawi Women Political Participation Barometer", A Research Paper for the Annual Regional Barometer on Women Political Participation, 2021.

Kalusa, Walima T. and Megan Vaughan, *Death, Belief and Politics in Central African History*, Lusaka: Lembani Trust, 2013.

Kanyinga, Karuti, "Devolution and the New Politics of Development in Kenya", *African Studies Review* 59/3 (2016), 155-167.

Kanyongolo, Edge, "The Constitution", in Nandini Patel and Lars Svasand (eds), *Government and Politics in Malawi*, Lilongwe: Capital Printing Press, 2013.

Kanyongolo, Fidelis Edge, "The Limits of Liberal Democratic Constitutionalism in Malawi", in Kings M. Phiri and Kenneth R. Ross (eds), *Democratisation in Malawi: A Stocktaking*, Blantyre: CLAIM-Kachere, 1998, 369-372.

Kanyongolo, Ngeyi and Bernadette Malunga, "Legal Empowerment; Laws Promoting Women's Participation in Politics", in Inge Amundsen and Happy Kayuni (eds), *Women in Politics in Malawi*, Bergen: CMI, 2016, 23-31.

Karim, Fertikh, "The Political Programme as Genre: The Sociology of Producing Party Programmes. The Example of Bad Godesberg", *Revue française de science politique* 64/5 (2014), 905-928.

Kaspin, Debora, "The Politics of Ethnicity in Malawi's Democratic Transition", *Journal of Modern African Studies* 33/4 (1995), 595-620.

Katumbi, N., J. Nyengere and E. Mkandawire, "Drivers of Deforestation and Forest Degradation in Dzalanyama Forest Reserve in Malawi", *International Journal of Science Research* 6 (2015), 889-93.

Katz, Elihu, and Paul F. Lazarsfeld, *Personal influence: The Part Played by People in the Flow of Mass Communications*, New York: The Free Press, 1965.

Kaunda, Jonathan Mayuyuka, "The State and Society in Malawi", *Journal of Commonwealth and Comparative Politics* 36/1 (1998), 58-63.

Kayambazinthu-Lora, Edrinnie and Edith Kalilombe Shame, "A Different Yardstick Gender and Leadership in the Political Discourse", in Inge Amundsen and Happy Kayuni (eds), *Women in Politics in Malawi*, Zomba: CMI and University of Malawi, 2016.

Kayira, Gift Wasambo, Paul Chiudza Banda and Amanda Lea Robinson, "Ethnic Associations and Politics in Contemporary Malawi", *Journal of Eastern African Studies* 13/4 (2019), 718-738.

Kayuni, Happy, "Budgeting in African Nations: The Case of Malawi", in Peter Haruna and Shikha Vyas-Doorgapersad (eds), *Public Budgeting in African Nations: Fiscal Analysis in Development Management*, London: Routledge, 2016, 168-85.

Kayuni, Happy, "Innovation and Thought Leadership in the Public Sector: Reflections in the Context of Malawi's Public Sector Reforms", Norhed Conference: Administrative and Political Governance for Inclusive Development, SUM, University of Oslo, 23 November 2016.

Kayuni, Happy, "The Gatekeepers: Women Political Participation in Phalombe and Chiradzulu Districts", in Inge Amundsen and Happy Kayuni (eds), *Women and Politics in Malawi*, Bergen and Zomba: Chr. Michelsen Institute (CMI), Department of Political and Administrative Studies, 2016, 81-92.

Kayuni, Happy and Ragnhild Muriaas, "Alternatives to Gender Quotas: Electoral Financing of Women Candidates in Malawi", *Representation* 50/3 (2014), 393-404.

Kayuni, Happy, Michael Chasukwa, Boniface Dulani and Gift Sambo, "Perceptions on the Legitimacy of Traditional Leaders in Democratic Malawi", *Journal of Public Administration and Development Alternatives* 4/1 (2019), 42-54.

Kenney, Meryl and Fiona MacKay, "Already doin' it for ourselves? Skeptical notes on Feminism and Institutionalism", *Politics & Gender*, 5:2 (2009), 271-80.

Kerr, A., "Disappearing Forests in Malawi: Causes and Solutions", *EEP* 153 Research Project, Santa Clara, CA, USA, 2015.

Khembo, Nixon, *Elections and Democratisation in Malawi: An Uncertain Process*, EISA Research Report No 10, Johannesburg/SA: Electoral Institute for Sustainable Democracy in Africa (EISA), 2010.

Khrishnamurthy, B. S., *A Review of Michael Gelfand, Lakeside Pioneer: A Social History of Medical Study of Nyasaland, 1875-1920*, Oxford: Basil Blackwell, 1964.

Killingray, David, "A New 'Imperial Disease': The Spanish Influenza Pandemic of 1918-19 and Its Impact on the British Empire", *Caribbean Quarterly*, 49/4 (2003), 30-49.

Kimathi, Leah, "Challenges of the Devolved Health Sector in Kenya: Teething Problems or Systemic Contradictions?" *African Development* XLII/1 (2017), 55-77.

King, Michael, "The Truth about Autopoiesis", *Journal of Law and Society*, 20/2 (1993), 218-36.

King, Michael and Elspeth King, *The Story of Medicine and Disease in Malawi*, Blantyre: CLAIM, 1992.

Kinsey, H. Bill, "Land Reform, Growth and Equity: Emerging Evidence from Zimbabwe's Resettlement Programem", *Journal of Southern African Studies* 25/2 (1999), 173-96.

Kishindo, Pascal, "Evolution of Political Terminology in Chichewa and the Changing Political Culture in Malawi", *Nordic Journal of African Studies* 9/1 (2000), 20-30.

Kondowe, Wellman and Flemmings Fishani Ngwira, "Projecting Voice in Political Discourse: A Study of Saulos Klaus Chilima's Discursive Strategies, Malawi", *Theory and Practice in Language Studies* 9/5 (n.d.): 500. doi:10.17507/TPLS.0905.03.

Krook, Mona Lena, *Quotas for Women in Politics: Gender and Candidate Selection Reform Worldwide*, Oxford: OUP, 2009.

Krook, Mona Lena, "Women's Representation in Parliament: A Qualitative Comparative Analysis", *Political Studies,* 58/5 (2010), 886-908.

Krook, Mona Lena, "Violence against Women in Politics; A Rising Global Trend", *Journal of Democracy* 28/1 (2017), 74-88.

Kuwali, Dan, "The End of Securocracy: The Future of Security Sector Governance in Malawi", *Malawi Law Journal* 6/1 (2012), 75-96.

Kuwali, Dan, "Addressing Contemporary Challenges to Security and Development in Malawi", Report of the Security Summit, 8-9 September 2015 Bingu International Conference Centre (BICC), Lilongwe

Kydd, Jonathan and Robert Christiansen, "Structural Change in Malawi Since Independence: Consequences of a Development Strategy Based on Large-Scale Agriculture", *World Development* 10/5 1982, 355-375.

Kymlicka, Will, "Nation-building and Minority Rights: Comparing Africa and the West", in Bruce Berman, Dickson Eyoh and Will Kymlicka (eds), *Ethnicity and Democracy in Africa*, Athens, Ohio: Ohio University Press, 2004, 54-71.

Laakso, Liisa and Adebayo O. Olukoshi, "The Crisis of the Post-colonial Nation-state Project in Africa", in Adebayo O. Olukoshi and Liisa Laakso (eds), *Challenges to the Nation-State in Africa*, Helsinki: Institute of Development Studies, University of Helsinki, 1996, 7-39.

Laisi, Elton, "Water Resources in Malawi: An Assessment of the Critical Issues Affecting Water Resources in Malawi and a Call for Attention Towards their Sustainable Use and Management", unpublished paper prepared for Malawi Water Week, Lilongwe, May 2015.

Lane, P., "Environmental Narratives and the History of Soil Erosion in Kondoa District, Tanzania: An Archaeological Perspective", *International Journal of African Historical Studies* 42/3 (2009), 457-83.

Leach, Melissa and Robin Mearns (eds), *The Lie of the Land: Challenging Received Wisdom on the African Environment*, Portsmouth, NH: Heinemann, 1996.

Lee, Rebekah and Meghan Vaughan, "Introduction: Themes in the Study of Death and Loss in Africa", *African Studies* 71/2 (2012), 163-73.

Leftwitch, Adrian, *States of Development: On the Primacy of Politics in Development*, Oxford: Wiley, 2001.

Leib, Ethan J., David L. Ponet and Michael Serota, "A Fiduciary Theory of Judging", *California Law Review* 101 (2013) 699-753.

Leithner, C. Anika and Kyle M. Libby, "Path Dependency in Foreign Policy", in *Oxford Research Encyclopedia of Politics*, Oxford: Oxford University Press, 2017.

Lewin, K., "Frontiers in Group Dynamics: Concept, Method and Reality in Science; Social Equilibria and Social Change", *Human Relations* 1 (June 1947), 5-40.

Leys, Colin, "The 'Overdeveloped' Post-colonial State: A Re-Evaluation", *Review of African Political Economy* 5, 1976, 39-48.

Lijphart, Arend, "Democracies: Forms, Performance and Constitutional Engineering", *European Journal of Political Research* 25/1 (1994), 1-17.

Lindberg, S.I., "Consequences of Electoral System in Africa: A Preliminary Inquiry", *Electoral Studies* 24 (2005), 41-64.

Lindberg, Staffan I., *Democracy and Elections in Africa*, Baltimore: Johns Hopkins University Press, 2006.

Lindberg, Steffanie, "It's Our Time to 'Chop': Do Elections in Africa Feed Neo-patrimonialism Rather Than Counter-Act It?" *Democratisation* 10/2 (2003), 121-40.

Luhmann, Niklas, "Operational Closure and Structural Coupling: The Differentiation of the Legal System", *Cardozo Law Re*view 13 (1992), 1419-40.

Luhmann, Niklas, "The Code of the Moral", *Cardozo Law Review* 14/3-4 (January 1993), 995-1010.

Luhmann, Niklas, "Legal Argumentation: An Analysis of its Form", *Modern Law Review* 58 (1995), 285-98.

Lusaka, Mwayi, "Dividing the Nation or Promoting Unity? Ethnic-based Associations and Production of Heritage in Malawi", in Kenneth R. Ross and Wapulumuka Mulwafu (eds), *Politics, Christianity and Society in Malawi: Essays in in Honour of John McCracken,* Mzuzu: Mzuni Press, 2020, 372-94.

Lwanda, John, "Politics, Culture and Medicine: An Unholy Trinity? Historical Continuities and Raptures in the HIV/AIDS Story in Malawi", in E. Kalipeni, S. Craddock, L. Oppong and J. Ghish (eds), *HIV and AIDS in Africa*, Oxford: Blackwell, 2004, 29-42.

Lwanda, John, "Kwacha: The Violence of Money in Malawi's Politics, 1954-2004", *Journal of Southern African Studies* 32/3 (2006), 525-44.

Lwanda, John, *Kamuzu Banda of Malawi*, Glasgow: Dudu Nsomba, 1993 and Zomba: Kachere, 2010.

Lwanda, John, *Malawi: The State We Are In?* Balaka: Montfort Media, 2019.

Lwanda, John and Emmie Chanika, "Democracy, Donors and Dependency: The Rises and Falls of Non-Governmental and Civil Society Organisations' Agency in Malawi Opposition Politics, 1992–2017", *The Society of Malawi Journal* 70/1 (2017), 19-54.

Lwanda, John Chipembere, *Promises, Power, Politics and Poverty: The Democratic Transition in Malawi 1961–1999*, Glasgow: Dudu Nsomba Publications, 1996.

Lwanda, John Chipembere, "Poets, Culture and Orature: A Reappraisal of the Malawi Political Public Sphere, 1953-2006", *Journal of Contemporary African Studies* 26/1 (2008), 71-101.

Mac-Ikemenjima, Dabesaki, "Violence and Youth Voter Turnout in Sub-Saharan Africa", *Contemporary Social Science: Journal of the Academy of Social Sciences* 12/3-4 (2017), 215-26.

Makwero, Martha T., "Delivery of Primary Health Care in Malawi", *African Journal of Primary Health Care and Family Medicine* 10/1 (2018), 1-3.

Malera, Grace, *The Socio-Legal Status of Malawian Women in Politics: Opportunities and Challenges*, A Research Paper, Denmark: Danish Institute for Human Rights, 2005.

Manda, Levi Zeleza, "Media in the Political Process", in Nandini Patel and Lars Svåsand (eds), *Government and Politics in Malawi*, Zomba: Kachere, 2014.

Mapanje, Jack, *The Chattering Wagtails of Mikuyu Prison*, London: Heinemann, 1993.

Marien, Sofie and Marc Hooghe "Does Political Trust Matter? An Empirical Investigation into the Relation Between Political Trust and Support for Law Compliance." *European Journal of Political Research* 50/2 (2011), 267-91.

Marvin, Barbara and Donald P. Whitaker, *Area Handbook for Malawi*, Washington, DC: American University, 1975.

Marwick, Maxwell, *Sorcery in its Social Setting: A Study of the Northern Rhodesian Cewa*, Manchester: Manchester University Press, 1965.

Masaka, Dennis, "Kwasi Wiredu's Consensual Democracy and One-party Polities in Africa", *South African Journal of Philosophy* 38/1 (2019), 68-78.

Mattes, Robert and Alejandro Moreno, "Social and Political Trust in Developing Countries: Sub-Saharan Africa and Latin America", in Eric M. Uslaner (ed), *The Oxford Handbook of Social and Political Trust*, Oxford: Oxford University Press, 2018, 357-82.

Mazrui, Ali, *Cultural Forces in World Politics*, Oxford: James Currey, 1990.

Mbali, M., "Aids Discourses and the South African State: Government Denialism and Post-Apartheid Aids Policy Making", *Transformation: Critical Perspectives in Southern Africa*, 54/1 (2004), 104-122.

McCracken, John, "Democracy and Nationalism in Historical Perspective: The Case of Malawi", *African Affairs* 97, no. 387 (1998), 231-49.

McCracken, John, "The Ambiguities of Nationalism: Flax Musopole and the Northern Factor in Malawian Politics, c. 1956-1966", *Journal of Southern African Studies* 28/1 (2002), 67-87.

McCracken, John, *A History of Malawi 1859–1966*, Woodbridge: James Currey, 2012.

Mehler, Andreas, "Political Parties and Violence in Africa: Systematic Reflections against Empirical Background", in Andreas Mehler, Matthias Basedeu and Gero Erdmann (eds), *Votes, Money and Violence: Political Parties and Elections in Sub-Saharan Africa*, Scottsville: University of KwaZulu-Natal Press, 2007.

Meier, Petra and Emanuela Lombardo, "Towards a New Theory on the Symbolic Representation of Women", Paper presented to APSA Annual meeting, Washington, DC, September 2010.

Meinhardt, H., *Free at last! Malawi's Democratic Transition*, Lilongwe: NICE, 2004, 414-418.

Messac, Luke, "Birthing a Nation: Political Legitimacy and Health Policy in Hastings Kamuzu Banda's Malawi, 1962-1980", *Journal of Southern African Studies* 46/2 (2020), 209-228.

Metcalfe, Les and Sue Richards, *Improving Public Management*, London: Sage, 1990.

Metoyer-Duran, Cheryl, "Information Gatekeepers", *Annual Review of Information Science and Technology* 28 (1993) 111-150.

Migdal, Joel S., *State in Society: Studying How States and Societies Transform and Constitute one Another*, Cambridge: Cambridge University Press, 2001.

Miller, Arthur and Ola Listhaug, "Political Parties and Confidence in Government: A Comparison of Norway, Sweden and the United States", *British Journal of Political Science* 20/3 (1990), 357-86.

Minde, I.J., G. Kowero, D. Ngugi, and J. Luhanga, "Agricultural Land Expansion and Deforestation in Malawi", *Forests, Trees, and Livelihoods* 11 (2001), 167-182.

Minnis, J.R., "Prospects and Problems for Civil Society in Malawi", in Kings M. Phiri and Kenneth R. Ross (eds), *Democratisation in Malawi: A Stocktaking*, Blantyre: CLAIM-Kachere, 1998, 145-65.

Mkandawire, Bonaventure, "Ethnicity, Language, and Cultural Violence: Dr. Hastings Kamuzu Banda's Malawi, 1964-1994", *Society of Malawi Journal* 63/1 (2010), 27-43.

Mo Ibrahim Foundation, 2019 African Governance Report, Mo Ibrahim Foundation, 2019.

Mosely, William G. and P. Laris, "West African Environmental Narratives and Development-Volunteer Praxis", *Geographical Review* 98/1 (2008), 59-81.

Moti, Ukertor, "Building Trust in Government for Good Governance: What can Nigeria and African Governments Learn?" *Nigerian Journal of Administrative Science* 10/1 (2013).

Moyo, Themba, "Language Politics and National Identity in Malawi", *South African Journal of African Languages* 22/4 (2002), 264-269.

Mozaffer, Shaheen and Andreas Schedler, "The Comparative Study Electoral Governance", *International Political Science Review* 23/1 (2002), 5-24.

Mpesi, Andrew, "Political Parties and their Manifestos: Inferring Party Policy Positions in Malawi since 1994", *Forum for Development Studies* 38/1 (2011), 25-42.

Mpesi, Andrew and Ragnhild L. Muriaas, "Food Security as a Political Issue: the 2009 Elections in Malawi", *Journal of Contemporary African Studies* 30 (2012), 377-93.

Mtegha, Michael, Justice, *Independent Commission of Inquiry into the 1983 Mwanza Incident*, Lilongwe: Malawi Government, 1995.

Mtika, M.M., "Political Economy, Labour Migration, and the AIDS Epidemic in Rural Malawi", *Social Science and Medicine* 64 (2007), 2455-2457.

Mulwafu, W.O., *Conservation Song: A History of Peasant-State Relations and the Environment in Malawi, 1860-2000*, Cambridge: The White Horse Press, 2011.

Mulwafu, Wapulumuka, "Afterword for Malawi Special Issue on Enduring Concerns and New Directions", *Journal of Southern African Studies* 46/2 (2020), 375-79.

Munene, Ishmael, "Our University: Ethnicity, Higher Education and the Quest for State Legitimacy in Kenya", *Higher Education Policy* 26 (2013), 43-63.

Muriaas, Ragnhild, Vibeke Wang and Rainbow Murray, "Introducing the Concept of Gendered Electoral Financing", in R. Muriaas, V. Wang and R. Murray (eds), *Gendered Electoral*

Financing: Money, Power, and Representation in Comparative Perspective, Oxford UK: Routledge Studies, 2020, 1-24.

Murrison, Katherine (ed), *Africa: South of the Sahara 2002,* 31st edition, London: Europa Publications, 2002.

Musopole, Augustine Chingwala, *uMunthu Theology: An Introduction*, Mzuzu: Mzuni Press, 2021.

Mutharika, Peter A., "The 1995 Democratic Constitution of Malawi", *Journal of African Law* 40/2, 1996, 205-220.

Mutharika, Peter A., "Towards a More Manageable Constitution", paper presented at the Constitution Review Conference, Lilongwe, 28-31 March 2006.

Mwakasungura, Kapote and Douglas Miller, *Malawi's Lost Years (1964-1994): and Her Forsaken Heroes*, Mzuzu: Mzuni Press, 2016.

Mwalubunju, Ollen, "Civil Society", in Nandini Patel and Lars Svåsand (eds), *Government and Politics in Malawi*, Zomba: Kachere, 2007, 267-96.

Najem, T. Pierre, "Good Governance: The Definition and Application of the Concept", in Tom Pierre Najem and Martin Hetherington (eds), *Good Governance in the Middle East Oil Monarchies*, London: Routledge, 2003, 1-18.

Nattrass, N., "Aids and the Scientific Governance of Medicine in Post-Apartheid South Africa", *African Affairs* 107, no. 427 (2008), 157-76.

Ndahiro, A. and J. Rwagatare (eds), *Rwanda: Rebuilding of a Nation*, Kampala: Fountain Publishers, 2015.

Neves, Marcelo, "From the Autopoiesis to Allopoiesis of Law", *Journal of Law Society* 28/2 (2001) 242-64.

Newton, Kenneth and Pippa Norris. "Confidence in Public Institutions: Faith, Culture, or Performance?" in S. J. Pharr and R.D. Putnam (eds), *Disaffected Democracies: What's Troubling the Trilateral Democracies*? Princeton: Princeton University Press, 2000, 52-73.

Ngigi, Samuel and Doreen Busolo, "Devolution in Kenya: The Good, The Bad, The Ugly", *Journal of Public Policy and Administration Research* 9/6 (2019), 9-21.

Ngongondo, C. et al., "Regional Frequency Analysis of Rainfall Extremes in Southern Malawi using the Index Rainfall and L-Moments Approaches", *Stochastic Environmental Research and Risk Assessment* 25/7 (2011), 939-55.

Ngwira, S. and T. Watanabe, "An Analysis of the Causes of Deforestation in Malawi: A Case of Mwazisi", *Land* 8/3 (2019).

Nkhoma, Bryson G., "Competition for Malawian Labour: *Wenela* and *Mthandizi* in Ntcheu District, 1936-1956", *Malawi Journal of Social Sciences* 21 (2013), 28-46.

Nohlen, Dieter, *Elections and Electoral Systems*, New Delhi: Macmillan India Limited, 1996.

Norris, Pippa (ed), *Critical Citizens: Global Support for Democratic Government* Oxford: Oxford University Press, 1999.

Nzunda, Matembo S. and Kenneth R. Ross (eds), *Church, Law and Political Transition in Malawi 1992-94*, Gweru: Mambo-Kachere, 1995.

O'Neil, Tam, Ngeyi Kanyongolo and Joseph Wales, *Women and Power: Representation and Influence in Malawi's Parliament*, London: Overseas Development Institute, 2016.

Okimoto, Tyler G. and Victoria L. Brescoll, "The Price of Power: Power Seeking and Backlash against Female Politicians", *Personality and Social Psychology Bulletin* 36/7 (2010), 923-936.

Olson, Mancur, "Dictatorship, Democracy, and Development", *The American Political Science Review* 87/3 (1993), 567-576.

Orr, Alastair, "'Green Gold'? Burley Tobacco, Smallholder Agriculture, and Poverty Alleviation in Malawi", *World Development* 28/2 (2000), 347-363.

Ortbals, Candice D. et al., *Gender and Political Violence: Women Changing the Politics of Terrorism*, Cham: Springer, 2018.

Ott, Martin, Bodo Immink, Bhatupe Mhango and Christian Peters-Berries (eds), *The Power of the Vote: Malawi's Parliamentary and Presidential Elections*, Zomba: Kachere, 2004.

Ott, Martin and Fidelis Kanyongolo (eds), *Democracy in Progress: Malawi's 2009 Parliamentary and Presidential Elections*, Zomba: Kachere, 2009.

Ott, Martin, Kings M. Phiri and Nandini Patel (eds), *Malawi's Second Democratic Elections: Process, Problems and Prospects*, Blantyre: CLAIM-Kachere, 2000

Paalo, Sebastian A., "Political Party Youth Wings and Political Violence in Sub-Sahara Africa: A Case of Ghana", *International Journal of Peace and Development Studies* 8/1 (2017), 1-14.

Pachai, Bridglal, "Land Policies in Malawi: An Examination of the Colonial Legacy", *The Journal of African History* 14/4 (1973), 681-98.

Packard, Randall M., "Maize, Cattle and Malaria: The Political Economy of Malaria Epidemics in Colonial Swaziland", *Journal of African History* 25/2 (1984), 189-212.

Packard, Randall M., *White Plague, Black Labour: Tuberculosis and The Political Economy of Health and Disease in South* Africa, Berkeley and Los Angeles: University of California Press, 1989.

Pangapanga, P.I. et al., "Unravelling Strategic Choices towards Droughts and Flood's Adaptation in Southern Malawi", *International Journal of Disaster Risk Reduction* 2 (2012), 57-66.

Patel, Nandini and Fidelis Edge Kanyongolo (eds), *Democracy Tested: The Case of Malawi's 2019 Tripartite Elections*, Pretoria: Pretoria University Law Press, 2021.

Patel, Nandini and Lars Svåsand (eds), *Government and Politics in Malawi*, Zomba: Kachere, 2007.

Patel, Nandini and Michael Wahman (eds), *The Malawi 2014 Tripartite Elections: Is Democracy Maturing*? Lilongwe: National Initiative for Civic Education, 2015.

Patterson, K. D., "Disease and Medicine in African History", *History and Africa* 1 (1974), 141-148.

Pennebaker, James, Darjo Paez and Bernard Rime, *Collective Memory of Political Events*, Mahwah, NJ: Lawrence Erlbaum Associates, 1997.

Phillips, Anne, *The Politics of Presence*, Oxford: Clarendon Press, 1995.

Phillips, Anne, "Democracy and Representation: Why Should it Matter Who Our Representatives Are?" in Anne Phillips (ed), *Feminism and Politics*, Oxford: Oxford University Press, 1998.

Phiri, Kings M., "Dr. Banda's Cultural Legacy and its Implications for Democratic Malawi", in Kings M. Phiri and Kenneth R. Ross (eds), *Democratisation in Malawi: A Stocktaking*, Blantyre: CLAIM-Kachere, 1998, 149-67.

Phiri, Kings M., and Kenneth R. Ross (eds), *Democratisation in Malawi: A Stocktaking*, Blantyre: CLAIM-Kachere, 1998.

Phoofolo, Pule, "Epidemics and Revolutions: The Rinderpest Epidemic in Late Nineteenth-Century Southern Africa", *Past and Present* 138 (1993),112-43.

Pierson, Paul, "Increasing Returns, Path Dependence, and the Study of Politics", *American Political Science Review* 94/2 (2000), 251-67.

Piscopo, J., "State Capacity, Criminal Justice, and Political Rights: Rethinking Violence against Women in Politics." *Política y Gobierno* 23/2 (2016), 437-58.

Pitkin, Hanna, *The Concept of Representation*, Berkeley: University of California Press, 1967.

Pogge, Thomas, *World Poverty and Human Rights,* Cambridge: Polity, 2005.

Pollini, J., "Environmental Degradation Narratives in Madagascar: From Colonial Hegemonies to Humanist Revisionism", *Geoforum* 41/5 (2010), 711-722.

Potts, Deborah, "Capital Relocation in Africa: The Case of Lilongwe in Malawi", *The Geographical Journal* 151/2 (July 1985), 182-196.

Potts, D. "Environmental Myths and Narratives: Case Studies from Zimbabwe", in P. Stott and S. Sullivan (eds), *Political Ecology: Science, Myth and Power*, London: Edward Arnold, 2000, 45-65.

Pound, Roscoe, "A Survey of Social Interests", *Harvard Law Review* 57/1 (1943), 1-39.

Power, Joey, *Political Culture and Nationalism in Malawi: Building Kwacha*, Rochester: University of Rochester Press, 2010.

Probst, Peter, "Mchape '95, or, the Sudden Fame of Billy Goodson Chisupe: Healing, Social Memory and the Enigma of the Public Sphere in Post-Banda Malawi", *Journal of the International African Institute* 69/1 (1999), 108-37.

Prowse, Martin and Paul Grassin, *Tobacco, Transformation, and Development Dilemmas from Central Africa*, Cham, Switzerland: Springer Nature and Palgrave Macmillan, 2020.

Ramesh, Ramasamy, "Does Trust Matter? An Inquiry on Citizens' Trust in Public Institutions of Sri Lanka", *Millennial Asia* 8/2 (2017), 123-145.

Ranger, Terence, "Conference Summary and Conclusion", in Paul Gifford (ed), *The Christian Churches and the Democratisation of Africa*, Leiden: E.J. Brill, 1995, 14-35.

Ranger, Terry, "The Influenza Pandemic in Southern Rhodesia: A Crisis of Comprehension", in David Arnold (ed.), *Imperial Medicine and Indigenous* Societies, Manchester: Manchester University Press, 1988, 173-5.

Raz, Joseph, *The Authority of Law: Essays on Law and Morality*, Oxford: Oxford University Press, 1979.

Regalia, Stephanie, "Malawi: The Road to the 2019 Tripartite Elections: Reflections on Corruption, Land, and Multiparty Politics", *Notes de l'Ifri* (January 2019), 6-26.

Reynolds, Andrew and Timothy D. Sisk, "Elections and Electoral Systems: Implications for Conflict Management", in Timothy D. Sisk and Andrew Reynolds (eds), *Elections and Conflict Management in Africa*, Washington: United States Institute of Peace Press, 1998.

Reynolds, Andrew et al., *Electoral System Design*, The New International IDEA Handbook, 2008.

Roberto M. Unger, "The Critical Legal Studies Movement", *Harvard Law Review* 96/3 (1983), 561-675.

Rocheleau, D.E et al., "Environment, Development, Crisis and Crusade: Ukambani, Kenya, 1890-1990", *World Development* 23/6 (1995), 1037-1051.

Rompel, Matthias and Reiner Gronemeyer, *Malawi: Economy, Society and Political Affairs*, London: ZED Books, 2020.

Ross, Andrew C., *Colonialism to Cabinet Crisis*, Zomba: Kachere, 2009.

Ross, Kenneth R., "Not Catalyst but Ferment: The Distinctive Contribution of the Churches to Political Reform in Malawi 1992-93", in Matembo S. Nzunda and Kenneth R. Ross eds., *Church, Law and Political Transition in Malawi 1992-94*, Blantyre: CLAIM-Kachere, 1995, 31-42.

Ross, Kenneth R., "A Practical Theology of Power for the New Malawi", in Kenneth R. Ross ed., *God, People and Power in Malawi: Democratisation in Theological Perspective*, Blantyre: CLAIM-Kachere, 1996, 225-67.

Ross, Kenneth R., "'Worrisome Trends': The Voice of the Churches in Malawi's Third Term Debate", *African Affairs* 103 (2004), 91-107, republished in *Mission as God's Spiral of Renewal*, Mzuzu: Mzuni Press, 2019, 298-319.

Ross, Kenneth R., and Wapulumuka O. Mulwafu (eds), *Politics, Christianity and Society in Malawi: Essays in in Honour of John McCracken*, Mzuzu: Mzuni Press, 2020.

Rousseau, Jean-Jacques, *The Social Contract*, ed. Maurice William Cranston, Harmondsworth: Penguin, 1968.

Ruteere, Mutuma, "More than Political Tools: The Police and Post-election Violence in Kenya", *African Security Review* 20/4 (2011), 11-20.

Saint-Martin, Denis, "Path Dependence and Self-reinforcing Processes in the Regulation of Ethics in Politics: toward a Framework for Comparative Analysis", in Denis Saint-Martin and Fred Thompson (eds), "Public Ethics and Governance: Standards and Practices in Comparative Perspective Research", *Public Policy Analysis and Management*, 14/2 (2006), 5-27.

Sartori, Giovanni, "The Party Effects of Electoral System", in Larry Diamond and Richard Gunther (eds), *Political Parties and Democracy*, Baltimore and London: Johns Hopkins University Press, 2001.

Schneider, Ben Ross and Sylvia Maxfield (eds), *Business, the State and Economic Performance in Developing Countries*, Ithaca and London: Cornell University Press, 1997.

Schoffeleers, Matthew, *In Search of Truth and Justice: Confrontations between Church and State in Malawi, 1960–1994*, Blantyre: CLAIM-Kachere, 1999.

Schultze, U. and R. Boland, "Knowledge Management Technology and Reproduction of Knowledge Work Practices", *Journal of Strategic Information Systems* 9 (2000), 193-212.

Seeberg, Merete B., Michael Wahman and Svend-Erik Skaaning, "Candidate Nomination, Intra-party Democracy, and Election Violence in Africa", *Democratisation* 25/6 (2018), 959-977.

Sen, Amartya, "Well-Being, Agency and Freedom: The Dewey Lectures", *The Journal of Philosophy* 82/4 (1985), 169-221.

Shepperson, George and Thomas Price, *Independent African: John Chilembwe and the Origins, Setting and Significance of the Nyasaland Native Rising of 1915*, Edinburgh: Edinburgh University Press, 1958.

Shoemaker, Pamela J., *Gatekeeping*, Newbury Park, CA: Sage, 1991.

Shumba, Jabusile M., *Zimbabwe's Predatory State: Party, Military and Business*, Scottsville: University of KwaZulu-Natal Press, 2018.

Sow, R., African Women's Decade 2010-2020: Mid-Term Review, A Research Report, Make Every Woman Count, 2016.

Steinmo, Sven, "The New Institutionalism", in Paul Barry Clark and Joe Foweracker (eds), *The Encyclopaedia of Democratic Thought*, London: Routledge, 2001.

Svåsand, Lars, "Democratisation in Malawi: Moving Forward, Stuck in Transition or Backsliding?" *Forum for Development Studies* 38/1 (2011), 1-24.

Svåsand, Lars, "The Concept of Opposition and the Structure of Opposition in Malawi", *Commonwealth & Comparative Politics*, 51/3 (2013), 306-325.

Swanson, M.W., "The 'Sanitation Syndrome': Bubonic Plague and Urban Native Policy in the Cape Colony, 1900-1909", *Journal of African History* 18/3 (1977), 387-410.

Tamm, Marek, "History as Cultural Memory: Mnemohistory and the Construction of the Estonian Nation", *Journal of Baltic Studies* 39/4 (2008), 499-516.

Tengatenga, James, *Church, State and Society in Malawi: An Analysis of Anglican Ecclesiology*, Zomba: Kachere, 2006.

Tengatenga, James, "*Moral Majority* redivivus: Assertive religious politics and the threat to religious freedom and citizenship in Malawi", *Stellenbosch Theological Journal* 5/3 (2019), 165-82.

Teubner, Gunther, *Law as an Autopoietic System*, trans. Anne Bankowska and Ruth Adler, ed. Zenon Bankowski, Oxford: Blackwell, 1993.

Thelen, Kathleen, "Historical Institutionalism in Comparative Politics", *Annual Review of Political Science* 2 (1999), 369-404.

Thelen, Kathleen, "How Institutions Evolve: Insights from Comparative Historical Analysis", in J. Mahoney and D. Rueschemeyer (eds), *Comparative Historical Analysis in the Social Sciences*, Cambridge: Cambridge University Press, 2003, 208-40.

Thomas, S., "Economic Developments in Malawi Since Independence", *Journal of Southern African Studies* 2/1 (1975), 30-51.

Thomson, J.A. *Deuteronomy: An Introduction and Commentary*, edited by D.J. Wiseman, Leicester: Inter-Varsity Press, 1974.

Thorold, Alan, "Regionalism, Tribalism, and Multiparty Democracy: The Case of Malawi", *South African Journal of International Affairs* 7/2 (2000), 135-139.

Tiessen, Rebecca, "Small Victories but Slow Progress", *International Feminist Journal of Politics* 10:2 (2008), 198-215.

Tiffen, M., M. Mortimore and F. Gichuki, *More People, Less Erosion: Environmental Recovery in Kenya*, London & New York: John Wiley, 1994.

Tostensen, Arne, *Malawi: A Political Economy Analysis. A Report Commissioned by the Norwegian Ministry of Foreign Affairs,* Oslo: 2017.

Turper, Sedef and Kees Aarts, "Political Trust and Sophistication: Taking Measurement Seriously", *Social Indicator Research* 130/1 (2017), 415-34.

Tushman, M. L. and R. Katz, "External Communication and Project Performance: An Investigation into the Roles of Gatekeepers", *Management Science* 26/11 (1980), 1071-1084.

UNDP, Human Development Report, Poverty and Human Development in Malawi, New York: UNDP, 2013.

United Nations Development Programme, *Public Sector Management, Governance and Sustainable Human Development*, New York: UNDP, 1995.

Vail, Leroy, "Introduction: Ethnicity in Southern African History", in Leroy Vail (ed), *The Creation of Tribalism in Southern Africa*, Stanford: University of California Press, 1989, 1-50.

Vail, Leroy and Landeg White, "Tribalism in the Political History of Malawi", in Leroy Vail (ed), *The Creation of Tribalism in Southern Africa*, Stanford: University of California Press, 1989, 146-84.

Van Den Berg, Peter A. J., "The Integrative Function of Constitutions: A Historical Perspective", in Fabian Amtenbrink and Peter A.J. van den Berg (eds), *The Constitutional Integrity of the European Union*, The Hague: T.M.C. Asser Press 2010, 13-54.

Van Rign, K., "The Politics of Uncertainty: The Aids Debate, Thabo Mbeki and the South African Government Response", *Social History of Medicine* 19/3 (2006), 521-535.

Vandenabeele, Wouter and Sylvia Horton, "The Evolution of the British Public Service Ethos: A Historical Institutional Approach to Explaining Continuity and Change", in Leo W.J.C. Huberts, Jeroen Maesschalck and Carole L. Jurkiewicz (eds), *Ethics and Integrity of Governance*, London: Edward Elgar, 2008, 7-24.

Vaughan, Megan, *Curing their Ills: Colonial Power and African* Illness, Cambridge: Cambridge University Press, 1991.

Vila, Bryan and Cynthia Morris (eds), *The Role of Police in American Society: A Documentary History*, Westport, CT: Greenwood Press, 1999.

Wahman, Michael and Edward Goldring, "Pre-Election Violence and Territorial Control: Political Dominance and Subnational Election Violence in Polarized African Electoral Systems", *Journal of Peace Research* 57/1 (2020), 93-110.

Walker, P., "Roots of Crisis: Historical Narratives of Tree Planting in Malawi", *Historical Geography* 32 (2004), 89-109.

Walker, Peter, "Democracy and Environment: Congruencies and Contradictions in Southern Africa", *Political Geography* 18 (1999), 257-84.

Wang, Vibeke, Happy Kayuni, Asiyati Chiweza and Samantha Soyiyo, "Relieving Women's Costs of Standing for Election: Malawi's 50/50 Campaigns", in Ragnhild Muriaas, Vibeke Wang and Rainbow Murray (eds,) *Gendered Electoral Financing: Money, Power, and Representation in Comparative Perspective*, Oxford: Routledge, 2020, 113-32.

Wantchekron, Leonard, "Clientelism and Voting Behaviour: A Field Experiment in Benin", *World Politics* 54 (2003), 399-422.

Wermter, Oskar, *Politics for Everyone and By Everyone: A Christian Approach*, Nairobi: Paulines Publications Africa, 2003.

Wiredu, Kwasi, "Democracy by Consensus: Some Conceptual Considerations", *Philosophical Papers* 30/3 (2001), 227-44.

Wiyo, K.A., L. Fiwa and W. Mwase, "Solving Deforestation, Protecting and Managing Key Water Catchments in Malawi using Smart Public and Private Partnerships", *Journal of Sustainable Development* 8 (2015), 251-61.

Wood, Richard, *The Welensky Papers: A History of the Federation of Rhodesia and Nyasaland*, Durban: Graham Publishing, 1982.

World Bank, "Progress Towards Sustainable Energy: Global Tracking Framework", Washington: World Bank, 2015.

World Bank, *Governance and Development*, Washington: World Bank, 1992.

World Bank, *Governance: The World Bank Experience*, Washington: World Bank, 1993.

World Bank, *Sub-Saharan Africa: From Crisis to Sustainable Growth*, Washington: World Bank, 1989.

World Bank, *The World Bank and Participation*, Washington: World Bank, 1994.

Wright, Christopher, *Deuteronomy*, Grand Rapids, MI: Baker Books, 1996.

Wroe, Daniel, "Briefing: Donors, Dependency, and Political Crisis in Malawi", *African Affairs* 111, no. 442 (2012), 135-44.

Zeleza, Paul Tiyambe, *Africa's Resurgence: Domestic, Global, and Diaspora Transformations*, Los Angeles, CA: Tsehai Publishers, 2014.

Zere, E., O. Walker, J. Kirigia, F. Zawaira, Magombo, F. and E. Kataika, "Health Financing in Malawi: Evidence from National Health Accounts", *International Health and Human Rights* 10/27 (2010), 1-11.

Zimmerman, Brigitte, "Voter Response to Scandal: Cashgate", in Nandini Patel and Michael Wahman (eds), *The Malawi 2014 Tripartite Elections: Is Democracy Maturing?* Lilongwe: National Initiative for Civic Education, 2015, 215-35.

Zulu, L.C., "Community Forest Management in Southern Malawi: Solution or Part of the Problem", *Society and Natural Resources* 21 (2008), 687-703.

Internet Sources

African Union Goals & Priority Areas of Agenda 2063. https://au.int/agenda2063/goals

Alapishvili, Levan, "The Civil-Military Relations and Democratic Control on Armed Forces in Caucasus—A Comparative Study", www.nato.int/acad/fellow/97-99/alapishvili.pdf> [15.6.2020].

Chirwa, Vera Mlangazuwaa, "Prisons in Malawi", Report of the Special Rapporteur on Prisons and Conditions of Detention on a visit from 17 to 28 June 2001, African Commission on Human and Peoples' Rights, available at:< https://www.achpr.org/public/Document/file /English/achpr30_misrep_specmec_priso_malawi_2001_eng.pdf, [13 July 2020].

Chirwa, Wiseman, Nandini Patel and Fidelis Kanyongolo, Democracy Report for Malawi. www.idea.int/publictions/sod (accessed June 2020).

Cubitt, Christine "An Introduction to Governance in Africa", *Governance in Africa* 1/1 (2014). DOI: http://dx.doi.org/10.5334/gia.ae.

Freedom House, "5 Governance Challenges for Africa", *Perspectives* 12 June 2015. https://freedomhouse.org/article/5-governance-challenges-africa.

Fukuyama, Francis, "What Is Governance?" CGD Working Paper 314, Washington, DC: Center for Global Development. 2013. www.cgdev.org/ content/publications/ detail/1426906.

Holmberg, Sören, Staffan Lindberg and Richard Svensson, "Trust in Parliament", *Journal of Public Affairs* 17/1-2 (2017). https://doi.org/10.1002/pa.1647.

Hutchinson, Allan and Joel I. Colón-Ríos, "What's Democracy Got to Do With It? A Critique of Liberal Constitutionalism", *Comparative Research in Law & Political Economy*. Research Paper No. 29, 2007. https://digitalcommons.osgoode. yorku.ca/clpe/245, [4.8.2020].

Keping, Yu, "Governance and Good Governance: A New Framework for Political Analysis", *Fudan Journal of the Humanities and Social Science* 11/1-8, 2018, https://doi.org/10.1007/ s40647-017-0197-4.

Messac, Luke, "Moral hazards and Moral Economies: The Combustible Politics of Healthcare User Fees in Malawian History", *South African Historical Journal,* 2014, 1-19, http://dx.doi.org/10.1080/02582473.2014.903292.

Organisation for Economic Co-operation and Development (OECD), *The State's Legitimacy in Fragile Situations: Unpacking Complexity, Conflict and Fragility*, Paris: OECD Publishing, 2010, accessed 10/11/20, https://doi.org/10.1787 /9789264083882-en.

Organisation for Economic Co-operation and Development (OECD), *Trust and Public Policy: How Better Governance Can Help Rebuild Public Trust*, OECD Public Governance Reviews, Paris: OECD Publishing, 2017, 13. http://dx.doi.org/10.1787/9789264268920-en.

Patel, Nandini and Michael Wahman, "The Presidential, Parliamentary and Local Elections in Malawi, May 2014", *Africa Spectrum* 50/1 (April 2015),79-92, available at SSRN: https://ssrn.com/abstract=3676322.

Said, J. and K. Singini, *The Political Economy Determinants of Economic Growth in Malawi*, ESID Working Paper No. 40, Manchester, UK: University of Manchester, 2014, www.effective-states.org.

United Nations, *Agenda 2030: Sustainable Development Goals*, New York: UN, 2015. https://www.undp.org/content/undp/en/home/sustainable-development-goals.html.

Wroe, Daniel, "Remembering Kamuzu: The Ambiguity of the Past in Malawi's Central Region", *Journal of Southern African Studies*, 41/1 (2015), 247-61. DOI:10.1080/03057070.2020.1721151.

Zeleza, Paul T., "Malawi Makes History: The Opposition Wins Presidential Election Re-run", https://ww.linkedin.com/pulse/ Malawi-makes-history-opposition-wins-presidential-election-zeleza.

Index

CPSIA information can be obtained
at www.ICGtesting.com
Printed in the USA
LVHW011509241221
707138LV00015B/1425

9 789996 076077